WASHINGTON AT THE PLOW

WASHINGTON
AT THE PLOW

The Founding Farmer
and the Question of Slavery

BRUCE A. RAGSDALE

THE BELKNAP PRESS OF HARVARD UNIVERSITY PRESS

CAMBRIDGE, MASSACHUSETTS & LONDON, ENGLAND ∘ 2021

Library of Congress Cataloging-in-Publication Data

Names: Ragsdale, Bruce A., author.
Title: Washington at the plow : the founding farmer and the question of
slavery / Bruce A. Ragsdale.
Description: Cambridge, Massachusetts : The Belknap Press of Harvard
University Press, 2021. | Includes bibliographical references and index.
Identifiers: LCCN 2021007199 | ISBN 9780674246386 (cloth)
Subjects: LCSH: Washington, George, 1732–1799. |
Agriculture—Virginia—Experimentation—History—18th century. |
Slave labor—Virginia—Mount Vernon (Estate) | Slavery—Virginia—
Mount Vernon (Estate) | Slaves—Emancipation—Virginia—Mount Vernon (Estate) |
Mount Vernon (Va. : Estate)—History—18th century.
Classification: LCC E312.17 .R35 2021 | DDC 306.3 / 6209755—dc23
LC record available at https://lccn.loc.gov/2021007199

For Rick

Contents

WASHINGTON AT THE PLOW

Introduction

The Life of a Husbandman

In late July 1787, during a brief adjournment of the Federal Convention, George Washington traveled with Gouverneur Morris from Philadelphia to a fishing camp near Valley Forge. In the early morning, while Morris went trout fishing, Washington rode to the nearby site of the former encampment of the Continental Army. He found the remaining works at Valley Forge in ruins, and the grounds of the encampment uncultivated. On his ride back to the fishing camp, he observed some farmers at work and stopped to speak with them. Washington learned about their cultivation of buckwheat, a crop he had recently introduced into his experimental system of farming at Mount Vernon. The farmers told him about the various uses they found for the crop, and Washington recorded their advice on sowing the seed. The chance exchange with the unsuspecting farmers was one opportunity among several Washington had to learn about improved agriculture during the summer he presided over the Federal Convention. He attended a meeting of the Philadelphia Society for Promoting Agriculture, which had inducted him as an honorary member soon after its founding in 1785. He visited the farm of his friend, Samuel Powel, president of the agricultural society, and together they toured the famous nursery of William Bartram. With other convention delegates, Washington observed a farmer's experiments with a soil amendment, which Washington then ordered sent from Philadelphia for application on the fields at his own farms.[1]

Agricultural improvement and the work of nation building were firmly joined in Washington's mind by the time he attended the convention to draft a new constitution. Soon after his return to Mount Vernon following resignation of his command of the Continental Army, Washington in February 1784 described the prospects for the new nation in the language of farming. "We have now a goodly field before us, & I have no wish superior to that of seeing it judiciously cultivated; that every Man, especially those who have laboured to prepare it, may reap a fruitful Harvest." Washington gave life to that metaphor in his ambitious plans for the reorganization of farming at his own estate and in his determination to prove the practicability of an agricultural system that he believed would be the foundation of commercial prosperity and political stability. Agriculture and commerce were inextricably linked in Washington's vision for the new nation, and he saw in the improvement of agriculture "the only source from which we can at present draw any real or permanent advantage; & in my opinion it must be a great (if not the sole) means of our attaining to that degree of respectability & importance which we ought to hold in the world." As he reminded a Maryland planter in the midst of debates on ratification of the Constitution, "in the present State of America, our welfare and prosperity depend upon the cultivation of our lands and turning the produce of them to the best advantage." A new agricultural order, based on grain farming and stewardship of the land, would promote settled communities and the shared commercial interests that Washington considered the only durable bond of political unions and the foundation of the "rising empire" he had envisioned even before the war for independence. The pursuit of agricultural improvement and exchange of scientific knowledge about farming promised to establish peaceful ties between the United States and European nations. Washington equated the promotion of agriculture with "the cause of humanity."[2]

The story of Washington's life as a farmer fundamentally reshapes the familiar biography of the general and president. A commitment to agricultural improvement defined Washington's pursuit of private opportunities and his expectations for the new nation. The public example of farming at Mount Vernon reflected his ideals of leadership and civic responsibility.

Farming framed much about his engagement with the world, near and far, in ways that extended well beyond the marketing of crops. Perhaps most significant, Washington understood slavery primarily through his management of agricultural labor and his recurrent efforts to adapt enslaved labor to new kinds of farming at Mount Vernon. An examination of Washington the farmer also offers a view of his personality and character barely glimpsed through study of his military or political career. Washington considered farming the activity best suited to his disposition, more rewarding than military service or public office, and his agricultural interests revealed a curiosity of mind and boldness of imagination that few discerned in other dimensions of his life. Agriculture was central to Washington's identity and reputation, and in his life as an innovative farmer, Washington defined a new role for an estate owner in an independent nation.

∘   ∘   ∘

Washington grew up in an agricultural society dominated by the production of tobacco that was sold on tightly regulated markets in Great Britain. By 1732, the year of his birth, the great tobacco planters who owned enslaved laborers and rich lands along Virginia's tidal rivers had gained tremendous wealth and controlled access to both economic opportunity and political authority within the colony. Even as many aspiring planters invested in new enterprises or increased their cultivation of grain, they continued to grow the tobacco that remained the most important means of obtaining British credit and manufactured goods. The tobacco trade with Great Britain also offered wealthy planters access to the center of the empire and the personal services of merchants, who represented Virginians in legal matters and family business. For all of the many advantages of tobacco cultivation, however, the limits of colonial Virginia's economic success and the costs of its dependence on British trade would become evident to Washington by the time he assumed direction of his own agricultural estate.

Washington's family moved when he was three years old from the farm where he was born in Westmoreland County to the later site of Mount Vernon, further up the Potomac. When he was six the family moved again, to a farm in King George County across the Rappahannock River from Fredericksburg. With each move, Washington's father, Augustine, worked to increase the value of his investment in the land. Washington's earliest memories of farming were probably from the lands along the Rappahannock, where his father relied on enslaved laborers to cultivate tobacco and grains. Washington's mother, Mary Ball Washington, managed the farm during her husband's two trips to England, and again following Augustine's death in 1743, when the eleven-year-old Washington inherited the property. Mary Washington controlled enough enslaved laborers to employ a white overseer, and under their management, one of the enslaved workers served as foreman of field hands as they continued to grow tobacco. For much of Washington's youth, his family faced a precarious economic position but was always attentive to new prospects. Through his parents' connections with far wealthier planter families and in the formative time spent with his older brother Lawrence at the expanding Mount Vernon plantation, the young Washington absorbed his first lessons in the successful management of an agricultural estate in Virginia.[3]

Washington came of age surrounded by the great planters of the Northern Neck, the area of Virginia lying between the Potomac and Rappahannock Rivers, and from those wealthy families he learned about emerging opportunities for Virginians with sufficient resources to invest. The Northern Neck was the colony's only proprietary grant, held by the time of Washington's birth by the Fairfax family, and the generous terms of the proprietors encouraged individuals to claim vast tracts of land. Even by the standards of land-hungry colonial Virginia, the large planters of the Northern Neck stood out in their zeal for land speculation, especially in the regions west of the Blue Ridge, as far as the Ohio River and its tributaries. Under the patronage of the Fairfax family, Washington received his first job as a surveyor on western lands recently added to the proprietary, and at sixteen he saw the potential for the expansion of commercial agriculture into the region.

The Northern Neck provided Washington with a distinctive perspective looking east toward Great Britain, as well. The Potomac was the most distant from London of the four great rivers of Tidewater Virginia, making commerce between those places more time-consuming and more expensive. Although most of the area's large planters remained involved in the tobacco trade, the tobacco they cultivated was never prized on London markets like that grown along York River to the south, and planters in the Northern Neck were more likely to explore grain cultivation and other investments, like the ironworks in which Washington's father was involved. Military service during the French and Indian War further convinced Washington of the commercial potential of the West, especially at the headwaters of the Potomac River where he spent much of his time as colonel of the Virginia Regiment. By the time he returned to manage farming at Mount Vernon, Washington had much broader experience than most Virginia planters and was eager to explore opportunities outside the traditional investments of the colonial Virginia gentry.[4]

The view from Mount Vernon provided its own broad horizons along the Potomac River that connected the estate to markets throughout the Atlantic and inland toward the western territory that Washington was convinced might enrich a new kind of empire, with the Northern Neck at its center. The agricultural possibilities of the estate were never far from Washington's mind, even during the several long absences necessitated by military service and public office. Washington took possession of Mount Vernon in 1754, but spent most of the next four years away in military service. He became a full-time farmer in 1759 following his marriage to Martha Dandridge Custis, and over the next decade and a half he dedicated himself to diversified agriculture and the acquisition of additional land and slaves. While serving as commanding general of the Continental Army from June 1775 to December 1783, he made only one brief visit to Mount Vernon and relied on correspondence with his estate manager in a largely vain effort to keep the farms operating, but during the five years following the Revolutionary War, he restructured the entire estate and put in place his most ambitious plan of farming. His duties as president of the United States again removed Washington from the day-to-day supervision of his farms beginning in April 1789. In March 1797, he resumed his close management of agricultural experiments and initiated new enterprises, including a distillery. At the time of his death in December 1799, Washington was in the midst of another reorganization of his farms, with new cycles of crop rotations intended to increase productivity and ensure the fertility of the soil. He remained the innovative farmer throughout his forty-five years at Mount Vernon.

On his final retirement in 1797, Washington lamented the long absences that had kept him from his preferred life as a farmer. Yet, on each return from public service he had brought a sharper vision for the reinvention of the traditional Virginia plantation through experiments for the improvement of agriculture and the demonstration of the public benefits of enlightened farming. In the 1760s he offered his fellow Virginia planters a model of diversified cultivation that would open commercial opportunities outside the confines of the British Empire. Following the Revolutionary War, Washington expected his innovations in farming to be among his most important contributions to the growth of the new nation. In his final and never realized plans for Mount Vernon, Washington at the close of his presidency hoped to prove that a landed estate in Virginia could prosper without reliance on enslaved labor.

For Washington, the project of agricultural improvement depended on collaboration among nations, with Great Britain exercising the greatest influence. At each stage of agricultural innovation at Mount Vernon, Washington formed deeper and deeper ties with Great Britain through exchanges of practical knowledge, plant material, and new farming implements. He shared with British agricultural leaders a cultural ideal that entrusted large estate owners with a responsibility to demonstrate improved farming practices. Before the Revolutionary War, as he became a wheat farmer and broke with the colonial dependence on British tobacco merchants, Washington educated himself in the methods of cultivation that had transformed British agriculture during the middle decades of the eighteenth century. In the years immediately following a destructive war and the disruption of the empire, Washington adopted a comprehensive system of farming based on the latest models of British husbandry.

In June 1785, Washington announced that he was "desirous of entering upon a compleat course of husbandry as practiced in the best Farming Counties of England." Washington saw no irony in his choice of an agricultural model for the independent nation. British husbandry in the second half of the eighteenth century was the ideal to which improving landowners in Europe and the United States aspired, and after 1785, Washington introduced the complicated system of crop rotations and livestock management that characterized the most advanced estates in Great Britain. His commitment to British husbandry strengthened as his disappointment with the state of farming in the United States grew. Washington's search for an experienced English farmer to guide his new initiatives attracted the attention of the leading agriculturalists in Great Britain, who offered their support for the farming pursuits of the man most Britons previously knew only as a military commander. The prominent agricultural writer Arthur Young was "very glad to find the General is a farmer." Washington soon became the most celebrated farmer of the age.[5]

Americans and Europeans alike compared Washington to Cincinnatus at the plow, recalling the Roman general who surrendered authority to return to his farm. This powerful representation of Washington's life as a farmer gave added political significance to his innovations as he figuratively returned to his own plow, and in the years after his resignation from the Continental Army he sought to reorganize his agricultural estate in ways that would further enhance his reputation and serve as a public example for the new nation. His fame as a farmer attracted the support of European monarchs, British agriculturalists, and American proponents of improvement, who variously presented Washington with newly designed farm implements, rare seeds, new breeds of livestock, and the latest publications on agriculture. A steady stream of visitors came to Mount Vernon to view a startling, new agricultural landscape designed by Washington himself.[6]

Those visitors also observed the large number of enslaved laborers who worked the land and constructed the massive farm buildings. The agricultural system that was essential to Washington's vision for the new nation and central to his identity and reputation was at his own estate inseparable from the work of the enslaved. Throughout his life as a farmer, Washington depended almost entirely on the labor of the enslaved workers he owned or controlled, and he was at the forefront of efforts in Virginia to adapt slavery to new types of farming. In the transition from tobacco to wheat, he found additional value in and productive work for the increasing number of enslaved people under his control. Long after he first expressed a "wish to get quit of Negroes" in 1778, Washington applied enslaved laborers to the far more demanding routines of cultivation and to the various trades required of the British system of farming while he made further efforts to replace hired laborers with enslaved artisans. Washington found no model

Fig I.1 Sculpture of George Washington by Jean-Antoine Houdon, State Capitol, Richmond, Virginia. Houdon, after consulting with Jefferson, Franklin, and Benjamin West, presented his version of Washington as Cincinnatus in modern dress, beside the plow that signified his return to farming after resigning military command. Photograph by David M. Doody, The Colonial Williamsburg Foundation.

or precedent for the scale and ambition of his efforts to merge the enlightened and scientific farming of Great Britain with Virginia's system of slavery.

◦   ◦   ◦

When a friend asked for advice about an investment in slaves, Washington in 1794 confided that with regard to that "species of property," "I do not like even to think, much less talk of it." Washington's written comments on the institution of slavery were infrequent and terse, but, in fact, he thought almost continuously about the management of enslaved labor and about the work of enslaved individuals. In the various records of farming at Mount Vernon, Washington left the most detailed documentation of his engagement with slavery and his conflicted attitudes toward the institution. The record of labor management at Mount Vernon, probably the most detailed for any Chesapeake estate in the second half of the eighteenth century, also describes Washington's frequent interaction with individual laborers. His agricultural ambitions defined the daily work and much about the personal lives of the enslaved at Mount Vernon, and his records of farming and labor offer the most complete, if always imperfect, portrait of enslaved individuals on the estate.[7]

Washington's successive schemes for agricultural improvement anticipated widespread efforts of slaveholders to apply enslaved labor to diversified farming as tobacco markets declined following Independence and again when demand for American grain soared in the 1790s. His adaptation of enslaved labor to new crops and crafts occurred during a period of relative stability in the enslaved population following the closing of the slave trade from Africa and before the rise of an organized internal slave trade forced many enslaved laborers in Virginia to the states to the southwest. During Washington's management of his estate, the enslaved population throughout the Chesapeake grew by natural increase, and the enslaved, including those at Mount Vernon, were able to establish remarkably strong families. As the agricultural economy shifted, enslaved laborers in the Chesapeake became skilled in an increasing variety of tasks.[8]

The Revolution profoundly changed slavery in ways that went far beyond the eclipse of Virginia's colonial agricultural economy. During the war, the incursion of British troops offered thousands of enslaved people in Virginia the opportunity to escape bondage, and the many more who remained enslaved at plantations learned of a language of freedom and examples of resistance. By the time Washington returned to Mount Vernon after his resignation from the Continental Army, he had witnessed the rise of an antislavery movement that called for the extension of the revolutionary principles of liberty to the enslaved. Even in Virginia, where antislavery sentiment was relatively weak, the assembly prohibited the external slave trade and enacted the first law permitting individual acts of manumission.[9]

While he relied more extensively on enslaved labor after the Revolutionary War, Washington implicitly acknowledged the new critique of slavery and the inherent contradiction between a British ideal of farming intended to usher in an era of peaceful prosperity and a system of labor that rested on coercion and a denial of individual freedom. As he presented his farms as a public example, Washington introduced protections for the minimal welfare of the enslaved in an attempt to reconcile his reliance on forced labor with his pursuit of improved agriculture and his aspiration to be recognized as an enlightened and humane estate owner. His efforts to balance those ultimately irresolvable tensions explain much about Washington's conflicted attitude toward slavery during the same years in which he privately offered his first support for the principle of gradual abolition.

An exploration of Washington's lifelong experience as a manager of agricultural labor and a focus on his efforts to apply enslaved labor to the course of British husbandry after 1785 offer a new perspective on Washington's eventual decision to free by the terms of his will the slaves under his ownership. Among the founders, Washington was the only large slaveholder to provide for the freedom of all the slaves he owned, but he offered no explanation of his motives or of his expectations. As several historians have recognized, Washington experienced or at least acknowledged no single turning point or revelation leading to his decision to free the slaves, and even after writing his will, he continued to search for new ways to organize enslaved labor more productively. At his death, he was planning to transfer a large number of laborers to cultivate his lands in the West. The path to emancipation was never direct, and it never met the expectations of either the antislavery advocates who appealed directly for Washington's support or of later generations who searched for the moral or humanitarian basis of his decision. Washington's criticisms of the institution of slavery were always complicated by his continuing demands for the labor of the enslaved in support of his agricultural vision.[10]

During the same years in which Washington implemented the full system of British husbandry and designed an ostensibly more rational and humane management of enslaved labor, he faced persistent calls to free the slaves he owned and to endorse a general emancipation as a fulfillment of his role as the champion of American liberty. Following the Revolutionary War, abolitionists in the United States, Great Britain, and France directly appealed to Washington to use his influence and example to advocate for the extension of personal freedom to the enslaved. Whether the entreaties came from close friends, like Lafayette, or antislavery leaders who approached him for the first time, Washington could not escape the implication that his ownership of slaves violated many of the fundamental principles of the American Revolution on which his reputation rested, just as his reliance on coerced labor challenged his identity as an enlightened estate owner, esteemed by British agriculturalists. Among the founders, Washington was the unique object of these antislavery appeals, and their coincidence with significant changes in his management of agricultural labor suggest the many ways in which Washington's concern for reputation drove his decisions about the ownership of slaves.

Washington found in the British system of farming an additional standard by which to measure the effectiveness of enslaved labor, and his assessment of that labor ultimately reinforced the arguments of the abolitionists who appealed to him. However many provisions Washington made to protect the families and physical well-being of the enslaved, slavery at Mount Vernon remained a harsh labor system from which he never eliminated violent punishment, and the complicated routines of farming introduced after 1785 slowly convinced Washington of the inflexibility and inadequacy of a labor system that rested on coercion and was destructive of trust and collaboration. As early as the fall of 1793, he privately resolved to find some way to free the slaves under his ownership, and by the close of his second presidential term, Washington acknowledged that slavery was antithetical to the kind of agricultural improvement that he believed would be a foundation of commercial prosperity and a demonstration of his own enlightened management. His newfound commitment to emancipation would be evident only in the extraordinary plans to reorganize his farms in ways that would make his estate more nearly like those of the great improving landowners of Great Britain. In this final and most improbable plan of agricultural improvement, Washington imagined a plantation without enslaved laborers.

∘   ∘   ∘

Washington brought a more rational system to the management of his estate, beginning with the original and often unique designs of his farming and financial records. Like many of his British counterparts, he searched for more regular ways to document the seasonal routines of farming from year to year. He relied on his ledgers and account books to monitor networks of exchange in the local community and trade with commercial centers throughout the Atlantic world. He applied the forms of accounting and bookkeeping to the supervision of enslaved laborers and the distribution of their provisions. With his scrupulous accounts of every kind of transaction, Washington created an unmatched record of the conduct of business in Virginia during the last third of the eighteenth century as he turned away from a colonial dependence on tobacco exports and produced commodities for sale on markets throughout the Atlantic world.

In accounts that measured days worked and others that assigned a monetary value to the labor of the enslaved, Washington devised the kind of records that would enable later slaveholders to adapt the labor force to the demands of highly competitive markets. Many historians have recently emphasized the degree to which slavery as organized in the United States in the first half of the nineteenth century accommodated and even facilitated the transition to a capitalist economy that depended on the rational calculation of costs and productivity and the uniform measurement of labor. Washington recognized the advantages of regularizing his accounts of labor, and he relied on his labor records to monitor and accelerate the pace of work, especially among enslaved artisans and at harvest time. In the anonymous enumeration of field laborers in his weekly work reports, Washington reduced the enslaved individuals to quantifiable units of production, as would the sophisticated accounting records adopted by large-scale cotton planters in the nineteenth century. Washington relied on the record of days worked to determine the most efficient allocation of enslaved laborers in the increasingly complicated tasks required of the British model of farming.[11]

In other ways, the accounts of labor reflected the personal relationships between the enslaved and the enslaver that characterized slavery in the Chesapeake during the late-eighteenth century. The weekly work reports designed by Washington were records of supervision rather than measures of the productivity of enslaved field laborers, and they reflected his definition of personal obligations that he tried to impose on the enslaved. Washington relied on the reports, with their credit and balance ledgers based on the number of laborers, to enforce his notion of the presumed "duty" of enslaved laborers to work six days a week, from sunrise to sunset. In the record of work completed each week on his several farms, Washington measured the days spent on tasks and recorded the reasons for individual absences from labor, but the reports seldom included any calculation of either the quantity or value of crops cultivated by the enslaved laborers. Washington rarely compared the costs of provisioning and housing the enslaved laborers with the revenue to be extracted from their work. Two years after introducing his weekly accounts of labor, Washington acknowledged to Arthur Young that he was "not able to give you the price of labour as the land is cultivated here wholly by Slaves." Correspondence from Young and other British agriculturalists informed Washington about the more careful calculations of labor costs and productivity on British farms, but the knowledge served primarily to distinguish further the labor systems of Great Britain and Virginia.[12]

Washington always sought to balance his pursuit of enlightened management and his idealized vision of a landed estate with the profitability that would make any system of farming viable, but profit alone was seldom the primary consideration in his decisions about crop rotations or the allocation of labor, particularly after 1785. As he reminded several farm managers, "*immediate* profit is not so much an object with me," preferring that they focus on the restoration of the land, the planting of new meadows and live hedges, and aesthetic refinement of the grounds of the Mansion House. Fields were to be configured "as well for appearance as profit." Like some of the wealthiest improving estate owners in Great Britain, Washington deferred short-term profits in his effort to demonstrate a viable and replicable system of farming, and like his associates among the agricultural improvement society in Philadelphia, he understood that the introduction of the British system of husbandry required a significant expenditure of capital. Despite chronic shortages of cash, Washington remained a very wealthy individual with no encumbering debts, and he willingly accepted the costs of the lengthy experiments he deemed essential to innovation.[13]

From the construction of a merchant mill to the establishment of a distillery, Washington risked investments in experimental enterprises and mechanical improvements, but almost always with the goal of increasing the value of his agricultural produce or making his estate more self-sufficient in the provisioning of the enslaved laborers. He encouraged the establishment of a mercantile community in the Potomac region, but his own commercial ventures were rare and short-lived. When he promoted corporate schemes for economic improvement, such as opening Virginia's rivers to navigation, it was in support of expanding commercial agriculture into the West, which he expected to advance his private interests as well as the political order of the region. Washington's most important investments beyond Mount Vernon were in the purchase and settlement of western lands, from which he hoped to derive income based on leases to a large number of tenants who would support an even more ambitious and British-inspired model of landed wealth. For all of his innovations and experiments, Washington approached opportunity as an eighteenth-century landed gentleman rather than a nineteenth-century entrepreneur.[14]

For as long as Washington managed farming at Mount Vernon, he was dedicated to experiment and to the exchange of agricultural knowledge with improving landowners throughout much of the Atlantic world, and in his agricultural innovations, Washington emerged most clearly as a figure of the Enlightenment. Through his extensive reading in agricultural treatises and his adoption of new methods of cultivation, Washington entered a community of agricultural improvement in Great Britain and established himself at the forefront of new farming in the United States. He participated in a steadily expanding network for the exchange of plant materials and livestock and benefited from the findings of naturalists spread throughout the British Empire. Agriculture remained the most powerful component of a broader cultural authority that Washington ascribed to Great Britain, and his deference to British custom shaped his perspective on the new nation's relations with Great Britain long after the sovereignty of the United States was secured.[15]

Washington discovered in the British definition of agricultural improvement, with its emphasis on private property and the decisive influence of knowledgeable gentry farmers, a new and professedly public-spirited role for the owner of a large landed estate in the United States. Before and after the Revolutionary War, Washington expected wealthy landowners like himself to accept the financial risks required for experiment and innovation, and he believed that only those with sufficient resources and access to books and learned correspondence would be able to offer smaller farmers a model for the reversal of ruinous methods of cultivation. He presented himself as a different kind of Virginia planter, committed to innovation and conversant in the principles of British husbandry, with its promise of steady gains in productivity and increased land values. Like the advocates of improvement in Great Britain, Washington offered his agricultural knowledge and innovation as a kind of civic responsibility. Throughout his life, he adhered to this explicitly elitist model of agricultural improvement, and his assertion of agricultural influence reinforced his deeply held preference for leading through example rather than persuasion or public advocacy.[16]

Washington's example of improvement and his emphasis on the civic benefits of his innovations found a striking parallel in the contemporaneous agricultural projects of George III. The king's early interest in farming provoked biting satire of "Farmer George," but George III initiated public-spirited efforts, including an experimental course of husbandry very similar to that pursued by Washington. Soon after he gained control of Windsor Great Park, with its nearly 4,500 acres of pleasure gardens, hunting grounds, and isolated farms, the king converted much of the land to experimental farms, and he hired an innovative firm of estate managers to introduce the most recent advances in crop rotations, livestock management, and the design of farm buildings. He encouraged the managers to focus on the larger social goals of the agricultural experiments, such as creating useful labor for "the industrious poor," and "trying experiments in Agriculture, to excite imitation where success might encourage it." George III actively directed many of the improvements and drew on his own considerable knowledge, much of it gained from the same agricultural treatises Washington read. Arthur Young was a favorite of both, and they concluded from their

Fig I.2 "The Farm Yard." Print by Henry Kingsbury, 1786. The agricultural improvements of George III were met with satire and derision of "Farmer George," frequently presented with Queen Charlotte as they carried out common farm chores, here in view of Windsor Castle. The many caricatures of the king offered no indication of his agricultural learning and his intent to demonstrate the national benefits of improved farming.

reading of Young that farming was the appropriate responsibility of a leader who wished to promote the economic prosperity and social order of a nation.[17]

The experimental character of Washington's agricultural improvements and his commitment to a commercially productive use of natural resources drew him to a particular ideal of stewardship of the land articulated by British agricultural writers and naturalists. Perhaps more than any of his contemporaries in the United States, Washington placed the restoration and maintenance of soil fertility at the center of his system of farming. He saw in the gullied and depleted landscape of so many Virginia farms the destructive effects of the long dependence on tobacco and corn and a labor system that encouraged the quick exhaustion of the soil. He had no interest in the practical experience of colonial farmers who found crude but effective ways to cultivate fertile lands, nor did he acknowledge the examples of Indian farming he frequently encountered in his travels west. He relied rather on British models of soil management and the experiments of farmers in the United States who read the same British treatises and adhered to the same methods described in them. For British agriculturalists, like Arthur Young, the study of soil was the greatest responsibility of landowners, and the concept of agricultural improvement adopted by Washington presumed a civic, even moral, obligation of estate owners to make the best use of land over time. Improvement in this sense depended on control of the land by learned and cosmopolitan estate owners who understood a science of agriculture and directed farming toward the lasting production of commercial crops.[18]

In his expansive authority over his estate of nearly eight thousand acres and the several hundred enslaved persons who labored there during his lifetime, Washington displayed his sense of command and his insistence on control and order. He was a demanding and rarely satisfied supervisor of both enslaved and free labor, and he was seldom comfortable delegating the management of farming or business affairs. Some thought they could identify in Washington's management of his estate the imperious habits of a military commander, with his references to labor gangs as "forces" and workers "marching & counter marching," but the military analogies failed to recognize the degree to which Washington as a farmer attempted to exercise a mastery checked only by his own sense of responsibilities. He frequently bypassed the hierarchy of managers and overseers to communicate directly with individual enslaved laborers and to issue his own orders for the work of field laborers. No detail was too small for his attention, and no misstep of others safe from his admonishment.[19]

Washington's lifelong engagement in farming offers a window on a personal self that remained a mystery for the many who observed him in public life and for subsequent generations that knew only the revered, stoic leader. As master of Mount Vernon, more than in any other aspect of his life, Washington asserted his personal will and resolve. Richard Peters, who knew him as a general, as a president, and, perhaps most closely, as a farmer, offered a retrospective character sketch that found Washington's "victory over his natural temperament, as one of the greatest he had obtained." In Washington's relationship with the overseers on his farms, with the merchants who marketed his produce, and with the enslaved across the estate that victory was incomplete. The enslaved frequently met with Washington's anger and his disparagement of their work. In business transactions and in the regulation of overseers, Washington exhibited the indignation and petulant sarcasm that he had learned to moderate in public life in the years following service in the French and Indian War. But Peters also identified in Washington's private life a "cheerfulness, pleasantry, and disengaged conversation" unfamiliar to those who mistook Washington's public circumspection for aloofness or indifference. Peters knew that in addition to the comforts of domestic life, Washington discovered in the routines of farming at Mount Vernon a personal gratification seen nowhere else in his life.[20]

After several years of closely supervising every aspect of farming at Mount Vernon, Washington found on reflection "the life of a Husbandman of all others, is the most delectable. It is honorable—It is amusing—and with Judicious management, it is profitable. To see plants rise from the Earth and flourish by the superior skill, and bounty of the labouror fills a contemplative mind with ideas which are more easy to be conceived than expressed." Washington in the sweeping reorganization of farming on his estate attempted to realize the ideal he had absorbed from British agricultural literature, with its celebration of the active, engaged landowner on whom improvement depended. He transformed the working landscape of the farms and imposed a new regimen on the enslaved field laborers, expecting to establish a rural order born of a knowledge gained from his extensive reading and his communications with improving farmers in Great Britain and the United States. That ideal of a balanced order rooted in nature and improved by human endeavor would instead remain in conflict with the system of enslaved labor on which Washington established agriculture at Mount Vernon.[21]

The examination of what remains the least familiar dimension of Washington's life deepens and complicates understanding of his public leadership and his self-identity. Farming was never just a private enterprise, and even less a gentlemanly pastime; it was for Washington a measure of his abilities and virtue similar to the tests of military command and public service, and he invested his agricultural improvements with a civic purpose that he believed would constitute an important part of his legacy. His awareness of the public audience for his agricultural innovations and the implications for his reputation established a critical context for his focus on the national benefits of improvement and, ultimately, for his decision to free the slaves on whom he had relied to carry out his agricultural vision. As a farmer, Washington responded to the pivotal opportunities that he believed would define a post-colonial economy and ensure the stature of the United States among the nations of the Atlantic world. In his determination to secure those opportunities through the example of farming at his estate and to join his efforts with those of a self-defined community of enlightened landowners, Washington would inescapably confront the fundamental contradictions of slavery and freedom in the founding era.

° *1* °

The Experiments of a
Virginia Planter

In March 1760, less than a year after Washington returned to Mount Vernon
following his marriage to Martha Dandridge Custis, he and Peter, an enslaved blacksmith, worked together to make a plow designed in part by
Washington. After that effort failed, Washington returned to the smith's
shop a week later to spend "the greatest part of the day in making a new
plow of my own Invention." The following day, the new plow was set to
work in the lower pasture and "Answerd very well." Since February, Washington had been supervising a new regimen of plowing across the estate
at the start of the first season of his full-time management of the farms at
Mount Vernon. Over several weeks in late winter and early spring, he relied on an enslaved man he referred to as Mulatto Jack and another he distinguished as Cook Jack to plow new ground for growing clover, lucerne,
and rye.[1]

As he directed the sowing of seeds he had ordered from London, Washington turned to Jethro Tull's *Horse-Hoeing Husbandry* for instruction
on the cultivation of lucerne and sainfoin, another fodder crop. He carefully recorded the placement of seeds in experimental beds "to try their
Goodness" and to measure the "several Virtues" of compost mixtures he
prepared. Washington refitted the mechanisms on his plows, both those
crafted by the blacksmiths at Mount Vernon and those shipped from

England, and he employed a succession of horses to determine which type was best suited to field work. Washington's new interest in fodder crops and plowing marked the initial step in his application of the methods of British husbandry that would guide his management of Mount Vernon as he made farming his principal occupation over the next decade and a half.[2]

By the spring of 1760, Washington aspired to be an enlightened landowner, committed to innovation and experiment, drawing on the knowledge found in British agricultural treatises and shared by a select group of Virginia planters. Following the British methods of agricultural improvement, Washington applied his learning to the practical tasks of farming, with daily visits to his fields where he became familiar with the soil and the growth of crops. His close observation of unfamiliar crops and of the use of new implements allowed him to measure precisely the results of his new ventures and to impose greater regularity on the seasonal patterns of farming.

Washington imposed the same demands for order and regularity on the enslaved laborers, who came under his closer observation and the stricter supervision of white overseers. Washington also recognized that agricultural change at Mount Vernon depended on the education of the enslaved in new skills. Mulatto Jack was almost certainly a novice at plowing, since he had until 1759 been enslaved on the Custis estates where no plows were used, but he and Cook Jack made themselves indispensable to Washington as the only slaves capable of managing a plow during this first season of new farming. When Washington ordered these men to other tasks, plowing came to a stop. As Washington diversified agriculture over the next decade, he purchased slaves who would bring valued skills to Mount Vernon, and he directed enslaved workers on the estate to carry out more difficult tasks that previously required the costly hire of free laborers. Washington's design of agricultural improvement would continue to drive his management of enslaved labor and give greater value to his investment in slaves, even as he moved away from the staple agriculture that had given rise to the Chesapeake system of slavery.[3]

◦   ◦   ◦

Washington first leased Mount Vernon in 1754 from the estate of his late brother Lawrence when, following the recent death of Lawrence's only child, he could anticipate that he would eventually inherit Mount Vernon and that it would likely be his primary source of income. Over the next four years during his service in the French and Indian War, he only intermittently managed farming at Mount Vernon, even admitting to an English tobacco merchant in 1757, "I am so little acquainted with the Business relative to my private Affairs that I can scarce give you any information concerning it." Until his resignation from the Virginia Regiment in December 1758, Washington relied on managers and overseers to pursue a familiar pattern of plantation management, with only limited efforts toward diversification.[4]

Tobacco was well established as the most important cash crop at Mount Vernon as well as at Washington's Bullskin Plantation to the west in Frederick County. Washington grew varieties of the premium sweet-scented tobacco at both estates, and during the 1750s, he usually sold his combined crop of tobacco through consignment to merchants in England. Alexandria merchant John Carlyle, who as commissary to the Virginia Regiment was in frequent contact with Washington, often managed the shipment of the tobacco, and from 1755 to 1758, Washington's brother John Augustine managed much of the farming and other estate business at Mount Vernon. On the recommendations of Carlyle and George William Fairfax, Washington opened correspondences with several English merchants, including Richard Washington of London. Washington expected his namesake, although no relation, to become his principal agent in London for both the sale of tobacco and the purchase of British goods to furnish Mount Vernon. In return for the consignment of tobacco, these merchants sent Washington basic farming implements such as hoes and scythes, and clothing for enslaved laborers. Richard Washington also sent tools used in the redesign of the house at Mount Vernon and the goods to furnish what its owner, even from his remote military posts, intended to make a genteel seat characteristic of a Virginia tobacco planter.[5]

On his infrequent visits to Mount Vernon during the French and Indian War and in correspondence with Carlyle and John Augustine, Washington encouraged new farming endeavors to supplement the uncertain returns from tobacco. Both of his estates produced wheat that was sold locally, and on at least one occasion shipped to a Norfolk merchant involved in the West Indies trade. Washington continued to acquire cattle and sheep for Mount Vernon, and he ordered the creation of new fields and meadows for the support of livestock and the cultivation of new crops. The gristmill at Mount Vernon, despite an unreliable flow of water, attracted the business of area farmers who brought their wheat and corn to be ground.[6]

The purchase and hire of additional enslaved laborers enabled Washington to take the first steps toward increased production of crops and greater self-sufficiency of labor on his plantations. Between October 1754 and January 1758, he or his agents purchased at least fourteen slaves and rented the labor of four more. Three of the purchased slaves were carpenters who worked on the construction of tobacco houses and slave quarters and the expansion of Washington's own house. Washington ordered Cleo, whom he purchased for £50 in 1755, to make clothes for the enslaved in what he considered her "leizure hour's," presumably after her work in the fields. In January 1756, John Carlyle, accompanied by Washington's brother, took the liberty of purchasing for Washington three slaves whom they deemed "So Good a bargin." Carlyle also purchased for Washington an enslaved woman and child sold by Governor Dinwiddie. The additional slaves, however, were insufficient to meet Washington's demand for labor at wheat harvest, and at Mount Vernon and Bullskin, overseers paid free laborers to thresh wheat.[7]

The overseers of both estates sought to convince a skeptical Washington that they had satisfied his expectations of detailed attention to farming and constant work from enslaved laborers. Humphrey Knight at Mount Vernon pleaded, "I hope you will not be Douptfull of my Diligence in your buseness. I'll Loose my life before any thing shall Go amiss." Christopher Hardwick, overseer at Bullskin, insisted that he never failed to apprise Washington of important business. Knight, with a casual reference to his violent oversight of labor, reported that he closely monitored the carpenters "and has whipt em when I could see a fault." He promised to work all of the enslaved laborers to Washington's advantage. The overseers' repeated assurances, in response to Washington's complaints about their management and infrequent written reports, were an early indication of the friction that would mark Washington's relationship with overseers throughout his life.[8]

Whatever frustration Washington may have felt about the management of his estates, he received during the growing season of 1758 encouraging reports about the potential for farming at Mount Vernon. George William

Fairfax assured Washington that his plantations had produced the finest crops of tobacco and corn that he had seen that year. John Carlyle affirmed that Washington's crops were the best of their kind in the county, and Humphrey Knight, who managed the crop, added, "I Dont See a better crop of Tob[ac]co any where." As he prepared to set aside his military ambitions, Washington could anticipate that the management of his agricultural estate might secure his private fortune and his public reputation.[9]

In the spring of 1759, Washington for the first time had the opportunity to direct a sustained course of farming at Mount Vernon, and through his marriage to Martha Custis earlier that year he gained the financial resources and the control of additional enslaved laborers that would enable him to expand the scale of production beyond anything he previously envisioned. The Mount Vernon estate to which Washington escorted Martha and her two children in April 1759 extended to nearly 2,800 acres, and Washington owned as many as twenty slaves who lived and worked at Mount Vernon. The details of the land were sufficiently unfamiliar to Washington that in October 1759 he decided to mark the exact boundaries of the estate. Relying on his surveying skills, Washington spent two days recording the pole distances along the perimeter of an estate that he described largely in terms of trees. The markers of a "crooked Elm" and a "stooping locust" were characteristic of Virginia deeds, but the survey notes also reflect an instinctive eye for the natural landscape and the agricultural potential of the soil. Washington further noted tenant properties and bogs that would soon be eliminated in his determination to consolidate and coordinate the use of arable land.[10]

Because Martha's first husband, Daniel Parke Custis, had died without a will, she was entitled under Virginia law to one-third of his personal property and to life rights to one-third of the Custis estate's land and slaves. These dower rights gave Washington access to the Custis cash reserves and the estate's favorable balance with London merchants, enabling Washington to purchase slaves in unprecedented numbers and to acquire surrounding land. Over the next sixteen years, he would more than double the acreage at Mount Vernon and buy more than sixty slaves. His first land purchase was the largest, more than 1,800 acres across Little Hunting Creek, bought from William Clifton. This problematic transaction eventually brought Washington control of what would form the basis of River

Plantation, the largest at Mount Vernon. Before and after coming into ownership of Mount Vernon following the death of Lawrence's widow, Anne Lee, in March 1761, Washington bought several other parcels that he incorporated into existing plantations or added to the Clifton property. By the summer of 1764, the Mount Vernon estate encompassed nearly 5,500 acres.[11]

Washington quickly merged his lands at Mount Vernon so that he could bring farming across the estate under his own coordinated management. He chose not to renew the leases of some of the tenants on the estate, and he bought out others. A few tenants continued to rent land on the periphery of the estate and to pay their annual rent in tobacco. Washington followed the same strategy with his newly purchased land on Clifton's Neck. A survey of the Clifton property, which Washington copied and annotated soon after purchasing the land in 1760, revealed a jumble of leaseholds. Washington determined to consolidate as much of the land as possible to establish new plantations. After removing or relocating several of the tenants, Washington reported in August 1764 that he had "long been pestered with a Tenent that lives in the very heart of the Plantations which I have settled in Clifton's Neck." He had already come to the man with various propositions, but "wanting him away now more than ever," Washington "attacked him again" and persuaded him to relocate to Frederick County where he could lease land owned by Washington's brother Charles. In a 1766 survey of the Clifton land, which he now referred to as his farm on Little Hunting Creek and the Potomac River, Washington documented the clear division of the plantation into three large fields, which could accommodate the three-year rotation of crops he instituted that year.[12]

Over the spring and summer of 1759, Washington purchased fifteen slaves, nearly as many as all his previous purchases combined. At the appraisal of the Custis estate that same year, Martha received the property rights to eighty-four slaves. The Washingtons brought at least a dozen of these individuals to Mount Vernon, where they worked and lived alongside the slaves Washington owned, although their legal status remained distinct. Washington controlled the dower slaves during his lifetime, but he could not sell any of them without compensating the Custis estate. If a dower slave married a slave owned by Washington, as often happened, the legal status of their children, like the condition of enslavement itself, was determined by the status of the mother.[13]

Washington drew on cash from the Custis estate for the several slave purchases made in Williamsburg during the spring session of the House of Burgesses in 1759. In August of that year, he drew £99 sterling from the Custis account with the Hanbury merchant firm in London to pay slave traders who had recently offered for sale in Maryland what they called "choice healthy Gold Coast SLAVES." The Africans purchased by Washington worked as field laborers at the outlying plantations at Mount Vernon. Hannah and her child, bought from a neighbor of the Custis estate in June 1759, may have been known to Martha and the slaves from the Custis estate; several years later, Washington listed her as the wife of Morris, one of the dower slaves brought to Mount Vernon in 1759.[14]

During the next four years, Washington continued to purchase slaves, some as individuals and some in groups as large as seven. Most of the individuals he purchased had already been enslaved in Virginia or Maryland, and several were sold as part of the settlement of estates. Washington also participated in sales that exposed the vast scale and brutality of the trade from Africa to the Chesapeake. The August 1759 sale in Maryland had offered 350 enslaved Africans transported on a single ship. Two years later, Washington went to Lower Marlborough, Maryland, to purchase "Sundry Slaves" from the ship *Africa,* which advertised "A Cargo of Choice Healthy Fine Slaves, consisting of Men, Women, Boys and Girls." Later in 1761, Washington purchased from Thomson Mason several slaves recently transported from either Africa or the Caribbean.[15]

The final division of slaves from Lawrence Washington's estate in 1762 brought his brother control of another five adults and two children. The recently acquired slaves, particularly those who had worked on Virginia plantations, brought a greater diversity of skills to Mount Vernon. Washington increased the number of carpenters, whose work was essential to the introduction of new crops and the construction of shelters for livestock. The carpenters made plow stocks, yokes for oxen, and tumbrils for the oxen to pull. Washington sent more than half the new slaves, and all but one of the enslaved women, to work in the fields. The new purchases, combined with the natural increase of resident slaves, brought the number of enslaved adults at Mount Vernon to sixty-eight by July 1765.[16]

In his purchase of slaves and land, Washington followed a well-established path of aspiring gentry planters in eighteenth-century Virginia, and he somewhat more cautiously sought to improve his advantages in the tobacco trade, the other traditional foundation of planter wealth. The Custis connection offered Washington an entrée to three prestigious British merchant firms that had managed the sale of the premium tobacco leaf grown on the Custis lands along York River. In May 1759, Washington introduced himself to Robert Cary & Company, the firm that usually received the greatest share of the Custis tobacco. More recently, Martha Custis had managed the estate's business with the Cary firm following the death of her first husband in 1757. Washington informed the Cary partners that by marriage he was entitled to one third of the Custis estate, and he assured the merchants that he would continue and perhaps increase the consignment of tobacco "in proportion as I find myself and the Estate benefitted thereby." Washington would soon add the tobacco cultivated at Mount Vernon and Bullskin to the Cary consignments. A merchant firm of the scale and reputation of Cary & Company offered Washington incentives to continue organizing his crop production around the London tobacco market. The Cary firm managed the valuable Custis stock in the Bank of England, it had longstanding relationships with buyers of premium tobacco, and it worked with the leading London shops and manufacturers that catered to the Virginia trade.[17]

Even as Washington recognized and pursued the potential benefits of trading with leading merchants like Cary & Company, he entered these commercial relationships with a skepticism and mistrust that would grow over the next few years. By the close of his service in the Virginia Regiment, Washington had come to doubt that British officers and administrators accepted colonial Americans as equal partners in the defense and promotion of imperial interests. He confronted each of the Custis merchants with a defensive tone that echoed this perceived lack of British respect for colonials. Early in his correspondence with the Cary firm, Washington criticized the merchants for their premature sale of Custis tobacco, when a short delay would have been to his advantage. When he asked the same merchants for an estimation of prices he could expect for his Potomac tobacco, he advised them to be well informed in their answer or "I might possibly think myself deceivd and be disgusted accordingly." Washington warned James Gildart, a Liverpool tobacco merchant, to be careful in his selection of goods for the estate because Virginians sometimes "suffer vile Impositions from the dishonesty of the Tradesmen." After returning to Mount Vernon from his disappointments in the Virginia Regiment, Washington found in each successive consignment of tobacco evidence that the trade in the staple crop was one more supposed benefit of the British empire that, in fact, placed Virginia planters at a perpetual disadvantage.[18]

The Custis estate had in many ways been a model of the reciprocal benefits of empire for British merchant and Virginia planter in the first half of the eighteenth century, and in his administration of the affairs of Daniel Parke Custis, Washington learned about the organization of one of the colony's wealthiest estates and largest producers of tobacco. In the year and a half between her husband's death and her marriage to Washington, Martha managed much of the Custis business and was appointed by a county court as administrator of the estate. At its April 1759 session, the Virginia General Court recognized Washington's legal authority to administer his wife's share of the estate and his responsibility for managing the two-thirds of the estate that would be divided between Martha's two surviving children.[19]

Between April and October 1759, Washington, working closely with the attorney John Mercer and consulting Martha, drafted accounts of the Custis assets and debts for the commissioners appointed to oversee the distribution of the estate among the three heirs. When he prepared to meet with Mercer in August 1759, he anticipated that it would "be necessary that Mrs. Washington shoud accompany me in order to clear up any doubtful matters." The various accounts, most of which Washington laboriously copied for his own records, detailed the vast holdings of the Custis estate and the organization of its working plantations. The estate extended to nearly eighteen thousand acres spread over six counties, and at the time of the appraisal controlled 283 slaves, valued at £8,958. Overseers directed work at individual plantations, and the estate was so large that Custis had appointed Joseph Valentine as a steward, in the terminology of English estates, to manage much of the business of the collective plantations.[20]

Washington made copies of the inventories of property in the six counties, familiarizing himself with the detailed lists of each slave by name and appraised value, the livestock numbering in the hundreds, and scores of farming implements. Despite its scale of operation and the cultivation of corn, wheat, and oats, the Custis estate adhered to an older model of tobacco production, with no evidence of the recent improvements in British agriculture that already attracted Washington's interest at Mount Vernon. Only on the Eastern Shore plantations were there "4 old plows," while the Tidewater plantations were firmly fixed in cultivation with the hoe. Nor were there implements of domestic manufactures. The extensive collection of Custis books Washington brought to Mount Vernon included older works on gardening and botany, but none of the British treatises of practical farming that he ordered for himself.[21]

In addition to the slaves, who were together valued at nearly £3,000, Martha's dower, which came under Washington's control and management, included Claiborne's Plantation, with 2,880 acres in King William County; the Bridge and Ship Landing Quarters, with a combined one thousand acres, in York County; a nearby mill; a house in Williamsburg; and several lots in Jamestown. The Custis estate was remarkable in Virginia for the size of its capital assets, and Martha, in her management of the estate, carried on her late husband's practice of making large loans to prominent Virginia families. The recovery of debts owed to both her and the Custis children would involve Washington in the business of several of those families and provide him with a unique perspective on the risks of mismanagement and reckless spending by the colony's largest landholders.[22]

At Mount Vernon, Washington divided the arable lands into working quarters, called plantations, similar to the Custis estate and other large tobacco growing estates. Before 1759, the cultivated areas at Mount Vernon consisted of the Home Plantation surrounding Washington's residence and Muddy Hole Plantation to the north, where tobacco was grown. Beginning in 1759, Washington organized Dogue Run Plantation on the creek of the same name and partially formed out of lands purchased in 1757. Williamson's Plantation, renamed Creek Plantation in 1761, comprised land formerly leased by tenants. Land purchased from William Clifton was consolidated as River Plantation, established by 1761. At the four outlying plantations, which together produced the estate's tobacco, Washington installed overseers, who, as of 1761, each managed the work of between four and ten enslaved field laborers. The Home Plantation grew wheat, hay, and other crops to support livestock, and was also the site of the largest orchards on the estate. By June 1761, nine enslaved field laborers worked at the Home Plantation. Also living and working in close proximity at the Home House were seven enslaved carpenters, two enslaved blacksmiths, and ten enslaved servants in the mansion. This organization of the estate and division of laborers defined much about the community and family connections for the enslaved, although marriages across plantations were common.[23]

Washington frequently coordinated the management of the Mount Vernon plantations with that of his Bullskin Plantation in Frederick County. In addition to combining the tobacco crops for marketing, he transferred farming implements and livestock between the estates, and he occasionally moved enslaved workers from one property to the other. Washington was less directly involved in the supervision of the plantation in King William County and the other Custis properties, where Joseph Valentine continued as manager, but he regularly visited these properties on his way to or from sessions of the House of Burgesses. Washington also directed the shipment to Robert Cary & Company of tobacco from the Custis properties under his direct control and those he managed as guardian for Martha's son, John Parke Custis. Washington understood the operation of the Custis plantations well enough to recruit an overseer from one of the York River quarters to work at Mount Vernon's River Plantation, and to transfer enslaved field workers who had not been among the initial removal of dower slaves to Mount Vernon.[24]

In important ways, Washington's ambitions for Mount Vernon diverged from the model of the Custis estate and the traditional focus on tobacco cultivation. By the time Washington assumed the management of his estate, Virginians were learning about new methods of farming that had dramatically increased productivity in Great Britain over the past several decades. Many of the changes dated to Jethro Tull's frequently reprinted book, *Horse-Hoeing Husbandry,* first published in 1731, which emphasized the importance of plowing for the preparation of the soil and the proper sowing of seeds. Even greater gains in wheat and barley production came from crop rotations and the widespread introduction of fodder crops, especially clover, that both restored soil fertility and allowed livestock to be raised in smaller spaces, thereby increasing supplies of manure for further enrichment of the land. These methods allowed for a much more intensive cultivation of land at the same time that the increased size of farms and consolidation of estates added other efficiencies. At least as significant as the changes in cultivation and animal husbandry or those in estate management was the widespread commitment to experiment and the dissemination of agricultural knowledge.[25]

The advocates of these farming practices sometimes referred to their methods as the New Husbandry, and the most enthusiastic and influential proponents represented a new type of farmer, as well. The literature of agricultural improvement introduced Washington to the emergence of a new rural order in Great Britain and the critical influence of the self-defined gentleman farmer. The widespread adoption of the New Husbandry coincided with a final wave of land enclosure and the consolidation of agricultural estates, facilitating the coordination of crop rotations and livestock breeding. The increasing concentration of landholding allowed estate owners to bring more land under cultivation and to control the methods of farming on the best land. A growing number of landless laborers provided a readily available workforce for estate owners.[26]

The New Husbandry was always more than a response to these practical opportunities; it represented a different and often self-conscious cultural role assumed by many of the British estate owners who now spent much of their time directing the farms on their lands. Improvement for these estate owners depended on daily supervision of cultivation, but even more important were their reading in a new type of agricultural treatise and their participation in networks for the exchange of scientific knowledge about agriculture. Beginning with the model of Tull, the publications associated with the New Husbandry represented something different in British writing on agriculture in their blend of practical information and scientific analysis. Many of the most effective and influential improvers were lesser gentry and highly capitalized tenants who shared their experiments and experience with one another and who provided an eager market for agricultural treatises. The number of agricultural publications increased dramatically after 1750, and these books, the same type of volumes that brought the New Husbandry to Washington and other farmers in the British colonies, were the most important means for spreading information about improved farming methods.[27]

In addition to their detailed instructions for the management of crops and livestock, the publications of the New Husbandry defined agricultural improvement as a public good that members of the landed gentry were best placed to serve. The gentry, uniquely among residents of the countryside, could bring to farming a learning and understanding of which the common farmer was thought incapable, and the gentry, unlike the aristocrat, had the practical skills to demonstrate models of cultivation for more general adoption. The emphasis on practical experience and scientific process fixed the New Husbandry in the Enlightenment belief in progress and the ability of humans to improve the world around them. Farming could be a way of understanding the natural world and controlling its resources for the benefit of society.[28]

Agricultural treatises frequently associated the efforts of the improving gentry with virtuous farmers of antiquity, like Virgil and Pliny, and the allusions to the ancients reaffirmed the professed civic purposes of the gentry who pursued the New Husbandry. "Among the Romans their senators ploughed; and the great examples they gave of virtue and industry laid the foundation of all their after greatness" wrote Edward Lisle in the *Observations in Husbandry,* which Washington received in 1759. The georgic verses of Virgil enjoyed enormous popularity in Great Britain at the time, and the term georgic came to define far more than a rediscovered style of verse about the countryside. Georgic denoted a pervasive ideal of rural life in which human endeavor transformed nature through labor, reason, and the aesthetic design of the landscape.[29]

The same ideals and practical knowledge inspired agricultural projects throughout much of Europe, where British models of improvement held sway as they did in the American colonies. Frederick the Great of Prussia, one of the first national leaders to present his agricultural improvements as a public model, hired an English farmer to introduce crop rotations. Agricultural treatises were exchanged between Great Britain and the Continent, although translations from English to European languages predominated. These publications and the correspondence between improving farmers of various nations reflected a commitment to the generous communication of agricultural knowledge from which Washington would benefit in the 1760s and in which he would later participate. Washington joined with enlightened British and European landowners in his eager demand for agricultural knowledge and in his belief that large estates with contiguous farms were the most advantageous sites to demonstrate a new, rational system of agricultural improvement in any society.[30]

Soon after he returned to Mount Vernon in 1759, Washington immersed himself in the literature of the New Husbandry as part of his self-education as a farmer. In May, in his first correspondence with Robert Cary & Company, he asked the London merchants to send "the newest, and most approvd Treatise of Agriculture," along with specific titles that indicated his knowledge of the favored books found in the collections of the small group of Virginia planters who embraced British models of agricultural improvement. On a trip to Williamsburg and the Custis estates in the fall of 1760, Washington consulted another planter's library to confirm the title of Thomas Hale's *A Compleat Body of Husbandry*, which he ordered from the Cary firm. Over the next several years, he received from London some of the essential British agricultural treatises, including Lisle's *Observation in Husbandry*, Batty Langley's *New Principles of Gardening*, and the first six volumes of *Museum Rusticum*. Washington relied on the office of the *Virginia Gazette* in Williamsburg to order other books, most notably Duhamel's *A Practical Treatise of Husbandry*, and his was one of the first copies in Virginia of what would become an enduring volume in American agricultural libraries well into the next century.[31]

The treatises that Washington gathered in his library in the 1760s introduced him to the culture of agricultural improvement then flourishing in England and Scotland, but new to Virginia. For decades, organized support for agricultural innovation in Virginia had focused on the traditional goals of mercantilism, with a search for crops that could be produced in the colony and shipped to Great Britain in exchange for credit and finished goods, much as the tobacco trade had long functioned. Silk and wine had been the objects of investment and experiment since the second half of the seventeenth century, and at the same time that Washington assumed the management of farming at Mount Vernon, a Committee on Encouragement of Arts and Manufactures, established by the Virginia Assembly in 1759 and chaired by Charles Carter of Cleve, promoted experiments with wine, olives, and cured sturgeon, all for export to Great Britain. Although Washington joined other prominent neighbors to invest in a vineyard, his acquisition of the British agricultural treatises signaled his intention to break from the mercantilist model on his own estate. Washington's goal was not simply to diversify crops, as Carter and many other Virginia planters had been doing through the middle decades of the eighteenth century. He planned to emulate British estate owners by integrating the cultivation of crops with the management of livestock and incorporating the latest advances in husbandry with the lessons of his own experiments.[32]

Landon Carter, brother of Charles and owner of Sabine Hall Plantation in Richmond County, had in the 1750s gathered British agricultural books in his library while he increased wheat cultivation and adopted the plowing, manuring, and crop rotations of the New Husbandry. John Baylor of Caroline County, a friend whose extensive library Washington had visited, purchased more recent British farming publications. That Baylor and Washington also purchased agricultural books through the Williamsburg shop of the *Virginia Gazette* indicates there was a broader audience for these practical guides, and Washington had opportunities to speak with other improving planters who served with him in the House of Burgesses. His most important sources of information about farming, however, were British books and British merchants who assisted him in the selection and purchase of the implements of husbandry.[33]

In his growing collection of agricultural books, Washington read about a world of voluntary associations in Great Britain and the collaboration of British landowners committed to sharing their own practical experience and the results of measured experiments. The members of London's Society for the Encouragement of Arts, Manufactures, and Commerce described their *Museum Rusticum* as "a channel of intelligence" that would share the recent advances in English agriculture with the gentry and nobility as well as with farmers and artisans. Other volumes, such as Francis Home's *Principles of Agriculture and Vegetation,* were written in response to the offer of premiums by improvement societies. Robert Maxwell's *The Practical Husbandman* sought to preserve and disseminate the transactions of the Society of Improvers of Knowledge of Agriculture in Scotland. The stated aim of many of these books was to establish fixed principles and rational systems that might lead farmers away from the destructive practices of the past.[34]

In the treatises Washington gathered in his library, the British authors and advocates of agricultural improvement often presented themselves as patriots, promoting the agriculture upon which "the Wealth and the Happiness of the Kingdom depend." Robert Maxwell dedicated *The Practical Husbandman* of 1757 to William Pitt, noting that the "greatest and best Men, in all Ages, have been Lovers and Encouragers of Husbandry."

The members of the Society for the Encouragement of Arts, Manufactures, and Commerce expected their *Museum Rusticum* would be "an honour to the kingdom, and a blessing to mankind." Others agreed that agricultural improvement should be a transnational project, through which Britons would share their notable advances in farming with a wider world. Hale's *Compleat Body of Husbandry* aimed to collect and disseminate the most useful agricultural lessons from various nations, so that "they may learn one from another." The publisher of the 1751 edition of Jethro Tull's *Horse-Hoeing Husbandry*, which Washington consulted, combined the patriotic and the imperial in his suggestion that the new methods should be introduced to the British colonies in America to protect the balance of trade and power. As an active reader of these treatises and in his adoption of the principles of the New Husbandry on a Virginia plantation, Washington was able to participate in these discussions, confident that he could contribute to the general prosperity of the empire.[35]

Many of the New Husbandry volumes that Washington read linked agricultural improvement to civic responsibilities in ways that reinforced the Virginia planter's sense of his own social authority. The authors favored by Washington argued that meaningful improvements in agriculture must be the work of gentry landowners who were actively engaged in the daily tasks of farming and who held influence over smaller farmers. *The Farmer's Compleat Guide* held that the proper advocate of agricultural improvement was "a gentleman who has a large farm in his own hands." Lisle, in *Observations in Husbandry*, declared that of all the advantages arising to a gentleman engaged in farming—health, character, material security—none was greater than that of doing good on the public stage. Washington would through much of his life as a farmer similarly present his improvements as a public example that he and other wealthy Virginians with access to British knowledge and superior farming implements were uniquely qualified to implement on their plantations.[36]

Washington had every reason to believe that his adoption of the cultivation practices of the New Husbandry would bring the same practical benefits to a Virginia plantation. Beginning in 1760 with the seminal text of Tull's *Horse-Hoeing Husbandry*, Washington initiated his practice of excerpting practical information, often in small notebooks that he could carry in his coat pocket when he rode to his fields, and the British books that he added to his library offered practical guidance and encouragement for his innovations. His early experiments with seed germination were almost certainly inspired by Home's *Principles of Agriculture and Vegetation,* which he had recently received from Robert Cary & Company. From Hale's *Husbandry,* which his London merchants sent in March 1761, Washington learned about the use of river mud as a soil enrichment, which he began to apply in 1762. In the same volumes of Hale, he read of the advantages of sowing turnips with a drill plow, one of which he ordered from Cary & Company in the fall of 1761. Duhamel's *Practical Treatise* persuaded Washington of the merits of the Rotherham plow, which he ordered from England soon after receiving the volume.[37]

While Washington remained invested in tobacco cultivation, his innovations in farming at Mount Vernon in the early 1760s were largely focused on other crops and inspired by the model of British husbandry. "The chief Art of an Husbandman is to feed the Plants to the best Advantage," wrote Jethro Tull, and much of the subsequent agricultural literature consulted by Washington offered instruction on the examination and preparation of soil. Washington undertook a series of carefully observed experiments to discern the optimal preparation of the soil for different crops. In April 1760, he designed a multi-compartment box with ten sections, each filled with a different mixture of soil and amendments, including three types of dung, mud, sand drawn from the river, and marl, a calcium-rich clay. With a specially made device, Washington planted three grains of wheat, oats, and barley in each compartment and then measured their progress, finding that the "black mould" from swamp land was the most effective.[38]

In a bed prepared with dung, Washington sowed clover, lucerne, and rye grass in numbered rows to compare their density of growth. Another field of lucerne was partially sowed by drills and partially sowed by raking in. A specially prepared bed was divided between trefoil clover and lucerne, "both done with design to see how these Seeds answer in that Ground." He extended his experiments to tobacco, planting five sorts of sweet-scented tobacco in equal allotments of dunged soil and soil left without amendment. At another quarter, Washington ordered tobacco to be planted in hills with and without marl, "giving both equal working and let them fare exactly alike in all Respects."[39]

Soon after he returned to Mount Vernon in the spring of 1759, Washington assured one of his English tobacco merchants that he would "conduct my own business with more punctuality than heretofore as it will pass under my own immediate Inspection." He imposed time-based metrics on the work of enslaved laborers and free artisans. In his agreement with an indentured joiner, John Askew, Washington required that any time lost, whether to sickness, negligence, or private business, would be made up at the end of the year, and Washington maintained an account of days worked. From the first of January 1760, Washington required weekly accounts of carpenters' work to be submitted by Will, purchased as a slave in April and now working as the lead carpenter at Mount Vernon. Washington entrusted the enslaved miller, Anthony, to deliver an account of the days worked by the free laborer hired by Washington to rebuild his mill.[40]

Washington devised his own work programs, which he expected enslaved laborers to follow. In early February 1760, on a daily circuit of his plantations, Washington noted with disapproval that a team of four enslaved carpenters had hewed only 120 feet on a shortened work day. He sat down to observe the carpenters as they worked at their own pace, while he measured the time expended and the lumber finished. Accounting for the length of the day, Washington calculated that two carpenters were each capable of hewing 125 feet of poplar wood a day, while two others could together saw 180 feet of plank. Washington would expect of the carpenters an increased productivity as the days lengthened into spring. He also noted the need for precise measurement of work with other types of wood.[41]

Overseers met with separate expectations of regularity as well as the frequent displeasure of Washington. Washington considered Christopher Hardwick at Bullskin in Frederick County to be a "Rascally Overseer," who abused livestock and ignored severely ill slaves. On a visit to one of his Mount Vernon plantations in January 1760, Washington found the overseer Robert Stephens absent, "According to Custom," and soon thereafter he "severely reprimanded young Stephens for his Indolence." A week later, Washington found Stephens "hard at Work with an ax—very extraordinary this!" John Foster provoked Washington's fury when he absented himself for several days from his charge at Dogue Run Plantation. Neither Stephens nor Foster lasted long under Washington's direct supervision.

Stephens had left by the fall of 1760 when Washington personally assumed direction of the tobacco harvest at Williamson's Tract; John Foster ran away from Mount Vernon in the spring of 1762.[42]

Washington hoped to enforce steady work by overseers and free artisans through written agreements that outlined responsibilities and the consequences of failure. John Askew, who came to work as a joiner in September 1759, signed an agreement to labor "duely from Sun rise to Sun set, allowing proper times only for Eating." When Burgess Mitchell arrived as overseer of the Home House plantation in May 1762, he agreed "to attend strictly to all orders and directions" from Washington, and to execute those directions "with the greatest care Expedition and exactness." Washington even required the overseer to behave in such a diligent and commendable manner as "to gain the good esteem & liking of his said employer." Mitchell acceded to Washington's stipulation that he would forfeit his wages and be turned off the estate if he failed to fulfill any article in the letter of agreement. Without further explanation or payment, Washington recorded that Mitchell departed less than three months after he arrived.[43]

In written agreements and terms of hire, Washington made the overseers responsible for the control of enslaved workers under their management. Edward Violette at Bullskin agreed to remain constantly at the Plantation, "looking after his People." Nelson Kelly at Dogue Run plantation was required to prevent the slaves from visiting other plantations without his consent. He also promised "to forbid strange Negroes frequenting their Quarters without lawful excuses," a provision that implicitly acknowledged that familiar slaves from other estates or free blacks often visited relatives and friends among the enslaved community at Mount Vernon. Washington initially managed the agricultural labor at the Home House farm, but by 1762, as the number of field workers increased, he hired an overseer with the explicit responsibility for supervising and working with the enslaved laborers at that farm. At the same time that overseers enforced steady labor, they were required by Washington to ensure the care of the enslaved under their management, "treating them with humanity and tenderness when Sick." The agreements with overseers made Washington's plantations more reliant on enslaved labor by discouraging the employment of hired workers, who had often assisted in the harvesting and threshing of wheat. The compensation of the overseers was henceforth to be reduced by deducting from their share of crop sales the proportionate costs of any free workers they hired.[44]

Washington hoped to impress upon the overseers his intention to have his tobacco managed as carefully as possible. Edward Violette and Nelson Kelly obliged themselves to grow the type of tobacco prescribed by Washington and to manage it according to his specifications. To promote the quality of the crop, Washington notified the overseers that he would always be in attendance when the tobacco arrived at the inspection warehouse and that he expected it to appear "very good, very neat, and very clean." Washington acknowledged that his emphasis on the quality of tobacco leaf might reduce the quantity grown, and he designed compensation accordingly. Overseers on the plantations that produced tobacco for market received a specified share of the proceeds from the sale of the crop and a bonus determined by the amount by which the sale price in Great Britain exceeded the price offered by buyers on the Potomac.[45]

When Washington shipped his first consignment of Potomac tobacco to Robert Cary & Company in spring 1761, he assured the merchants of his careful management of the crop and asked for advice on the future preparation of his crop, "for I am more anxious about the quality than quantity of what I ship." At the subsequent suggestion of the merchants, Washington agreed to remove the stems from some of his tobacco, but insisted on shipping leaf with and without the stems so that he could judge if the sales price justified the additional effort. The same year, he divided his shipment into three lots, each with a different kind of tobacco, and he asked the Cary merchants to report on the market value of each sort. Unfortunately, the merchants misunderstood the instructions, according to Washington, who suggested that they might want to read the letter again. When the Cary partners criticized some of the shipment, Washington conceded that the narrow leaf in question had been planted by mistake, and without his approval.[46]

During the first full season under Washington's direction, tobacco production at Mount Vernon and Bullskin increased from slightly more than twenty thousand pounds to more than thirty-two thousand pounds. Packed into thirty hogsheads, the combined Potomac crop grown in 1760 was shipped to Robert Cary & Company, while Washington consigned to

Richard Washington only the lower-quality tobacco he received in payment of rent from tenants. In the following season, the Mount Vernon and Bullskin plantations produced more than fifty-two thousand pounds of tobacco for export, and Washington again consigned his entire Potomac crop to Cary & Company. This crop, only the second grown under Washington's direct supervision, would be the largest produced at either Mount Vernon or Bullskin. The combined yield fell to just under thirty-eight thousand pounds in 1762, to about thirty-five thousand in 1763, and to twenty-seven thousand in 1764. When the tobacco grown in 1762 was shipped to Cary & Company, Washington made up for the deficiency with fifteen hogsheads of inferior rental tobacco. He further apologized for the quality of his own crop, assuring the merchants that much of it was of a sort that he would never again raise.[47]

Despite Washington's close management, neither the careful instruction of the overseers nor the experiments in improved cultivation increased the quality or the quantity of the tobacco grown at Mount Vernon. Each season seemed to bring new obstacles to a successful tobacco crop. In 1762, the Potomac region suffered one of the most severe droughts in memory. In 1763, a wet spring, a summer drought, and an early frost combined to ruin Washington's crop. When Washington attempted to repeat his experiment with different sorts of tobacco, the weather destroyed the plants and reduced his anticipated crop by half. During the first several years of Washington's management of Mount Vernon, the continuing war between Great Britain and France required merchant ships to wait for convoys, and insurance was so expensive that Washington chose not to insure for the full value of his crop. He hoped the prospect of peace in 1763 would restore the fortunes of merchants and planters, but, in fact, the free flow of the tobacco trade brought a decline in prices that had reached their wartime peak in 1759.[48]

Early in their correspondence, Washington asked the merchants of Robert Cary & Company what prices he might expect for Potomac tobacco if it were grown in the same manner as the best tobacco cultivated along the York and James Rivers. He quickly learned that neither plant stock nor skillful management could ensure the prices offered for the York River leaf esteemed on the small but lucrative domestic market in England. By the 1760s, most tobacco grown along the Potomac was sold directly to British buyers in Virginia, often the Scottish merchants who sold the cheaper grades of tobacco to growing markets on the European continent. Washington repeatedly reminded the merchants of Robert Cary & Company that he could have received a better price for his tobacco if he had sold directly to traders in Virginia, as he had done in 1759, but he continued the correspondence with the firm to maintain the personal contact with London and to facilitate the large annual order of goods for the estate.[49]

When Washington in May 1764 learned from Cary & Company that he had fallen more than £1,800 in their debt, it proved to be a moment of reckoning for his participation in the tobacco trade and for the management of the entire estate. Although he claimed to be at a loss to understand the size of the debt, Washington conceded that to pay for slaves and land, he had depended on cash from the Custis accounts and drawn too heavily on the sterling balance with Cary & Company to provide Martha's son, John Parke Custis, his share of the Custis personal estate. The debt was deepened by the failure of four bills of credit, totaling more than £400, submitted to Cary & Company by Washington over the past three years. Always protective of his reputation, Washington wanted the merchants to acknowledge that the debt was a result of "Mischances rather than Misconduct." Washington insisted that, had his crops proved good and sold well, he would have had a favorable balance with his London merchant, but his hunger for slaves and land had revealed the limits of a trade that would no longer support the expansion of estates as it had earlier in the eighteenth century.[50]

The alarm of the debt and the repeated disappointments in the traditional consignment tobacco trade emboldened Washington to advance the kind of diversification that had excited his interest since 1759. After the harvest of the crop planted in the spring of 1764, Washington sharply curtailed the production of tobacco on his Potomac lands. In 1765 he planted small crops at just two of his Mount Vernon plantations and abandoned tobacco altogether at Bullskin. In 1766 he grew no tobacco at all on his Potomac lands, and Mount Vernon ceased to be a tobacco plantation. Washington would henceforth rely on tobacco from the more productive dower lands in King William County to meet his obligations with Robert Cary & Company. At the same time, he lessened his reliance on the credit extensions of his tobacco merchants, assuring them that he would reduce his annual order of goods from London while the debt was outstanding. To reduce his expenditures further, Washington suspended for several years the purchase of slaves and of additional lands adjoining Mount Vernon.[51]

Wheat replaced tobacco as the most important cash crop at Mount Vernon. Washington had already taken a significant step to expand the marketing of wheat when in January 1763 he entered into an exclusive contract with the Alexandria merchant firm of Carlyle & Adam. Beginning with the next wheat crop at Mount Vernon and continuing for seven years, Washington would sell all of the wheat raised for market to the partnership of John Carlyle and Robert Adam for a fixed price per bushel of three shillings, nine pence of Virginia current money. Washington agreed to deliver the wheat to landings in Alexandria, at which time the merchants and their millers would assume all further risk.[52]

Like most estates in mid-eighteenth century Virginia, Mount Vernon had long produced wheat, the surpluses of which were most commonly sold in the colony. Since mid-century, demand for North American wheat had increased in Europe and the Caribbean, and by the 1760s merchants like Carlyle & Adam began to serve those markets. In 1764, the Mount Vernon plantations delivered 257 bushels of wheat, less than a third of their production, to Carlyle & Adam; a year later they delivered their entire crop of 1,112 bushels, as the grain became the most important responsibility and the largest source of income for the overseers on each farm. Overseers, for the portion of the crop negotiated with Washington, received the contract price per bushel of wheat of three shilling, nine pence.[53]

In 1765, at the same time that Washington phased out tobacco plantings and increased wheat crops, he devoted other land at Mount Vernon to the cultivation of hemp, and he encouraged his overseers with the promise of a share of the market sale. Parliament repeatedly had offered a bounty for the colonial production of hemp, usually without much effect, but more recently Virginia planters had shown interest in the crop. At least by 1763, hemp had been grown commercially at Washington's Bullskin Plantation in Frederick County, a region in which hemp was becoming the most important agricultural commodity. For his Mount Vernon plantations, Washington secured hempseed from his own plantation in Frederick and purchased more from a Fredericksburg merchant, the likely source of the English seed he tried in 1765. That year, the overseers at Muddy Hole,

Dogue Run, and River plantations all grew hemp and experimented with the several methods of rotting the crop, by which the fibers used in rope making were freed from the stems. Washington also invested in the equipment for the final processing of hemp and for weaving it into coarse cloth.[54]

The introduction of hemp at Mount Vernon was part of Washington's broader exploration of agricultural opportunities in the face of the declining prospects for tobacco at his Potomac estate. He inquired into the market for corn and grains through the wine trade to Southern Europe, where demand was high. In 1763, he considered the more active cultivation of farmlands on his property to the west, and he negotiated with a former overseer, Christopher Hardwick, to manage 240 acres in Hampshire County, hoping to bring "Tobacco Hemp Grain Beef Porke Butter and other Things to Market." Washington provided Hardwick with an enslaved laborer, Troy, who had worked in the fields at Mount Vernon for a year, and he committed to buy as many as five additional enslaved Africans from "some Guinea Ship," as well as to supply Hardwick with livestock and farming implements. Washington, however, was seldom comfortable managing an overseer from afar, and he closed out his account with Hardwick several months before the partnership was to go into effect.[55]

Washington had better luck when for the first time he hired a manager to assist in supervising all of the activities across his Mount Vernon estate and at the plantation in Frederick County. Lund Washington, a distant cousin, had managed the Virginia and Maryland estates of Henry and William Fitzhugh before he came to Mount Vernon in the fall of 1764. He would remain as the estate manager for over twenty years, and he also served as a kind of assistant or secretary to Washington. In his early years at Mount Vernon, Lund hired and paid free workers, delivered wheat to Carlyle & Adam, and purchased livestock for the estate. Lund arrived with sufficient agricultural knowledge to instruct the overseer at Bullskin in the cultivation and processing of hemp. The hire of Lund followed Washington's recognition that in the absence of the owner, an estate required "a Person of Character to manage the whole."[56]

As he adopted new crops with different seasonal routines, Washington sought to maximize his gain from the labor of the slaves on his plantations. Wheat and hay harvests required the timely coordination of laborers across the estate, regardless of their primary work. A growing number of enslaved carpenters, smiths, and laborers at the Home House farm joined the field workers to complete wheat harvests at the outlying plantations. Washington directed the work of laborers in moving a tenant's house off one of the newly organized farms and again when they repaired the mill dam. The carpenters, smiths, and field laborers from the Home House were employed in the harvest of sixty acres of wheat at River and Creek plantations in July 1763, and the carpenters spent extended days working in the corn-fields under John Chowning at River Plantation and Josias Cook at the Creek Plantation. In an early instance of measuring the working days of slaves in monetary terms, Washington deducted from each overseer's al-lotted share of the crop an estimated cash value of the work of the enslaved laborers from the Home House.[57]

The scale and complexity of operations across the estate heightened Washington's demand for closer supervision and control of enslaved laborers. He was particularly concerned that overseers curtail night visits between the several plantations, but as he soon discovered, the larger number of enslaved field workers, living at separate quarters, opened an opportunity for collaborative resistance and flight. In August 1761, just a few days after Washington traveled to Maryland to purchase several slaves recently transported from Africa, four enslaved field workers escaped from Mount Vernon. Although they left from Dogue Run plantation, one of the men, Neptune, worked at River Plantation, suggesting some coordination across the estate. The four men, ranging in age from twenty-five to forty, had each been at Mount Vernon for about two years.

Although group flight was relatively uncommon in Virginia and espe-cially at Mount Vernon, it was most likely to involve Africans, and the run-aways in the summer of 1761 were all African born. Two of them, Neptune and Cupid, had been transported on the same ship from which Washington purchased them, and in Washington's view, they spoke "unintelligible En-glish." Peros, "esteemed a sensible judicious Negro," had been enslaved for many years at a Custis property near Williamsburg, and Jack, more re-cently transported from Africa, had lived in Middlesex County and was probably one of the nine slaves purchased there by Washington in 1759. None of the enslaved men, to Washington's knowledge, had experienced recent conflict with anyone at Mount Vernon or met with the anger of their overseers, which Washington assumed the likeliest provocations for most runaways. While individual runaways had sometimes remained near the estate and occasionally returned of their own accord, this group, Washington suspected, would "steer some direct Course (which cannot even be guessed at) in Hopes of an Escape." Each failed in that escape, and upon recapture, Washington was intent on reclaiming their labor. He returned each individual to field work but on separate plantations, three at Mount Vernon and one at Bullskin, where Neptune again ran away and was again recaptured in 1765.[58]

Washington considered another runaway sufficiently dangerous that he decided in 1766 to sell the slave, Tom, to a buyer in the Caribbean, even though Washington acknowledged that Tom was a highly skilled field worker as well as foreman of a work gang on Mount Vernon's largest plantation. Tom had only recently attempted to run away, and the fact that he was also a "rogue" in Washington's estimation "was by no means remarkable." The decision to sell Tom in exchange for a shipment of liquor and sweetmeats marked some unexplained limit to Washington's willingness to manage slaves and their perceived recalcitrance as long as he was able to extract their valuable labor. Abram and Cloe, two enslaved field laborers who worked at River Plantation under Tom's direction, had run away two months before Tom did, and upon their recapture, Washington sent them back to work in the fields, as he had with the four men who ran away in 1761. The banishment of Tom to the harsh work of the sugar islands may have been intended as an example to be made of a slave with a certain degree of privilege, but his sale and separation from the plantation community remained an infrequent form of punishment at Mount Vernon, where Washington was more concerned with securing the maximum labor from each slave.[59]

However many "rogues" he identified among the enslaved workers, at no time before the Revolutionary War did Washington indicate that his reliance on slavery might impede the transition to wheat or the broader project of agricultural improvement at Mount Vernon. In fact, his renewed purchases of slaves beginning in 1767 and his transfer of more than twenty additional slaves from the Custis estates to Mount Vernon in 1770 suggest that Washington was confident that enslaved labor, closely supervised and apportioned across the estate's arable land, would enable him to establish a thriving operation based on mixed agriculture and livestock management.

The challenge, as it had been with tobacco, was to cultivate enough good land to employ the enslaved field workers to his advantage, preferably on a consolidated estate that he could personally manage.[60]

The implementation of Washington's vision of agricultural diversification had since 1759 depended on a greater variety of skills among the enslaved laborers. In his 1759 indenture agreement with the John Askew, Washington required the joiner to "use his best endeavour's to instruct in the art of his trade any Negro or Negroes which the said George Washington shall cause to work with him." In 1760, Anthony, a dower slave who may have learned the trade at a Custis estate, was serving as Washington's miller and lived at the mill with his wife, Betty. Anthony was succeeded by another enslaved miller, George, who continued at the mill for more than five years. Mulatto Jack not only worked as a plowman, he frequently traveled west to Bullskin and south to the plantation in King William County, delivering farm implements and livestock as well as acting as a courier for Washington's letters. On at least one of the outlying plantations, as was typical of other large Virginia estates, one of the enslaved workers served as a foreman of the gang of field workers. By 1765, Washington enumerated eleven enslaved tradesmen, a term that encompassed carpenters, millers, and blacksmiths, at the Home House.[61]

∘   ∘   ∘

In the parlance of mid-eighteenth-century Virginia, Washington, by rejecting tobacco cultivation at Mount Vernon, became a farmer rather than a planter. His identity as a farmer would involve far more than his choice of crops. The term connoted for him a commitment to experiment and innovation, and responsible stewardship of the land under his cultivation. Being a farmer also meant adopting the principles of the New Husbandry and making practical use of implements designed for the most advanced British agriculture. Washington believed that this course of farming would depend for its success on his knowledge and his ability to direct the operations of his estate, which he understood to include the adaptation of an enslaved labor force to the work required of a new kind of agriculture. The pursuit of this agricultural model also redefined his relationship with Great Britain.

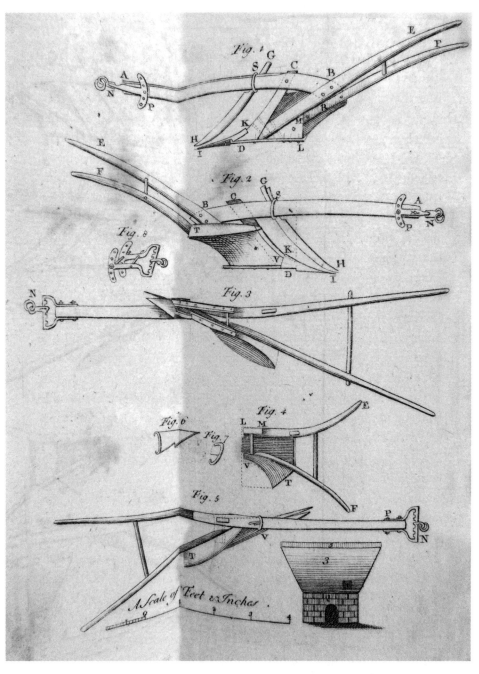

Fig 1.1 Illustration of the Rotherham plough, from Robert Maxwell, *The Practical Husbandman,* 1757 (fig. 1, plate 1). Washington in 1765 ordered a Rotherham plow from the Yorkshire town for which it was named. The plow was described in two treatises Washington added to his library by 1764, and he relied on tobacco merchants in Great Britain to obtain this and other farming implements to support his transition to wheat cultivation.

Courtesy of Mount Vernon Ladies' Association.

Washington's transition to farmer was made possible by his existing commercial ties with British tobacco merchants, even as he moved away from that traditional staple crop of colonial Virginia. The tobacco merchants, who were Washington's most important personal link to the center of empire, offered him access to the knowledge and materials he needed to establish a new agricultural foundation for his estate. Washington relied on the British tobacco merchants, particularly Robert Cary & Company, for the seeds, the plows, and the scythes required to cultivate wheat, and also the grasses and fodder crops to support livestock husbandry and soil improvement. The Cary merchants selected agricultural treatises relating to improved farming and provided access to the mechanical improvements Washington read about in British publications. In March 1765, Washington used a single consignment of his tenants' tobacco, shipped to Liverpool merchants, to procure a Rotherham plow. He insisted that this implement, one of the essential designs of the New Husbandry, must be purchased in the Yorkshire town where it had been invented, "for none but the true sort will answer the end of my sending for it."[62]

Washington's connections with tobacco merchants in London and other British ports enabled him to pursue a course of farming that strengthened his identification with a community of improving landowners in Great Britain. The farming implements he ordered for use by enslaved field laborers provided a material link with the transformation of English agriculture over the middle decades of the eighteenth century. Washington might continue to chafe under the perceived slights of London shopkeepers who sent defective wheat sieves he dismissed as useless lumber, but the trade also brought him plows and sheep shears from the prominent ironmonger Theodosia Crowley, seeds from "an eminent Hop Merchant in Southwark," and farm implements from traders who supplied the leading agricultural estates in England.[63] This shared material culture and common farming practice allowed Washington to participate in a new kind of partnership with Great Britain, while his agricultural innovations eroded the older commercial ties of empire.

° *2* °

The Agricultural Foundations
of Independence

The Stamp Act crisis of 1765 brought a new urgency to Washington's plan for agricultural improvement and the diversification of his estate. Like so many colonists in British North America, Washington decried the revenue act as unconstitutional and an attack on the colonies' liberties. He also perceived a threat that was as much commercial as political. He considered the Stamp Act to be part of a larger design by which Parliament and the British ministry, in their demand for more revenue from the American colonies, disregarded and endangered the reciprocal benefits of trade within an empire based on the exchange of colonial agricultural commodities for British manufactures. "The whole produce of our labour hitherto has centred in Great Britain," he wrote, "what more can they desire?" Washington suspected that, following as it had recent restrictions on colonial trade and other burdensome acts, the stamp tax was one more step toward additional duties on colonial imports from Great Britain. He hesitated to predict the political consequences of the opposition to the Stamp Act, but was confident that further duties on imports would drive trade from Virginia into new markets. He asked his politically influential London merchants to explain "where then lyes the utility of these Measures?"[1]

In September 1765, just a few weeks before the Stamp Act would require a tax to be paid on publications and routine business and legal documents,

Washington warned the Cary & Company merchants that British demands for revenue would accelerate the broader economic shift already beginning to redefine the relationship between Great Britain and the North American colonies. "The Eyes of our People (already beginning to open) will perceive, that many of the Luxuries which we have heretofore lavished our Substance to Great Britain for can well be dispensed with whilst the Necessaries of Life are to be procurd (for the most part) within ourselves," he predicted. "This consequently will introduce frugality; and be a necessary stimulation to Industry—Great Britain may then load her Exports with as Heavy Taxes as She pleases but where will the consumption be? I am apt to think no Law or usage can compel us to barter our money or Staple Commodities for their Manufactures, if we can be supplied within ourselve upon the better Terms." Once freed of their reliance on British-supplied goods, colonists in America would venture into trade outside the empire. Washington took immediate steps to fulfill his own prediction by ordering from Cary & Company the implements required for cloth manufactures at Mount Vernon, and within a year, a weaver he hired had established a workshop capable of manufacturing large quantities of cloth to provision the enslaved laborers on the estate and for sale.[2]

The steady reduction in tobacco cultivation at Mount Vernon became a hardened and politicized resolution to abandon the crop in 1765. Washington recognized that his own disappointment in the tobacco trade reflected a larger transformation of the commercial relationship that had shaped the plantation system of the colonial Chesapeake. It was now evident to Washington "that it only suits the Interest of a few particular Gentlemen to continue their consignments of this commodity to that place, while others shoud endeavour to substitute some other Article in place of Tobacco, and try their success therewith." His first reaction was to inquire of several British merchant firms what other commodities, such as hemp and flax, might fill the place of tobacco, but the imperial crisis of 1765 also convinced Washington to focus agricultural production on crops that could be shipped to markets outside of Great Britain.[3]

Following the repeal of the Stamp Act in March 1766, Washington gratefully acknowledged the political support of London tobacco merchants but advised them to promote new patterns of trade that would be mutually beneficial for planters in Virginia and merchants and manufacturers in Great Britain. When one firm assured him that its partners had done everything in their power to oppose the act and then to seek its repeal, Washington cautioned: "I coud wish it was in my power to congratulate you with success, in having the Commercial System of these Colonies put upon a more enlargd and extensive footing than it is because I am well satisfied that it woud, ultimately, redound to the advantages of the Mother Country so long as the Colonies pursue trade and Agriculture, and woud be an effectual Let to Manufacturing among themselves." His own vision of that enlarged and extensive colonial commerce would over the next ten years guide his most important choices about what crops to cultivate and where to market them.[4]

Wheat became the primary focus of farming at Mount Vernon, and the cultivation and processing of the grain determined the seasonal rhythms of work for most of the enslaved laborers on the estate. The transition to wheat as the estate's principal cash crop required more careful preparation of the fields than the traditional practice of sowing the grain in ground previously cleared for corn, a method Washington admitted to be "slovenly but easy." Washington directed hired ditchers and enslaved field workers to clear new land and to drain swamps on each of the outlying plantations, a process that continued until, by 1774, wheat was grown on more than a thousand acres of the estate. A three-year rotation of wheat, then corn, then a season of leaving the land fallow was intended to restore the soil. The scale of wheat cultivation also required a new infrastructure on the plantations, and the enslaved carpenters built barns with wooden floors for storing harvested wheat before it was threshed. New fencing protected cultivated fields and penned many of the increasing numbers of livestock. Substantial land was devoted to growing corn for the provisioning of the enslaved and for sale of the surplus. Fodder and other grain crops supported the livestock. Nearly all of this coordinated agricultural work revolved around the increased production of wheat. In mid-1774, Washington explained to tobacco merchants in London that "the whole of my force is, in a manner confind to the growth of Wheat, & Manufacturing of it into Flour."[5]

The amount of wheat brought to market rapidly increased after 1765, when the field laborers stopped working on tobacco. As manager, Lund Washington recorded two thousand bushels of wheat produced in 1765, when the final and much reduced tobacco crop was planted. By 1768 the plantations produced more than 4,700 bushels of wheat. The following year, a season in which Washington thought wheat did better than ever, the plantations produced over 6,700 bushels, the highest yield ever under his ownership. With the exceptions of 1771 and 1772, when first weather and then a blight reduced the crop, the Mount Vernon plantations continued to produce between five thousand and six thousand bushels of wheat a year through 1775.[6]

Across a seven-year span from 1765 to 1772, Washington doubled the amount of wheat sown. The increase in wheat harvests also reflected the higher productivity that came with sowing new lands and improved cultivation. By 1767, the number of bushels of wheat produced per field laborer reached the maximum levels of the best Chesapeake grain producers, and with the transition from tobacco to wheat complete, revenue per laborer doubled between 1764 and 1767. The abandonment of tobacco also allowed Washington to divert labor to the cultivation of various fodder crops, which in turn made possible the use of more draft animals in plowing.[7]

As wheat became the cash crop of his estate, Washington educated himself about each stage in the process of growing and processing the grain. He made frequent, nearly daily visits to his working plantations at critical stages in the cultivation of wheat, closely observing the progress of the crop and the work of the enslaved field laborers. His understanding of the task of cradling wheat and the specificity of his orders for scythes from London suggest he had handled the implements and conferred with the laborers who carried out the work. He instructed the London scythe maker to make them "exactly three feet 10 Inches in the Cut. pretty strait in the Back for the greater ease in delivering the Grain out of the Cradle—all to have the same bend—the Plate, or Rim at the back to be stout & strong." He insisted that the ironmonger in London follow his precise specifications so that "if one Scythe gives way in the throng time of Harvest another can be put to the same Cradle immediately, without loss of time." Washington expected to receive the finest implements crafted for improved wheat culture in Great Britain, and with those tools to achieve the most efficient use of labor.[8]

Washington relied on agricultural treatises, especially the *Practical Treatise on Husbandry* based on Duhamel and *The Farmer's Compleat Guide,* for information on the latest advances in wheat culture. He read about

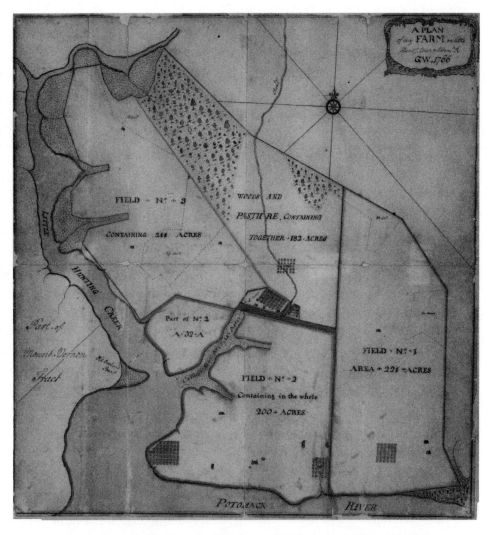

Fig 2.1   George Washington. *A plan of my farm on Little Huntg. Creek & Potomk. R.,* 1766. After abandoning tobacco cultivation at Mount Vernon in 1765, Washington made this survey of the farm he organized as River Plantation, with three large fields that accommodated a rotation of wheat, corn, and a season of fallow. By 1766, twenty enslaved field laborers worked at this, the largest plantation at Mount Vernon. Retrieved from the Library of Congress, www .loc.gov/item/74693204/.

sequences of plowing and harrowing, which he then compared in the fields. Following the method described in *The Farmer's Compleat Guide,* Washington, as an experiment, steeped wheat in brine and alum before sowing in an effort to strengthen the stalks. He compared four types of wheat, and he experimented with harvesting wheat damaged by the rust that was a persistent threat to the crop. He annotated his copy of Duhamel with uniform conversions for the measurements of the results of several dozen experiments with wheat. Washington was particularly attentive in observing the maturation of the grain, and in 1769 he experimented with harvesting wheat at three stages of ripening. His goal was not only to increase the weight and value of the grain, but also to identify varieties that would ripen in succession, allowing for a more efficient allocation of labor in the harvest.[9]

A successful harvest depended on the timely coordination of enslaved laborers and hired workers. The harvest brought together field laborers from all the plantations and the enslaved carpenters whom Washington put to work in the fields each year when the wheat was ready and quick work was necessary to protect the crop from rain. He frequently referred to "my Harvest People" or "my whole force" as laborers from across the estate moved from one plantation to the next. The harvest at each plantation began with the cradlers, initially hired white men, who cut the wheat in the field. Following in the cradlers' path came a succession of enslaved laborers with their own tasks—"Rakers and carryers," bundlers and stackers, and the driver of the oxcart that took the wheat to a barn. Water carriers and cooks served the field laborers whom Washington kept working throughout the long summer days.[10]

Washington was intent on moving the harvest along as quickly as possible while minimizing his reliance on hired laborers, especially the cradlers whose wages he found to be too costly. The key was to determine the minimum number of cradlers needed to keep the other laborers fully employed but also able to maintain the pace, and Washington sometimes adjusted the number of cradlers in the middle of a day when he judged the progress to be too slow. After several years of observing the work of harvesting, Washington decided to divide the cradlers and the assisting laborers into three gangs. "The Stops & delays by this means are not so frequent & the Work much better attended to as every Mans Work is distinguishable."[11]

Following the harvest of 1769, a season in which Washington had hired nine cradlers, he concluded "it was evidently to my advantage to employ my own hands to Cradle the Wheat rather than to hire white men to do it." By closely managing the teams of enslaved laborers and by selecting several types of wheat that could be harvested in succession, Washington believed he could dispense with the hired cradlers. By 1771, he reported that the harvest at his largest plantation employed "Ten Cradles 8 of which were my own Negroes." A year later, Jonathan Palmer, an experienced cradler hired by Washington to work year-round with the carpenters, became an instructor for six young cradlers.[12]

Cradling was just one of the new skills at which the enslaved became adept following the transition to wheat cultivation. As Washington sought to extract ever-greater labor from the slaves, he made a concerted effort to train individuals in specific skills and trades, as he did with cradling. Plowing and harrowing became routine in the cultivation of corn as well as wheat on all of the plantations. In an agreement with a local blacksmith, Peter Gollatt, Washington in 1770 bound a young enslaved man, Nat, along with another slave owned by John Parke Custis, to learn the trade of blacksmithing. Nat, on whom Washington had paid taxes as a tradesmen since 1763, rejoined the tradesmen at Mount Vernon at the close of his three-year term with Gollatt. When Washington in 1771 signed a ten-month agreement with Benjamin Buckler to work as a carpenter, a shoemaker, and a cradler at harvest time, he also required Buckler to supervise "several Negro carpenters" and "to use his utmost endeavours to hurry & drive them on to the performance of so much work as they ought to render."[13]

The emphasis on the pace of work that ought to be rendered was repeated in an agreement with another white carpenter, Caleb Stone, in 1773, among the earliest references to Washington's notion of an obligation or duty of the enslaved to deliver a certain level of work. To ensure that presumed obligation was met, and in a provision that may have been license for violent coercion, Washington vested in each of the hired carpenters "sufficient power and authority which he is to make use of & exercise with prudence & discretion." At the same time that he delegated this command over the slaves on his estate, Washington in the written agreement with Buckler noted that the carpenter was a stranger, and he reserved the right to dismiss him if he learned anything disparaging about his character.[14]

Washington frequently employed the enslaved carpenters to carry out work that was far more varied than their trade designation implied. They were an integral part of the annual harvest teams at the plantations, and they in some years assisted in planting corn. They joined with field laborers in the spring fishing that became one of the most consistently profitable ventures at the estate. The carpenters built roads connecting plantations and worked on repairs to the milldam and millrace. For a number of years, Washington had hired enslaved carpenters out to neighboring plantations, but after 1765 he found more and more ways to use their labor on his estate. The transition to wheat had created a greater demand for coopers to make barrels, and the complexity of farming methods depended on new types of agricultural buildings and additional housing for hired and enslaved laborers. Among the enslaved, the carpenters developed the widest range of skills and carried out the most varied work.[15]

In 1766, the first agricultural season without any cultivation of tobacco at Mount Vernon, Morris, an enslaved carpenter, became the overseer of Dogue Run Plantation. He would serve as overseer there for nearly twenty-five years, and Washington and his manager frequently referred to the plantation at Dogue Run simply as "Morris's." Like many of the slaves given greater responsibilities by Washington in the 1760s, Morris had been enslaved at the Custis estate, and he was among the first group of dower slaves that the Washingtons brought to work at Mount Vernon in 1759. Although slaves had served as overseers on large Virginia estates in the early eighteenth century, the reliance on enslaved overseers had become less common in the middle decades of the century. Morris was the first of several enslaved overseers at Mount Vernon, and he directed the work of twelve to fourteen adult field laborers in the years before the Revolutionary War. Washington, often on Christmas Day, annually paid Morris £2.10.0, "for encouragement." Enslaved overseers also received a larger share of provisions of food and clothing, and in contrast to most field laborers, lived with their wives. Morris's wife, Hannah, was transferred from Muddy Hole Plantation to Dogue Run in 1766. The enslaved overseers, unlike their white counterparts, did not receive any share of the profits from the crops produced under their supervision.[16]

Davy, who had worked as a field laborer at the Mill Plantation since 1765, was after 1770 listed as the first among the field workers at that plantation, where Washington no longer employed a white overseer. Cash payments to Davy, recorded by Washington with those made to Morris, and a special provision of clothing indicate that Davy had assumed the role of overseer for the first time. Davy, later recognized as Davy Gray, would be the longest serving and most experienced enslaved overseer at Mount Vernon, directing the work at several plantations until after Washington's death. When Washington organized Ferry Plantation on recently purchased land in 1771, he hired no white overseer for three years, relying on Michael, a long-time enslaved carpenter also skilled at cradling wheat, to direct the field laborers. While he was at Ferry Plantation, Michael received an annual cash payment, distributed along with those given to Morris and Davy Gray, as well as the special provision of clothing. After Washington hired a white overseer for Ferry Plantation in 1774, Michael returned to work as a carpenter.[17]

The enslaved overseers and foremen were the most conspicuous examples of individual slaves whose work and lives were changed by the transition to wheat and by Washington's efforts to replace hired white laborers with slaves skilled in various tasks related to grain cultivation. The distribution of cash "for encouragement," no matter how meager the amount, made clear to the overseers their enhanced worth to Washington. Whatever modicum of protection or autonomy that recognition of such worth secured for the enslaved individuals with the skills prized by Washington, their gains rested on his far greater success in applying enslaved labor to a new kind of agriculture. After 1765, Washington found new value in the enslaved labor he controlled, and he was invested ever more deeply in slavery as he became a successful farmer of wheat. The only caution he acknowledged about his reliance on slavery arose from a heightened recognition of the precarious investment in human property. To a friend in financial difficulties, Washington in 1767 stressed the risks of "such hazardous & perishable Articles as Negroes, Stock, & Chattels, which are to be swept of[f] by innumerable distempers, & subject to many accidents & misfortunes." Earlier that year, he complained, "God knows I have losses enough in Negroes to require something where with to supply their places." However many slaves died—and he almost never recorded their deaths before the 1780s—Washington steadily increased the size of the enslaved labor force at Mount Vernon through acquisition and transfer from his other plantations, and he gained ownership of still more slaves through his legal right to possess the children born to the enslaved women. The number of enslaved adults on whom Washington paid taxes in Fairfax County grew from 68 in July 1765 to 120 in July 1774.[18]

After a three-year hiatus during which he attempted to reduce the debt owed his London merchants, Washington in October 1767 resumed the purchase of slaves. He often bought less expensive slaves offered at the settlement of estates, and he purchased others to gain their demonstrated skills. On his way to Williamsburg, he purchased from the recently widowed Mary Ball Lee four slaves, including two brothers: William Lee, who became Washington's long-time valet, and Frank Lee, who was a servant in the Mansion House at Mount Vernon. The following day, while still in Westmoreland County, Washington bought from another estate a woman named Sarah, whom he sent to work as a field laborer at River Plantation. Over the next eight years, Washington purchased at least fourteen more slaves and authorized an overseer to acquire others. Washington bought field workers, such as Bath, purchased from Carlyle & Adam in 1770, and carpenters, including James and Isaac, purchased in April 1773. He also acquired slaves in settlement of debts owed him, such as the man and boy offered by Thomas Moore in 1770. Several slaves purchased after 1772 were sent to work on land Washington acquired in western Pennsylvania.[19]

When he instructed a business partner to purchase slaves in the Caribbean, "if choice ones can be had under Forty pounds Sterl.," Washington offered a rare explanation of what kind of enslaved laborers he sought to acquire. Daniel Jenifer Adams in 1772 carried flour and salted fish from Mount Vernon for sale in Barbados or whatever island offered the best market, and Washington preferred that the proceeds from the sales be "laid out in Negroes," or in rum and sugar if slaves were not available. "If the Return's are in Slaves let there be two thirds of them Males, the other third Females—The former not exceeding (at any rate) 20 yrs of age—the latter 16—All of them to be strait Limb'd, & in every respect strong & likely, with good Teeth & good Countenances—to be sufficiently provided with Cloaths." Washington received neither slaves nor rum from the ill-fated partnership, but he continued to purchase individual slaves as late as the spring of 1775, two months before he assumed command of the Continental Army.[20]

The largest single addition to the enslaved labor force at Mount Vernon came not through a purchase, but with Washington's decision to transfer slaves from the dower plantations in Tidewater. In November 1770, the overseer of Washington's plantation in King William County boarded twenty-one individuals, including six children, on a small ship so tightly loaded with people and their belongings that there "was not Room to put any thing Else a board." Then the enslaved people waited on the crowded ship through the afternoon and night while the overseer attempted to recapture Perros, who had run away to avoid the relocation to Mount Vernon. The ship left without Perros, who, following his return or recapture, continued to work at the plantation in King William County.[21]

Of the fifteen adults who arrived at Mount Vernon on board the ship, nine would by the following spring be working as field laborers at the estate's newest plantation. Washington organized Ferry Plantation in 1771 out of more than four hundred acres that he had recently taken possession of from John West, Jr., and John Posey. Washington wanted to recover the land, much of which had once been owned by his brother, so that he could profitably work enslaved laborers from dower lands that he hoped to lease to a tenant. With both an opportunity to rent the former Custis plantation and a determination to bring all of his farming operations under his direct supervision, Washington needed more land on which to work the additional dower slaves, "there being too many to distribute among my other Quarters." He explained to Posey that the purchase of the land would provide "a certainty of a place (in this Neighbourhood, where I want to draw all my force to) to put some of the Hands upon."[22]

The newly arrived dower slaves joined with the carpenter Michael, a man named Harry, and Lucy from the Mill plantation to prepare the land at Ferry Plantation for the sowing of wheat. Harry, almost certainly the same man who had worked at the Mansion House since at least 1766, ran away from Ferry Plantation in late July 1771, just months after arriving at the new farm. His flight, like that of Perros, underscores the threat to family and community connections inherent in any relocation of slaves from one plantation to another, even within the boundaries of a large estate like Mount Vernon. Within five days, Washington had paid for the recapture of Harry and his return to Ferry Plantation.[23]

Washington had in 1765 begun to consolidate enslaved laborers under his direct supervision at Mount Vernon. He dispensed with an overseer at his Bullskin Plantation and found tenants to lease parcels of that tract near the Shenandoah River. In the spring of 1766, he listed fourteen new enslaved adults at Mount Vernon, having likely transferred most of them from the Bullskin Plantation. The overseer at Bullskin, after managing a final harvest of wheat and hemp, moved to King William County where he served as an overseer of one of the dower plantations under Washington's control. Most of the arable land at Bullskin would remain in the hands of tenants, and tenancy became Washington's preferred way of improving and drawing income from arable land too distant for his direct management of farming.[24]

When Washington purchased more than 2,600 acres in Fauquier County and Loudoun County in 1767, he surveyed parcels for twelve tenants with whom he signed leases for the lifetime of the tenants and their children. Washington and the other trustees appointed for the sale of the land deemed it well suited for corn, wheat, or tobacco, but rather than farm the land himself or send an overseer and enslaved laborers, Washington relied on the tenants to improve the property and to increase the long-term value of the farmland. Through the leases, Washington sought to protect the fertility of the soil by restricting the number of laborers who could work the land and requiring tenants to preserve a prescribed number of acres of woodland to support subsequent occupants. Tenants were also required to plant large orchards, surrounded by fences, and further obligated by the lease to construct a residence and to build sufficient barns or tobacco houses for the amount of land. With the payment of the first three years' rent not due until the third year, tenants had the opportunity to make the necessary capital investments.[25]

∘   ∘   ∘

In 1769, Washington assumed political leadership in organizing the first of several nonimportation associations that he hoped would encourage widespread adoption of the same kind of diversification he had undertaken at Mount Vernon. Following Parliament's imposition of the Townshend Duties, Washington again recognized that Virginia's dependence on British trade rendered it particularly vulnerable to parliamentary demands for revenue. He decried the threat to established colonial prerogatives, which he privately declared no one should hesitate to defend with arms, but he believed that, before a last resort to arms, colonists might persuade the British officials "by starving their Trade & manufactures" to recognize American rights as they had following the Stamp Act protests. Washington also looked beyond the immediate political crisis to recognize that with a commercial boycott "there are private, as well as public advantages to result from it." He expected the plan of nonimportation, which George Mason drafted in collaboration with him, to encourage long-term changes in plantation management throughout the colony. With many families "reduced, almost, if not quite, to penury & want, from the low ebb of their fortunes, and Estates daily selling for the discharge of Debts," an association to prohibit British imports would "contribute more effectually than any other I can devise to immerge the Country from the distress it at present labours under."[26]

Washington was instrumental in gaining approval for the nonimportation association that members of the recently dissolved House of Burgesses adopted in May 1769, and over the following six years he shaped subsequent commercial associations, always with a focus on laying a foundation for greater economic independence. He feared that Parliament's assertion of authority to tax the colonies, left unchecked, would lead to further legislation that would prohibit colonial manufactures and thereby perpetuate the reliance on British commerce and credit. The associations designed to promote home manufactures and agricultural diversification would protect Virginia planters against the demands of British merchants. In 1774, as he helped to draft the county resolves that would be a model for the Virginia Association, Washington insisted on a delay in the enforcement of any nonexportation provision so that farmers would have time to plan for a permanent transition from tobacco to crops that would support manufactures and independent trade. By that time, he had made significant progress in selling his agricultural produce on markets outside the restrictions of the British Empire.[27]

In June 1769, as he reorganized his estate to comply with the first nonimportation association, Washington decided to construct a merchant mill that would enable him to produce the high-quality flour in demand in Europe and the Caribbean markets. After consulting with a well-known mill owner and a millwright, Washington decided to build the new mill downstream from the old one to take advantage of a more dependable flow of water and to facilitate access for ships loading flour and for wagons from the nearby road connecting Alexandria and Colchester. To construct the mill and a millrace nearly two miles long required the work of numerous hired white laborers and the assistance of enslaved laborers sent by Washington to the site. A millwright, John Ball, oversaw much of the work, while another hired artisan quarried the stone for the foundation from the nearby estate of George William Fairfax. Washington frequently visited the site, spending long days to ensure the proper level of the ground and to mark the foundations of the mill building. Throughout much of 1770, he recorded the progress of the laborers and encouraged a faster pace of work, offering the ditchers an additional eighteen pence per rod dug "if they woud be brisk and stick to it." On his return from a two-month trip west, Washington in December 1770 found the mill nearly finished and ready to receive the first flow of water to sharpen the millstones. In early April, after a day supervising work at the milldam, Washington saw the water of Dogue Run enter the race and turn the two sets of millstones, one of them to be constantly used for grinding his own wheat.[28]

At the older mill, which had operated since 1759 primarily to grind corn and wheat for consumption on the estate, Washington relied on enslaved millers Anthony and George. For the potentially lucrative merchant mill, Washington departed from his practice of training enslaved laborers in new skills, and he hired at considerable expense William Roberts, a skilled millwright and miller from Pennsylvania. In October 1770, Lund Washington signed an agreement with Roberts, who agreed to carry out all of the work necessary for the operation and maintenance of the mill. Roberts and his apprentice would construct flour casks when they were not running the mill. Washington agreed to pay Roberts £80 in Virginia currency a year, twice the next highest yearly wage of any hired worker at Mount Vernon in the 1760s and 1770s. In the summer of 1771, Washington ordered the construction of a house for the miller.[29]

Within a few months of when the mill began to run, Washington decided to replace the disappointing Virginia millstones with the finest sort imported from Great Britain. Enclosing the specifications provided by William Roberts and another millwright, he ordered a pair of French burr millstones, "an Article of more consequence than all the rest" of the items in his lengthy request for goods from London. Washington stipulated that the millstones were to be produced by John Cooper & Sons, one of London's leading millwright firms, the partners of which were members of the Society of Arts, an influential group of mechanics and agriculturalists. Washington's relationship with his London merchants, Robert Cary & Company, again gave him access to the highest-quality agricultural technology in Great Britain. He authorized them to negotiate the cost of the millstones: "I should not Incline to give any extravagent Sum for them on the one hand nor miss of getting a pair of good ones by limiting the price on the other." Regardless of the price, the sooner he could receive them the better. Washington would use the superior burr millstones for his merchant business.[30]

With his mill in full operation, Washington gained much greater flexibility in marketing his wheat crop. He could decide to sell his annual crop as flour or as unmilled wheat, as prices would favor, and most of his crop was milled into flour. He could also initiate his own trading ventures. By 1771, he was free of the Carlyle & Adam contract by which he had committed to sell his wheat crop to the Alexandria merchants for seven years. Under that contract, the merchants were responsible for milling and selling the wheat once it was delivered, so for several years after making wheat his principal cash crop, Washington had little direct involvement with markets for the commodity. Washington's transactions with Carlyle & Adam, however, taught him about the potential hazards of a trade that offered few of the financial services provided by established tobacco merchants in Great Britain.

By 1767, Washington was so displeased with the business practices of Carlyle & Adam that he threatened to end all communications with that firm. In one of the longest letters he ever wrote, filled with indignation and sarcasm, Washington rebuked the merchants for their perceived mistreatment and disrespect. It was only a more extreme demonstration of the kind of anger Washington had directed at his London tobacco merchants when he believed they had mistreated him. He was offended that Carlyle and Adam "seem to squint at my veracity" and that they dismissed the meticulous care he took in the preparation of his wheat. Beneath Washington's personal umbrage were more substantive complaints about the merchants' failure to pay on the delivery of the wheat and their unwillingness or inability to pay interest on what they owed Washington. The merchants' most disturbing conduct had been their casual disregard of the "solemn contract" in which Washington had carefully defined the acceptable quality of wheat and agreed to a price that "the most judicious People of this County" thought too low. To the merchants' admission that they had signed the agreement without closely examining it, Washington replied that he could not use such excuses to avoid paying interest or penalties to his correspondents in England and Madeira when they expected his timely remittances. At issue were not just fairness and trust, but the reliable flow of payments in a complicated commercial network on which the operation of Washington's estate depended.[31]

If the merchants could not pay him on delivery of his crop, he implored them to explain, "How then am I to make remittances for Goods to Cloath a numerous Family, Supply a House in various necessaries, & support it in all its various expences?" Washington reminded them that most of the goods he imported were necessary supplies, such as clothing for the enslaved and basic implements for farming and carpentry. For all of the disadvantages and excessive charges of the tobacco trade, the exchange of Virginia crops for finished goods had efficiently supplied large estates like Mount Vernon. As he shifted to wheat production, Washington enjoyed an advantage over other large planters engaged in grain production because he was able to supply his estate with British goods, as long as he continued to ship tobacco to Robert Cary & Company on his account from the dower plantations in Tidewater. As he explained in 1769, "I only grow Tobacco to Supply my Family with Goods." The transition to wheat at Mount Vernon would remain incomplete until Washington found other sources for consumer goods and plantation supplies, or until the traders in grain enabled him to make more reliable payments to the merchants who shipped him finished goods.[32]

The steady supply of flour encouraged Washington to take advantage of rising demand in the Caribbean and Europe. As he had explained to Carlyle and Adam, it behooved the producers of large quantities of wheat to find more distant markets. Through his network of mercantile correspondents, Washington followed reports of prices in markets as far-flung as Barbados, Lisbon, and London as well as in Philadelphia and Norfolk. Much of the wheat delivered to Carlyle & Adam and the salted fish from Mount Vernon had sold in the Caribbean, where there was demand for these two most valuable commodities produced at the estate. Washington merged cargoes of flour and fish in his own first venture to the Caribbean, made in partnership with Daniel Jenifer Adams of Maryland in 1772. The partnership with the unscrupulous Adams proved disastrous, but in its quick collapse Washington formed a further connection with a Jamaican merchant, Robert McMickan, who managed the sale of several shipments of flour, corn, and fish from Mount Vernon.[33]

Washington found himself the reluctant owner of Daniel Jenifer Adams's ship, which provided an unexpected opportunity to venture into new markets. Rather than sell the ship at a certain loss and in spite of having no interest in becoming a shipper, Washington refitted the brigantine in Alexandria and "in the opinion of Many People, made a good Vessel of it." Washington renamed the ship *Farmer* to make clear his true ambitions, and he sent it to Jamaica, filled with flour and fish. In the fall of 1774, *Farmer* sailed for Lisbon with four thousand bushels of corn, and returned with salt after stopping in Turks Island. The voyages entailed numerous expenses unrelated to the commodities trade and burdened Washington with the persistent problems of hiring seamen in Virginia. After the Continental Association restricted imports, Washington sold the ship in the spring of 1775 to a Maryland merchant.[34]

In April 1772, Washington served on a committee of the House of Burgesses that presented a bill to prevent fraud by providing for the more stringent inspection of all flour milled for export from Virginia. The enacted statute described flour as a valuable article of commerce and provided the same kind of government regulation that had long protected confidence in Virginia's tobacco trade. In compliance with the act, Washington in December 1772 registered the "G. Washington" brand that would be marked on every cask he exported. He first ventured into European markets for flour in 1773 with a shipment to Madeira of eighty barrels of his highest quality flour, which he proposed to consign to his wine merchants as payment for his order of four pipes of wine for his own consumption. Through the Norfolk merchant Thomas Newton, Jr., Washington shipped the same Madeira firm ninety barrels of a lesser quality flour, for which European buyers were paying higher prices than could be gained on the Norfolk market. The proceeds of that flour were also to be applied to the purchase of wine, to be shipped directly to Washington's wharf. For many years, Washington had ordered his Madeira wine through Robert Cary & Company in London, paying with tobacco receipts or buying on credit, with the additional costs entailed in either form of payment. Flour gave him the means to trade directly with the wine merchants, even as he relied on the Cary company to cover any possible costs in excess of the sale of his flour.[35]

Thomas Newton, who served in the House of Burgesses with Washington, was a dependable source of information about flour and wheat prices on both sides of the Atlantic, and beginning in 1773 he became the most important trader of Washington's flour. Washington sent him large quantities of superfine flour, as well as the lower grades known as middlings and "ship stuff," which were regular products of the milling process. The superfine flour, which carried the inspectors' certificate of quality, was sold by Newton for more than Washington could have received at the mill. Newton thought Washington would be best served by steady buyers among Norfolk bakers, who needed a dependable supply of the high-quality flour that Washington's mill was capable of producing. Newton sold some of Washington's flour to a baker who "has all flying to him for bread." While his largest shipments of flour went to Norfolk in 1773 and 1774, Washington thought flour might be the basis of a new and more advantageous trade between the colonies and Great Britain. In June 1774, at which time he admitted that commerce between Great Britain and Virginia would likely be suspended because of the worsening imperial crisis, Washington inquired of Robert Cary & Company how his highest quality flour would sell in London and whether the firm would accept his regular commission of up to two hundred barrels.[36]

For several seasons after 1765, Washington had explored British markets for the hemp and flax grown at Mount Vernon, but received scant encouragement from merchants. The Hanburys were reluctant to enter the trade, and James Gildart in Liverpool found what little American hemp came to British markets to be poorly prepared and disparaged by British ropemakers. Washington planted hemp crops at two Mount Vernon plantations in 1766, and as late as 1770 sold slightly more than two hundred pounds to Alexandria merchant Robert Adam, for which he received the bounty for hemp, but the fibers from hemp never became a viable export crop for him. Wheat and fish brought the surest revenue, and it was wheat above all that defined the estate, from determining the work of the enslaved field laborers to shaping the reconfiguration of the agricultural landscape.[37]

Beginning in 1769, Washington resumed his purchase of nearby land and soon added more than a thousand acres to his estate, which by 1772 extended to over sixty-five hundred acres. In addition to the four hundred acres that Washington organized as Ferry Plantation, he added several parcels to expand the boundaries of the estate and others to consolidate his farmlands. While surveying one of the new parcels, Washington discovered twenty acres of land that had never been patented, and he quickly gained title from the Fairfax proprietary. The continuing financial problems of his neighbor John Posey gave Washington the opportunity to purchase a narrow strip of land with a value far greater than its six acres would suggest. He acquired Posey's valuable ferry landing and fishery, as well as control of the entire riverfront along Ferry Plantation.[38]

At each of the outlying plantations, the ground cleared for grain cultivation and the new meadows and pastures for livestock offered broad vistas across a rolling countryside. Despite the persistence of "rough & stumpy ground" in some wheat fields and the numerous crude dwelling houses provided for enslaved families, the agricultural landscape at Mount Vernon more nearly approached the georgic ideal of English estates, and Washington was eager to display his improved plantations to family and guests. During harvests, Martha and her daughter, Patsy, accompanied Washington to watch the work that brought together large gangs of laborers. Washington invited guests to accompany him on his daily inspection of the plantations, and the new mill became the special destination for visitors. When a group of women and their daughters stayed at Mount Vernon in November 1771, Washington "Rid to the Mill with the Ladies & back again." With another house party, Washington guided the guests to the mill and the fishery during the April run of herring. The artist Charles Willson Peale, after three days working on the first life portrait of Washington, spent an afternoon visiting the mill with his sitter.[39]

The farmland designed for wheat cultivation at Mount Vernon opened spaces for the foxhunting that became the favorite sport of Washington. Often in the company of members of the Fairfax family and other neighbors, Washington, beginning in 1768, hunted several times a week, especially during the winter months. The chases could go on for six, even seven hours, taking Washington and his party to every part of the estate. At Muddy Hole Plantation, he supervised the cutting of new paths for fox hunting. Washington became just as avid a breeder of foxhounds, often in collaboration with his hunting companions. The style of foxhunting that he adopted had developed in Great Britain in the early eighteenth century, often in close association with the kind of agricultural improvements that he sought to emulate in Virginia. It was a sport that depended on consolidated estates and access to great expanses of land. Washington commonly mixed foxhunting with his own supervision of work at the farms, taking the hounds with him on his inspection of the plantations. Washington continued to hunt regularly until late winter 1775, and resumed the sport with less frequency when he returned to his estate in the 1780s. The enslaved laborers on the outlying plantations regularly saw Washington on horseback in pursuit of the fox and heard the dogs as well as the English hunting horn that Washington specified be "large & loud."[40]

o   o   o

The commitment to agricultural improvement and wheat cultivation framed Washington's renewed expectations for the West, which had so long been a focus of his interest and speculation. At the same time that he organized nonimportation associations in Virginia, Washington became an ardent advocate of opening the upper reaches of the Potomac River to commercial navigation. He served on the House of Burgesses committee that in December 1769 prepared a bill to clear the river for navigation, and after the failure of that bill, he and other supporters won approval for an act in 1772 by which the Virginia Assembly established two private companies for the construction of canals on the Potomac and James Rivers. In urging support for the Potomac project, Washington spoke of the promise of a new path of commerce between Great Britain and "that immense Tract of Country which is unfolding to our view." The success of that trade was predicated on the simultaneous expansion of commercial farming into western lands possessed by Indian nations. The trade in agricultural produce would support independent mercantile establishments in the Chesapeake and be the first step toward an anticipated colony on the Ohio, thus setting the foundation of what Washington anticipated would be "a rising Empire," his oft-repeated phrase, first evoked in advocacy of his dream of a Potomac waterway.[41]

The prospect of extending commercial agriculture beyond the mountains was so enticing that Washington set aside his resolution to consolidate enslaved labor and agricultural resources under his own supervision at Mount Vernon. He would invest in the labor needed to confirm his title to new lands and to initiate the kind of farming he thought would maximize the value of that land. Even while restrictions on settlement beyond the Appalachians remained in place, Washington asked William Crawford, an associate from surveying and military expeditions, to identify land he could purchase in western Pennsylvania once the British relaxed or rescinded the Proclamation of 1763. Washington considered the proclamation to be merely "a temporary expedien[t] to quiet the Minds of the Indians," and he urged Crawford to proceed in secret to mark out lands so as to keep others from settling there. Washington insisted that the Pennsylvania land be suitable for productive farming. "Ordinary, or even middling Land woud never answer my purpose or expectation," Washington instructed Crawford, "No: A Tract to please me must be rich."[42]

Crawford obtained for Washington warrants for the survey of over sixteen hundred acres in Pennsylvania, in five separate parcels to circumvent the colony's restriction on the amount of land granted one person. When Washington in October 1770 first visited his Pennsylvania tract at the Redstone settlement along the Youghiogheny River, he found "as fine Land as ever I saw—a great deal of Rich Meadow." From there, Washington continued with Crawford into the Ohio country and along the Great Kanawha River. There they passed through vast areas of land that Washington and other veterans hoped to claim under a grant fulfilling Governor Dinwiddie's 1754 proclamation, a promise made to encourage enlistment in the Virginia Regiment.[43]

Throughout the journey, Washington observed the country with the eyes of an experienced farmer who instinctively recognized which still-wooded lands would be best for meadows and which best for the cultivation of grain. He recorded the predominant types of trees on different areas of land, searching for the stands of cherry and walnut that grew in the richest soil, or the sugar trees and ash that indicated the next richest. His notes on locations suitable for gristmills and on the navigability of the rivers reflect his intention to establish ties between western farmers and eastern markets. When he met with Guyasuta, the Six Nations chief who had accompanied him on his first journey to the West in 1753, Washington assured him of the peaceful intentions of the Virginians and of their interest in the kind of trade the Indians welcomed, but their extended conversation about land and even the path of Washington's journey surely exposed Washington's design to settle large numbers of white farmers on the lands of Indian nations in the Ohio country. Washington recognized that despite the recent concessions of the Six Nations, other Indians in the region, including the Shawnees and Delawares, "view the Settlement of the People upon this River with an uneasy & jealous Eye."[44]

His acquisition of western land revealed Washington at his most avaricious and competitive, but he anticipated no quick profits from the lands, the settlement of which he believed would determine the political order of the region as well as add to his fortune. Washington wanted large tracts to be organized under the direction of wealthy Virginia planters who had the resources and influence to introduce a particular model of commercial farming. He wanted to keep the lands out of the possession of officers who lacked the means to establish farms on their smaller grants, and he worked quietly and often anonymously to purchase the land rights of other veterans, aiming to claim so large a tract that it would be worth his expense of settling.[45]

To secure his claim to the Pennsylvania land, Washington entered into partnership with Gilbert Simpson, a former tenant at Mount Vernon, who in October 1772 proposed to settle the property with three or four laborers and a small number of horses and cows. Since the land was so well suited for corn and for meadows, Simpson thought the partnership would in a few years add something to Washington's fortune and provide a good living for himself. Washington, somewhat uncharacteristically, agreed to the proposal, and Simpson moved to the land, known as Washington's Bottom, along with an enslaved man, Orson, for whom Washington paid Simpson £55. Washington also sent two slaves from Mount Vernon to work the land, and he advised Simpson to plan for the long term in establishing a system of farming.[46]

Simpson proved incapable of any such planning, and within weeks of reaching the Pennsylvania lands in the spring of 1773, he threatened to abandon the project. He complained that one of the slaves sent by Washington was "a worthless hand" and the other "knew nothing of work." Yet when Simpson returned to Loudoun County, he left the new farm in the charge of one of the enslaved laborers, who, he now assured Washington, was "as trusty I believe as most white men." Simpson eventually returned to the Youghiogheny after Washington agreed to send two more enslaved young men from Mount Vernon, and work began on the mill that Washington considered essential for the success of the settlement. The partnership with Simpson, however, was a continuing frustration to Washington, who complained that he could never hear of the mill under the direction of "that confounded fellow" Simpson "without a degree of warmth & vexation at his extreame stupidity." The outbreak of war with Indians drove away many of the surrounding white settlers who would have provided business for the mill, and Simpson's continued mismanagement left Washington with little reason to believe that his reliance on a distant farm manager would succeed.[47]

In 1774 and 1775, the farm under Simpson's supervision became the staging ground for an even more ambitious effort to settle farms on thousands of acres that Washington claimed as part of the bounties offered soldiers during the French and Indian War. After treaties with Indian nations removed some of the restrictions imposed by the Proclamation of 1763, Washington successfully petitioned the Virginia governor and council to authorize veterans of the Virginia Regiment to claim two hundred thousand acres south and east of the Ohio River. Again with the assistance of William Crawford, Washington gained control of an eventual thirty-three thousand acres. A grant of nearly eleven thousand acres along the Great Kanawha was the object of Washington's first effort to establish farms and homesteads within the three years required by Virginia statute.[48]

Washington's long-term objective was to lease the land to tenants, and he estimated that the tract would support up to three hundred families. In a broadside published in Virginia and Maryland newspapers, Washington offered prospective tenants generous time to clear and till the land before they would need to pay the moderate rents. He boasted of a "luxuriency of soil" and meadows "almost fit for the scythe." Washington also investigated the possibility of recruiting German immigrants, so as "to settle my lands with Industrious people," and he met with representatives of a large group of Scottish farmers looking for land in America. Neither of those ventures proved feasible in 1774, nor had the advertisements for tenants attracted settlers. In the meantime, Washington relied on his own resources and laborers to establish the first farms. In preparation, he purchased indentured servants and convicts in Baltimore and Alexandria. He also purchased at least two slaves to work on the lands in the Ohio country and sent others from Mount Vernon.[49]

After the outbreak of hostilities with Indians in the region delayed an initial expedition, Washington in January 1775 sent a skilled farmer, James Cleveland, who had worked as overseer of Mount Vernon's River Plantation, to lead the effort to clear and fence five acres on each lot to be rented. Washington also sent two hired white laborers from Mount Vernon, William Stevens and William Skilling, to oversee the initial work. In written agreements with the several managers of the expedition to settle the claimed lands in the Ohio country, Washington attempted to ensure strict supervision of the indentured servants and slaves. He was particularly worried about controlling the white servants. Indeed, so sure was he that they would attempt to run away that he prepared descriptions to be placed in newspaper advertisements for their recovery. He advised William Stevens to pull all of the canoes out of the water once they reached the tract, without telling the servants the reason for it, and he authorized Cleveland to sell any of the white servants who proved difficult to manage. Washington's concerns were justified. Four of the servants with Cleveland sought refuge with nearby Indians, and Cleveland spent more money on the recovery of runaway servants than the sale of their indentures would bring.[50]

The priority of the expedition was to meet the minimal requirements for the claim, but Washington also emphasized his desire to ensure the long-term productivity of the land. He urged the managers to build gristmills, to plant orchards, and to raise cattle. He also hoped to increase his own stock of draft animals and instructed Cleveland to "buy me all the Buffaloe Calves you can get and make them as gentle as possible," so that he could raise a breeding line. By the fall of 1775, Cleveland had finished all the work required by Washington and secured upwards of fifteen thousand acres for his claim, but soon after the Indians' defense of their land forced Cleveland to abandon the project. When one of Washington's hired workers returned to the Great Kanawha site to retrieve the lone slave who had continued to work there, he discovered that Indians had burned the newly constructed buildings. Before he returned to Virginia, Cleveland sold some of the remaining servants and left the slaves owned by Washington with William Crawford in Pennsylvania. By that time, Washington had turned his attention almost entirely to his command of the Continental

Army. Any new, significant work on his western lands would have to wait until after the Revolutionary War. Nothing about these first efforts to secure title to the Ohio lands undermined Washington's belief in the lucrative value of western lands or weakened his determination to push agricultural settlement into territory possessed by Indians, but the experience further dissuaded him from directing his own agricultural initiatives from afar.[51]

On the eve of the Revolutionary War, Washington explained to a prominent English correspondent the perils of not closely managing a large Virginia estate, the nature of which was such "that without close application, it never fails bringing the proprietors in Debt annually, as Negroes must be clothed & fed, taxes paid, &c. &c. whether anything is made or not." The efforts to settle western lands had taught Washington anew about the importance of that "close application" to the management of an agricultural estate and the need for personal supervision, especially of bound labor, if a planter was to extract the maximum gain from that labor and maintain authority over the laborers. He barely needed to add "that Stewards (in this Country at least) far removed from the inspection of a Superior, are scarce ever to be entrusted." He pointed to the "melancholy proofs" in Virginia newspapers, which regularly advertised the sale of distressed estates. Washington knew the fate of those estates firsthand from his ongoing efforts to recover substantial debts owed by several families to him or to the Custis heirs, and his engagement in the business of those families further convinced him that the owners of extensive plantations must manage their own estates or suffer a similar fate.[52]

Washington offered these observations in a report on his administration of the court-directed sale of George Mercer's valuable estates in Loudoun and Frederick Counties, which together included ten thousand acres of land, ninety slaves, and large herds of livestock. While the slaves attracted buyers, the land sold for less than anyone expected. "That Colo. Mercer has been a considerable loser in the management of his Estate here, nobody will deny," noted Washington. Mercer, who with his brother owed more than £3,200 to the Custis estate in bonds now held by Washington, had moved to England and left his estates in the hands of overseers, one of whom Washington described as "a consummate rascal." Washington's efforts to recover debts owed by the brothers Bernard and Thomas Moore, both of whom had borrowed large sums from Martha Custis before her marriage to Washington, offered further evidence of how quickly loans not based on a reasonable assessment of agricultural capacity, compounded by the burden of five percent annual interest charges, could doom a once prosperous estate. As Washington told his neighbor John Posey, who owed him £700 and wanted to borrow £500 more, interest "woud be such a Moth in your Estate as woud inevitably destroy it."[53]

Although he declined to extend more money to Posey, Washington understood that he was enmeshed in a complicated web of loans that connected him with many indebted gentry families and that the failure of one endangered many others. He offered Posey the only favor in his power, which was to delay pressing for repayment as long as he could without endangering his own financial well-being. Like Posey, James Mercer and Bernard Moore begged for Washington's indulgence as they waited to receive payments from their own debtors and as they held onto sufficient land and slaves to produce crops that might help them reduce their debts. Washington as often as not relented, whether out of sympathy with the frequent appeals to long-standing family ties or out of recognition that foreclosure seldom delivered him the full amount owed. He was willing to loan money or delay collection as long as there was some possibility his patience would prevent the dispersal of an estate. If it became necessary to sell off an estate's assets, he advised starting "with the Sales of such things as can be best spared, & so raising to Negroes, & even Land if requisite."[54]

In the recovery of large debts and as executor of less troubled estates, Washington repeatedly participated in the sale of slaves, and he became invested in enslaved laborers in ways that extended far beyond the ownership of those whose labor he controlled at Mount Vernon. Washington had seldom sold slaves he owned, and then only as punishment for individuals he wanted to remove from his estate. For indebted Virginia planters, however, slaves were often the most easily liquidated property they owned, and the Mercers, the Moores, and John Posey all offered Washington slaves as security on loans or as payments on their debts to him. Thomas Moore offered to transfer ownership of slaves rather than force Washington to wait until he had the money to reduce his debt to the Custis heirs. James Mercer assured Washington that "the Slaves included in your mortgage are equal to any in the Colony, for which I wou'd not take double the Sum they are engaged for." Washington reluctantly accepted the mortgage from Mercer despite his concern that slaves were "a very uncertain & precarious Security." After Bernard Moore sold nearly all of his estate, he asked Washington and other friends to loan him money without interest for the purchase of slaves to work what land he had left. Washington gave Moore £100 "to be laid out in Negroes for his use, and Wifes; after the decease of whom, to be sold for the benifit of myself & other's."[55]

Almost inevitably, the acceptance of property in slaves as security for debts led to the sale and forced relocation of some of those enslaved individuals, and Washington often participated in such transactions. When Thomas Moore offered his entire King William County estate for sale in 1770, Washington purchased a man, Frank, and a boy, James, along with a bay mare, and credited Moore's account for the combined prices. Washington was one of twenty managers of a lottery by which much of Bernard Moore's estate, including more than fifty slaves, was sold in December 1769, although the four tickets Washington purchased did not win him either slaves or land. Washington had been more directly involved in the recent sale of much of John Posey's estate, which included "about twenty-five choice SLAVES, consisting of men, women, and children," as well as valuable land in Fairfax County.[56]

The eccentric and unstable Posey had let his estate fall into such disrepair that Washington pressured him to sell his assets in October 1769 before a court ordered him to liquidate them. Washington urged another of Posey's creditors to support an immediate sale, arguing "it is a fact very well known that his Negroes & stock never can be disposed of at a more favourable juncture than in the Fall when they are fat and lusty and must soon fall of[f] unless well fed which I am sure cannot happen in the present case for very good reasons too obvious to mention." Posey, for once, was "perfectly Sober" when he agreed to the sale on the condition that Washington would attend. A widely distributed notice announced "the money arising from the sales to be paid into the hands of *George Washington.*" At the sale, Washington secured for himself two hundred acres adjacent to Mount Vernon. He purchased none of Posey's slaves, but the proceeds from their sale helped to pay off the debt to Washington, just as Posey's sale of slaves in 1767 had provided an initial payment to Washington.[57]

Washington also managed the public sale of slaves when he served as executor of estates, such as that of Thomas Colvill. Soon after Colvill's death, Washington placed an advertisement in the *Virginia Gazette* for the "Sale of Colo. Colvills Negroes," and he attended the sale in February 1767. After the death of Colvill's wife, Frances, Washington managed the public sale of the several remaining slaves bequeathed to her. At that sale at Fairfax County courthouse in February 1773, Washington purchased two slaves: Ned, whom he sent to work with the field laborers at River Plantation, and Murria, a young girl.[58]

In November 1774, Washington was the sole manager of the public auction of an exceptionally large number of slaves owned by George Mercer. Upon arriving at Mercer's lands in Frederick County, Washington was disappointed to find only ninety slaves for auction when a hundred and ten had been promised, but he soon reported, "The Negros, Horses, and Stock, have all sold exceeding high." Washington and John Tayloe, who also held Mercer's power of attorney but did not participate in the auction, had placed in the *Virginia Gazette* notice of the sale with a description of the fertile lands and the large number of livestock to be auctioned in addition to the slaves. "Among the slaves are two good Blacksmiths, two Carpenters, and an exceeding trusty and skilful waggoner." Years later, Mercer's overseer boasted that he had made the slaves "all Look well from the greatest to the Least young and old according to their ages." It was probably the largest slave sale in which Washington had participated since he had bought slaves from the ships of traders from Africa in 1759 and 1761, and it was certainly the largest sale he ever directed.[59]

Washington was by 1775 more deeply invested in slavery than ever before. Enslaved laborers carried out most of the work on his estate, including the range of tasks required for wheat cultivation and processing. Their labor made possible various initiatives to achieve some measure of commercial independence for his estate. Washington engaged in and gained from a range of financial transactions in which Virginia planters used slaves as commodities and securities. In his purchase and relocation of slaves to help settle his western land claims, and in his support for the hire of enslaved laborers to construct canals around the falls of the Potomac, Washington pointed to the territorial expansion of slavery.[60]

Only once in the years before the Revolutionary War, at the height of the imperial crisis in 1774, did Washington obliquely acknowledge any fundamental injustice of race-based slavery, when he warned that British assertions of political authority over the colonies threatened to "make us as tame, & abject Slaves, as the Blacks we Rule over with such arbitrary Sway." The analogy between British policy and enslavement was a common, even clichéd, element of patriot rhetoric, often displayed without irony and without reference to the slavery found throughout the British colonies. What set Washington's comment apart was its reference to his own unchecked authority over the slaves at his estate. Still, this recognition of his arbitrary sway had no discernible impact on his investment in enslaved labor in the years before the Revolutionary War.[61]

◦   ◦   ◦

By the early months of 1775, Washington had reason to believe that he had protected his estate and his investments in land and labor against the impact of an increasingly likely rupture with Great Britain. He had effectively removed his estate from the narrow limits of a colonial, staple economy and reoriented it toward growing markets throughout the Atlantic. He proved to be skilled at agricultural innovation and at exercising authority over enslaved laborers as they carried out the varied tasks of grain cultivation and domestic manufactures. Aside from his efforts to settle his claimed land to the west, Washington heeded his own advice about the indispensable need for a landowner's direct management and supervision of a Virginia estate. His success in the transition to wheat and in the adoption of the New Husbandry methods of cultivation persuaded him that the improvements in farming demonstrated at Mount Vernon would promote the establishment of an ordered agricultural society and secure commercial opportunities for the "rising empire" he imagined for Virginia and the other colonies joined in a Continental Congress.

° *3* °

Mount Vernon in Wartime

During nearly eight-and-a-half years of service as commander of the Continental Army, Washington was, with the exception of one brief visit, absent from Mount Vernon and removed from the direct supervision that he considered essential to the successful management of labor and farming on a Virginia estate. After he accepted the commission as commander in June 1775, Washington depended on his long-time farm manager, Lund Washington, to assume greater responsibility for the operation of his estate. As much as he disliked turning over supervision of Mount Vernon, Washington had more faith in his cousin, who had over ten years' experience on the estate, than he could ever have had with the "common hands" that he considered the only alternative, and he praised Lund for his fidelity and hard work, traits he seldom attributed to overseers. After three years away from Virginia, and anticipating several more years before he returned, Washington in February 1778 wrote from Valley Forge to assure Lund that his care of the estate was the only thing that made it tolerable to be absent. Fearful that something would "induce you to leave my business, whilst I, in a manner, am banished from home," Washington offered to increase Lund's wages. Washington was confident that Lund understood his vision for farming at Mount Vernon. "To go on in the improvement of my Estate in the manner heretofore described to you—fulfilling my plans—and keeping my property together, are the principal objects I have in view during these troubles." No one who worked for Washington ever completely escaped his criticism, and before he returned to Mount Vernon, he severely chastised Lund for failing to send more regular accounts of the estate's business and for his poor judgment in boarding a British naval vessel anchored off Mount Vernon in 1781. Through most of his long absence, however, Washington trusted Lund and confided in him about the most sensitive matters as he came to insist that the management of his private estate reinforce his public reputation.[1]

Despite his experience and his knowledge of the estate, Lund was at least initially overwhelmed by the new responsibility and his perception of the demands from Washington. During the first winter away from Mount Vernon, Washington expected the work of the estate to continue with little interruption, and he sent detailed instructions for new improvements. Lund did not understand how he could oversee the transplanting of cherry trees, the replanting of a vineyard, and the clearing of swampland while he was attempting to manage the construction of a fence around the pasture, the preparation of flax for weaving, and the threshing of harvested wheat. At the same time, Lund directed the work on the expansion and redesign of the Mansion House, including the making of bricks and hauling of stones for the chimneys. His frustration fell on the enslaved laborers at the Home House farm, whom he characterized as lazy or too old for work, while others were incapacitated by injury. Lund also assumed responsibility for many of Washington's business affairs, including the ongoing efforts to recover debts owed by the Mercer family and the collection of rents from tenants. Although Lund claimed that he wrote every week, Washington, as he had during every previous absence from his estate, demanded ever more frequent and detailed reports from his manager.[2]

Whenever Martha Washington was in residence at Mount Vernon, Lund deferred to her direction, as well. Washington regularly conferred with his wife about the estate's business and entrusted her with management of the household accounts in his absence. In the first years of the war, Martha distributed the cash that Lund used to pay for the daily expenses of the estate, and Lund delivered all sums paid into Washington's account to her just as soon as he was able to count the money. She held the keys to Washington's closely guarded study and to his even more restricted desk, and

Lund relied on her to provide important business documents to him. Although Martha left the keys in Lund's custody when she went away, Lund was uncomfortable with the privilege. He told Washington he declined to look in the desk or other parts of the study without her presence. At times, Lund seemed to consider Martha one supervisor too many. With barely disguised condescension, he reported to Washington the repeated times that Martha was unable to find a document or left business correspondence unanswered. He complained that "Mrs Washingtons Charitable disposition increases in the same proportion with her meat House," leaving him with insufficient food for the laborers in the harvest fields. After Martha began to spend winters with her husband at the army's encampment, Lund assumed control over the distribution of the household cash.[3]

Little would be routine about managing the Mount Vernon estate and Washington's properties during the Revolutionary War. As early as October 1775, Lund prepared to defend Mount Vernon against a possible British raid and a reported plot to kidnap Martha Washington. While Martha organized her husband's papers and books for safekeeping, Lund searched for a secure storage location away from the Potomac shoreline. He assured Washington that fifty well-armed men could defeat a raiding party of four times that number if it attempted to scale the steep hill below the Mansion House. In the event of a British attack, Lund, if he had the muskets, "woud endeavour to find the men Black or White, that woud at least make them pay dear for the attempt." When in January 1776 rumors spread of a threatened British attack near Alexandria, Lund predicted that a hundred men would come from throughout Fairfax and the surrounding counties to defend Washington's estate. Already, upon hearing of the threat, William Stevens had crossed the ice-covered Potomac from Maryland, prepared to defend Washington's property. (Stevens also came to collect his wages for recent work on Washington's lands in the Ohio country.)[4]

Lund faced another potential threat to the security of the estate and his authority over its labor force when Virginia's last royal governor, Lord Dunmore, in November 1775 issued a proclamation offering freedom to any slave or indentured servant who left a rebel's possession to serve with the British Army. In the spring and summer of 1775, Dunmore's repeated threat to emancipate slaves in Virginia had alarmed whites in the colony and beyond, and persuaded slaves and servants to join his force. Among the white servants who fled to Dunmore was Joseph Smith, an English-born painter indentured to Washington. Smith ran off in the summer of 1775, while working under the supervision of Washington's brother-in-law, Fielding Lewis. Lund and Lewis advised that it would be impossible to recover Smith from Dunmore, but Lund assured him that "if he comes up here and indeavours to Land at mt Vernon Raising the rest, I will shoot him, that will be some Satisfaction." After Smith was wounded and taken prisoner by Virginia forces, Lund advised Lewis to sell the servant to the backcountry "after Whipg him at a Publick whiping Post."[5]

By early December, Lund was more concerned about the impact of the "much dreaded proclamation" on other indentured servants and slaves. "What effect it will have upon those sort of people I cannot tell—I think if there was no white Servts in this family I shoud be under no apprehension about the Slaves." A hired craftsman working on the redesign of the Mansion House confided in Lund that nearly all the indentured servants would leave if they could make their escape. Lund acknowledged that "Liberty is sweet," and promised Washington that he would make an example of anyone who tried to create unrest. A month later, he reported that the servants behaved as well as usual. "As to the Negroes I have not the least dread of them." Washington made no reference to the bound laborers on his own estate, but he was far more fearful than Lund that slaves in Virginia would join "that Arch Traitor to the Rights of Humanity, Lord Dunmore." He warned that Dunmore "will become the most formidable Enemy America has . . . if some expedient cannot be hit upon to convince the Slaves and Servants of the Impotency of His designs." In particular, it was the possibility of slaves joining the British forces that convinced Washington that it was necessary for Dunmore to be "instantly crushd, if it takes the force of the whole Colony to do it." Washington told John Hancock, then president of the Continental Congress, that the fate of America depended on the removal of Dunmore from Virginia.[6]

Following Dunmore's Proclamation, as many as a thousand enslaved men, women, and children sought refuge with the British forces, and many of the men fought in the Ethiopian Regiment organized by Dunmore. Most of the slaves who fled to the British were from the lower Tidewater, many of them maritime laborers, but few from as far away as Mount Vernon had any realistic chance of reaching Dunmore's protection. Through most of the war, intermittent British raids into the Chesapeake, including the lower Potomac, and the passage of Sir William Howe's fleet to the head of the bay in August 1777 did not directly affect Mount Vernon, but any appearance in the region of British forces usually attracted slaves seeking refuge from other estates in the Chesapeake. On the rare occasions that British ships or troops came near Mount Vernon before 1781, they offered a chance for servants and slaves to escape. Lund's fears about the indentured servants proved justified in July 1776, when three servants from Mount Vernon went off with the HMS *Roebuck,* which was part of Dunmore's fleet looking for provisions along the Potomac. As isolated as the incident was, the flight of the servants, like the widely circulated reports of the slaves who escaped to Dunmore and the British forces, demonstrated how quickly war could open previously unimaginable paths to freedom for the enslaved.[7]

◦   ◦   ◦

From his encampment in Cambridge, Massachusetts, Washington in the summer of 1775 instructed Lund to prepare the estate for the possibility of a prolonged conflict that would disrupt all familiar commerce. The Continental Association, in effect since the previous December, prohibited the importation of British manufactures and British-traded goods, making it imperative that the spinners on the estate increase their output. The production of cloth, most of it distributed to the enslaved laborers, would be a central enterprise of the estate throughout the war years, diverting labor and requiring expanded cultivation of the flax used in the weaving workshop. As spinning wheels became increasingly scarce, Lund hastened to buy more and soon had nine working. Enslaved carpenters made hemp brakes, formerly imported from England. Lund set what he called "a parcel of Little people"—enslaved children—to spinning, only to complain that their work was slow and awkward. By January 1776 the spinners had enough thread to make 150 yards of linen, and by year's end, William Keaton, the hired weaver, had supervised the enslaved spinners and weavers in the manufacture of more than 750 yards of woolen and linen cloth. Lund, however, complained that Keaton did "not weave fast enough for our family." By 1779, another hired weaver, Hugh Archer, was overseeing the weaving of cotton sheeting and tablecloths as well as coarse woolens and linen, yet still these home manufactures never met all of the estate's needs.

The hired tailor, Andrew Judge, used the woven fabric to make clothes for enslaved laborers and provided the enslaved house servants with livery suits similar to those formerly imported from Great Britain.[8]

The enforcement of the Continental Association's provision for non-exportation of American commodities began September 10, 1775, closing off the most profitable markets for flour from Mount Vernon's mill. In anticipation of the export ban, which he had strongly supported, Washington in August 1775 directed Lund to cease buying wheat from neighboring growers, and he expected a prolonged decline in sales of the grain on which he and so many Virginia planters had come to depend. When his brother Samuel proposed buying a gristmill in the fall of 1775, Washington asked incredulously, "Have you considered the times? where are you to get a Market for anything you raise?" Washington encouraged Lund to continue sowing wheat at his estate, and even to undertake experiments in newly prepared fields, but crop yields fell precipitously under Lund's management. Washington and Lund discussed selling wheat and corn to traders in New England or in the French islands of the Caribbean, and Washington delegated such decisions to Lund, who could respond to local opportunities as they appeared.[9]

From 1773 to 1775, the last three years in which Washington supervised the cultivation of wheat, the estate produced on average more than 5,500 bushels a year; in 1776 and again in 1777, the combined plantations at Mount Vernon delivered to the mill fewer than 1,900 bushels. In 1778 and 1779, the crop was reduced to several hundred bushels, and some plantations produced no marketable wheat. In 1776, Lund reported that a weevil had begun to destroy wheat in Fairfax County, and three years later, more out of desperation than any realistic expectation, he insisted "there surely must be an End to the Fly" that continued to destroy wheat. Without Washington's careful supervision of ditching and draining, fields were often too wet to plow or to sow. Lund admitted that "it gives me Real concern and uneasiness, that we are mak[in]g nothing—all our Wheat destroyd, our Mill idle, and but a short Crop of Corn." When wheat prices rose in 1778, Lund had little to sell and found the most recent crop worse than those of previous years.[10]

Early in the war, Lund thought it strange to pay the miller high wages while the mill stood idle, but the miller, William Roberts, had a signed contract with Washington, and he was, all agreed, a remarkably skilled miller and millwright. By late summer 1778, after the succession of miserable wheat crops, Lund asked Washington if they should consider replacing Roberts with someone who would work for lower wages, perhaps someone with "a more Happy disposition." Lund added that "Roberts has Faults—he is fond of Drinkg too much & when in Liquor is apt to be ill natured," and that he spent much of his time trading horses, which he then pastured at Washington's expense. Roberts delivered to Washington his own version of his management of the mill, and, whether because of that representation or Lund's acknowledgment that few millers were as good as Roberts, he was still in place as miller and millwright when business revived following the war.[11]

To compensate for the diminished crops, Lund resumed the purchase of wheat, and the mill produced enough flour to sell to merchants as well as supply the estate. Lund purchased over nine hundred bushels of wheat from area farmers in 1777, and another four hundred in 1778. Most of the flour sales were to merchants in Alexandria, where Josias Watson purchased the largest amount—over a thousand barrels between 1777 and 1783—but the volume remained a mere fraction of prewar sales. Watson and other Alexandria merchants, including Robert Hooe, also purchased corn from the Mount Vernon plantations. Corn production fared better than wheat, but much of it went to provisioning enslaved and hired laborers on the estate and to fattening hogs and cattle.[12]

After the nearly complete failure of the wheat crop in 1778, Washington, stating the obvious, told Lund he could not support himself if he made nothing. For several years Lund considered reintroducing tobacco, and asked the enslaved overseers, Morris and Davy Gray, to prepare land for the old staple at the plantations under their supervision. Although Washington encouraged tobacco at other plantations, as well, Lund expected a poor crop. Lund also needed to reserve the same "Strong Land" required for tobacco for growing the flax that was essential for supplying the estate with cloth. When Morris finally grew tobacco, which he did for several years toward the end of the war, he and the field laborers produced no more than could be used to pay taxes and church duties. At Washington's suggestion, Lund explored the production of saltpeter made from barnyard litter, and he paid "a Dutch Man" for staying six days and instructing him in the art of distilling whiskey. When Lund read about New Englanders making rum and molasses from cornstalks, he reasoned that this use of a readily available commodity could produce more revenue than tobacco. By August 1778, he had overseen the construction of a mill for pressing cornstalks and put up kettles to boil the juice for molasses, but in the next month he abandoned the experiment as too expensive. Such projects, arising out of wartime austerity, showed Lund to be resourceful and inventive in searching for ways to supply the estate and to keep the enslaved laborers productively employed, but they introduced no sustainable production for market.[13]

Lund took advantage of isolated opportunities to sell the estate's produce to armies. In 1776, two Virginia regiments purchased corn; over the next two years Lund sold corn, shad, and bacon for the use of the Continental Army. With salt in short supply, Lund found a way to cure more fish with brine and smoke so that he could meet the demand of the army and still supply the enslaved at Mount Vernon, recognizing that "our people being so long acustom'd to have Fish when ever they Wanted woud think it very hard to have none at all." When soldiers of the French army came through Northern Virginia in 1781, they purchased corn and livestock from Mount Vernon.[14]

A more lucrative wartime enterprise was the joint investment made by Washington, John Parke Custis, and Lund in a mercantile ship, fitted out and armed under the direction of Alexandria merchants Jenifer & Hooe and commissioned to intercept British vessels. Together, Washington and his partners owned a one-eighth interest in the privateer *General Washington,* which after its launch in April 1778 carried a small amount of corn from Mount Vernon on its first voyage to Nantes. The partners invested not to market their own crops, however, but to profit from the capture of British prize ships and their cargoes, several of which the *General Washington* brought into United States ports. After returning from France, the ship made voyages to St. Eustatius, Amsterdam, and Newport, providing varying profits for the investors. Washington also bought goods out of the return cargoes, including fine women's clothing and large quantities of rum, sugar, and salt from St. Eustatius. The proceeds from these voyages could never offset the decline in the sale of agricultural produce or the loss of other sources of revenue. Neither was Washington able to rely on the once steady rental income from his lands in Fauquier, Loudoun, and counties beyond the Blue Ridge. Some tenants refused to pay rents as long as the war closed markets, and others were emboldened by a rent strike led in part by James Cleveland, formerly an overseer at Mount Vernon and more recently the manager of Washington's effort to settle lands in the Ohio country.[15]

The organization of the plantations at Mount Vernon, and also the residences of the slaves, remained largely unchanged during the war, except that the Mill Plantation, at which Davy Gray had served as overseer since 1770, ceased to be organized as a separate unit by 1778. Gray, who became overseer of the Muddy Hole Plantation, and the other enslaved overseer, Morris, continued to receive small cash payments in acknowledgment of their responsibilities, and the first wartime payment was presented to Morris by "Order of Mrs Washington." Morris and Gray also received supplemental provisions of pork, as provided to white overseers, and Lund purchased for each of them a pair of leather breeches. Soon after Lund assumed management of the estate, he found many of the slave cabins to be in such derelict condition that he ordered the carpenters to make them habitable for the winter, and Washington directed that some new cabins be constructed. When the estate weavers could not keep up with the need for clothing to distribute to the enslaved, Washington encouraged Lund to purchase the least expensive linen, "without making the poor Negros suffer too much," although he made the distribution of provisions conditional on what he expected in return. The enslaved laborers, he wrote, "certainly have a just claim to their Victuals and cloaths, if they make enough to purchase them."[16]

∘   ∘   ∘

As the war continued, Lund came to understand his service to Washington and his protection of the interests of the estate as a kind of civic responsibility. He declined when Washington proposed to increase his salary, and later refused another offer to compensate for the depreciation of currency as the war went on for years. He assured Washington that he would never leave his employ or expect additional pay "while you are encountering every danger and difficulty, at the Hazard of your life and repose, give[in]g up all domestick happiness, to serve the publick and me among them."

Although he thought of establishing his own home, "all this I will forego and endeavour the best I can for you whilst you are away." So too did Lund recognize that his management of the estate and its business would affect the public reputation of General Washington. He assured Washington "I find my self equally anxious to discharge a Debt against you, as I am to pay one of my own."[17]

Washington encouraged Lund in his consideration of the public appearance of ostensibly private business dealings. By 1779, Washington was especially distressed about the impact of depreciated currency on standing financial obligations. He feared that his refusal to accept paper money could by his closely watched example injure public credit, but he also found himself the great loser when debts contracted before the war could be discharged at the face value of the currency. These personal losses deepened his pessimism about the decline in public virtue as manifested in "the infamous practices of Speculators, monopolizers, & all that tribe of gentry." As Lund reported, even the miller William Roberts was demanding that his wages be adjusted to make up for the depreciation. Washington insisted that "No Man has, nor no man will go further to serve the Public than myself—if sacraficing my whole Estate would effect any valuable purpose I would not hesitate one moment in doing it." He recognized that, if he alone honored the depreciated currency in settling old debts, "it is not serving the public but enriching individuals and countenancing dishonesty." Since he was too far removed from Virginia to understand prevailing business practices, Washington suggested that Lund "pursue the advice of, some sensible Whigs." Although his inclination was to refuse such payments in future, Washington would agree to accept the paper money for old debts if the others believed it would advance "the great cause we are imbarked in."[18]

The tension between Washington's private interest and his regard for public reputation was never greater than when he approached the most dramatic change in his estate management during the Revolutionary War. In the early months of 1778, Washington for the first time considered selling slaves for financial gain. Even more significant was his professed desire to lessen his reliance on enslaved labor, or as he put it, "to get quit of Negroes." Washington asked himself whether, in the event of American victory in the war, it would be in his interest "to have negroes, and the Crops they

will make; or the sum they will now fetch and the interest of the money."
As a financial calculation, he had no doubt of the advantage to be gained
by selling slaves, assuming he sold them after the devaluation of currency
had reached its lowest level. His greater misgiving was selling slaves at a
public venue.[19]

Over many months in dialogue with Lund, Washington struggled to define the conditions under which he would be willing to sell slaves. He
strongly preferred private sale or the barter of slaves for one of the adjoining
parcels of land he was so eager to add to Mount Vernon. Washington
wanted to sell only slaves who gave their consent, and he did not want any
sale to result in the separation of husband and wife, or parents and children.
Lund agreed he would attempt to negotiate a private sale or an exchange
of land for slaves, but he reminded Washington the most advantageous way
to sell would be at a public sale. He also discovered that the enslaved had
their own strategies for avoiding or delaying sale. By early April 1778, Lund
had reached an agreement for the sale of Bett to a man from Botetourt
County, "but her Mother appeard to be so uneasy about it, and Bett her-
self made such promises of amendment, that I coud not Force her to go
with the Man." When Lund negotiated the sale of Phillis to another man,
he could "not get her to utter a Word of English," and the buyer left,
thinking she could not speak. Lund then concluded that he would be unlikely to sell slaves unless he held a public sale with no regard for the
consent of the individuals offered for sale.[20]

Months later, a frustrated Lund twice implored Washington to "tell me
in plain terms, whether I shall sell your Negroes at Publick sale or not, &
how many of them & indeed Who." After a hasty note that he feared did
not reflect the care and thought required of so important a subject, Washington in late February 1779 sent Lund his lengthiest comments about the
sale of slaves, but still he hesitated to make a decision. If Lund had not acted
as a consequence of the earlier message, Washington asked for more time
to "revolve the matter in my mind more fully," and "to draw some more
precise conclusions than at present." The message arrived too late; more
than a month earlier, Lund had recorded the cash sale of nine slaves for
£2,303, far less than the amount Washington had anticipated. Included in
the sale were Bett and Phillis, as well as Orford, who had recently returned
to Mount Vernon with other slaves who had remained in Pennsylvania

following their evacuation from the Ohio country three years earlier. Another of the nine, Jack, was probably the man of that name who had been in Pennsylvania with Orford. Lund left no indication of how the five women and four men were selected for sale, although in a letter now lost he had referenced individuals who might be sold. Bett's earlier promise of "amendment" likely referred to some behavior that had drawn the disapproval of Lund, but the long discussions of the potential sale had focused largely on prices and the terms of the sale, with no mention of removing individuals Lund considered troublesome.[21]

When Washington told Lund that every day he longed "more & more to get clear of" slaves, he did not explain his intent beyond the immediate financial calculation. On the eve of the Revolutionary War, Washington had shown neither an inclination to reduce his investment in enslaved laborers nor any reluctance to participate in public slave sales, such as the widely advertised Mercer sale he managed in November 1774. As late as 1775, he was purchasing slaves and finding new ways to extract their labor on his lands to the west. In those ventures and at Mount Vernon, Washington found enslaved laborers to be far more reliable workers than the indentured servants, whom he considered a much higher risk of running away or disrupting other laborers. The diversification of the estate had created work for all but the youngest and oldest of the enslaved at Mount Vernon, but the disruptions of the war had greatly lessened the demand for labor. The first discussion of slave sales came as Washington recognized that his estate was barely able to support itself. Yet his expressed wish "to get quit of Negroes," not just sell a group of slaves for needed cash, arose from something more than wartime expediency.[22]

Washington's desire to "be clear of" or "to get quit of" the enslaved at his estate was in 1779 more of a sentiment than a plan, but its expression alone indicated a striking new perspective on slavery that Washington had gained since entering service in the Continental Army. As commander of the army, Washington was at the center of unanticipated discussions about the potential role of free Blacks and of slaves in the military conflict with Great Britain. After he and his council of generals in October 1775 unanimously agreed to prohibit the enlistment of enslaved men in the Continental Army and by a large majority agreed to prohibit the reenlistment of free Blacks, Washington two months later authorized the reenlistment of free Blacks after learning "that the free negroes who have Served in this Army, are very much disatisfied at being discarded." Faced with a choice that would recur throughout the war, Washington also recognized that the alternative to the enlistment of free Blacks and slaves was the risk that the African American recruits might join the British forces to secure the advantages or freedom they expected from military service. In 1778, Washington acceded to requests from military and civilian leaders in Rhode Island who proposed to organize a battalion of free Blacks and slaves, and several other states followed with the enlistment of both free Blacks and slaves. Discussion of the enlistment of slaves, and the provisions for their emancipation at the end of their service, exposed Washington to new antislavery arguments that emerged during the Revolution. The most impassioned appeal for the enlistment of slaves came from Washington's highly trusted aide-de-camp, John Laurens, who spoke with Washington about his proposal to organize a battalion of slaves from his native South Carolina. Laurens argued that bringing slaves into military service would "advance those who are unjustly deprived of the Rights of Mankind to a State which would be a proper Gradation between abject slavery and perfect Liberty."[23]

Washington had no expectation of improving the condition of the enslaved or extending rights to them when he considered sales as the first step toward disengagement with slavery on his estate. Rather, he assured himself that "if these poor wretches are to be held in a state of slavery, I do not see that a change of masters will render it more irksome," as long as families stayed together. (Washington certainly knew that this was not true. He knew that some slaveholders were far more brutal than others and that no sale agreement could ensure that family units remained intact.) In his protracted indecision about selling slaves, Washington was concerned above all with the appearances of any such sale. His protection of slaves from the destruction of immediate family ties or forced removal was not entirely new; Washington in 1773 had agreed not to send an enslaved man to his Pennsylvania lands when that unnamed individual protested leaving Fairfax County, and recently Lund had on Washington's behalf sold a man who wished to live closer to his family in Maryland. But by 1778 what had been an occasional regard for the pleas of individual slaves became a principle that Washington aspired to observe in his management of enslaved laborers. He was even more insistent that he not be involved in the public sale of slaves. The terms and conduct of a slave sale would thus ensure that his public reputation reflected his determination to disassociate himself from what he saw as some of the worst cruelties of slavery.[24]

Although Washington disingenuously claimed that the social ramifications of enlisting slaves was "a subject that has never employed much of my thoughts," he believed that arming slaves presented a threat to American military success and ultimately to the property of slaveholders throughout the theater of war. His greatest fear was that if the states organized battalions of slaves, the British would do the same, leading to a contest to see "who can Arm fastest." Washington also worried that the enlistment and subsequent emancipation of enslaved men would "render Slavery more irksome to those who remain in it" and "be productive of Much discontent in those who are held in servitude." When he recommended that the army hire Blacks as wagoners, he added that any hires "ought however to be freemen, for slaves could not be sufficiently depended on. It is to be apprehended they would too frequently desert to the enemy to obtain their liberty; and for the profit of it, or to conciliate a more favorable reception, would carry off their waggon-horses with them." Washington, like many of his officers, believed the British always held the greater appeal for slaves hoping to escape bondage, and he would see dramatic evidence of that when the British sailed up the Potomac in 1781.[25]

The HMS *Savage* anchored a quarter mile from Mount Vernon in April 1781 after the ship had taken on board more than thirty slaves seeking refuge from the estate of Robert Carter in Westmoreland County. The captain, Thomas Graves, sent a party ashore seeking provisions from Mount Vernon, but Lund initially rebuffed the crew. While anchored near Mount Vernon, Graves recorded that thirteen slaves, followed two days later by another five, reached the shelter of the *Savage*. All but one of the individuals had escaped from Mount Vernon. Lund, apparently hoping both to recover the slaves and to save the estate's buildings from destruction, accepted the captain's invitation to meet on board, and he later offered the ship a large supply of provisions. Lafayette, by then an ardent opponent of slavery, wrote Washington from Alexandria that news of the escape of "Many Negroes" from Mount Vernon did not concern him "as I little Value those Concerns," but he was extremely disturbed that Lund, "who in Some Measure Represents you at your House," would supply the same British sailors who just a few days before had burned several houses on the Maryland shore. Washington confided in Lafayette that Lund had mistakenly seen himself as "more the trustee & guardian of my property than the representative of my honor."[26]

Before Lafayette's letter arrived, Washington received a full report from Lund, to whom he sent the harshest reprimand. "To go on board their Vessels—carry them refreshments—commune with a parcel of plundering Scoundrels—and request a favor by asking the surrender of my Negroes, was exceedingly ill-judged," he wrote. "It would have been a less painful circumstance to me, to have heard, that in consequence of your non compliance with their request, they had burnt my House, & laid the Plantation in Ruins." Washington had little doubt that unless a superior naval force arrived in the Chesapeake, the British incursion would result "in the loss of all my Negroes, and in the destruction of my Houses—but I am prepared for the event." He would, however, make every effort to recapture the slaves who had absconded with the British, and in that he would rely on Lund, who owned several of the slaves.[27]

The escape of the seventeen slaves enumerated by Lund marked an unprecedented scale of resistance by the enslaved at Mount Vernon. Only in 1761, when four African-born slaves ran away, had Washington faced an organized group flight from his estate. He had understood most of the instances of individual slaves running away as attempts to hide from likely punishment, to visit family members, or to avoid forced relocation away from family and community. In 1781, however, Washington experienced at his own estate what he knew had happened wherever British forces went throughout the United States during the war—the escape of enslaved people, often in large groups, with the aim of securing lasting freedom under the protection of the British. The greatest flight of slaves in Virginia took place in the first half of 1781 when incursions by Benedict Arnold, Lord Cornwallis, and the naval force that included the *Savage* offered several thousand slaves the chance to seek their freedom. Those who fled from Mount Vernon represented the diversity of the enslaved population on the estate. Frederick, "an overseer and valuable," was forty-five and had been a foreman at River Plantation since 1765. Gunner, the same age and also "valuable," was a brickmaker brought to Mount Vernon in 1774.

Among the other tradesmen were Strephon, a cooper, and Wally, a weaver. The African-born Sambo had been among the slaves Washington sent to work on his lands in Pennsylvania. Peter, Lewis, and Frank were each described by Lund as "an old man." Three women—Deborah, Esther, and Lucy—joined the larger group of men. Several of the men were still "lads."[28]

Many of the thousands of Virginia slaves who escaped in 1781 followed the British army to Yorktown where, during the final days of the siege and in the face of dwindling provisions, Cornwallis ordered them expelled from the army's encampment. Hundreds died of starvation and disease. The terms of capitulation allowed for Americans to repossess property, including slaves, held by the British, and Lucy and Esther were retaken at Yorktown. Six of the men who found refuge on the *Savage* were recaptured in Philadelphia; others from Mount Vernon may have been among the dead at Yorktown. The recaptured slaves were returned to Mount Vernon, where in 1786 Esther was a field laborer at River Plantation, Sambo worked as a carpenter, and Gunner was a laborer at the Home House farm. At least three of the slaves who fled from Mount Vernon traveled with the British to New York, and embarked for Nova Scotia in 1783. Henry Washington, called Harry by Lund, had been enslaved at Mount Vernon since 1765 and later moved from Canada to Sierra Leone, where he became a farmer.[29]

As the British prepared to evacuate New York in spring 1783, Washington made a personal appeal for the return of American-owned slaves in accordance with the terms of the provisional Treaty of Paris. The commanding British officer, Sir Guy Carleton, refused to comply, telling Washington that the Blacks freed by British proclamations were no longer property as defined by the treaty. To deliver up the former slaves to possible execution and severe punishment, Carleton added, "would be a dishonorable Violation of the public Faith pledged to the Negroes." After his conference with Carleton, Washington conceded to Virginia governor Benjamin Harrison that "the Slaves which have absented from their masters will never be restored to them," but even into his service as president, Washington would continue to seek British compensation for the lost slaves. Whatever reservations he had about owning slaves and however much sympathy he had for the antislavery appeals of Laurens and Lafayette, Washington consistently defended the property rights of slaveholders and endeavored to recover any slaves who escaped from his estate or household. In addition to his official representation to Carleton, Washington was among the slaveholders who hired a Fairfax County neighbor to travel to New York to search for escaped slaves.[30]

○   ○   ○

Throughout his long absence, Washington's attention frequently turned to Mount Vernon with thoughts of the estate he hoped to reshape after the return of peace. Along with frequent instructions for Lund about routine cultivation on the plantations and the care of livestock, he also guided his manager in the design and improvement of the agricultural landscape. When the framing of the expanded Mansion House was nearing completion in the summer of 1776, Washington chose the trees to be planted in groves on either end of the house. He wanted locust trees at the north end, while the south end was to be planted with "all the clever kind of Trees (especially flowering ones) that can be got." Crab apple, poplar, dogwood, and other native trees would be "interspersed here and there with ever greens such as Holly, Pine, and Cedar, also Ivy." Both ends were to be planted to frame views to the working estate, in the prevailing English style that erased the distinctions between the gardens surrounding a landowner's house and the improved farmlands around. The grove to the north was to be planted "so as to Shew the Barn &ca in the Neck," across Little Hunting Creek at River Plantation. Also in the English style, the trees were to be set out to imitate nature, "Planted without any order or regularity." Three years later, Washington asked Lund if he had opened the "visto" to Muddy Hole Plantation, another of the constructed views that would visually order the farming landscape for both enslaved laborers and visitors.[31]

Within a few months after leaving Mount Vernon, Washington was urging Lund to experiment with planting live hedges for practical use as well as ornament. Washington approved of honey locust or hawthorn hedges between cultivated fields and pastures, but thought cedar or other evergreens would look best. Lund supervised enslaved labors in their collection of cedar berries for planting these live hedges intended to replace rail fence. Washington also wanted ornamental plantings of trees to grace the working parts of the estate. He ordered Lund to plant tall, straight locust trees to define a lane to the new spinning house; a similar line of trees was to be planted along the millrace. His instructions displayed his un-canny memory of the landscape across his estate. From winter encamp-ment in New Jersey in December 1778, he directed Lund to a stand of hickory leading to Dogue Run, and "the Corner tree on the run decayed (a Beech)."[32]

Even in the most difficult times of the war, Washington found diversion in the traditional pursuits of a Virginia planter, taking particular interest in the acquisition and breeding of horses. In December 1776, on the eve of the battle of Trenton, when he admitted to being "distressed by a number of perplexing circumstances," he sent two horses to the care of Lund and announced his intention to find another for the matched team of four that pulled Martha's coach. In early 1778, while at Valley Forge, Washington sent a breeding stallion to Lund, who requested more information about the pedigree; "if his Ancesters are of Royal Blood, & he handsome much money may be made by him." With no other impressive horses standing at stud in the area, Lund had high expectations for "Steady," and over the next several years he collected fees from the owners of several dozen mares bred with the stallion at Mount Vernon. Washington continued to follow the breeding business at his estate and in March 1781 asked Lund to send a list of all the mares and colts. From his headquarters in New Windsor, New York, Washington told Lund that the report on horses and other live-stock, as well as an account of the landscape at the Mansion House, "would be satisfactory to me, and infinitely amusing in the recital, as I have these kind of improvements very much at heart."[33]

Since 1759, Washington had sought to consolidate under his ownership all the land on what he called "my own Neck," the area between Little Hunting Creek and Dogue Creek. The land, for which he hoped to ex-change slaves, would further unify the Mount Vernon estate. Although he was determined to avoid any further debt, he was willing to acquire the property "by any means in my power, in the way of Barter for other Land—for Negroes . . . in short for any thing else (except Breeding Mares and Stock of other kinds)." With Lund as his liaison, Washington ap-proached the owners of land he had long coveted. During the war years, Washington added two tracts of land to Mount Vernon. The larger was the 480 acres purchased by Lund from Thomas Hanson Marshall in 1779 and then transferred to Washington in exchange for an equal number of acres at an outlying part of the estate. In the spring of 1783, Washington purchased from William Barry 118 acres that gave him control of the land surrounding his mill. Still eluding him were the more than five hundred acres owned by Penelope French along Dogue Creek between Washington's Ferry Plantation and the mill. Washington admitted that in these wartime purchases he was motivated more by his ideal of a unified estate than any practical need for arable land. In negotiations for one of the land sales, he feared that he might "run the hazard of paying too severely for the gratification of a mere fancy, (for it is no more) of putting the whole neck under one fence; as it is well known that I stand in no need of Land or meadow for all my purposes."[34]

Still, Washington was eager for Lund to put the land bought from Marshall into meadow, and portions of both newly purchased tracts were incorporated into the existing Dogue Run Plantation. In anticipation of a life once again focused on farming, Washington began to think about how he would restore the productivity of his lands. He and Lund concluded that the three-year rotation of wheat, corn, and a fallow, which had been in use since the mid-1760s, was exhausting the soil, and the profits from the mill would depend on finding some way to prepare the land for higher yields of wheat. The entire estate, moreover, needed to be reorganized and brought under stricter management. "As my public business is now drawing to a close," Washington confided to Lund in June 1783, "I cannot avoid looking towards my private concerns, which do not wear the most smiling countenance." Washington had drawn no money from his estate for eight years, and the accounts he finally received in 1783 revealed that for the past five years the estate had not produced enough to pay his manager. At the close of Washington's military service, the estate provided "the *only means* by which myself & family—and the character I am to maintain in life hereafter—is to be supported." His income, as well as his reputation, would once again depend on the success of farming at Mount Vernon.[35]

For all of the dislocations of war, service as commander of the Continental Army exposed Washington to new farming practices and provided him with a critically fresh perspective on Virginia farming. Observing the lands surrounding Newburgh, New York, Washington learned that northern farmers, experienced in the cultivation of grasslands, had improved the land far beyond what anyone had achieved in Virginia.

"Improved Meadow in this part of the country, many miles from any large towns, sells from thirty to sixty pounds or more. But my countrymen are too much used to Corn blades & Corn shucks, & have too little knowledge of the profit of grass lands." From Juan de Miralles, the Spanish agent to the United States, Washington learned of mules bred from Spanish jackasses to be superior draft animals—longer lived, cheaper to feed, and easier to manage than horses or oxen.[36]

Washington returned to farming at Mount Vernon with a far deeper understanding of how agriculture would determine the new nation's peaceful engagement with other nations. When near the close of his service as commander-in-chief of the Continental Army he reflected on what would define the United States as a nation and secure the promise of the Revolutionary War, he considered the "unbounded extension of Commerce" as one of the blessings of an enlightened age that made the time of the nation's origin such an auspicious moment in history. If the United States hoped to engage in the reciprocally beneficial trade among nations, it needed more than a unified government that could enforce treaties and ensure the nation's credit: it needed to produce the kind of agricultural exports that could open connections with markets throughout the Atlantic world. Commerce in Washington's view also involved trading more than goods; it encompassed the exchange among nations of ideas and learning, including those related to the experimental farming embraced by landowners in Great Britain and much of the European continent during the last third of the eighteenth century.[37]

From his early reading of Lord Sheffield's *Observations On the Commerce of the American States,* with its call for the continuation of navigation acts restricting American commerce and its arrogant dismissal of the United States' capacity to respond, Washington recognized the threat that British neo-mercantilism posed to the principles of benevolent commerce and reciprocity that he hoped would prevail after the war. While he accepted the need to grant the Congress authority to protect trade with retaliatory or discriminatory regulations, Washington's commitment to liberal commerce and to a free engagement with the enlightened world found its most important expression in his pursuit of agricultural improvement at his own estate. He shared this persistent faith most freely with his former French comrades, particularly Chastellux and Lafayette. Acknowledging that such halcyon days might now be out of reach, Washington told Chastellux that his greatest wish was that "all restrictions of trade would vanish." "We should exchange produce with other Countries, to our reciprocal advantage: the Globe is large enough, why then need we wrangle for a small spot of it?" To Lafayette, Washington described himself at his estate "as a Citizen of the great republic of humanity at large," hoping to see mankind "connected like one great family in fraternal ties." Washington's openness to the liberal thought of France, like his later confidence in the great agricultural leaders of Great Britain, shaped his expectations of the relationships among nations in the wake of the independence of the United States.[38]

Lafayette, among the first to inform Washington of the provisional Treaty of Paris, wrote from Cadiz in early February 1783. Along with his congratulations, he shared a vision of the peacetime role that the man he called his adoptive father could play. "Were You But Such a Man as julius Cæsar or the king of Prussia, I should Almost Be sorry for You" at the conclusion of war, Lafayette wrote, but unlike other great military commanders, Washington had waiting for him vital civic work to provide "the finishing Stroke that is Wanting to the Perfection of the temple of Liberty." Washington's influence would be best employed "in inducing the People of America to strengthen their fœderal Union." But before Lafayette described the need for Washington to secure the powers of Congress and the defense of the new nation, he first suggested Washington join him in a plan "Which Might Become Greatly Beneficial to the Black part of Mankind." Lafayette proposed to Washington that they jointly purchase "a small Estate Where We May try the Experiment to free the Negroes, and Use them only as tenants." He told Washington that his example would inspire the emulation of others, and if they succeeded in America, Lafayette promised to carry the model to the West Indies. Lafayette added "If it Be a Wild scheme, I Had Rather Be Mad that Way, than to Be thought Wise on the other tack."[39]

In reply, Washington for the first time offered a tacit endorsement of the abolition of slavery in the United States. He wrote Lafayette that the proposal "to encourage the emancipation of the black people of this country from the Bondage in wch they are held, is a striking evidence of the benevolence of your Heart." Although Washington refrained from putting his full thoughts on paper, he went so far as to add "I shall be happy to join you in so laudable a work; but will defer going into a detail of the business, 'till

I have the pleasure of seeing you." In the summer of 1784, after spending several weeks at Mount Vernon, the historian William Gordon reminded Washington of his expressed wish "to get rid of all your Negroes" and of Lafayette's wish "that an end might be put to the slavery of all of them." Knowing that Lafayette was then visiting Mount Vernon, Gordon added that he "should rejoice beyond measure could your joint counsels & influence produce it, & thereby give the finishing stroke & the last polish to your political characters." Gordon, echoing Lafayette, asked Washington if it would be possible to establish "the industrious" among the enslaved as copyholders, similar to sharecroppers, who would have an incentive to make the produce of their labor more profitable and by their efforts "excite the lazy to exertions." Gordon disavowed any interest in immediate emancipation of slaves, but he was "for gradually releasing them & their posterity from bonds, & incorporating them so in the states, that they may be a defence & not a danger upon any extraordinary occurrence."[40]

In their private conversations, Lafayette and Gordon impressed upon Washington their belief that slaves were capable of becoming productive and independent laborers within the United States, and both Lafayette and Gordon were determined to find ways to educate enslaved people in the skills to support themselves after emancipation. Whatever Washington's response, these conversations, as well as Lafayette's later investment in a plan to establish slaves as tenants, offered Washington models for extricating himself from slavery in ways that extended freedom to enslaved individuals, in contrast to his earlier plan to get "quit of Negroes" by selling slaves to buyers who would continue to hold them in bondage. In their separate appeals, Lafayette and Gordon also stressed the opportunity for Washington to use his unparalleled public influence to set an example for other slaveholders and by so doing to burnish his reputation. The discussions about the proposals for some kind of tenantry for the enslaved, and particularly the ease with which Lafayette raised the ideas with Washington, were evidence of how dramatically white dialogue about slavery had changed during the Revolutionary War. Such conversations with Virginia slaveholders would have been barely imaginable before 1775. No slaveholder, particularly Washington, who had been so closely involved in debates on the enlistment of slaves and the recovery of slaves who escaped to the British, could after 1783 return to their estates without some recognition of the ways in which so many enslaved persons had in the midst of the war challenged their bondage. Washington also learned of the rise of a new form of antislavery advocacy among a small but influential group of whites as well as Blacks. Upon his return to Mount Vernon, Washington declined to embrace anything as radical as the plan proposed by Lafayette, but neither did he dismiss it out of hand. Washington understood that the management of his estate henceforth would serve as a public example, closely watched through much of the Atlantic world. That understanding would have its own impact on the new system he devised for the supervision of enslaved laborers, although not on their condition of servitude until many years later.

○   ○   ○

Washington expected that the arrival of peace and his subsequent return to farming would open a new life "under my own Vine & my own Fig tree." That favorite biblical phrase was less a dream of a rural idyll than a reflection of Washington's belief, shared with many of his contemporaries in Great Britain as well as the United States, that a dedication to agricultural improvement would supplant military conflict and the wasteful expenses of empire. The vine and fig tree passage from the book of Micah, so frequently quoted by Washington during and after the Revolutionary War, described for him a kind of independence rooted in the possession of one's own productive land and in the safety of a place "where none shall make them afraid."[41]

In his farewell to the troops of the Continental Army in November 1783, Washington described similar prospects for those "retiring victorious from the Field of War to the Field of Agriculture." He recommended that only a small number of soldiers continue in the military establishment he had prescribed in detail, leaving the overwhelming majority of the Continental troops to enter civil society and "prove themselves not less virtuous and usefull as Citizens, than they have been persevering and victorious as Soldiers." Some would find productive labor in commerce, manufacturing, and fisheries, but above all, it was farming that offered the opportunity for the troops to enjoy the blessings of the "Independence and Sovereignty" they had won through their perseverance. Washington expected "the extensive and fertile Regions of the West, will yield a most happy Asylum to those, who fond of domestic enjoyment, are seeking for personal independence."[42]

Agriculture was fundamental to Washington's vision of the United States at peace with European nations, and of the mutually beneficial commerce that would bring those nations together in common interests. That vision guided his introduction of an entirely new system of farming on his estate in the years after he resigned his command of the Continental Army. Several years after returning to Mount Vernon, Washington shared with his former comrade in arms, the Marquis de Chastellux, his enduring belief that agricultural improvement and reciprocal exchanges between nations would bring about a new era of peace. "For the sake of humanity it is devoutly to be wished that the manly employment of agriculture and the humanizing benefits of commerce would supersede the waste of war and the rage of conquest—that the swords might be turned into plough-shares, the spears into pruning hooks—and, as the Scripture expresses it, the nations learn war no more." Washington hoped that his own turn from military command to enlightened farming would demonstrate how nations might fulfill that prophecy.[43]

· *4* ·

New Farming in a
New Nation

Not long after returning to Mount Vernon following the Revolutionary War, Washington concluded that farming in the United States, and particularly as practiced in Virginia, was unprofitable and destructive of the land. After nearly two years at home he lamented, "I never ride to my plantations without seeing something which makes me regret having continued so long in the ruinous mode of farming, which we are in." Throughout much of Virginia, the damages to the land "need no other proof of the fact than the gullied, and exhausted State of them, which is every where to be met with." To reverse the decline he saw all around him, Washington in 1785 embarked on a sweeping reorganization of every aspect of farming at his estate. Over the next several years, he transformed the agricultural landscape and imposed a far more demanding work regimen that redefined much about the lives and labor of the more than two hundred enslaved people at Mount Vernon.[1]

The model for his reinvention of farming was as notable as its scale and ambition. Washington intended to demonstrate the advantages of improved cultivation by making Mount Vernon more nearly like the great agricultural estates of Great Britain. He was hardly alone in his opinion that "no Country has carried the improvment of Land & the benefits of Agriculture to greater perfection than England." Enlightened landowners throughout much of Europe as well as in parts of the United States aspired to adopt the principles of husbandry that in recent decades had increased crop yields and the value of livestock in Great Britain. The recently established Philadelphia Society for Promoting Agriculture in announcing its aims to the public decried "the very imperfect state of American Husbandry" and offered its first premium for experiments in crop rotations "agreeable to the English mode of farming." Washington, however, was nearly unique in his single-minded resolve to adhere to British practices at his estate, and he remained more dedicated to British principles of husbandry and more closely engaged with British agriculturalists than perhaps any other large landowner in the United States.[2]

The agricultural vision of Washington was made even more distinct by his unquestioning determination to adapt enslaved labor to British farming practices. The British treatises that Washington read and the agricultural-ists with whom he corresponded had surprisingly little to say about the management of agricultural labor, and they certainly had no models to offer a large slaveholder in Virginia. From the beginning of the reorganization of his estate in 1785, Washington focused on new ways to manage enslaved laborers in the methods of farming he introduced. He directed the several enslaved overseers and coordinated the work of the many field laborers and artisans in what he wanted to function as an all-encompassing system of farming.

It was the concept of a system that distinguished Washington's initia-tives in the 1780s from his earlier adoption of the crops and cultivation methods associated with the British New Husbandry. Washington had long relied on British agricultural treatises to guide his innovations in farming, but now, like the members of the Philadelphia society with whom he worked closely, he wanted to adopt a more comprehensive, integrated system of farming as found on the improved estates of England and, in-creasingly, of Scotland. The absence of anything that could be considered a system of farming was, in Washington's opinion, to blame for the unpro-ductive and ruinous state of agriculture in the United States. He wrote the renowned British agricultural expert Arthur Young that farming in the United States did not merit the "epithet of system," and that he was among the select group of Americans "who are endeavouring to get into you reg-ular & systematic course of cropping as fast as the nature of the business will admit." If that proved successful, he continued, "we shall make a more respectable figure as farmers than we have hitherto done."[3]

○   ○   ○

The new plan of farming at Mount Vernon was part of a broader restoration of his estate and business affairs that consumed much of Washington's attention in the mid-1780s. The war had, as he described it, deranged his affairs during the long years when he received no income from farming or his other enterprises. In the first year after his resignation from the Continental Army, Washington spent long hours organizing his business papers and devoted two months to a trip west in hopes of salvaging his earlier investments there. Then, facing the likely departure of Lund Washington as estate manager, Washington turned his attention to his farms. In the early months of 1785, he resumed his frequent rides on a circuit of the estate's working plantations, and in June he announced his intention to introduce a farming system based on his long and close study of British agricultural treatises.

Washington believed he needed the guidance of an experienced English farmer who would live at Mount Vernon and advise him, the overseers, and the field laborers in the most advanced methods of British husbandry. To find such a farmer, Washington turned to his close friend and former neighbor George William Fairfax, who was living with his wife, Sally, in Bath, England, having moved there to take care of family legal matters before the war. Washington asked Fairfax on what terms he would be able to hire "a knowing Farmer, I mean one who understands the best course of Crops; how to plough—to sow—to mow—to hedge—to Ditch & above all, Midas like, one who can convert every thing he touches into manure, as the first transmutation towards Gold: in a word one who can bring worn out & gullied Lands into good tilth in the shortest time." He proposed to place the farmer in charge of a plantation with 250 acres of arable land, worked by about ten enslaved field laborers and properly stocked. He would pay standing wages, rather than the share of crops usually allotted to a white overseer, and thereby avoid disappointing a good English farmer who would come without "a just idea of the wretched condition of our Lands—what dressings they will require, & how entirely our system must be changed to make them productive." If Washington could afford the kind of steward that managed large English estates, the man would live in the Mansion House and share his table, as had Lund; a "common Farmer" would live on the farm where he worked.[4]

Fairfax was well placed to answer Washington's request. He was a vice president of the Bath and West of England Society, perhaps the leading agricultural society in Great Britain at the time. Fairfax had frequently presided over that society's meetings from its founding in 1777, and he was in regular contact with leading proponents of agricultural improvement in England and Scotland. He relied on Edmund Rack, the secretary of the Bath society, to begin the search for a farmer who would meet Washington's requirements, and Rack forwarded a copy of Washington's letter to Arthur Young. Rack was likely also the source of the copy of Washington's letter published in England and Scotland in the first months of 1786. The excerpts from the letter describing Washington's criticism of agriculture in his own country and his decision to hire an English farmer appeared in print paired with a letter from the eminent British historian Catherine Macaulay, written following her ten-day visit to Mount Vernon in June 1785. Macaulay "found that Fame had not exaggerated the private or the public qualities of that modern Colossus of human virtue, General Washington." She also sent her unnamed correspondent, almost certainly her close acquaintance Edmund Rack, a parcel of seeds that Washington had collected for a new plantation he was establishing. The combined letters, submitted to *The Gentleman's Magazine* by a self-proclaimed "Cincinnatus," offered an unfamiliar view of the former American rebel virtuously pursuing the same enlightened husbandry that engaged British estate owners. *The Scots Magazine, The Edinburgh Magazine,* and various British newspapers reprinted the letters from Washington and Macaulay, which also appeared in American newspapers within a few months.[5]

Publication of the letters in the Bath newspaper attracted the interest of a young farmer who wrote directly to Washington with an offer of his services and assurances that he understood every aspect of the English style of husbandry. By that time, Fairfax and Rack had selected a farmer to travel to the United States and to present himself for the consideration of Washington. James Bloxham had served for fifteen years as a farm manager for William Peacey, a tenant on a large estate in Gloucestershire and himself recognized as one of the area's best farmers, according to Fairfax.

Peacey insisted that he knew of no equal to Bloxham in the essential work of improved farming; he was skilled in plowing, sowing, hedging, and ditching, and he understood the management of livestock from their "Breeding up to the Slaughter." After meeting several farmers, Fairfax considered Bloxham the best choice and booked his passage on a ship to the Chesapeake without waiting for further word from Washington. If Washington chose not to engage Bloxham, Fairfax would offer a tract of his own Virginia land for the English farmer, who was determined to relocate to the United States.[6]

The arrival of Bloxham at Mount Vernon in April 1786 proved an inauspicious start to the new course of farming. Washington and Bloxham signed articles by which the Englishman agreed to serve as a farmer and manager of husbandry for one year and to suggest plans for the improvement of the farms and the livestock, but within two months, he threatened to return to England at the end of the year. He found nothing amenable about Mount Vernon, starting with the summer air. He described the plows as the worst the world had ever seen, and he complained it was impossible to conduct any kind of business on the farms. Bloxham feared he was in danger of being poisoned by the slaves, whom he described to Peacey as very disagreeable people. Back in England, he noted, farmers like Peacey and himself would not be troubled with such laborers, but, he added, the general has got them "and he must Keep them."[7]

Washington was infuriated with "the old man," who "scarcely has sufficient knowledge of his own mind to determine whether to continue more than the present year." He was particularly incensed that Bloxham had arrived with such unrealistic expectations of an estate that was only just emerging from the impact of the war. If the plantations had already met the standards of the best farming counties in England, Washington explained to Peacey, he would have had no reason to hire the English farmer. After Bloxham's family decided to come from England, he was more content and assumed the responsibilities defined by the agreement, including the improvement of farm implements and the instruction of the enslaved field laborers in the best methods of cultivation. Washington, however, while acknowledging Bloxham's knowledge and industry, remained skeptical of the farmer's ability to manage the scale of change required at Mount Vernon.[8]

Far more encouraging was the support that Arthur Young offered Washington in his adoption of British husbandry. Young was by the 1780s Great Britain's most respected agricultural writer, as well as a tireless self-promoter always eager to attach himself to famous landowners. He had recently made a connection with George III, as the monarch caricatured as "Farmer George" undertook substantial agricultural improvements at the royal farms. Now Young had the opportunity to advise the most celebrated farmer in the new United States. Moved, he claimed, by "the spectacle of a great commander retiring in the manner you have done from the head of a victorious army to the amusements of agriculture," Young offered Washington whatever practical support he could provide from England, be it related to livestock, farming implements, seeds, or the hire of experienced laborers. Young also forwarded the first four volumes of his new periodical, the *Annals of Agriculture*.[9]

Washington already knew of Young through his published works, and he unhesitatingly replied with detailed requests for plows and an assortment of seeds essential for the rotation of crops advocated by Young and many other British agriculturalists. He also inquired of Young whether a skilled plowman might be willing to come to Virginia for annual wages and housing. Young discouraged Washington from hiring an English plowman, who would be expensive and unnecessary given the ease with which his new plows worked the soil. He instead offered more implements and seeds, and, most important, ongoing advice while Washington adopted the new system of farming. In a correspondence extending over eight years, Washington found in Young a kindred spirit in whom he confided his disdain for agriculture in the United States and his determination "to pursue a course of husbandry which is altogether different & new." To demonstrate the value of that new system of farming would, according to Washington, require resolution and a practical guide, and, he declared to Young, "Your annals shall be this guide."[10]

Even before the arrival of Bloxham or the offer of assistance from Young, Washington returned to the British agricultural books he had accumulated in the 1760s, and he ordered more recent publications, including *The Gentleman Farmer*, by Henry Home, Lord Kames of Scotland. Since its publication in 1776, *The Gentleman Farmer* had become one of the most popular practical guides for estate owners in Scotland and England. Washington copied excerpts from Kames into more than one hundred pages of a note-book, and he redrew the designs for the harrow that he described as "a very useful, indeed absolutely necessary instrument in Husbandry." Lord Kames was one of Scotland's premier jurists, and like Washington, he saw in the improvement of agriculture an opportunity, even an obligation, to combine private interest and public good. "How pleasing to think, that every step a man makes for his own good, promotes that of his country!" As his book title suggested, Kames believed that farming was the most vir-tuous and patriotic employment for landed gentry, who might "rouse emulation" among tenants and small farmers. Although Washington never distinguished between English and Scottish agriculturalists, Kames's book was the first of the increasingly important Scottish influences on his ap-plication of improved husbandry. Kames intended his book to guide farmers in every temperate climate, but he especially wanted to erase the agricultural past of Scotland, with its wastelands and unkempt fields. Kames, like the Scottish agriculturalists with whom Washington later cor-responded, shared with improvement advocates in the United States the hope "that agriculture will soon be as familiar among us, and as skillfully conducted, as in England."[11]

In his notes on Kames, Washington twice recorded the observation that "No branch of husbandry requires more skill and sagacity than a proper rotation of crops." Crop rotation was at the heart of what defined a system of improved agriculture in Great Britain by the 1780s, and the most prized skill of a landowner was the ability to determine the succession of crops that would maximize production of grain while sustaining the fertility of the soil particular to an estate. On both sides of the Atlantic, estate owners dedicated to this model of agricultural improvement assumed that the com-plexity of crop rotations, the cycles for which ran as long as seven years, required the direction of the sort of "gentleman farmer" for whom Kames and most other British agriculturalists wrote. Washington concluded that a productive system of rotations depended on "a *course* of experiments by intelligent and observant farmers." Even George III prescribed his own ro-tation of crops as a mark of his practical knowledge and commitment to the civic example of his experimental farms.[12]

Throughout the rest of his life, Washington would seek to perfect the rotation schemes that might cure the ills of farming in the United States. Two goals guided his experiments: first, to introduce crops that would be useful on a farm and valuable on the market; and second, to devise the sequence of rotations and soil dressings that would maintain the fertility of the land. During the Revolutionary War, Washington and his manager, Lund Washington, recognized that the rotation of wheat, corn, and a season of fallow, a system they implemented in the 1760s as a certain improvement over tobacco culture, depleted all but the best land, and Washington directed Lund to experiment with a better preparation of land for wheat. After his return to Mount Vernon, Washington cited knowledge of a course of crops as the most important skill he hoped to find in a new farm manager, but after deciding to implement the full course of British husbandry, he assumed responsibility for devising his own sequence of rotations.[13]

For his individual plantations, Washington initially developed rotation charts based on the model forms he copied from Kames. While he acknowledged that rotations that worked in one country might not succeed in another, he diverged from British practice only in the inclusion of a season for corn, which remained an essential staple for provisioning the enslaved on the estate. Washington intended for his rotations to be experimental, varying the sequences from farm to farm. The seven-year cycles usually began with corn or wheat, the two crops most likely to exhaust the soil. He then planned for fields to be planted with seasons of clover and grasses, followed by turnips and barley, and finally, a season as pasture, although the variations were nearly endless.[14]

The success of the rotations depended on a reliable supply of seeds for new crops, especially the cultivated, or "artificial," grasses, the legumes that restored the soil, and the root crops that prepared the soil for grain and served as fodder for livestock. Merchants in Philadelphia and Baltimore provided the seeds for sainfoin, burnet, timothy, and various sorts of clover, and new types of wheat and barley. Other varieties of grasses, beans, and wheat arrived from England, sent by Arthur Young and Bloxham's old employer, William Peacey. Washington insisted that neither the condition of the seeds nor the time of their arrival interfere with his complex plan of rotations. "An imposition of bad Seeds," he wrote, " is a robbery of the worst kind; for your pocket not only suffers by it but your preparations are lost—& a season passes away unimproved."[15]

In late December 1785, Washington spent two days surveying his Dogue Run Plantation with the goal of reconfiguring the fields. The seven-year rotations required an equal number of even-sized fields at each plantation, and Washington intended to demarcate the fields with a permanent arrangement of ditches and hedges. After surveying the plantations, he ordered hired ditchers and enslaved laborers to undertake the massive job of creating a new farming landscape across the estate. Over the next few years, Washington hired white ditchers and purchased the remaining time of an indentured servant from Germany, Daniel Overdonck, who was skilled in ditching. His agreement with another ditcher, James Lawson, obliged the hired man to instruct enslaved workers in his trade. A group of enslaved laborers selected from different parts of the estate worked together as ditchers under the supervision of Lawson and Overdonck, even though the latter arrived with no knowledge of English. The enslaved ditchers were all men, and as they moved from farm to farm, they coordinated their work with women who prepared ground for hedging and men who fixed the posts and rails.[16]

On each of his plantations, at the center of the reconfigured fields, Washington attempted to realize the British ideal of neatly organized and well-designed farmyards, with substantial barns and stables for the better protection of livestock and harvested crops. With the rise of the New Husbandry, British estate owners constructed new kinds of farm buildings that accommodated the changes in agricultural management. Crop rotations depended on areas for the storage of the hay crops and root vegetables, used to feed livestock. The threshing of wheat, especially as it became mechanized in the late eighteenth century, required covered areas at the center of barns. Well-designed farmyards facilitated the collection of the manure so essential to soil fertility. The centralized farm buildings also supported a closer supervision of labor. Wealthy estate owners for the first time commissioned professional architects to design what had previously been vernacular and utilitarian buildings, and by the 1780s, British pattern books offered advice for smaller farmers on the designs of barns and farmyards. The Philadelphia agricultural society at its inception in 1785 offered a prize for the best design of a farmyard "suitable to this climate and circumstances of common farmers," and Washington encouraged the society to continue its support for improved farmyards, which he considered "the basis of all good Husbandry."[17]

After reading the first volumes of the *Annals of Agriculture,* Washington asked Arthur Young to send him a plan for a barn and farmyard to serve a farm of about five hundred acres. Young responded with an elaborate plan and directions for the use of a multifunction building that incorporated aspects of the most advanced barn designs from the great estates of England. In the second volume of the *Annals,* in an article from which Washington took notes, Young described the farm buildings on the Holkham Hall estate of Thomas William Coke, one of Britain's foremost agricultural innovators. According to Young, the barns at Holkham were "ornaments" that framed the approach to a great mansion more splendidly than any landscape designed by Capability Brown. Travelers encountering the "new-built farm-houses, with barns and offices, substantially of brick and tile," could only conclude "*we approach the residence of a man, who feels for others as well as for himself.*" In his design for Washington, Young centered the barn on a large threshing floor, a common practice in Great Britain, but scarcely known in Virginia, where wheat was usually trod by horses in the open air or threshed by hand. A great door allowed the entrance of wagons carrying wheat, and the threshing floor was large enough for three laborers to clean the wheat of a five-hundred-acre farm over the winter months.[18]

Initially Washington decided to build a barn precisely as Young described it, but he soon made the substantial addition of a farmyard of his own design, influenced by the plan sent by the Philadelphia agricultural society. He provided stalls for dairy cows and pens for other livestock. Archways allowed laborers to remove dung from the stalls, and the mangers were designed for efficient distribution of corn and hay. Above the stalls and mangers, hay could be stored in a dormered half-story, "so arranged as to look well." Washington placed the barn between Ferry Plantation and the new farm organized on land acquired from Penelope French. A visitor from France in 1788 described the partially constructed barn as "a vast pile," adding "All this is quite new to Virginia, where there are neither barns nor provisions for cattle." Washington believed the completed barn to be "the largest and most convenient one in this Country."[19]

Construction of this building of unprecedented scale and complexity challenged Washington to sequence the work of enslaved laborers from various parts of the estate. In early 1788, he sent five enslaved ditchers to gather the lumber needed to fire the brick kilns, and he set the enslaved carpenters to work cutting floor planks. Washington pressured merchants

Fig 4.1 Arthur Young, by John Russell, 1794. Great Britain's most prominent agricultural writer by the 1780s, Young sent Washington farming implements and seeds as well as volumes of his *Annals of Agriculture* and the plan of the massive barn constructed at one of the Mount Vernon farms. Washington compiled an agricultural survey of the United States for Young, but he ended their correspondence following Young's repeated requests to publish his letters.
Photograph © National Portrait Gallery, London.

to deliver other lumber in time for the carpenters to dress it before they joined the field laborers in the annual harvest of hay. In April a hired brick-maker, Charles Hagan, worked with Gunner and Sam, enslaved laborers from the Home House farm, to begin making bricks. Three other enslaved men joined the brickmakers, and women field-workers built a fence around the first brick kiln to deter theft. By summer, Hagan and the slaves ordered to work with him had constructed two more kilns, one of which alone fired thirty-five thousand bricks. In the fall, Washington hired an additional brickmaker to supplement production of the materials required for the barn's two bricked stories. Because of the steady operation of the kilns, the hired brickmakers received pay calculated by the number of nights they worked as well as the days.[20]

At the completion of the new barn in the spring of 1789, Washington ordered Gunner and Tom Davis, another enslaved laborer from the Home House, to inspect the barns at the other plantations and to use their new skills to make necessary repairs to the brickwork. The renovation of the barns was part of a comprehensive examination of the buildings at each farm and the construction of agricultural buildings that would serve the new course of husbandry, while also improving the appearance of the estate. On the advice of James Bloxham, Washington provided shelters for cattle, and he instructed his farm manager on the proper brick foundations for the stercorary, or dung repository, to be constructed near the stables. Washington ordered the construction of new corn houses at several farms and the refurbishing of overseers' houses. At Dogue Run, where the enslaved "complain much of the Leakiness of their Houses," Washington wanted new coverings on the cabins and other cabins moved there. The scattered houses and farm buildings at the Ferry and French's plantations were concentrated near the new barn at the center of the unified farm.[21]

The most ambitious building project for the new course of farming was the unique treading barn designed by Washington and constructed at Dogue Run Plantation between the fall of 1792 and the spring of 1794. Washington had since the 1760s used horses for treading wheat, and although it was the common practice in parts of Virginia and Maryland, he considered the open-air method "a very execrable one." He had read of the advantages of second-story threshing floors, the elasticity of which allowed for the collection of far more grain than on dirt or a ground-level floor. In his design for the treading barn, Washington provided an earthen ramp for the horses to enter on the second level, where the animals then trod the wheat in a circular path framed by a sixteen-sided exterior wall. As the hooves of the horses separated the wheat grains from the straw, the grains fell through the precisely measured slats between the white oak floorboards to a brick-enclosed ground floor. There workers gathered the wheat berries for winnowing before they carried the cleaned grain to the nearby gristmill. The design of the barn, with its complicated framing and sloping rafters, was Washington's own.[22]

To guide Thomas Green, the frequently unreliable joiner and head carpenter, Washington sent from Philadelphia elaborate instructions and drawings for every detail of the treading barn. He specified the dimensions for more than twenty cuts of lumber, some to be purchased and "the rest to be got by my own People." To ensure that his plans would be properly executed, and as a caution against Green, who "never will overcome his propensity to drink," Washington insisted that his farm manager, Anthony Whitting, be on site at the laying of the foundation to ensure the proper placement of the window bars and the sills that would secure the chamber of threshed wheat. For further protection against the theft of grain, Washington

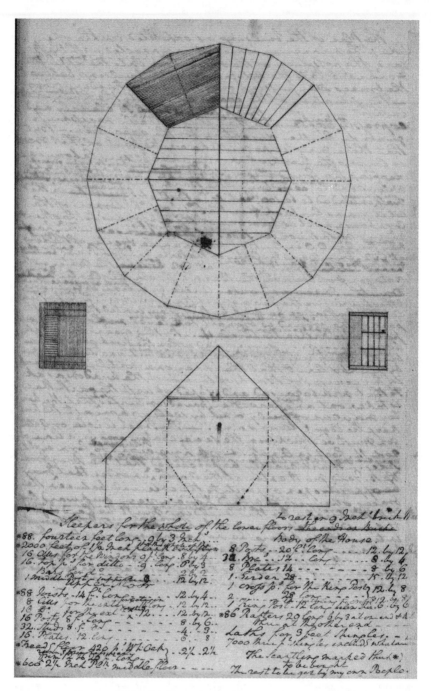

Fig 4.2 Plan for a Sixteen-Sided Barn, October 28, 1792. Washington's original design allowed for horses to tread out wheat in a circular path under cover from the weather. The grains fell between carefully spaced floor planks and were gathered on a lower level secure from theft. The enslaved carpenters carried out most of the complicated construction, despite Washington's doubts about their attention to detail. George Washington Papers, Series 4, General Correspondence, Manuscripts Division, Library of Congress.

urged his subsequent farm manager to keep the key in his own possession or to ensure that the overseer at Dogue Run never left it out of a locked box.[23]

Once the Dogue Run barn was in operation, Washington anxiously awaited reports of how the new method of treading worked, and he advised his manager how to experiment with the proper spacing of the floorboards to maximize collection of the cleanest grain. For months, Washington asked his manager to assess the effectiveness of the treading barn compared with treading on the ground, but the first season of use provided no sure answer except that the wheat was cleaner and the barn deterred theft. While the Dogue Run barn was under construction and in the early months of its operation, Washington considered building a similar treading barn at River Farm, but in May 1795 he instead drafted plans for another barn modeled on that designed by Arthur Young, with a covered threshing floor and granaries. Washington was eager to replace the derelict barn at River Farm for fear that "some very disasterous accident may befal not only the horses, but negros also, in a high wind, or storm." The new barn would, like that at Union Farm, be built on a scale more common in Great Britain than Virginia—of brick, two stories high, and covering sixty by thirty feet of ground, with additional space for cattle sheds. Its construction, by Washington's detailed calculation, would require 140,000 bricks to be made on the site. By April 1796, Tom Davis and Muclus, enslaved bricklayers, were progressing with work on the walls, while four enslaved carpenters constructed the barn doors.[24]

◦   ◦   ◦

The agricultural innovations introduced by Washington after 1785—the multiyear rotation cycles, the ditching and hedging of new fields, and the construction of farm buildings—imposed significant new demands on the enslaved laborers. Their work extended to longer hours, in every season of the year and every type of weather. The introduction of new crops and new methods of cultivation entailed almost constant experiments, so that no season of work was the same as the year before. Families of the enslaved were separated as more men moved to artisan jobs at the Home House, and the women field laborers took on more burdensome work, including plowing and harrowing with draft animals. Washington, always an exacting manager, expected ever greater skill and care from the enslaved agricultural workers under his control, and his first practical step toward the adoption of the new course of farming was to devise a unique system of monitoring and documenting the work of the enslaved field laborers and workers in associated trades.[25]

Beginning in November 1785, Washington compiled a weekly accounting of all work completed by the enslaved at the Mount Vernon plantations. On each Saturday, the overseers on the four outlying plantations and the lead carpenter presented Washington with a report of tasks that the laborers under their direction had carried out over the preceding week. The reports noted any increase or loss in the number of livestock at each plantation, but otherwise they were concerned almost entirely with the work of the enslaved and an account of their days. During the five months in which Washington prepared the reports, he frequently noted the specific days devoted to certain work and regularly recorded the gender divisions of labor: "Women all grubbing until Friday—3 of the Men at home House cutting wood for Christmas," read one entry. "Three days with one Man & 4 Women cleaning wheat," another noted. He reported "3 plows at Work (with women)." Washington identified many of the enslaved by name, indicating his personal familiarity with laborers at the outlying plantations, and he recognized the particular skills or responsibilities of individuals. He also documented any workdays lost to sickness. Throughout the rest of his life, Washington referred to the weekly reports or farm reports, but these were primarily records of the allocation of enslaved labor rather than any measure of agricultural production or financial accounting of the farms.[26]

The reports became one of the most important means by which Washington exercised closer daily management of his plantations following the long-planned departure of Lund Washington, who had served as estate manager for over two decades. Washington's nephew George Augustine Washington would in the spring of 1786 assume many of Lund's responsibilities, but Washington announced his own "fixed determination (whatever else may be left undone) to attend to the business of my plantations." The model of British husbandry that Washington aspired to emulate rested on the active management of the estate's owner, and the unique design of the weekly reports was part of Washington's early recognition that his implementation of the complicated work of the New Husbandry would require stricter allocation and supervision of enslaved labor.[27]

Beginning in April 1786, the weekly reports were prepared by George Augustine Washington, and after him a succession of farm managers continued to deliver them until the end of Washington's life. The scope of the reports expanded to include a wider range of labor, such as that of the enslaved ditchers, spinners, and bricklayers. Other revisions measured more precisely the allocation of laborers. When John Fairfax, overseer of the Home House farm, began in early 1787 to submit weekly reports on agricultural work, he presented the information in charts that accounted for the total number of workdays in the week, with breakdowns for labor carried out by men, boys, and girls. The detail and frequency of the reports allowed Washington to direct farming even when he was away from Mount Vernon. During the summer of 1787, after transcribing the information submitted by the overseers each Saturday, George Augustine Washington sent the weekly reports to Philadelphia, where his uncle served as president of the Federal Convention. Washington scrutinized and questioned the information, asking for clarification of matters so small as a suspected miscount in the number of peas sown. He also found ways to standardize the format for easier review and comparison.[28]

By the time Washington departed Mount Vernon for his first term as president of the United States, the reports reflected the most significant change in format. Although the reports included no record of monetary exchanges, by April 1789 the farm manager was preparing them in the style of the double-entry bookkeeping by which Washington had always carefully recorded financial transactions. Each plantation or team of workers was debited for the number of enslaved people working six days a week, and credited for the days spent on the weekly tasks. Thus, for the week ending September 18, 1790, the Dogue Run Plantation was debited for the work of eleven women and seven men, for a total of 108 workdays. The credit side of the ledger recorded twenty-four workdays plowing in newly sown wheat, twenty-one days beating and preparing flax, fourteen days treading and cleaning wheat, and twelve days harrowing the wheat field and hauling rails for fencing. Field laborers spent another twenty-five workdays tending the tobacco that Washington planted in a brief experiment with the old staple crop. The field laborer Charity was listed "in child bed," and Brunswick was sick, accounting for another twelve days.[29]

Washington had since the 1760s occasionally made time-based records of labor, initially for indentured servants whose obligations were usually defined by a term of service. The time-based accounting of the slaves' work, however, was a significant innovation, original to Washington, while reflecting parallel trends in other slave societies where estate owners pursued more efficient, scientific agriculture. In the British colonies of the Caribbean, plantation owners had maintained similar work logs as early as the 1740s, and a 1755 handbook on plantation management in Barbados recommended fortnightly lists of where every slave was employed on an estate. By the 1780s, Caribbean planters were using preprinted log sheets for their work reports, and, like Washington, they measured the labor of slaves by workdays rather than completed tasks. (In the nineteenth century, the weekly accounting of slaves' work would become standardized and commercialized through the sale of formatted plantation account books, and the developer of one of the most successful account books cited Washington and his work reports as an inspiration.)[30]

Each new farm manager, in signed articles of agreement, was required to submit "regular weekly reports from each Farm & class of people," and they were also responsible for getting regular accounts from the overseers at the plantations. Washington in 1793 sent the interim manager Howell Lewis a ream of paper from Philadelphia "for the purpose of supplying the Overseers &ca with Paper to make their reports on . . . and let them know that it is to be applied to this purpose only." From the initiation of the reports and continuing thereafter, the enslaved overseers participated in this new method of supervising labor, and although they may not have prepared written reports, they were a critical part of the collection of data. When Samuel Vaughan visited Mount Vernon in 1787, he noted the "Negro overseers, who every saturday night give an exact account of the Stock the increase, decrease, condition, work done, &c &c."[31]

The comprehensive reports of work at Mount Vernon brought to the management of enslaved labor the same insistence on system and accounting that characterized so much about the improved British husbandry adopted by Washington. Whether practiced in Great Britain, the British

Caribbean, or Virginia, the British model of agricultural improvement rested on the landowner's ability to coordinate increasingly complicated and interconnected activities across an estate or plantation, and that coordination necessitated regular documentation and accounting. Washington, always a fastidious record keeper, searched for more precise ways to document and to evaluate the new system of farming. His long habit of noting weather conditions in his diary became regularized in the "Meteorological account of the weather," with three daily readings of temperature and cloud conditions, which opened each weekly report by 1789. At the same time that he introduced the weekly reports in November 1785, Washington inventoried the livestock and farm equipment at his plantations, and newly hired overseers and managers agreed to make regular inventories of all farming implements. Washington initiated new account books to document every kind of transaction related to labor on the estate. The overseer's account book, maintained from 1785 to 1798, recorded the distribution of clothing and provisions to the enslaved adults and children at each plantation and to the hired laborers and overseers. The store books tracked the acquisition and distribution of tools and supplies for the work of the farms, as well as the weekly allowances of liquor provided hired laborers and the enslaved overseers.[32]

His diaries had always served as his principal record of agricultural work, and beginning in 1785 Washington formulated more systematic ways to organize information about seasonal work and agricultural experiments. Washington drew from his diaries to compile a separate notebook of running "Notes & observations" on the first two years of his new system of farming. He then indexed the document by nearly fifty topics, including each crop and tasks such as plowing, harrowing, and hoeing. From his collation of the indexed citations he created reference notes for each topic to guide him through subsequent seasons of cultivation.[33]

In February 1786, Washington personally conducted the first comprehensive census of all the enslaved persons on the estate, with a focus on the labor at each plantation and the Home House. He named 216 individuals, with notations on the usual work of each of the able adults. Agricultural laborers were already concentrated at the four outlying plantations, while the artisans and tradesmen worked and resided at the Home House farm. The census lists seventy-nine laborers across the four working plantations, with the largest of these, River Plantation, accounting for the greatest number, twenty-seven. For each of the outlying plantations, Washington listed the laboring men, followed by the laboring women and the children. Women made up the majority of enslaved laborers on every outlying plantation, and by larger margins than in the years before the Revolutionary War. He recorded ages only for the children, indicating how far they were from daily labor, which he usually demanded of them after the age of twelve. The census also indicated the mother of each child and the wives of the enslaved overseers, but Washington otherwise made no indication of the marriages that connected many of the enslaved across the several plantations and that he frequently referenced in other contexts. He designated the dower slaves, who made up slightly more than half of the entire number. [34]

The census information and the surveys of the plantations prepared Washington for the arrival of James Bloxham from England and for the first full growing season under the new farming schemes. After his arrival in April 1786, Bloxham resided at Ferry Plantation but advised Washington on all of the farms. During the first summer he worked alongside field laborers in the hay and wheat harvests. By early fall, he was directing the laborers at Dogue Run in a new method for preparing and sowing fields. Washington, despite his initial irritation with him, encouraged Bloxham to bring his family from England. In November 1786 Washington also agreed to offer an annual salary of twenty-five guineas to Caleb Hall, whom Bloxham described as "a compleat Wheel Wright, Waggon builder, and Plow & Hurdle maker." Bloxham had proposed the hire of Hall, a former neighbor in Gloucestershire, and Washington added the incentive of another five guineas after the first year, if the arrangement proved satisfactory. Washington claimed he made the offer to please Bloxham, but he always placed enormous confidence in anyone with British farming experience. (Hall declined to move to the United States.)[35]

Bloxham proved to be particularly skilled in the sowing of seeds, especially the new sorts that Washington received from England. Washington further relied on Bloxham to advise on the cultivation of barley, buckwheat, and oats. He called on Bloxham for instruction in the use of harrows and rollers to fix seeds in the soil. When a plow ordered from Arthur Young arrived at Mount Vernon, Bloxham found it worked well, and Washington put him in charge of caring for it. Washington, however, remained distant from Bloxham, to whom he referred almost invariably as "the Farmer." He pointed out petty errors and misjudgments on Bloxham's part, even those that he admitted were of little consequence. When Bloxham introduced a new method of sowing wheat during his first summer in Virginia, Washington staged his own competing experiment on adjoining land and waited to see "which method will succeed best." In his diaries and correspondence, Washington made relatively infrequent references to the man in whom he had invested such high expectations. As early as August 1787, Washington considered employing Bloxham as a conventional overseer of the adjoining the Ferry and French's plantations if they were to be merged, and by November 1788 Bloxham was serving in that reduced position, with responsibilities that differed little from those of other overseers.[36]

By the winter of 1790, Washington and his manager, George Augustine Washington, were considering the dismissal of Bloxham. George Augustine "thought the wages you allow'd Mr Bloxham greatly beyond what his services merited, and in no other point of view do I consider him preferable to the Overseers of this Country but in the business of seeding." George Augustine thought a good overseer could do the same job for at least one-third less than what they paid Bloxham. But the dissatisfaction of Washington and his manager extended far beyond the cost of the wages. Long before Washington left Mount Vernon for his inauguration as president, he had shared with George Augustine his conclusion that Bloxham "had no capacity for the management of Negroes." In March 1790, George Augustine informed Bloxham that Washington would not extend his employment past the end of the year, and Bloxham asked if Washington would "liberate him" before winter set in. George Augustine advised Washington that summer would be a difficult time to engage another overseer, but he had no objection to Bloxham's hasty departure, "for He has not much to recommend him." By July, Bloxham and his family had moved to a rented house outside Alexandria.[37]

Several years later, Washington recalled Bloxham, "tho' perfectly acquainted with every part of a farmers business, . . . yet, finding it a little troublesome to instruct the Negros, & to compel them to the practice of *his* modes; he slided into *theirs.*" Bloxham's service at Mount Vernon had begun with his own expression of contempt and fear of the enslaved Blacks with whom he worked, and his service ended with Washington's assessment that the English farmer was incapable of managing the enslaved field laborers who provided nearly all of the agricultural labor on the estate. In the disappointing tenure of Bloxham, Washington for the first time confronted evidence that agricultural knowledge and experience by themselves were inadequate to the implementation of British models of improvement on a Virginia estate reliant on enslaved labor. As long as Washington required the enslaved laborers on his estate to learn new skills and to carry out greater responsibilities in the fields, he would expect his managers and white overseers to enforce the same strict authority over them that he exercised.[38]

Bloxham had worked not only with the enslaved field laborers he tried to manage; he worked alongside the several enslaved overseers who directed labor at the Mount Vernon farms. During the critical years when Washington introduced the British system of crop rotations and ordered the extensive reconfiguration of the agricultural landscape, he relied on enslaved overseers at four of the five plantations involved in commercial farming, more than at any time before or after. Morris had been overseer at Dogue Run Plantation since 1766, and continued there until 1790. Davy Gray, who had served as overseer at the old Mill Plantation as early as 1770, was overseer at Muddy Hole by 1778. Following the death of a longtime white overseer, John Alton, Washington in December 1785 sent Gray to be the overseer at River Plantation, the largest at Mount Vernon, and Washington selected Will, the enslaved seedsman at the Home House, to replace Gray as overseer at Muddy Hole. Another enslaved overseer, also named Will, had supervised work at the farm Washington acquired from Penelope French in 1786. He continued to serve as overseer until Bloxham assumed the combined oversight of the French's and Ferry plantations in the fall of 1788, at which time, Will remained as an overseer or foreman of labor at French's. For the indispensable work of the enslaved carpenters who manufactured farming implements and constructed utilitarian buildings on the plantations, Washington designated Isaac, whom he had purchased in 1773, to serve as overseer of the carpenters beginning in 1786.

The enslaved overseers were differentiated by a full suit of clothing, valued at nearly three times that of the field laborers. In addition to the annual provision of shirts, trousers, and shoes, the enslaved overseers at the plantations received an allotment of thirteen gallons of rum, three hundred pounds of pork, and a half bushel of salt. As the overseer of the carpenters, Isaac received the same clothing and rum, but a smaller provision of pork. While serving as overseers on plantations, Morris, Davy Gray, and Will lived with their wives, an increasingly rare arrangement as Washington reallocated labor for the new system of farming. Molly, the wife of Davy Gray, moved with him from Mill Plantation to Muddy Hole, then to River Plantation, and back to Muddy Hole. The choice of enslaved overseers, of course, saved Washington the cost of wages, but he never spared that expense when he believed he needed a different kind of authority over the laborers in the fields. As long as he was in direct command of the daily work of farming at Mount Vernon, he relied on the enslaved overseers for their experience and knowledge of the land. Davy Gray supervised work at four plantations over the course of thirty years and probably knew the farmland as well as anyone, with the possible exception of Washington.[39]

With the transition to crop rotations and the associated reduction in wheat production, the hired overseers, such as Hezekiah Fairfax at Ferry Plantation, received fixed wages rather than the earlier provision for a share of the proceeds from the cash crops produced under their supervision. Subsequent hires received annual wages determined by the size of the farm and the experience of the overseer. Washington never quite reconciled himself to the standing wages for overseers, "as *their* profits, whatever may be *mine,* are the same whether they are at a horse race or on the farm." The elimination of compensation by shares encouraged the overseers to observe the prescribed crop rotations rather than increase the production of cash crops, and Washington continued to pay wages while insisting that farm managers exercise closer supervision of the hired overseers, since "they can have no interest in acting otherwise than they are directed."[40]

The acquisition of French's land, which Washington had long coveted, was the last major addition to the Mount Vernon estate. The 552 acres and the adjacent 142 acres recently purchased from the estate of Harrison Manley at last gave Washington control of the entire neck of land between Little Hunting Creek and Dogue Run. As he acknowledged when he attempted to purchase the land in 1782, the acquisition would be "at the expence of my judgment." On closer examination of the property in 1786, Washington described the French land as eroded and exhausted in many places. He calculated that it was likely to bring him less income than he could gain from the land he had bought on Hunting Creek for the sole purpose of exchanging it with French. Yet, when Penelope French refused to sell her land outright, Washington accepted a complicated transaction by which he assumed a recent seven-year lease on the land and the hire of twenty-three slaves for £136 a year and further agreed that at the end of the lease he would make annual payments of £150 to French for the remainder of her life. Washington acceded to the valuation of the land and slaves by any third party French selected. He insisted that he did not want the land "for a farthing less than the value; for to make money by it was never my object."[41]

His object was to introduce the new system of crop rotations, and in the fall of 1786, Washington urgently needed the French and Manley lands to merge with his adjacent plantations and to form new ones out of the whole. By late November he was surveying his new purchases, and he organized the new land and the adjoining Ferry Plantation into mirror images of one another, each with seven fields and divided by a wide lane leading to the site of the great barn he would build according to the design of Arthur Young. The consolidation of land during the latter stages of enclosure in Great Britain had facilitated an expanded scale of cultivation and the more efficient coordination of rotations and livestock management across large estates. By the second half of the eighteenth century, the unification of the great British estates also gave rise to an aesthetic ideal of agricultural improvement that merged intensive cultivation with the design of a park-like setting, under the dominion of a single landowner. Washington by 1786 achieved that valued consolidation with his control of the almost eight thousand contiguous acres on the neck of land he had long considered "my own."[42]

During the first six months of 1787, Washington directed work to align French's Plantation with the other plantations by clearing fields, filling gullies, and plowing the land for a full rotation of crops. He regularly sent enslaved field laborers from Muddy Hole and Dogue Run to assist and instruct the hired slaves who worked at French's. Together they processed the corn, wheat, and tobacco planted during the previous season by the former tenant whom Washington was obliged to assist with all crops in the ground when he assumed the lease. After preparing the ground for wheat, the field laborers reconfigured the tobacco houses at French's to serve as protected areas for threshing the grain. In the midst of his merger of plantations and groups of enslaved field laborers, Washington recorded a rare allegation of sabotage. In early March 1787, he found that the corn house "at French's was burned down in the Night, either by carelessness or design. The latter seems most likely, but whom to suspect was not known."[43]

Washington brought a surveyor's perspective to the organization of fields and the system of cropping. He carefully demarcated plots of land for experiments, such as the sixteen square rods of ground that he marked off in four equal parts to test the effect of a soil amendment. He frequently recorded the measured controls in his experiments with the separation of furrows and depth of plowing. His precise measurement extended to every detail of farming. After a winter day spent riding to all of the plantations, Washington "ascertained how many of the following Sorts of Seeds there are in a lb. Troy—The weight of a bushel of each & how much an acre will take of each sort to sow it." The accompanying chart recorded 298,000 Timothy seeds in a pound and 13,410,000 in a bushel, with one-thirteenth of the total volume made up of chaff. Similarly meticulous calculations were offered for other grasses, barley, and the several beans Washington introduced for soil enrichment. The determination of the ideal rate of sowing seeds per acre became for Washington a quest comparable to his search for the proper sequence of crop rotations.[44]

Sometime in late 1785 or 1786, Washington consulted eight agricultural treatises for information on crops and methods of cultivation, and he collated the excerpted notes from each work by topic in the soft-covered notebooks he preferred for agricultural notes. All of the books on which he relied were British publications, some from his existing library and others purchased after he decided to adopt the new system of farming. Washington's notes signaled his intention to begin his rotations with the crops recommended by British agricultural writers. The notes and excerpts emphasized how each crop, whether new or familiar, figured within the larger farming system. Some crops prepared the land for subsequent, more profitable cultivation. "Bulbous rooted crops," like turnips, carrots, and parsnips, "are most successful in dividing & pulverizing the ground." Some otherwise useful crops were "robbers" and must be followed by restorative ones. Buckwheat promised the dual advantages of serving as a green manure and growing so luxuriantly that it cleared the weeds before the next crop was sown. Washington took note of the use of grasses and root crops to support livestock as an essential part of any successful farming system. Arthur Young reminded Washington that "in England husbandry never prospers but in proportion to the attention to cattle," and Washington, acknowledging the negligence of Virginia farmers, determined to improve his livestock through the establishment of better meadows.[45]

A French visitor reported that it was Washington's stated "intention to set his country the example of cultivating artificial meadows, so rare in it, yet so necessary." In matters as specific as the choice of grasses for fodder, Washington was attentive to public example and his assumed responsibilities as a wealthy landowner committed to a particular model of agricultural improvement. To John Beale Bordley, a member of the Philadelphia Society for Promoting Agriculture and an influential advocate of crop rotations, Washington explained his confidence in the example of the landed gentry as well as his expectation of what he later described as "a spirit of emulation" among smaller farmers. "Experiments must be made-and the practice (of such of them as are useful) must be introduced by Gentlemen who have leisure and abilities to devise and wherewithal to hazard something. The common farmer will not depart from the *old* road 'till the *new* one is made so plain and easy that he is sure it cannot be mistaken, and that it will lead him directly to his object. It is right perhaps it shd be so—for new ways are thorny and require time for amelioration."[46]

Bordley sent Washington several copies of his own 1784 pamphlet comparing the crop rotations of England with those he carried out in experiments at his Maryland farm, but Washington believed his most recent plan of rotations would be more effective than Bordley's practice of planting corn and wheat in succession without any restorative crops. Washington followed British practice as closely as possible, making exceptions only to accommodate what he deemed the inferior quality of plowing in the United States and variations in weather. He was confident the rotations would improve pastureland and halt erosion, but by his best estimate this most recent rotation would produce only 75 percent of the wheat grown under his old system.[47]

The experimental character of the rotations demanded frequent revision in the ongoing effort to balance conservation of the land with increased revenue from wheat. In 1790, Washington and Anthony Whitting, his English-born farm manager, drafted alternative proposals for a seven-year rotation of crops on a single field, and for both plans Washington calculated the cost of seed, the likely yields, and the value of market crops. He drafted a plan typical of British husbandry, except for its inclusion of a single season for corn. Wheat was sown only once in seven years, and a generous three years of clover prepared for the cycle to begin again with corn. Whitting wanted to push the land to produce more wheat, with fewer restorative crops and the most exhausting grains in quick succession. Washington acknowledged that Whitting's plan had an advantage "of no small magnitude" in its potential to bring more wheat to market, given that wheat "is the one article I shall ever raise money from, All the others will be consumed, wasted, or turned to little or no account." He hesitated, however, to risk the potential damage to the soil. If he followed Whitting's proposal to plant more frequent rotations of wheat, the lands "would not only grow worse under such a routine, but would absolutely sink under it."[48]

Washington was determined to restore the fertility of his lands, even at the risk of lower profits. "To crop them hard" without the intervening restoration of the soil would, he wrote Whitting, be "like pushing a horse that has a long race to perform to his full speed at first; the result of which must be, that he will grow slower and slower every round he takes, until he is unable to move." To his next farm manager, William Pearce, Washington explained, "I know full well that by picking & culling the fields I should be able, for a *year* or *two,* to make larger crops of *grain,* but I know also, that by so doing I shall, in a few years make nothing, & find my land ruined." The solution was to increase the amount of manures on the fields and to establish "a judicious succession of Crops." Washington reminded manager James Anderson that a regular rotation system and the more careful management of fewer acres of arable ground were more important than immediate profit.[49]

At some point around 1793, Washington significantly revised his plans for crop rotations. He drafted in exhaustive detail comparisons of six possible rotations for Dogue Run Farm, and for each plan he calculated the number of required plowings, the projected crop yields, and the likely cash value of the marketable crops. The rotation plan that would be most favorable to the land would also produce the smallest marketable crop. Other plans were based on proven British models, but Washington worried that the estate's land could not bear the demands on the soil and that the uncertain seasons in Virginia would reduce the yields below British standards. For the instruction of manager William Pearce in late 1793, Washington outlined for each of the farms new rotation plans that marked his most significant departure from British practice. On all but one of the farms, he dispensed with clover and cultivated grasses, relying instead on manure and plowed-in buckwheat to restore the soil between wheat and corn crops. Clover and grasses would now be planted on new and enlarged meadows that supported the growing number of livestock. In his detailed calculations, Washington determined the timing and number of required plowings—as many as thirteen hundred a year on the larger farms—and estimated how much of the corn produced would be consumed by the enslaved residents on each farm, but in all of his planning for this change in cultivation, he made no other reference to the demands on the enslaved laborers who would carry out the work.[50]

In none of these plans was Washington able to eliminate the cultivation of corn, which he considered the crop most destructive of the land at Mount Vernon. When he first announced his intention to follow a complete course of British farming, he cited his exclusion of tobacco and the planned reduction of corn crops as the defining characteristics of more enlightened farming that rejected the legacies of colonial staple agriculture. By the summer of 1787, Washington vowed to be rid of "Indian corn" altogether, and he directed his manager "that *all* the Corn ground at *all* the Plantations, should be laid down in either Wheat or Rye, as shall be best suited to the land." Washington, however, found it nearly impossible to dispense with corn cultivation as long as he relied on a large enslaved labor force. Each year from 1786 to 1789, he was forced to buy corn to supply the minimal needs of the slaves' diet. As he told a friend in 1788, "my wish is to exclude Indian Corn altogether from my system of Cropping, but we are so habituated to the use of this grain, and it is so much better for negros than any other that [it] is not to be discarded." Rather than abandon corn, Washington would search for ways to grow it more profitably and with less injury to the land, but the crop demanded more time from the field laborers than any other. He rarely sold any corn after 1785. In 1798, Washington negotiated a long-term contract for the purchase of corn to supply his new distillery and at the same time attempted to reduce the acreage devoted to the crop on his farms, but corn remained a part of the last rotation he drafted in 1799.[51]

Early in his implementation of the new course of farming, Washington concluded from his review of plowing that "this business should never stop," and in the new rotations of 1793, the plow was more important than ever. The enslaved drivers of plows, including an increasing number of women, worked throughout the year breaking up ground in new fields, creating furrows for sowing, cultivating the soil between rows of corn, and harrowing in seed. Washington was always searching for new types of plows to meet the needs of different soil types and different crops. He asked Arthur Young to send two of "the simplest, & best constructed Plows," in the hopes that they would be as useful as the old Rotherham plow that had been "ruined by a bungling Country Smith." Washington found the plows received from Young worked well, despite the initial resistance of the field laborers who thought them too heavy. Washington increasingly employed drill plows, which dropped seed as they cut furrows in the soil, and he developed his own models. The enslaved carpenters and blacksmith, sometimes working with a hired joiner, became skilled in the manufacture and repair of drill plows.[52]

Washington continued to search for other mechanical advances that might make agricultural labor more efficient. He first read about a new threshing machine invented by William Winlaw in the *Annals of Agriculture* and asked Arthur Young to determine if it would be worth shipping one to Virginia. Before learning of Young's skepticism about the machine, Washington contacted John Beale Bordley, who reportedly had a similar machine on his Maryland estate. He was also interested in Bordley's report of a machine for sowing clover. Although he acknowledged "many of these newly invented things meet the approbation of the moment, but will not stand the test of constant use, or the usage of common labourers," Washington eagerly pursued the promise of advances in agricultural implements and machinery. The most fantastical machine to draw his attention was the "Hippopotamus" dredging apparatus designed to pull mud from the bottom of a river for use as a soil amendment. The inventor in Philadelphia sent drawings of the machine, with its crane powered by horses turning a mill on a floating barge. Washington, who had long thought the mud of the Potomac might provide an endless source of manure for cultivated fields, examined the plans with high expectations, but decided to carry out more experiments with the fertilizing properties of the mud before commissioning his own machine.[53]

For all of the diversification of crops and livestock, wheat remained the most valuable market commodity in the agricultural system Washington introduced, and milling the key to successful marketing of the crop. After years of enduring the drunken rages of the miller, William Roberts, Washington in February 1785 dismissed the person he described as a madman. Yet Roberts was, in Washington's opinion, an honest man, who understood "the manufacture of wheat, as well as any miller upon the Continent," and he was also a millwright, a skill few millers possessed. Washington admitted that he had spent not one shilling on repairs during the fifteen years Roberts managed the mill. Furthermore, the superfine flour milled under Roberts's supervision had an excellent reputation and sold for a higher price in the United States and in the West Indies than any other produced in Virginia. Roberts, however, had exacted commensurate increases in his own wages over his years of service, and Washington refused to tolerate his violent behavior any longer.[54]

To replace Roberts, Washington called on the Philadelphia milling firm of Robert Lewis & Sons to recommend a sober miller "who understands the manufacturing business *perfectly.*" After advertising for someone to serve "His Excellency General Washington," Lewis & Sons engaged their former apprentice, Joseph Davenport, "a plain Man of few words, & no great address," but a good miller and cooper. He was not a millwright, but he was capable of maintaining record books and accounts. As stipulated by Washington, Davenport agreed to supervise the three enslaved coopers at the mill, and by February 1786, Ben, an enslaved miller, was working alongside him. Washington initially found in Davenport a steady and reliable worker, but he considered him less skilled than Roberts in the management of the mill. Years later, he declared him "a very indolent man!"

when he failed to carry out an experiment to test the relative market value of wheat and flour. Nevertheless, Washington had no inclination to dismiss Davenport as long as the reputation of the mill's flour was maintained, and Davenport continued to work as the miller until his death in 1796.[55]

◦　　◦　　◦

In late 1788, by which time Washington fully anticipated he would soon be leaving Mount Vernon to return to public life, he found that several years' experience with his new course of farming led him "to reflect how much more delightful to an undebauched mind is the task of making improvements on the earth; than all the vain glory which can be acquired from ravaging it, by the most uninterrupted career of conquests." For several years, he had dedicated himself to those improvements on the earth that would promote commerce and earn the new nation the respect of nations throughout the Atlantic world. The prospect of his extended absence while serving as president forced Washington to consider whether the system of farming he had presented as a kind of civic responsibility could succeed without his daily supervision. His involvement in every aspect of agricultural enterprise had only deepened his long-standing belief that the success of a Virginia plantation, reliant on enslaved labor, depended on the presence and active management of the estate owner. Responding to his nephew's complaint that he could not manage an estate and practice law at the same time, Washington surely had his own imminent departure in mind when he agreed: "to manage a Virginia Estate *well* there cannot be a divided attention—because with all the attention that can be given they are rarely productive."[56]

Washington made every effort to prepare his manager and overseers to exercise that needed level of attention in his absence. George Augustine Washington remained as manager, but his chronic health problems limited his ability to supervise daily work, and Washington expected of him only a general supervision of the business of the estate. Most agricultural work would be directed by two white overseers, to whom Washington sent New Year's Day instructions for the coming year and a new plan of rotations for each plantation. Washington required John Fairfax, the overseer at what Washington now referred to as the Mansion House rather than the Home House farm, to assume broader responsibilities in the direction of work at three of the outlying farms, two of which had enslaved overseers, and the third, an overseer who had just arrived at the estate in December 1788. James Bloxham, then serving as overseer of the French's and Ferry plantations, received from Washington instructions for the coming year at those farms.[57]

Washington's instructions revealed how much work remained to be done to implement the full course of British husbandry, which he expected to require at least another year. Some of the newly drawn fields had yet to be prepared for the designated crops on which the rotations depended. Much of the fencing and ditching was incomplete. River mud needed to be collected and "ameliorated" before it was spread as manure. Experiments had yet to determine the proper sequence and combination of crops. With considerable reservations, Washington decided to plant small amounts of tobacco at each of the farms in hopes of securing additional revenue during the transition to the new course of farming. As he explained to Fairfax and Bloxham, he hoped that preparing the soil with plows would increase his chances of success, but frankly admitted that his object in trying tobacco was to gain some profit. The effort would prove to be both short-lived and disappointing.[58]

Bringing the system of rotations into practice would "require much exertion," which Washington thought could only be extracted from the slaves through strict management and authority. For each plantation, Washington prescribed work for the slaves he referred to as the "hoe people"— field laborers, most of them women, whose tasks were most likely to vary from season to season. Washington also tried to impart to the overseers his general principles of managing enslaved agricultural labor. He compared two hypothetical farm managers, equally disciplined and controlling the same number of able laborers, but one of the overseers accomplished far more in a year. The difference, Washington explained, was in the planning and foresight that would ensure the most efficient allocation of labor throughout the seasons. The new system of agricultural improvement required an unprecedented degree of coordination and supervision, and Washington expected the overseers to enforce his demands for labor from the enslaved while he was absent. In his instructions for John Fairfax, he emphasized the responsibility of the manager of labor: "To request that my people may be at their work as soon as it is light—work 'till it is dark—and be diligent while they are at it can hardly be necessary, because the propriety of it must strike every manager who attends to my interest, or regards his own Character." As he prepared to depart his estate in 1789, the supervision and control of the enslaved laborers appeared to Washington as the fundamental difficulty in implementing a British model of husbandry at Mount Vernon. From the distance of New York and then Philadelphia, he would find this challenge only increased.[59]

° *5* °

Enslaved Agricultural Labor
at Mount Vernon

When Washington returned from a meeting of the Potomac Company in July 1786, he rode immediately to the fields where he could observe the wheat harvest just underway. Before reaching the Mansion House for breakfast, he counted at Muddy Hole Plantation six cradlers at work, including the enslaved overseer Will, and Tom, a cooper who usually worked at the mill. With them was Jack, a field laborer from Dogue Run, "who tho' newly entered, made a very good hand; and gave hopes of being an excellent Cradler." At Ferry Plantation, Boatswain and the postilion Joe, both from the Home House, worked as cradlers with Caesar. Over the next ten days, Washington made daily visits to the plantations to monitor the progress of the harvest and to assess the work of individual laborers. He took special note of those who left their usual work to assist in the harvest while the wheat was ripe and the weather clear. At River Plantation, he watched Tom Davis, an enslaved bricklayer, "who had never cut before, and made rather an awkward hand of it." Two women from the Home House, Myrtilla and Dolshy, worked with the combined gangs from Muddy Hole and Dogue Run to complete the harvest at the first plantation and then the other. A group of young boys and girls who had never worked in the fields before assisted in making hay after two hired white men cut the grass under the direction of James Bloxham. Upon the completion of the harvests at the Ferry and River plantations, Washington "Gave the People employed in it the remainder of the day for them selves." It was a rare respite in the increasingly rigid work schedule he imposed.[1]

As soon as the season's grain harvest was finished, Washington compiled a list of changes he intended to introduce for the following year. His first objective was to make the enslaved laborers at each plantation carry out the harvest by themselves, without help from elsewhere on the estate and without hired white laborers. Washington believed he could accomplish that goal by prescribing an exact sequence of cradling, raking, and binding based on his observations. Cradling would begin earlier to allow a smoother cut and time for the straw to cure for two days before it was raked and gathered. For every two cradlers, Washington would assign four rakers and one binder. The children, he concluded, would be competent to carry the bundles. He expected these changes to have the effect that the work "will be done with more ease, regularity and dispatch, because it becomes a sober settled work—there being no pretext for hurrying at one time, and standing at another." By making each raker follow a single path, "the authors of bad work may be discovered and every person marked." Washington further intended to eliminate any possibility for time not spent on productive work. If the enslaved laborers remained on their assigned plantations, with their tools at hand, they would be prepared to undertake other work if weather interrupted the harvest. Washington envisioned days filled with the regular and deliberate work he prescribed for the enslaved field laborers, and he spent much of the next few years devising ways to extend that "sober settled work" throughout the agricultural calendar. He also resolved to rely more exclusively on the enslaved laborers he owned, finding ways for them to perform all the varied tasks of the more complicated system of farming.[2]

Under the new farming regimen, work for the following season began almost as soon as the wheat harvest was over. Sometimes as early as August and continuing into October, field laborers sowed the wheat that would be harvested the following summer. The threshing of wheat could wait until winter or even spring, but that used for seed needed to be threshed and cleaned before fall. The sowing of rye and timothy coincided with that of wheat. Much of the fall was spent gathering and processing the other grains grown over the summer. The field laborers at each plantation hauled rye and oats to barns where they cleaned the grains. Corn required substantial labor at every stage of its cultivation, and in late fall and early winter, the husking of corn frequently brought "hands gathering" for the work. Usually in late December, a group of enslaved men butchered hogs for the meat that was distributed to the overseers and used by the Washington family. In 1786, over a hundred hogs were slaughtered.[3]

During the winter months, the field laborers spent much of their time constructing or repairing the fences that divided fields and separated the meadows and pastures. The increased number of livestock, particularly the draft animals that pulled the plows and harrows, created more need to assemble and relocate pens. If the ground was not frozen, field laborers in January grubbed in the swamp land, pulling up roots and stumps to prepare it for cultivation, and broke up the ground in the fields. By February, weather permitting, plows were running everywhere. Winter was also the season for field laborers to gather dung and then cart it for scattering in the fields. When snow or cold prevented work in the fields, the laborers dressed the flax used by weavers making clothes for all the estate's enslaved laborers and their families. Threshing wheat continued in February and March.

In early spring, the field laborers worked more regularly to clear and to break up ground for the plows. The sowers put in oats as one of the earliest crops, followed by fodder grasses and barley in early April. Men and women drove the plows and then crossed the fields of oats with harrows. By late April, they were planting corn, some of it in the traditional practice of hilling, but increasingly sowed with the drill plows constructed by the carpenters and smiths on the estate. When corn was planted in rows with the drill plows, sowers returned to plant potatoes and carrots between the rows, in a practice Washington thought would reduce the erosion associated with corn. Later they sowed turnips. Once the crops were growing, the field laborers began weeding with hoes, and in some of the cornfields the plow drivers turned the soil between rows. June frequently brought hurried tasks so that all field laborers would be available for the harvest that began with hay crops and continued with wheat. July was also the harvest time for flax and rye. Some years the plow drivers turned the buckwheat into the soil as a green manure; other years the field laborers harvested it as a fodder crop.

Throughout the year, the essential work of preparing the ground and cultivating crops fell to the field laborers whom Washington designated "hoe people." Washington regarded their labor as particularly onerous and undesirable, as evidenced by his threat to make a bricklayer "a common hoe negro" if he did not improve his work. He made a similar threat to send a group of seamstresses at the Mansion House to work as "common laborers" under the overseers at the plantations if they did not increase the pace of their shirt making. The majority of the "hoe people" were women, and when Washington recorded their work he seldom referred to them by name. He clearly knew them as individuals and named them when they were sick or gave birth, but in the record of their routine work the enslaved women in the fields remained largely anonymous. The women field laborers often worked together in small groups, occasionally with one enslaved man directing their tasks. The adoption of British husbandry and the introduction of more sophisticated farm implements did little to relieve the drudgery and physical burden of those who still worked with hoes. Outside the growing season, much of their time was spent clearing and grubbing fields to prepare the soil for plowing. They were consigned to monotonous tasks like cutting down corn stalks. While the men prepared posts and cut tenons in rails, the women used the framing to construct fences.[4]

Women were more likely than men to work spreading dung in the fields, and in late winter months they often filled gullies with brush and corn stalks to halt further erosion. Although men worked in most of the tasks associated with the diversification of farming, such as sowing and mowing, the most challenging new task for the women was to join with the men in plowing and harrowing with draft animals. After childbirth, an enslaved woman typically returned to the fields in less than a month. Although able to stop work to care for their sick children, women were no more likely than men to be listed in the weekly reports as sick themselves.[5]

The work of the field laborers depended on that of the enslaved carpenters, ditchers, and spinners. In the spring of 1786, before the harvest Washington monitored so closely, Isaac and three other carpenters manufactured many of the implements used to gather the wheat. They made new rakes and cradles, and mended others. They fixed sneads, or handles, to the scythes. They also constructed harrows, likely based on the drawings

Washington traced from his edition of Lord Kames's *The Gentleman Farmer*. Over the next several years, the carpenters regularly constructed plows, carts, and axletrees. They made nine-foot rake handles and plow beams, using ash cut for the purpose from the estate's woods. After 1789, the enslaved carpenters worked with the hired joiners, or house carpenters, in the construction of the great agricultural structures, like the barn at the Ferry and French's plantations, while they continued to produce many of the implements used in fieldwork.[6]

The ditchers made possible the division of fields for the system of crop rotations, and they maintained the boundaries at each plantation. Ditching was skilled work for which Washington had previously hired white men. After a white ditcher, the indentured servant Daniel Overdonck, left Mount Vernon in late 1788, the enslaved ditchers who had trained under him became a dedicated corps of five or six men working across all the plantations and at the mill as needed. Under the supervision of the Mansion House overseer, they drained swampland for the creation of arable fields and meadows. They maintained the millrace and dug the ditches that separated other fields. Washington considered their work "a kind of trade" that he could employ across the estate, and he exempted the ditchers from his expectation that enslaved laborers work only on the plantation where they resided.[7]

The spinners and seamstresses on the estate, often working with a hired tailor, were by the mid-1780s able to produce much of the clothing worn by the enslaved field laborers and artisans. What had once been purchased from Great Britain or Philadelphia was now fabricated largely from the wool and flax produced on the estate. In 1786, field laborers received a spring distribution of coats, breeches, shirts, and trousers, and for the women, a summer "petty coat." In November they received one pair of shoes and stockings. Most of the spinners and seamstresses were enslaved women, although they were often joined by men who were incapable of work in the field.[8]

Despite Washington's recurrent attempts to make each plantation self-sufficient in labor, the annual harvest of grains and hay still drew artisans away from their workshops and to the fields. The harvest remained a group activity that interrupted the focused tasks that characterized labor during most of the year. As Washington reminded a farm manager, "Hay time &

Harvest will not wait, and is of the highest importance to me, every thing else must yield to them." Carpenters were the most frequent additions to the force of field laborers at harvest, but ditchers, bricklayers, and spinners also joined in the work. Washington supervised all of them, sometimes visiting each plantation twice a day at the busiest time of a harvest. The annual harvests of hay and grains coincided with intense work in other fields, as plow drivers prepared soil for the sowing of the next season's wheat, and other crops at the height of the summer required regular weeding by plow drivers and hoe workers. While in the fields, Washington frequently reallocated labor in response to weather conditions or the urgency of the work, and he, rather than an overseer, directly commanded the field laborers to shift from one task to another. During the harvest of 1788, when he was perhaps more closely involved than ever before or after, Washington noted that "I ordered the People" to different work or to a different plantation. Although he never recorded the independent decisions of the laborers, the complexity of sequencing the tasks and the variety of simultaneous work at each plantation would have depended on the self-management of experienced field laborers.[9]

Washington was largely successful in finding steady if not settled year-round work for the enslaved laborers he controlled. This was particularly true during the first several years of the new course of farming, when the demand for more arable land and the intense cultivation required to restore the soil placed an enormous burden on the field laborers. Over the next decade, the regular experiments and the introduction of new crops provided challenging work for the able workers among a steadily increasing enslaved population at Mount Vernon. The laborers were engaged in the frequently shifting work that blended new cultivation practices with the physical burden of preparing and maintaining the soil. Their work was alleviated only by the significant increase in the use of draft animals for plowing, harrowing, and carting, and by the customary rest on Sundays, at Christmas, and again on Easter and Whit Mondays.

Throughout these new seasonal routines of work, Washington was a daily presence on the plantations, and his personal supervision brought him into even more frequent interaction with individual laborers. A Scottish visitor who accompanied Washington on his daily circuit of the working plantations reported in the fall of 1785 that Washington "strips off his coat and labors like a common man." Washington, to be sure, was not assisting the field laborers in their work, but he was determined to understand the practical tasks of the field and to impart to the enslaved laborers his presumed knowledge of cultivation. Over the next few years, he took every opportunity to be with the field laborers, whom he frequently called "my people," as they carried out new and often experimental tasks.[10]

∘   ∘   ∘

The cultivation of the land by enslaved agricultural laborers was for Washington the most salient characteristic of farming on his plantations, and he identified the management of the enslaved laborers as the most significant challenge to the successful adoption of the model of British husbandry that drove his reorganization of the estate. He believed each task of cultivation, each experiment in new crops, and each application of new farming implements needed to be incorporated within a system of supervision and enforcement for which no British agricultural treatise would offer guidance. The reliance on enslaved labor differentiated Washington not only from the practitioners of improved husbandry in Great Britain, but also from a broader community of enlightenment leaders with whom he shared visions of a new era of harmony among nations throughout the Atlantic world. At the same time that Washington undertook his comprehensive efforts to extract more labor and greater efficiency from the enslaved, he confronted a new and growing antislavery movement, often advocated by individuals on either side of the Atlantic who simultaneously celebrated him as the champion of American independence. On the eve of Washington's return to Mount Vernon, Lafayette and William Gordon urged him to free the slaves he owned as the culminating act in his defense of the revolutionary ideals of liberty. Other prominent antislavery leaders, including many who knew him only as the public hero, turned directly to Washington to set a powerful and personal example by endorsing abolition and by manumitting the slaves he owned, and these appeals surrounded him as he reassessed the management of enslaved labor on his estate. Even as a private farmer, Washington could not escape the antislavery expectations placed uniquely on him.

In retirement at his estate, Washington received a succession of appeals from antislavery advocates who asked for his endorsement of some form of abolition. A Massachusetts merchant, recently back from London, visited Mount Vernon in January 1785 and delivered a set of abolitionist publications authored by the British antislavery leader, Granville Sharp, who personally requested that the pamphlets be presented to Washington. In May 1785 Washington met at Mount Vernon with the British Methodist leaders, Thomas Coke and Francis Asbury, who solicited his support for a petition calling on the Virginia General Assembly to enact a general emancipation. According to Coke, Washington explained that he had shared with the leading men of his state his support for the principle of their cause, but he declined to sign the petition. He indicated to the Methodist clergy that if the assembly took the petition under consideration, he would present his support by letter. Several months later, James Madison, a member of the assembly, informed Washington that although several prominent members professed support for the petition, the assembly rejected it without debate, thereby eliminating any possible call for Washington's public comment.[11]

That Washington was a slaveholder as well as the hero of the Revolutionary War made him all the more compelling an object of the abolitionists' appeals. After the failure of the antislavery petition in Virginia, Robert Pleasants called on Washington to extend to the slaves under his ownership the same "Liberty and the Rights of Mankind" that had been the cause of the Continental Army. Pleasants, a Quaker plantation owner in Henrico County, Virginia, who had freed and then hired the slaves on his estate, called attention to the paradox, if not outright hypocrisy, of those who fought for the cause of liberty and now sit down "in a state of ease, dissipation and extravigance on the labour of Slaves." He speculated that Washington's continued ownership of slaves resulted from a mix of habit and racial prejudice, but he stressed the urgency of emancipation, which he described as a sacrifice that "the Lord is requiring of this Generation." Washington as "the Successful Champion of American Liberty" had a unique opportunity to crown all his earlier military achievements with support of abolition. "Thy example & influence at this time, towards a general emancipation, would be as productive of real happiness to mankind, as thy Sword may have been." Washington made no known response to Pleasants, but he filed the letter among his papers.[12]

In private correspondence, Washington in the spring of 1786 reiterated his support for gradual abolition enacted by a state legislature. He assured Philadelphia merchant Robert Morris that on the subject of slavery "there is not a man living who wishes more sincerely than I do, to see a plan adopted for the abolition of it—but there is only one proper and effectual mode by which it can be accomplished, & that is by Legislative authority: and this, as far as my suffrage will go, shall never be wanting." In reply to Lafayette's announcement of his own recent efforts in support of abolition, Washington wrote, "Would to God a like spirit would diffuse itself generally into the minds of the people of this country." With the failure of the petition to the Virginia Assembly, Washington despaired of seeing that spirit, but he assured Lafayette of his support for gradual abolition, carried out by legislative authority.[13]

No public pronouncement in favor of abolition followed these private assertions in 1786 or at any later moment in Washington's life. Washington was scarcely alone among Virginia slaveholders who voiced support for the principle of abolition and then declined to offer any public encouragement for antislavery legislation. He professed support for abolition, however, at the same time that he increased his reliance on enslaved laborers in every aspect of the new and complicated course of British husbandry he was establishing at Mount Vernon. Nothing in his organization of the labor force or in his new methods of supervision indicated any expectation of changes in the status of the enslaved.

Nor did Washington ever explicitly link any modifications in his own management of enslaved labor to his exposure to antislavery arguments. But in the years following the Revolutionary War he adopted a management system that differed in principle and practice from his organization of enslaved labor before the war. Only incidentally, over the course of the first several years of his new farming initiatives, did Washington reveal several resolutions to mitigate what he perceived to be the most brutal and inhumane aspects of the institution of slavery. He also demonstrated a heightened, self-conscious concern with protecting his reputation as a slaveholder. Without any apparent knowledge of similar developments in the Caribbean, Washington quietly adopted practices associated with the amelioration movement, by which planters sought to make slavery more efficient, more humane, and more easily adapted to British models of agricultural improvement.

When amelioration efforts appeared on plantations of the British Caribbean beginning in the 1770s, some planters explained their new focus on improving working conditions and diet explicitly in terms of the financial advantages to be gained by reducing sickness and mortality among the enslaved. For others, however, such as Joshua Steele in Barbados, amelioration of the condition of the enslaved was a frankly humanitarian effort that anticipated some form of gradual abolition. A small number of Chesapeake planters adopted comparable changes in management in response to similar impulses rather than as a result of any direct influence of the Caribbean examples. In Virginia and Maryland, where mortality was significantly lower than in the Caribbean and the enslaved population was growing by natural increase, the changes in slave management were more likely to reflect humanitarian sentiments or self-professed benevolence. For some, including Washington, amelioration efforts represented mixed and even contradictory intentions to make slavery function more efficiently while demonstrating the enlightenment of the landholder in the face of a rising critique of slavery. Amelioration in the Chesapeake as well as the Caribbean frequently merged with the adoption of agricultural improvement. Jefferson after his return from France resolved to make the management of slaves more "rational and humane" at the same time that he adopted the program of agricultural improvement he learned about from Washington and others. Across the range of ameliorative changes adopted by planters both sympathetic and hostile to antislavery arguments were common efforts to make enslaved labor more efficient and to replace coercive force with persuasion and incentives.[14]

Among the deliberate changes Washington made in managing the growing number of enslaved people under his control were decisions to end all participation in the commercial slave trade, to protect slave marriages and families, to provide adequate food and medical care, and to restrict violent punishment. Washington believed that by fixing these minimal conditions on their treatment, he could establish a kind of transactional relationship through which he expected the enslaved to provide him with their labor in return. The new terms of managing enslaved laborers were a critical part of what Washington hoped to demonstrate through the implementation of a new course of farming on a Virginia estate, and he initially believed his new system of supervising labor would be a further demonstration of his enlightenment.

Following his return to Mount Vernon, Washington, who steadily purchased slaves up until 1775, was reluctant to participate in any commercial exchange of slaves, even expressing a "great repugnance to encreasing my Slaves by purchase." During the Revolutionary War, he thought the sale of slaves might be a first step toward fulfilling his wish "to get quit of Negroes," but by 1785 he was as reluctant to sell as to purchase any slaves. (His only purchase of slaves after 1785 was intended to relieve the financial burden of a relative rather than to gain a new source of labor. In 1788, Washington agreed to purchase thirty-three slaves valued at more than £1300 from the estate of his late brother-in-law, Bartholomew Dandridge, which remained in debt for a loan made by Martha Custis in 1758. Washington left all of the slaves in the possession of Dandridge's widow and exercised almost no role in the management of the laborers.) Washington, however, was so deeply invested in slavery and so frequently involved in commercial transactions with other slaveholders that he faced several decisions that challenged his determination to end his purchase or sale of slaves.[15]

In 1785, as he prepared to rent his settled lands in western Pennsylvania, Washington wanted to avoid any sales or transfers counter to the wishes of the enslaved persons who remained on his lands. (He never mentioned the option of manumission, by then legal in Pennsylvania and Virginia.) Washington's preference was to bring the enslaved individuals to Mount Vernon, but only "if the measure can be reconciled to them." He reminded his Pennsylvania agent, Thomas Freeman, that Simon's African countrymen and Nancy's family would be glad to see them back at Mount Vernon, and he promised to employ Simon as a carpenter alongside his shipmate, Sambo. If Simon or Nancy, the only ones originally from Mount Vernon, or any of the other slaves declined to relocate to his estate, Washington told his agent he would "not suffer them to go down the river, or to any distance where you can not have an eye over them." None chose to move to Virginia, even though it meant sale to new owners. After Freeman sold the nine individuals to five different buyers, he informed Washington that he would "not have Sold the Negroes but they would not be Prevailed with to come down from any Argument I could use." The sale also exposed Washington for the first time to the impact of the Pennsylvania Abolition Act of 1780. Freeman reported that the enslaved girl Dorcas, for whom he expected to receive £30, sold for less than half that amount because, under the terms of the act, she would be free at the age of twenty-eight.[16]

Although he stated his aversion to acquiring slaves by purchase, Washington was willing to make an exception if he could gain the skilled labor he wanted for his new course of farming. In 1786 he seriously considered accepting slaves as a payment on the long-delinquent debt owed by the Mercer family, and in his negotiations with John Francis Mercer, Washington agreed to accept six or more slaves, provided they were all men who could carry out specialized work. He wanted to employ three or four as ditchers at a time when he was still hiring white ditchers to direct the work and to instruct enslaved men on the estate. He agreed to accept the same number of enslaved men to work as artisans. Washington further stipulated that the designated individuals must be healthy "and none of them addicted to running away." In his strict calculation of labor needs and with a disregard for the potential disruption of family connections, Washington insisted "women, or Children, would not suit my purposes on *any terms.*" Mercer prepared for Washington a list of all the enslaved laborers he would offer, with detailed descriptions of their skills, family connections, and appraised market values. Mercer also noted his reluctance to divide families "which have long continued together," but would do so if necessary. To accommodate Washington's preference, Mercer added to the list the names of six enslaved men, and it was those individuals whom Washington agreed to accept, as long as the younger ones were ready to learn a trade from the white artisans hired for the purpose. After Mercer offered other means of repayment in lieu of the slaves, Washington readily agreed. "The money will be infinitely more agreeable to me than property of that sort," but he also left open the possibility of procuring the slaves on more favorable terms "if I should want any of those people."[17]

While again insisting he was opposed in principle to the purchase of additional slaves, Washington in 1787 authorized Henry Lee to buy for him an enslaved bricklayer recently advertised for sale. If the man proved to be "in the vigour of life" and a good worker, Washington had much work for him in the construction of his new barns. He had no interest in the purchase if the man had a family that came with him or from whom he was reluctant to separate. John Lawson of Dumfries, not Lee, purchased the enslaved bricklayer, Neptune, whom he then agreed to sell to Washington. Neptune, however, protested the sale and relocation that would separate him from his wife, who lived on a neighboring plantation. After Lawson persuaded Neptune that Washington would permit him to visit his wife, Neptune arrived at Mount Vernon in April 1787. Although Neptune did "not profess to be a workman," Washington found he had enough knowledge of bricklaying to learn the trade, but when he told Neptune he planned to purchase him, Neptune seemed "a good deal disconcerted" because of the separation from his wife. Washington complained to Lawson of his own embarrassment, "as I am unwilling to hurt the feelings of any one." Neptune soon presented himself before Lawson at Dumfries, twenty miles from Mount Vernon. He acknowledged that he had left Mount Vernon to avoid being sold so far away from his wife, but that he would agree to be hired to Washington. Neptune then delivered to Washington the letter explaining Lawson's proposed terms of hire.[18]

Although Washington may not have hired Neptune (no further record of him survives), the discussions with the enslaved bricklayer revealed how the ties of marriage and family provided the enslaved with the most powerful means to exert some limited influence over the conditions of work and their place of residence. Washington rejected a merchant's proposed exchange of slaves from Mount Vernon because he did not believe "it would be agreeable to their inclinations to leave their Connexions here, and it is inconsistent with my feelings to compel them." He agreed to keep Peter Hardiman, the enslaved stable worker owned by David Stuart, because Hardiman seemed unwilling to leave his wife and children. At the death of his mother, Mary Ball Washington, Washington offered to accept ownership of an enslaved man long resident at Mount Vernon, even though he deemed his monetary value far below other slaves in his mother's estate. "I shall readily allow the difference, in order that the fellow may be gratified, as he never would consent to go from me." On other occasions, Washington surrendered claims to slave property or debt repayment if he thought the transaction would force a sale or family separation.[19]

Fig 5.1 Edward Savage, "The East Front of Mount Vernon," c. 1787–1792. Savage's sweeping view sets the Mansion House in the context of the working estate, with a rare view of a residence for enslaved laborers to the right. The House for Families was constructed in the 1760s and razed in the early 1790s, when families of the enslaved moved to new quarters behind the greenhouse. Courtesy of Mount Vernon Ladies' Association.

Washington's professed regard for family connections, however, did not protect the family units of enslaved laborers on his estate. By 1799, over 70 percent of the individuals recognized as married in the estate records lived apart from their spouses, on separate farms, often at a distance of several miles from one another. Children of these marriages usually lived apart from their fathers, who were more likely to work and live at the Mansion House, where the workshops were located. Washington permitted visits only on Sundays, and, with limited success, he ordered overseers to prevent nighttime visits during the week. Although in his effort to prevent theft he instructed his manager to "absolutely forbid the Slaves of others resorting to the Mansion house," Washington made an exception for those "as have wives or husbands there."[20]

Prompted, as he said, "by motives of Justice," but equally concerned with his own reputation as well as the deterrence of theft, Washington insisted that the enslaved be provided with adequate food. He expected his farm managers to determine exactly what amounts of corn meal the enslaved families needed, explaining that his "wish & desire is that they should have as much as they can eat without waste and no more." On a visit to Mount Vernon during his presidency, Washington received repeated complaints from individual slaves who reported that changes in the distribution of food left many hungry. Washington also suspected that the overseers failed to distribute the full rations. He ordered his farm manager to distribute sufficient food, whether it be a peck or a bushel of corn a week. "In most explicit language I desire they may have a plenty; for I will not have my feelings again hurt with Complaints of this sort, nor lye under the imputation of starving my Negros and thereby driving them to the necessity of thieving to supply the deficiency." At hearing the reports of want, Washington initially suspected that some of the enslaved were stealing corn to feed the poultry they kept in the quarters or to share "with strange Negros," but he accepted the assurances of the enslaved overseer Davy Gray that the new ration was inadequate. At Dogue Run and Union farms, Washington heard further complaints, "which altogether hurt my feelings too much to suffer this matter to go on without a remedy." The following year he received complaints from enslaved laborers who had not received their usual allotments of fish and who hinted that one of the white overseers, Hiland Crow, had surreptitiously sold the provisions. Rather than investigate the overseer, Washington limited access to the storehouse to a single individual who would distribute the fish to each farm.[21]

Although he acknowledged that the practice was falling out of favor among other improving estate owners, Washington continued to distribute liquor to the laborers during harvest, "as my people have always been accustomed to it." He instructed his manager to be sparing in the allotment of spirits when the cost increased in the 1790s, but rum and whiskey were part of special tasks throughout the year. In the harvest of 1786, each of the plantations received gallons of rum along with one hundred pounds of beef from a cow butchered for the purpose of feeding the workers while in the field. When the fishery was in operation each spring, the laborers working there received multiple deliveries of rum, and, one year, whiskey drawn from a thirty-two-gallon barrel purchased in Alexandria. Rum was available to those butchering hogs during the Christmas holiday, and throughout the year, the enslaved received rum when they were sent to Alexandria for deliveries by boat.[22]

The provision of adequate food was the most basic obligation that Washington believed he owed the enslaved, followed by medical care. The written agreements with overseers required them to "be very careful of the Negroes in sickness," and to distribute sweet milk to sick persons and children. In medical care, as in so many other matters, Washington suspected the negligence of the white overseers, whom he accused of ignoring illness and injury in those under their supervision. He wrote one manager: "I am sorry to observe that the generality of them, view these poor creatures in scarcely any other light than they do a draught horse or Ox; neglecting them as much when they are unable to work; instead of comforting & nursing them when they lye on a sick bed." The burden for ensuring medical care fell then on the managers, whom Washington expected to discern with a heartless precision when a doctor's attendance was necessary. In Washington's estimation, if the call came too late, "in the last stage of the complaint it is unavailing to do it. It is incurring an expence for nothing." Just as he thought the manager could determine the precise amount of food needed by the enslaved, and provide not "an oz. of Meal more," so Washington expected the managers to uncover illness that was feigned as carefully as they determined when it was life threatening. He reminded William Pearce that he never wanted the enslaved to work when "they are really sick, or unfit for it," but he warned Pearce to investigate complaints of illness that might instead be the effect of fatigue from traveling about the estate at night.[23]

The instruction that Whitting must deliver to the slaves "every thing that is proper for them" reflected Washington's belief that he had, with his provisions and protections, established mutual responsibilities for both slaveholder and slave. The presentation of the work reports in the form of financial ledgers was the very embodiment of Washington's conviction that the enslaved and the enslaver owed each other something, and the slaves' side of the ledger could not be balanced until it accounted for every day of their labor. As he later explained his management of the enslaved, "it has always been my aim to feed & cloath them well, & to be careful of them in sickness; in return, I expect such labour as they ought to render." Washington defined the labor he expected in return as a duty of the enslaved.

He expected the managers and overseers to see that "my people can be brought into good habits, & a regular discharge of their duty." He wanted the hired head of the carpenters "to make the hands entrusted to his charge, do their duty properly." What Washington defined as a duty of the enslaved required "that, every labourer (male or female) does as much in the 24 hours as their strength, without endangering their health, or constitution, will allow of."[24]

On at least one occasion, Washington compared the costs of the provisions distributed to the enslaved and the value of their labor. When he agreed in 1786 to hire enslaved laborers from Penelope French as part of the terms of a land purchase from her, Washington drafted a memorandum detailing the provisions he distributed annually to the enslaved laborers and their children. To clothe ten adults, Washington would provide sixty ells of coarse linen, fifty yards of cotton, one pair of shoes and socks for each adult, and five blankets among them. The thirteen children would receive clothing valued at between one-third and one-half that distributed to the adults. For the twenty-three individuals hired from French, Washington projected an annual allotment of three barrels of corn per person, ten barrels of salted fish to be shared by all, meat "now and then," and occasional distributions of milk and fat. He anticipated the need for a doctor to attend the enslaved about six times a year, and for the services of a midwife at least twice a year. Washington paid county taxes of twenty shillings on each enslaved adult and ten shillings on each child. He estimated the cost of farming implements for each adult field laborer at £1 per year. Washington balanced the estimated costs of the provisions and equipment against the projected yield of cash crops, with eighty acres devoted to corn "for a gang chiefly composed of breeding women," and eighty acres in wheat. As long as he paid the additional rent to French, he expected to lose money on his operation of the new plantation. As with any purchase or extended hire of laborers, Washington stood to gain from any births by the enslaved women. Several years after he first hired the slaves of French, he explained that "the chance of the increase of the Negroes, & consequently their work, was placed against the decrease; & no deaths have happened, whilst five or Six are not of full size for half sharers."[25]

The overseer's account book for 1786, the first full year of the new system of farming, measured costs of food and clothing by the market values of

A list of Negros the property of Mrs French, in possession of George Washington, by virtue of a Contract which is to terminate with the life of the former. —

Names	Ages &c	Remarks
Will	Old but hearty	Looks after the Stock — repairs the Fences — and keeps them in order. —
Abram	In his prime	A good Ploughman — Cradler and Mower of Grass — a good seedsman & can stack.
Paschall	In his prime	A very good Mower, both of Grain & Grass — and an excellent Ditcher. —
Tom	about 28	A good Mower — and an excellent Ploughman — but unfortunately, from some tumour in his head, it is feared that blindness, partial if not entire, will ensue. — He has been constantly attended by Doc^r Craik — and has been visited by two other Doctors. —
Isaac	about 29	An excellent Scytheman, a good Ploughman — and handy at any other business on a Farm. —
Moses	about 26	A good Ploughman, and Carter
James	about 21	A stout young fellow & Cradler — has been employed mostly at the Distillery

Fig 5.2 "A list of Negros the property of Mrs. French, in possession of George Washington" (excerpt). In the summer of 1799, Washington compiled a list of the forty enslaved persons whom he leased from his neighbor Penelope French and now proposed to return. In his description of the adults, Washington offered his most detailed assessment of the laboring skills of individual field laborers he closely observed in the tasks of his new system of farming. Courtesy of Mount Vernon Ladies' Association.

what was consumed at each plantation, even though almost all of these goods were produced at Mount Vernon. In addition to what was distributed directly to the enslaved overseers, each plantation received roughly one thousand herring per person and slightly more than three barrels of corn per person. The account book recorded the market value of clothing, most of it also produced on the estate, and the costs of tools and supplies from the estate's store and of seeds purchased for sowing that year. The expenses for each plantation included the taxes paid on the number of tithables and, for the parish levies, the number of children as well as adults. Each plantation was debited for the value of the smiths' and carpenters' work, including the value of the carpenters' days spent in the harvest. The accounts thus monetized the value of the work of these artisans who were not a part of the labor force of the respective plantation, although none of these individuals was hired, and no monies exchanged. On the credit side, only some of the crops produced and livestock sold were recorded, although accounts recorded the monetary value of commodities, such as wool and fodder crops, which were used on the estate rather than sold on the market. These accounts and the broader range of records suggest Washington relied on an estimation of market values of labor, provisions, and farm supplies to measure the effectiveness of his allocation of artisans across the estate. For the most part, the extensive, labor-related records initiated after 1785 focused on what, in Washington's mind, the enslaver and the enslaved owed one another.[26]

Like many slaveholders in late-eighteenth century Virginia, Washington seldom wrote about or otherwise documented the violent punishment of the enslaved, but in the process of adopting the new course of husbandry and implementing the weekly reports, he explicitly discouraged the use of what he called "correction" or "severity" to extract labor from the enslaved. He instructed his several white overseers to rely instead on constant supervision as the only "sure way of getting work well done, & quietly by negroes; for when an Overlooker's back is turned, the most of them will slight their work, or be idle altogether. In which case correction cannot retrieve either; but often produces evils which are worse than the disease." After he suspected an overseer of repeatedly failing to spend the full day supervising the enslaved laborers at the Mansion House, Washington warned "the only way to keep them at work without Severity, or wrangling, is always to be with them." Washington advised managers to secure the labor of the enslaved through supervision and verbal warnings, for reasons he cited as both practical and humane. In the farm manager's supervision of the enslaved, Washington expected Anthony Whitting to prevent "all irregularities & improper conduct," and emphasized that "this oftentimes is easier to effect by watchfulness and admonition, than by severity; & certainly must be more agreeable to every feeling mind in the practice of them."[27]

Constant and vigilant supervision of enslaved laborers was Washington's proposed alternative to whipping. Hiland Crow, in Washington's opinion, was a capable overseer, but he was too often away visiting friends or entertaining them at his house rather than supervising the field laborers at Union Farm. The result of this inattention, Washington concluded, was "idleness, or slight work on one side, & flogging on the other." The flogging created "dissatisfaction," and it had on one or two occasions created what Washington described only as "serious consequences." Washington distinguished between what he considered "just & proper" whipping and that which violated his sense of excessive force, and he expected farm managers to enforce his standard of limits on violent punishment and to regulate the overseers in the same. George Augustine Washington assured his uncle that he had not "improperly" imposed a punishment on an enslaved field laborer "by my intrusting it to the execution of an Overseer." In fact, Jenny, suspected of intentionally destroying harvested flax, had been found not responsible for the act, but George Augustine in reporting her subsequent death of natural causes wanted to make sure Washington would never think him "capable of inhumanity." When Washington instructed manager William Pearce to punish Abram as an example, he further stipulated that the overseer at Union Farm, where Abram worked, not be allowed to administer the punishment of the runaway. Washington did "not trust to Crow to give it to him; for I have reason to believe he is swayed more by passion than judgment in all his corrections."[28]

Washington's reference to "all" of Hiland Crow's corrections suggests that punishment was frequent, while the assumption that violent punishment might be guided by judgment rather than passion indicates the limits of Washington's intended protection of the enslaved. Despite his infrequent and brief visits to Mount Vernon while president, Washington was

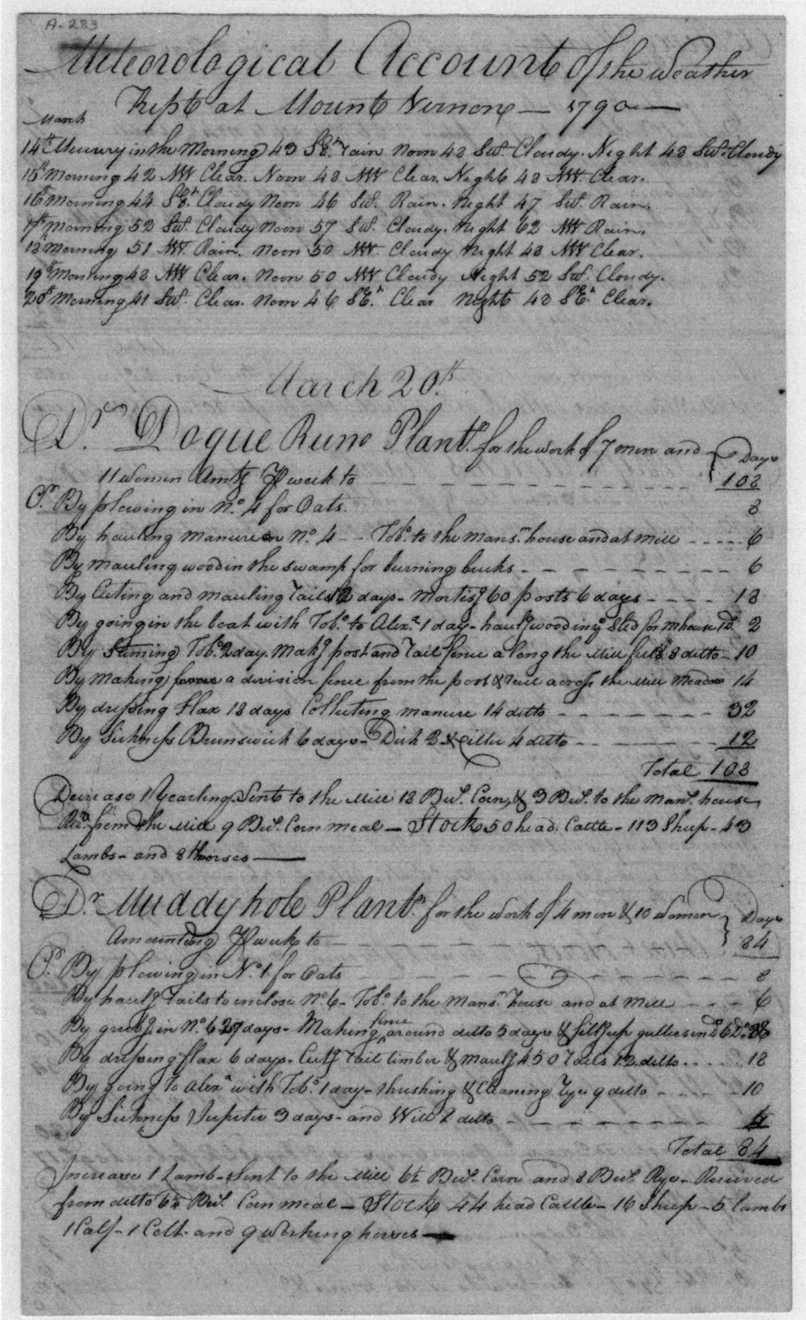

A-283

Meteorological Account of the Weather kept at Mount Vernon — 1790 —

March

14th Showery in the Morning 43 S.E. rain. Noon 42 S.W. Cloudy. Night 43 S.W. Cloudy

15th Morning 42 N.W. Clear. Noon 48 N.W. Clear. Night 42 N.W. Clear.

16th Morning 44 S.E. Cloudy Noon 46 S.W. Rain. Night 47 S.W. Rain.

17th Morning 52 S.W. Cloudy Noon 57 S.W. Cloudy. Night 62 N.W. Rain.

18th Morning 51 N.W. Rain. Noon 50 N.W. Cloudy Night 48 N.W. Clear.

19th Morning 48 N.W. Clear. Noon 50 N.W. Cloudy Night 52 S.W. Cloudy.

20th Morning 41 S.W. Clear. Noon 46 S.E. Clear Night 43 S.E. Clear.

March 20th

Dr. Dogue Run Plant. for the work of 7 men and 11 Women Amtg. 1 week to — Days 108

Cr. By plowing in No. 4 for Oats. 8

By hauling manure on No. 4 — Tob.o to the Mans.n house and at mill — 6

By mauling wood in the swamp for burning bricks — 6

By Cutting and mauling rails 12 days — Morties.g 60 posts 6 days — 18

By going in the boat with Tob.o to Alex.a 1 day — haul.g wood in.g sled for m house 1 — 2

By Stemming Tob.o 2 day. Mak.g post and rail fence along the Mill field 8 ditto — 10

By making a division fence from the post & rail across the Mill Meadow 14

By dressing Flax 18 days Collecting manure 14 ditto — 32

By Sickness Brunswick 6 days — Dick 2 & Gillie 4 ditto — 12

Total 108

Decrease 1 Yearling Sent to the Mill 12 Bu. Corn & 3 Bu. to the Man.n house Rec.d from the Mill 9 Bu. Corn meal — Stock 50 head Cattle — 113 Sheep — 40 Lambs — and 8 Horses —

Dr. Muddy hole Plant. for the work of 4 men & 10 Women Amounting 1 week to — Days 84

Cr. By plowing in No. 1 for Oats — 8

By haul.g rails to inclose No. 6 — Tob.o to the Mans.n house and at Mill — 6

By grub.g in No. 6 29 days — Making fence around ditto 5 days & fill.g up gullies in d.o 2 — 36

By dressing flax 6 days. Cutt.g rail timber & maul.g 450 rails 12 ditto — 18

By going to Alex.a with Tob.o 1 day — thrashing & Cleaning Rye 9 ditto — 10

By Sickness Jupiter 3 days — and Will 2 ditto — 6

Total 84

Increase 1 Lamb — Sent to the Mill 64 Bu. Corn and 8 Bu. Rye — Received from ditto 64 Bu. Corn meal — Stock 44 head Cattle — 16 Sheep — 5 Lambs 1 Calf — 1 Colt — and 9 Working horses —

Fig 5.3 Farm Report, work done on the Mount Vernon farms, during week 14–20 March 1790. Beginning in 1785, Washington received weekly reports of the work completed by enslaved laborers at each of his plantations and in the workshops. By 1790, the reports designed by Washington were prepared in the form of double-entry bookkeeping, with each plantation debited for the number of enslaved laborers and credited for the days worked or the reasons for absence. Courtesy of Mount Vernon Ladies' Association.

aware of the overseer's use of the lash and was alert to evidence of unauthorized whipping. When a friend asked for a recommendation of Crow as overseer, Washington acknowledged he received "too frequent complaints of ill treatment" by Crow, although he added, "I never discovered any marks of abuse." In his assessment, Crow's skill as an agricultural manager outweighed his suspected cruelty. Washington told his friend that Crow would make a valuable overseer "if he is intended to be under your own eye." Tobias Lear wrote a friend that Washington never approved of a whipping without an investigation into the alleged offense, but neither this process nor Washington's instructions to the supervisors of labor shielded the enslaved from the regular threat of violence.[29]

Any determination of Washington to limit physical punishment remained in conflict with his demand for more labor. By 1793 he conceded to his farm manager that if any of the enslaved refused to do their duty or were impertinent, "correction (as the only alternative) must be administered." During his long absences from Mount Vernon during the presidency, Washington threatened to punish individuals who failed to carry out the work demanded of them. If the bricklayer Muclus did not demonstrate more industry, Washington authorized that he be both "severely punished and placed under one of the Overseers as a common hoe negro." Isaac deserved "severe punishment" for his idleness and carelessness with the tools in the carpenter shop. The enslaved ditchers "ought to have been severely punished" for something as seemingly inconsequential as the "villainous manner" in which they repaired a fence at the mill. When Anthony Whitting wrote that he had given the enslaved seamstress Charlotte a good whipping for what he characterized as "impudence" and that he was "determined to lower her Spirit or Skin her Back," Washington replied that the treatment of Charlotte was "very proper."[30]

Washington required farm managers to enforce whipping or other punishments for various kinds of behavior unrelated to the performance of work, such as running away, stealing, or fighting. He expected Whitting to punish both individuals involved in any fight, unless the manager could be certain that only one person was at fault. After a slave he identified as Matilda's Ben continued to misbehave following punishment for assaulting another slave, Washington explained to Whitting that if the young man "should be guilty of any attrocious crime, that would affect his life he might be given up to the Civil authority for tryal; but for such offences as most of his colour are guilty of, you had better try further correction; accompanied with admonition and advice. The two latter sometimes succeed when the first has failed." This instruction to Whitting is among the few surviving documents in which Washington characterized behavior by race as well as condition of servitude. He reaffirmed his preference for the verbal warnings that might avert violent punishment, but he also made clear that he would enforce his own system of discipline and control separate from any court of law. He stipulated punishments for infractions small and large. When William Pearce reported that someone broke into the smokehouse and stole several pieces of bacon, Washington ordered him to find the thief "& bring him to punishment." After an enslaved man from a neighbor's property visited River Farm and brutally beat his wife who lived there, Washington sent orders to Pearce that if the man ever came back "you are to give him a good whipping, & forbid his ever returning." After complaining about the loss of sheep and hogs and imposing strict restrictions on the number of dogs at each plantation, Washington declared to Whitting that "if any negro presumes under any pretence whatsoever, to preserve, or bring one into the family, that he shall be severely punished, and the dog hanged." Washington's expectation that an example be made of Richmond for stealing money from a hired servant or Abram for running away suggests that whippings were conducted in front of other members of the enslaved community. The enslaved individuals who voiced complaints to Washington about Hiland Crow must have expected him to enforce limits on violence, but Washington's frequent threats of severity, often expressed in anger and frustration, exposed the tenuous and conditional protections against punishment.[31]

From Washington's perspective, the most serious betrayal of the presumed duty of an enslaved laborer was the act of running away. During the years in which he established a new system of slave management and up until the end of his life, even as he developed a more critical perspective on slavery and considered emancipation, Washington defended the private property rights of slaveholders. When the enslaved servant owned by an Alexandria merchant visiting Philadelphia approached a Quaker group to help him win his freedom in court, Washington was so incensed that he wrote Robert Morris to express his concern. He assured Morris that he did not want to hold slaves in bondage, but considered the Quakers' efforts to "seduce" enslaved persons into freedom an assault on property rights that would deter anyone with enslaved servants from doing business in Philadelphia, then the nation's commercial center. Washington was particularly concerned that the Quakers had "tampered" with slaves who are "happy & content to remain with their present masters." Several months later, Washington engaged in a complicated deception to return a runaway enslaved valet owned by William Drayton, who had stayed at Mount Vernon on his journey from a meeting of the Confederation Congress to his home in South Carolina. When Jack, the enslaved valet, ran away and returned to Mount Vernon, Washington devised a plan by which he sent Jack on an errand to Baltimore, where an associate of Washington had arranged his recapture and passage to Charleston.[32]

By the time of his presidency, Washington defended his right to recover slave property at the same time that he sought to shield his reputation, particularly in those sections of the country where popular sentiment might oppose the recapture of escaped slaves. When Paul, one of the enslaved field laborers hired from Penelope French, ran away in 1795, Washington offered to share with the French family the costs of recapture, but he asked that his name not appear in a printed advertisement or in any other way be associated with the effort. After the farm manager, William Pearce, placed an advertisement in an Alexandria newspaper that offered a reward for the capture of Paul, who was described as a runaway from one of the president's farms, Washington explained that he "had no other objection to the advertising of Paul than that of having my name appear therein; at least in any papers North of Virginia." When Ona Judge, the enslaved servant of Martha Washington, escaped in 1796, Washington's steward placed an advertisement in the Philadelphia newspaper that identified Judge as absconding "from the household of the President of the United States." In his determined efforts to recapture Judge and the enslaved chef, Hercules, who ran away from Mount Vernon in February 1797, Washington relied primarily on private correspondents and the work of hired agents.[33]

Just as running away continued to be the most serious perceived challenge to the authority of Washington and his overseers, so Washington considered sale and separation from family to be the most serious punishment he inflicted on any enslaved person. As he had before the Revolutionary

War, Washington sold a man to the Caribbean in 1791 as a punishment. The offense of the man he designated as Waggoner Jack went unspecified in the account book that recorded his transportation to the islands and the return in wine and commission on the sale. Washington instructed the farm manager to warn Ben and his parents "in explicit language that if a stop is not put to his rogueries, & other villainies by fair means & shortly; that I will ship him off (as I did Waggoner Jack) for the West Indias, where he will have no opportunity of playing such pranks as he is at present engaged in." While most runaways were punished and sent back to work after their recapture, Washington in 1795 approved the sale of a young man named Anderson who had run away from John Dandridge, who managed more than thirty slaves owned by Washington in New Kent County.[34]

∘   ∘   ∘

From the time Washington recognized that he would be leaving to serve as president, he and his manager steadily replaced the five enslaved overseers serving as late as the fall of 1788, and by early 1793, only Davy Gray, by then at Muddy Hole, remained among them. Morris, who had been overseer at Dogue Run Plantation since 1766 became sick in 1790 and was initially replaced by Will, the former overseer at Muddy Hole. Will remained as overseer of Dogue Run until he was replaced by a hired man in late 1791. Another enslaved overseer named Will, at French's Plantation, was replaced by James Bloxham in late 1788. In March 1789, as Washington prepared to leave for his inauguration, he placed Isaac, the overseer of enslaved carpenters, under the supervision of Thomas Green, a hired joiner in whom Washington had little confidence.[35]

Anticipating that he would be away from Mount Vernon for months at a time over at least the next four years, Washington decided to rely on white overseers to enforce a rigorous schedule of year-round work, even though he had little faith in most of the hired overseers. William Garner at River Plantation was a "rascal," who "never turned out of mornings until the Sun had warmed the Earth; and if *he* did not, the *Negros* would not." Washington accused Henry Jones at Dogue Run of allowing the field laborers to remain idle "to bribe them against a discovery of his own idleness." Although Hiland Crow at Union Farm was a skilled farmer, he was too often away from home, "the consequence of w[hi]ch (supposing the negros had been idle during his absence) was, that he and his charge were perpetually at varience."[36]

In a detailed evaluation of the overseers prepared for the arrival of manager William Pearce, Washington in December 1793 reported "Davy at Muddy hole carries on his business as well as the white Overseers, and with more quietness than any of them. With proper directions he will do very well, & probably give you less trouble than any of them, except in attending to his care of the stock, of which I fear he is negligent." Washington's opinion of Davy Gray stood in sharp contrast to his view of the white overseers. Henry McCoy at Dogue Run appeared to Washington "a sickly, slothful and stupid fellow." James Butler at the Mansion House had no authority over the enslaved laborers, and Crow at Union Farm, though knowledgeable, was negligent in the supervision of the enslaved as well as the horses. Washington warned Pearce, "Thomas Green (Overlooker of the Carpenters) will, I am persuaded, require your closest attention, without which I believe it will be impossible to get any work done by my Negro Carpenters." Only William Stuart at River Farm escaped Washington's harsh assessment. Stuart was industrious and worked long days, and he also seemed "to live in peace & harmony with the Negroes who are confided to his care. He speaks extremely well of them, and I have never heard any complaint of him." The only fault Washington could find in Stuart was that he talked too much and "has a high opinion of his own skill & management."[37]

On his intermittent visits to Mount Vernon while president, Washington spoke directly with enslaved laborers, interposing himself between them and the manager or overseers and gathering information on his own terms. On several visits he received multiple complaints from the enslaved. He learned that the reduction in the amount of cornmeal distributed to the quarters left families hungry. On his ride to the plantations, Washington looked for signs of physical abuse, and he listened to complaints about mistreatment by white overseers. The enslaved workers at the plantations evidently considered Washington receptive to their appeals. When in 1790 George Augustine proposed to move Davy Gray from oversight of Muddy Hole Plantation to be overseer of the larger farm at Dogue Run, Gray protested that his earlier bout of jaundice left him too weak to take on the greater responsibility, and he was confident that Washington would agree not to relocate him. George Augustine informed Washington of Gray's appeal, and though no response survives, Gray continued to supervise Muddy Hole until the end of Washington's life. Washington trusted Gray enough to consult with him about complaints from other slaves.[38]

The success of Gray as an overseer never persuaded Washington to employ another enslaved overseer in place of the hired men, who, with the exception of Stuart, turned over with disruptive frequency. George Augustine Washington in 1790 proposed to avoid "the expence and frequently the perplexity of white Overseers" by installing James, an enslaved carpenter, as overseer of one of the plantations, and he believed James "might answer as well as an Overseer as any white man." Washington rejected the proposal, as he would refuse a later suggestion that he place Will, formerly the enslaved overseer at Muddy Hole and Dogue Run, as overseer at the Mansion House. Washington was willing to entrust Will with special responsibilities, including tasks not subject to immediate supervision, but he was concerned that Will "feels hurt in being superceded in his Overseership."[39]

In his written hiring agreements with the overseers and in his instructions to the managers who supervised them, Washington demanded that the overseers be present and with the slaves under their supervision throughout the workday. Washington ordered an overseer to "see the labourers at their work as soon as it is light in the morning" and each overseer should "be constantly with some part or other of his People at their work." "With me, it is an established maxim, that an Overseer shall never be absent from his people but at night, and at his meals." Even when the enslaved were not working, Washington expected the overseers to exercise a certain supervisory authority. He discouraged their entertainment of friends, other than family "now and then," and he expected the overseers to remain on the plantation except on Sundays, when, as he specified for one, "he may occasionally go to Church." The burden of enforcing these agreements, particularly during Washington's absences, fell on the farm managers, who Washington expected to hire overseers of "good character" and reputation, "& knowing in the management of Negros."[40]

Anthony Whitting arrived at Mount Vernon in 1790 with experience managing enslaved agricultural labor on a similar estate of even larger acreage on the Eastern Shore of Maryland. The Shrewsbury Farm had been owned by General John Cadwalader, Washington's fellow officer in the Continental Army, and since Cadwalader's death in 1786, Whitting had been the manager of farming at the estate. There he supervised nearly 50 adult slaves and more than 30 enslaved children in the same kind of improved farming found on Washington's estate. The field laborers at Shrewsbury worked with a large inventory of plows, harrows, and scythes, and cared for the varied livestock. When Whitting presented himself as a candidate for overseer at Mount Vernon, George Augustine Washington found his manner of conversation "much superior to what is met with among people of that pursuit," and Whitting quickly moved from overseer of one plantation to manager of all farming at the estate. As overseer, Whitting was required by the articles of agreement drafted by Washington to "be particularly attentive to the Negroes which shall be committed to his care," and as manager he was advised by Washington that the example he set, "be it good or bad, will be followed by all those who look up to you. Keep every one in their places, & to their duty." Washington reminded Whitting of something at the core of his own approach to the management of labor, enslaved or hired. "One fault overlooked begets another—that a third—and so on—whereas a check in the first instance might prevent a repetition, or at any rate cause circumspection."[41]

A member of the Cadwalader family had cautioned Washington that Whitting, though knowledgeable about agriculture and the economy of a farm, was too indulgent of his pleasures. During Whitting's three-year tenure, he gained Washington's considerable confidence, in large part because of his knowledge of the practice of husbandry in his native England, but following the death of Whitting in June 1793, Washington received reports of the manager's drinking and his association with "bad company" at Washington's house in Alexandria. He had been, Washington concluded, "a very debauched person," unable to govern the overseers or to manage the details of the estate's business. Whitting, following James Bloxham, became for Washington one more example of a knowledgeable English farmer unprepared to supervise enslaved Blacks. Washington warned a subsequent manager of the inherent risks of hiring English farmers or European tradesmen unfamiliar with slavery: "Rather than persevere in doing things right themselves, & being at the trouble of making others do the

like, they will fall into the slovenly mode of executing work which is practiced by those, among whom they are."[42]

After the death of Whiting, Washington searched for a new farm manager who would bring both knowledge of mixed agriculture and experience in the supervision of enslaved laborers. He believed that he was most
likely to find that ideal manager on the Eastern Shore of Maryland, where
Whiting had previously worked and where there was the greatest concentration of large estates operating under the same farming system as Mount
Vernon. It was also on the Eastern Shore where Washington was confident
that he would find someone who met his second requirement: "a residence
of some years in a part of the Country where the labour is done by Negroes." It was that experience with the management of enslaved labor that
Washington deemed essential to the direction of the several large farms
under separate overseers. Washington made inquiries that brought him the
names of managers on some of the largest and most successful estates on
the Eastern Shore, and he then consulted with his friend, Eastern-Shore
resident William Tilghman, to ensure that no measures taken on his behalf would have the appearance of enticing a manager away from an estate
owner to whom he was engaged.[43]

Among those whom Washington consulted in Maryland was Jacob
Hollingsworth, an innkeeper in Elkton. Washington occasionally stayed at
the inn while traveling between Virginia and Philadelphia, as did Thomas
Jefferson, who had hired a farm manager recommended by Hollingsworth.
As Jefferson prepared to introduce at Monticello the crop rotations he had
discussed with Washington and others in Philadelphia, he searched for a
farmer from the area around Elkton because, as he explained to Hollingsworth, "the degree of farming there practised is exactly that which I think
would be adopted in my possessions, and because the labour with you
being chiefly by Negroes, your people of course understand the method
of managing that kind of laborer." Jefferson informed his son-in-law and
manager "the farmers there understand the management of negroes on a
rational and humane plan." Hollingsworth assured Jefferson that the manager he identified for work at Monticello was "as neat a Farmer as Any in
our Ne[i]ghbourhood," and able to manage Negroes "tho not in a very
harsh manar." Jefferson, apparently alluding to an earlier conversation, told
Washington he had "engaged a good farmer from the head of Elk (the style

of farming there you know well)," and expressed his hope the farmer would assist him in the adoption of Arthur Young's model of husbandry.[44]

Washington did not hire the manager suggested by Hollingsworth, selecting instead William Pearce, a long-time manager of a Ringgold family estate in Kent County, Maryland. Pearce would prove to be the most satisfactory farm manager with whom Washington ever worked, and from the beginning of their relationship, Washington demonstrated a surprising trust in Pearce. In their written agreement and in early conferences, Washington emphasized the necessity of reestablishing the accountability of the overseers and all superintendents of laborers, "for it may be received as a maxim that if they are away or entertaining company at home, that the concerns entrusted to them will be neglected, & certainly go wrong." To that end, Washington delegated unprecedented control over overseers, all of whom Pearce was authorized to hire or discharge, according to his own judgment.[45]

By the time Washington hired William Pearce, experience in the management of enslaved laborers had become a priority in any hire involving supervisory duties at Mount Vernon. The disappointment with Bloxham and Whitting was reinforced by other hires of artisans and overseers inexperienced in the management of enslaved labor. As early as 1787, Washington had dismissed a suggestion to hire the newly arrived brother of Cornelius Roe, a bricklayer at Mount Vernon, because, as Washington wrote George Augustine, "I can hardly believe that a raw Irishman can be well qualified to manage Negros." When Washington met the Irish immigrant James Butler in Philadelphia in 1792, he was so impressed with his knowledge of farming and livestock that he hired him to manage the Home House farm, but from their first meeting, Washington was apprehensive that Butler "will be at a loss in the management of Negros—as their idleness & deceit, if he is not Sufficiently cautioned against them, will most assuredly impose upon him." When he first saw him at work at Mount Vernon, Washington thought Butler lacked the requisite "activity & Spirit." By the end of the year he was persuaded Butler "has no more authority over the Negroes he is placed, than an old woman would have; and is as unable to get a proper days Work done by them as she would." After Butler was dismissed as an overseer, Washington provided him with a certificate attesting to his honesty and hard work, further explaining "I part with him for no other cause than for his not being accustomed to the management of negros prone to, & who had been long in the habits of idleness."[46]

The perceived inadequacies of Butler included his appearance and demeanor, both of which Washington considered essential components in the exercise of authority over enslaved laborers. His initial reason for doubting the ability of Butler to manage slaves was "his clumsy appearance, and age." Washington had also questioned the wisdom of hiring Roe's brother because "his appearance may be very much against him." Washington doubted the Scottish carpenter he hired in Philadelphia would have any authority over the enslaved carpenters at Mount Vernon, "as he appears to be a simple, inoffensive man." When Washington was approached by a man who hoped to replace Butler as overseer, he explained to William Pearce the need to balance the applicant's bearing against his experience: "He is a tolerably good looking man and has the appearance of an active one—but how far any man, unacquainted with Negros, is capable of managing of them, is questionable."[47]

Despite his largely successful efforts to train enslaved laborers in the varied skills he required for his increasingly complex farming operations, Washington continued to hire some artisans with valuable skills, even if those individuals did not have experience in the supervision and direction of enslaved laborers. British experience continued to hold sway with Washington. James Donaldson, the Scottish carpenter whom Washington met and hired in Philadelphia in 1794, brought to Mount Vernon essential skills as a wheelwright and manufacturer of plows. Washington anticipated that Donaldson would be valuable for making equipment for the farms and repairing spinning wheels, as well as for training enslaved artisans in the same skills, and the agreement presented by Washington required Donaldson to instruct any of the enslaved carpenters who were committed to his care and management. Washington expected Donaldson to "take pains to teach those who work with him," especially the experienced carpenter, Isaac, and a boy named Jem, that they would learn more about making essential agricultural implements, including plows, harrows, and carts. Two months after the arrival of Donaldson, however, the farm manager confirmed Washington's suspicions that the man might be inadequate to the job of managing the enslaved carpenters. Although a good and industrious workman, Donaldson "has not spirit and activity enough to make the hands entrusted to his charge, do their duty properly." Washington so doubted Donaldson's ability to manage the enslaved artisans that he was willing to hire an additional, if less talented, carpenter "more competent to the Management of the Negros," to work alongside him.[48]

Donaldson was one in a succession of hired artisans Washington expected to instruct slaves who then might be able to assume the greater variety of tasks that supported the agricultural improvements adopted after 1785. The ditcher James Lawson was required by articles of agreement to train any slaves put under his direction, and to keep them closely at their work "without relaxing (under the idea of being an overseer) or neglecting, in any shape whatever, his own labour." John and Rachel Knowles, hired as a bricklayer and spinner, respectively, agreed "to take under their directions and carefully instruct such Negroes as the said George Washington may think proper in the different duties required of them." Once Thomas Green assumed supervisory duties as joiner and carpenter, Washington expected him to instruct in his trade any enslaved carpenters placed under his direction.[49]

As Washington recognized, the hire of artisans unfamiliar with slavery or of overseers with insufficient authority threatened to disrupt the racial and social order at his estate. In the weeks following Donaldson's arrival at Mount Vernon, Washington was anxious that the carpenter and his family might "get disgusted by living among the Negros," but he was equally concerned that Donaldson might become too friendly with the enslaved carpenters or other laborers. He instructed William Pearce that Donaldson should be "kept as seperate, and as distinct as possible from the Negros—who want no encouragement to mix with, & become too familiar (for no good purposes) with these kind of people." A month later, Washington again asked Pearce to caution Donaldson "against familiarities with the Negros." Washington was especially concerned that the overseers at the plantations would associate too closely with the slaves under their supervision. When John Allison became the overseer at the Mansion House in 1794, Washington feared "that he would be too familiar with those he overlooked, and of course would carry no authority." The renegotiated articles of agreement with Thomas Green as overseer of carpenters in 1790 required "that neither he nor his family will have any connection or association with any of the Negroes except those immediately under his direction and with those but where it relates to their business." The agreement apparently had little effect, since among the many criticisms Washington later directed against the carpenter was that "he is too much upon a level with the Negroes."[50]

Washington believed the authority of the farm managers depended on some kind of social distance from the white overseers as well as the enslaved. He cautioned William Pearce that "to treat them civilly is no more than what all men are entitled to, but my advice to you is, to keep them at a proper distance; for they will grow upon familiarity, in proportion as you will sink in authority, if you do not." The reserve and detachment that Washington expected from every supervisor of labor introduced the potential for suspicion and mistrust in nearly every personal interaction among overseers, hired laborers, and the enslaved. Washington assumed the need for a social order that divided whites between those who might dine at his table and those who did not enter the Mansion House, and he expected all of the whites to maintain a greater separation from Blacks, even as they spent their days together in close work. No surviving record reveals Washington's acknowledgment of what he knew well, that hired white men fathered children with enslaved women.[51]

On varied occasions, often in the field where the practical evidence surrounded him, Washington recognized the agricultural skill and knowledge of the enslaved. When peas failed to come up as usual at Muddy Hole plantation in 1786, Washington noted "this my Negros ascribed to planting them too early, whilst the earth was too cold—& not sufficiently dryed." When he briefly reintroduced tobacco cultivation in 1789, Washington consulted with the enslaved overseer at French's plantation, as "Frenchs Will understands the managemnt of it better than I do." Washington included the enslaved overseers in the direction of his agricultural experiments, and conferred with the plow drivers, although he disagreed with their assessment, about the performance of a new plow sent from Arthur Young.[52]

His most detailed recognition of the agricultural skills of laborers appeared in an annotated list of the slaves Washington hired from Penelope French. Intent on reducing the number of slaves under his management during his retirement, Washington in the summer of 1799 proposed to return these hired slaves to French. He suggested the two parties select disinterested persons who would produce a valuation of the slaves, "after comparing the old with the young—and the chances of increase and decrease," and then determine an annuity to be paid to Washington during the remaining term of the agreement. Washington had an incentive to present the hired slaves in a favorable light, but the specificity of his comments and his knowledge of their work reflected a lifetime of monitoring and assessing individual laborers on his estate. What is perhaps most striking about Washington's summary is how many of the individuals he described excelled at their work. Pascal was a "very good Mower, both of Grain & Grass, and an excellent Ditcher." Tom, also good at mowing, was "an excellent Ploughman," despite the serious impairment that would eventually leave him blind. Julius, though physically impaired since infancy, was "a very good Carter, and can do any other work." Isaac's skills spanned the seasons of work: "an excellent Scythesman, a good Ploughman, and handy at any other business on a Farm." Sabine, at sixty, was "a good working woman, notwithstanding her age." Daphne "Ploughs very well," and Washington said the same of Grace and Siss. Other women carried out only "common work," and Washington described them largely by their appearance. Milly was "a full grown woman, and likely," and Hannah "nearly at her full growth and a woman in appear[anc]e." Will, once an overseer and later a foreman, was now "old, but hearty" and tended the stock and repaired fences. Only Lucy prompted Washington's suspicions. At about fifty-five years old, she was "Lame, or pretends to be so," but Washington admitted she was "a good knitter, & so employed."[53]

Washington compiled the collective profile of individuals whom he viewed through their performance of the essential tasks of the husbandry he had adopted at Mount Vernon. From his perspective, theirs were lives defined by a cycle of labor that began with the "work in the Crops" assigned the four girls and two boys between the ages of twelve and sixteen and that continued with the plowing, mowing, and sowing by the two men, each described as "in his prime." Those in their twenties and thirties often carried out specialized work beyond the repetitive tasks of the so-called "hoe people." Sixteen children living at Union Farm awaited the age at which they too would join their siblings and mothers in the fields; none had fathers at the same farm. The individuals hired of French comprised well over half of the slaves working on what was by 1799 the most productive of the four farms devoted to commercial agriculture. Several years after French's slaves were combined with those already working at Ferry Plantation, one of Washington's farm managers considered the residents of the united plantation the most difficult to manage on all of the estate, perhaps because the labor force had been drawn from separate units or because it had the lowest incidence of family formation and the fewest married couples living together. By 1799, however, Washington described the slaves hired from French "as orderly, and as well disposed a set, as any equal number in the Country," particularly in the absence of Paul, who had run away for a second and final time in 1795.[54]

Any acknowledgment of agricultural skill was frequently overshadowed by Washington's unrelenting complaints about the work of enslaved laborers. The perceived carelessness and negligence of laborers regularly provoked his contempt, which he often expressed in a tone of petulant frustration. The seedsman "foolishly" sowed barley in wet soil. Nat was a "clumsey fellow" incapable of following directions. On a short visit to Mount Vernon while president, Washington "felt both mortification & vexation, to find an ignorant Negro sowing these Seeds contrary to my reiterated direction." Fences were ineptly constructed, with posts a strong man might break across his knee and rails so long and weak "as to warp, & be unable to bear the weight of a child in getting over them." When Washington considered the advantages of consolidating the flocks of sheep on the several plantations, he hoped they could be "placed under the care of a trusty negro if there be such an one," and then concluded, in a sweeping dismissal of the entire enslaved labor force, "I know not the Negro among all mine, whose capacity, integrity, and attention, could be relied on for such a trust as this."[55]

When Washington decided he needed new types of farming implements and mechanical equipment after 1785, he complained about the unwillingness or inability of the enslaved to undertake new tasks. He was frustrated that the blacksmith "is too great a bungler to entrust anything to him that requires skill, or exactness." No matter how good the model of a threshing machine brought over by English farmers, Washington warned Henry Lee that its utility on an estate reliant on enslaved laborers and incompetent overseers would "depend *absolutely* upon the simplicity of its construction; for if there be anything complex in the Machinery, it will be no longer in use than a mushroom is in existence." Washington's secretary, Tobias Lear, explained to the English promoter of a new plow design that the offer of the plow would not only violate the president's rule against accepting gifts, it would likely be of little value at the Mount Vernon plantations. Washington, Lear reported, had learned "from repeated experiments, that all machines used in husbandry that are of a complicated nature, would be entirely useless to him, and impossible to be introduced into common use where they are to be worked by ignorant and clumsy hands, which must be the case in every part of this country where the ground is tilled by negroes."[56]

The enslaved carpenters were an idle set of "Rascals," and, in Washington's estimation, would require an entire week just to build a chicken coop. They appeared particularly incompetent and indolent compared to the free laborers Washington observed in Philadelphia; "buildings that are run up here in two or three days (with not more hands) employ them a month, or more." As much as he criticized Thomas Green as overseer of carpenters, Washington hesitated to discharge him during the complicated construction of the sixteen-sided barn at Dogue Run, "for I am Sure, none of my Negro Carpenters are adequate to the framing, & executing such a Barn as I am about to build." He refused to trust "my Negro Carpenters or any other bungler."[57]

Suspicions of dishonesty and laziness crept into every aspect of Washington's management of the enslaved, and often of the men who oversaw them. Convinced that Alexandria provided a market for stolen goods, Washington wrote his manager, "I have such an opinion of my Negros (two or three only excepted); and not much better of some of the whites—that I am perfectly sure not a single thing that can be disposed of *at any price,* at that place, that will not, and is not, stolen, where it is possible." His distrust extended to the youngest of the enslaved workers. Whenever any of the children at the Mansion House were assigned to work, Washington wanted the overseer, John Fairfax, "to keep some person with them which will not only make them work but who will see that the work is well executed—and that the idleness which they appear every day in the practise of, may be avoided." Washington feared that with little incentive for the enslaved, who had no expectation of a change in their status, or for the overseers, who were paid regardless of output, the labor system at his estate invited deception and complicity. Too many of the overseers and hired white artisans were heedless of the example they set, "because all of them have discernment enough to know that no man can, with propriety, or a good conscience, correct others for a fault he is guilty of himself; the consequence of which is, that indolence & sloth take possession of the whole."[58]

Washington found in the close management of enslaved labor a negation of the essential principles he believed guided all productive work. In articles of agreement with overseers and hired workers and in instructions to his managers, Washington again and again repeated the trio of character traits—industry, sobriety, and honesty—that he believed to be the foundation of all productive work and of trust. Only a regard for reputation would ensure adherence to these virtues, and he had no expectation of securing these habits from the enslaved, whose social isolation and bondage were destructive of trust and cooperation. The occasional money that Washington or managers gave favored enslaved laborers as an encouragement or in recognition of the completion of special tasks highlighted the inadequacies of other calls to work, and these modest payments were so infrequent, and limited to so few laborers, that the impact was negligible for all except those who received them. In his parting instructions to Thomas Green in the spring of 1789, Washington explained that work was a bargain intended for mutual benefit, and that failure to do the job was a kind of robbery. He was mystified that the white overseers paid so little attention to their own reputations, which he considered all that anyone had to carry them through their working lives. Yet Washington understood that a reputation for reliable work and skill offered little incentive for those who were enslaved. "Having (I am speaking generally) no ambition to establish a *good* name, they are too regardless of a *bad* one; and of course, require more of the masters eye." The extent to which the need for the master's eye was compatible with improved agriculture would remain a persistent doubt in Washington's mind.[59]

◦ *6* ◦

Cincinnatus and the World
of Improvement

In April 1784, less than four months following Washington's resignation from command of the Continental Army and his return to Mount Vernon, the French Minister to the United States, the Chevalier de La Luzerne, visited Washington at his estate and noted that the general "dresses in a gray coat like a Virginia farmer, and nothing about him recalls the recollections of the important part he played" in the Revolutionary War. Over the next five years and again following Washington's retirement from the presidency in 1797, hundreds of other visitors, friends as well as strangers, came to pay their respects to the hero of the Revolution. Like La Luzerne, many of those seeking the general would find the farmer, greeting them in "bespattered boots," eager to display his experimental crops, his gristmill, or his design for a drill plow made by the enslaved carpenters. Those who were willing accompanied Washington on his daily visit to his plantations, riding the half-day circuit. When Benjamin Henry Latrobe visited Mount Vernon in 1796, Washington held the British-born architect in conversation for hours, well into the dark of a summer evening, discussing the condition of crops in Virginia, the relative merits of various English plows, and problems of soil exhaustion related to corn crops. A visitor from Poland noted that Washington "answered with kindness all questions I put to him on the Revolution," but "his favorite subject is agriculture." Another noted of Washington that "his greatest pride now is to be thought the first farmer of America."[1]

Washington had quickly become "quite a Cincinnatus," as many visitors remarked in the 1780s. Cincinnatus was known to the eighteenth-century Anglo-American world through the writings of Livy, Cicero, and Cato, who held up the image of "Cincinnatus at the Plow" as a model of republican virtue. The representation of Washington as Cincinnatus became for the new republic a symbol of disinterested leadership and the refusal of arbitrary power, and Washington's life as a farmer made the symbolism all the more compelling. Dedication to agricultural improvement blended with military valor and public service to define the civic virtues of Washington.[2]

On his return to Mount Vernon, Washington fostered the image of his rural life detached from political contest and military conflict. To his close friend, the Marquis de Chastellux, Washington, with reference to a favorite phrase from Joseph Addison's *Cato,* announced that, "free from the bustle of a camp & the intrigues of a Court, I shall view the busy world, 'in the calm lights of mild philosophy.'" Washington described himself to Chastellux and his other French comrades, Lafayette and Rochambeau, as "a private Citizen on the banks of the Potomack," free from the burdens of public service. That rural life, however, attracted widespread public interest in the agricultural pursuits of the new Cincinnatus. Washington the farmer was celebrated in his own country and in much of Europe, and his figurative return to the plow became a metaphor for the dreams of a new order among nations. At his estate, Washington displayed his experiments and improvements before visitors, known and unknown, in a demonstration of a public example and his personal virtue. His deepening personal connections with European and American advocates of agricultural improvement and scientific investigation shaped Washington's perspective on how the United States might engage the world and how he might participate in an enlightened community that sought to establish a new foundation for peace.[3]

∘   ∘   ∘

The widely shared enthusiasm for Washington's agricultural pursuits became evident when he set out on his first significant improvement project following his return to Mount Vernon. Washington decided to become a breeder of mules, both for his own use as draft animals and to encourage their use by other farmers. He knew of the animals' reputed superiority to horses in their strength and longevity and for the economy with which they could be fed, but mules were infrequently bred in most parts of the United States and were often too small for effective draft work. Mules are the off-spring of a male donkey or jackass and a mare, and are unable to repro-duce themselves, so any breeding program depended on a reliable stock of jackasses. Washington recalled his wartime conversations with the Spanish agent to the United States, Juan de Miralles, who spoke of the vir-tues of mules bred from Spanish jackasses. Miralles had promised to pro-cure one of those prized jackasses, normally prohibited from export from Spain, but he died while visiting Washington at the Morristown encamp-ment in 1780. In July 1784, Washington asked the Alexandria merchant Robert Townsend Hooe, whose partner, Richard Harrison, was resident in Cadiz, if the trading firm might be able to procure a Spanish jackass for him. "An ordinary Jack I do not desire," and Washington was sufficiently knowledgeable about the animals to request one "at least fifteen hands high; well formed; in his prime; & one whose abilities for getting Colts can be ensured."[4]

The request set in motion a sequence of communications involving the highest diplomatic circles in Europe and raised expectations of pro-moting further ties between the new nation and an important ally from the Revolutionary War. Harrison contacted the United States chargé d'affaires in Madrid, William Carmichael, who in turn spoke to the Conde de Floridablanca, the chief minister to the king, about Washington's re-quest. Floridablanca reported that not only would King Charles III permit the export of the jackass for Washington, the monarch also or-dered that two of the best specimens in Spain would be sent "as a proof of his esteem for so distinguished a character." Jefferson, after reports from Carmichael, wrote Washington from Paris about his satisfaction at the testament of the king's favor and his excitement about the public ben-efits of the breeding project. He had tried to procure one of the jackasses himself, but now hoped instead to acquire two female asses—jennies—from Spain, so that "we may be enabled to propagate and preserve the breed."[5]

When Washington received an early report from Harrison about the extravagant price of a Spanish jackass, he countermanded his order, and then gave similar instructions to Lafayette, to whom he had sent a separate inquiry about procuring breeding asses. His initial disappointment with the cost made him all the more grateful for the generosity of the king, and he asked Floridablanca "to assure his Majesty of my unbounded gratitude for so condescending a mark of his royal notice & favor." To Lafayette he wrote, "I have long endeavoured to procure one of a good size & breed, but had little expectation of receiving two as a royal gift," and "Royal Gift" was the name he bestowed on the lone Spanish jack that survived the sea journey. Washington received another unexpected gift of a Maltese jack and two jennies procured by Lafayette, who also sent Chinese pheasants and partridges from the French king's aviary. A Baltimore newspaper account of the costly gifts and the handsomely paid French attendant who delivered the animals greatly agitated Washington, who feared that the report would be reprinted in French and British newspapers and be interpreted as a willingness on his part to accept inappropriate gifts. Washington ultimately accepted the animals, but only after making several attempts to reimburse Lafayette.[6]

In October 1785, a Boston newspaper printed the report of a man at Cape Ann, Massachusetts, who witnessed the arrival of "the largest Jack-Ass I ever saw, of a peculiar species," sent as "a present to His Excellency General Washington, with a farrier to attend him." The following day, Thomas Cushing, lieutenant governor of Massachusetts, sent Washington the same news and promised to care for the animal until Washington could arrange for transport. Washington dispatched his overseer John Fairfax to Boston with instructions that anticipated every possible obstacle to safe delivery. "You know too well the high value I set upon these Jacks, to neglect them on the road in any instance whatsoever." He wanted Fairfax to meet with an interpreter before leaving Boston to learn from the Spanish attendant what to feed the jack, what hours to travel, what blankets would be needed at night. Before Fairfax left Boston, Cushing received word that the second jackass from the king had died at sea, a casualty of a great storm.[7]

Newspapers along the route reported the progress of Royal Gift and his attendants as they traveled from Boston to Mount Vernon. The fall 1785

Fig 6.1 "General Washington's Jack Ass" in *Weatherwise's Town and Country Almanack, for the year of our Lord, 1786* (Boston, 1785). Washington received a jackass from Spain's King Charles III and in 1786 began to breed the mules that would eventually outnumber other draft animals on his farms. The arrival of "Royal Gift" attracted the attention of newspapers and planters eager to bring their mares for breeding with the prized Spanish jackass, normally prohibited from export. Courtesy of Mount Vernon Ladies' Association.

edition of the popular *Weatherwise's Town and Country Almanack* featured an illustration of "General Washington's Jack Ass." Even before the arrival of Royal Gift in Virginia, Washington received requests to share the benefits of what were expected to be two jacks. Tench Tilghman wrote on behalf of several people on the Eastern Shore of Maryland who hoped Washington might share one of the jackasses to promote the breeding of mules in that region, where plowing was widely adopted and planters needed less expensive draft animals. As soon as Fairfax returned to Mount Vernon with Royal Gift and his Spanish attendant in early December, Washington invited a ship captain from Alexandria to interpret the conversation with the Spaniard. In February, the enslaved carpenters began to fashion the posts and rails for the yard behind the new greenhouse where Royal Gift would stand next to Washington's prize Arabian stallion, Magnolio, and John Fairfax advertised the stud services of the Spanish jack, "the first of the kind that ever was in North-America." The advertisement assured readers that "the usefulness of mules, bred from a Jack of his size, either for the road or team, are well known to those who are acquainted with this mongrel race."[8]

The first efforts of Royal Gift disappointed and perplexed Washington, who for many years had closely managed the breeding of horses and his beloved fox hounds. The failure of the "very bony and stout made" jackass to perform at stud elicited some of Washington's rare and generally awkward attempts at humor. When he invited his nephew Bushrod to bring mares for breeding, he warned that Royal Gift was "too full of royalty, to have any thing to do with a plebean race." When William Fitzhugh sent several mares to be bred, Washington assured him "when my Jack is in the humour they shall derive all the benefits of his labours—for labour it appears to be," adding "I am not without hope, that when he becomes a little better acquainted with republican enjoyments, he will amend his manners, and fall into a better & more expeditious mode of doing business." Washington strangely imputed to the Spanish king Royal Gift's disappointing performance. The jack seemed to follow "what one may suppose to be the example of his late royal Master, who cannot, tho' past his grand climacterick, perform seldomer, or with more Majestic solemnity, than he does." The arrival of the first jenny solved the problem with the reluctant Royal Gift and eased Washington's frustration. When he returned a mare to

Fitzhugh, Washington explained "A female ass which I have obtained lately, has excited desires in the Jack, to which he seemed almost a stranger; making use of her as an excitement, I have been able to get several mares served." By the end of the following season, Washington was able to assure a Maryland planter, "Royal Gift never fails."[9]

With the arrival of the Maltese jack and the two jennies sent by Lafayette, Washington had the stock to begin his breeding project in earnest. To ensure that the benefits of the Spanish jack would not end with its own breeding life, Washington ordered another jenny from Surinam through the assistance of Alexandria merchants, who shipped as payment twenty-five barrels of superfine flour from Washington's gristmill. In his November 1785 census of livestock on his estate, Washington designated thirty-three mares he would breed with Royal Gift after his safe arrival. In 1788, he resolved that he would use his mares only to breed mules, and to that end he agreed to exchange the celebrated Magnolio with Henry Lee in return for land in Kentucky. Washington greatly expanded his stock of mares for the sole purpose of breeding mules. In the summer of 1789, he contacted merchants in New Jersey and Pennsylvania to procure at least twenty mares, and as many as twice that number if suitable ones could be found. Even with a greatly expanded stock of mares, the breeding of mules was a slow and often disappointing process, with many lost foals and the death of mules. In 1790, George Augustine Washington apologized for "the ill success which has attended the propigation of Mules," and in 1793 Washington complained, "I make a miserable hand of breeding Mules." Despite the setbacks, by the end of Washington's life each of the farms at Mount Vernon had more mules than any other draft animals. Washington also received revenue from the steady business of planters from throughout the Chesapeake who paid pasturage and stud fees to breed their mares and jennies with the several jacks at Mount Vernon in the 1790s.[10]

When he first inquired about the possibility of importing a Spanish jackass, Washington had explained to Hooe that breeding mules would provide a private convenience for himself and "a public benefit to this part of the country." In his correspondence with Lafayette, Washington was more explicit about the anticipated benefit of bringing a breeding jackass to his estate and to a region where planters relied so heavily on enslaved labor: "The Mules which proceed from the mixture of these Animals with the horse, are so much more valuable under the care which is usually bestowed on draught cattle by our Negroes, that I am daily more anxious to obtain the means for propagating them." The breeding of mules was one of the few major improvement projects of Washington's that had no parallel in Great Britain, and like other departures from British husbandry, it was rooted in Washington's perception of the special challenges of managing enslaved labor. He also wanted to provide other farmers a more economic draft animal. Washington explained to Arthur Young that through his breeding program, "I hope to secure a race of extraordinary goodness, which will stock the Country. Their longevity & cheap keeping will be circumstances much in their favor." Young wished him luck but had serious doubts based on failed experiments in Ireland, and he held fast to his opinion that oxen made the best animals for farm labor.[11]

Mules would offer Washington more than their hard work; they would be a proud display of his commitment to innovation. He told Young that "in a few years, I intend to drive no other in my carriage." The jacks and their progeny also provided a new way to collaborate with other important advocates of agricultural improvement throughout the United States. Several planters from Maryland, where livestock improvement was more advanced than in Virginia, brought their jennies and mares to breed with Royal Gift. From New York, John Jay reported that a plan by a group of farmers to establish a society for the breeding of horses and mules had been discouraged by the scarcity of suitable jackasses. He speculated that Royal Gift might be the foundation of "as good a Race of those animals as any in the world." In response, Washington invited Jay to send a jenny to Mount Vernon for breeding with any of the jacks without the usual charge. When Washington made his southern tour as president in 1791, the planters in Charleston and the surrounding area were so excited about the prospect of breeding mules that they convinced Washington to send Royal Gift to stand at stud for a season in South Carolina. Jeremiah Wadsworth, a leader in breeding improved livestock, sent an offer from the partners in a Connecticut firm who were eager to purchase one of the jackasses bred from Royal Gift.[12]

Royal Gift traveled by land to South Carolina, where he attracted the interest of the most prominent political and agricultural leaders. Charles Cotesworth Pinckney, Ralph Izard, Jacob Read, and Thomas Bee were among those who brought their mares and jennies to breed with the famous Spanish jackass. Unfortunately, the journey had taken a serious toll on Royal Gift's health, and few of the mares or jennies foaled. Royal Gift never recovered enough to stand at stud or to return to Virginia, and he died in South Carolina in 1796. Washington was most regretful that the relocation of Royal Gift from Virginia to South Carolina had yielded "so little public or private advantage." Despite the sad end of the Spanish jackass, Washington's success with the jackasses bred from Royal Gift at Mount Vernon and his support for breeding programs throughout the United States furthered public acclaim for his agricultural innovations.[13]

The leaders of the several agricultural societies established in the 1780s venerated Washington as the great patron of improvement in the United States and recognized the significance of his transition from revolutionary military leader to experimental farmer. The Philadelphia Society for Promoting Agriculture, organized in March 1785, elected Washington as a corresponding member, with the expectation that following the military service that contributed so much to the independence of the country, Washington would "chearfully, become a Member of a Society whose Views are solely directed to the Increase of it's Advantages, by cultivating one of the most usefull Arts of Peace." The South Carolina agricultural society, established later that year, elected Washington one of its first honorary members, a recognition "due to the man, who by his gallantry & Conduct, as a Soldier, contributed so eminently to stamp a Value on the Labours of every American Farmer; and who by his Skill and Industry in the Cultivation of his own Fields, has likewise distinguish'd himself as a Farmer." Washington readily accepted both honors, and he offered his encouragement to other improvement societies that elected him as a corresponding member and sent their published transactions.[14]

Washington attributed to the many local societies for the encouragement of agriculture "the perfection to which husbandry is now arrived in England." He believed the English example, like that previously developed by Scottish agriculturalists, demonstrated the likeliest path to improvement in the United States. The British societies facilitated the exchange of learning and experience among improving landowners, and Washington expected comparable groups in the United States would apply the principles of improved husbandry to their local conditions. "To a liberal communication of experiments must this Country be indebted for those profitable courses of crops which are best adapted to our climate—our soil—and our circumstances." In the 1780s, private societies in the United States and Canada reestablished networks for the exchange of scientific and agricultural experiments with Great Britain. Washington was interested in those societies that focused on large-scale commercial farming and the introduction of British husbandry in the United States, and he expected wealthy landowners to provide the leadership for agricultural change. Societies like that in Philadelphia were organized by urban residents who owned country estates, and among the founding members of the Philadelphia society were wealthy leaders of the patriot cause, most of whom had personal connections with Great Britain or France. Washington remained convinced that it would be through the investments and innovations of wealthy and knowledgeable landowners "that the Community may derive advantages from the experiments and discoveries of the more intelligent."[15]

After the founding of the Philadelphia society, Washington hoped every state in the union would establish similar organizations, and he was frustrated by his fellow Virginians' failure to establish one. He tried to persuade Alexander Spotswood to organize an agricultural society in the area around Fredericksburg, which Washington believed to have both land suitable for experiment and the greatest concentration of innovative farmers in the state. He knew that, like Spotswood, several of his associates in the area, including Charles Carter and William Fitzhugh, could afford to conduct the kind of experiments that would benefit the public. Washington, however, never offered to participate in the organization of an agricultural society, and no such group formed as a result of his suggestions. Despite his repeated calls for the collective promotion of improvement, Washington refrained from playing any public role in fostering those efforts, preferring to rely on personal influence and trusting in the strength of his example.[16]

The Philadelphia society became the most important of the institutional connections in the United States for Washington's farming pursuits, but his participation in the society was largely through private correspondence and friendship with its influential members, including the founding president, Samuel Powel, and Richard Peters. Washington received from the society a publication on crop rotations, samples of wheat from the Cape Colony in southern Africa, and a copy of the essay on farmyards that was awarded one of the society's premiums. While serving as a delegate to the Federal Convention, Washington in July 1787 attended a meeting of the Philadelphia society in Carpenter's Hall, and he visited the farms of some of its leading members. Sometime in the mid-1790s, the society fell into what its members later recalled as "a long sleep," likely contributing to Washington's growing disenchantment with the various agricultural societies in the United States and his disappointment that more had not been established. While the example of local agriculture societies in Great Britain and Ireland went unheeded, those nations moved forward with the organization of national societies that Washington anticipated would be among the most beneficial institutions in either country.[17]

In the years after 1785, Washington developed closer and more formative ties with British agriculturalists who demonstrated the innovation and initiative he found lacking among their counterparts in the United States. He relied on his British correspondents for practical advice, and he increasingly engaged them on matters related to agricultural policy and the political economy of their respective nations. During his presidency and the difficult negotiations to protect the new nation against the competing forces of Great Britain and France, these correspondences served to remind him of the potential for common enterprises among nations and of the larger significance of the agricultural changes Washington sought to perfect at his own estate. Washington more readily confided in British rather than American agricultural leaders about his deepening disappointment with the practice of farming in the United States.

The dialogue with British agriculturalists began with Arthur Young, who presented himself as a "brother farmer," and whose influence went far beyond the practical assistance he provided Washington in the selection of crops and advice on cultivation. The first volume of the *Annals of Agriculture,* from which Washington copied extensive notes on practical experiments, also introduced him to Young's anti-mercantilism and his sharp critique of what Young considered Britain's wasteful spending on warfare and empire. Young's opening essay, with its summation of the dilemma facing the British nation—"America is Lost! Must we fall beneath the blow? Or have we resources that may repair the mischiefs of the late unfortunate contest?"—had attracted the close attention of George III, who noted its warnings about the inevitable costs of defending distant imperial holdings

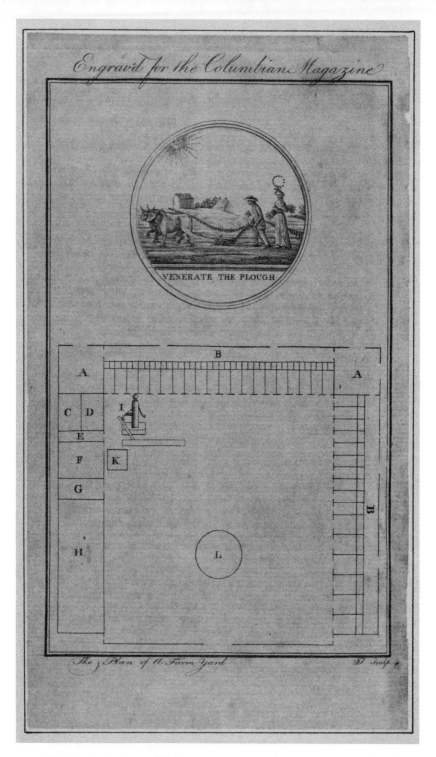

Fig 6.2   "The Plan of a Farm Yard - Venerate the Plow," *Columbian Magazine*, 1787. Washington received the farmyard plan and an accompanying essay, which were awarded a "Venerate the Plough" medal from the Philadelphia Society for Promoting Agriculture. He drew on the plan in the design of his own farmyard adjacent to the great barn at Union Farm. Washington was in frequent correspondence with the society, of which he was an honorary member. Library of Congress, Prints and Photographs Division, LC-DIG-ds-04633.

and of sacrificing the potential benefits of trade with an independent United States. Young argued that the money spent, first to defend and then to defeat the American colonies, would have been more productively invested in the reclamation and cultivation of wastelands in Great Britain, land that still awaited enclosure and improvement by the methods Young so tirelessly promoted.

Young's essay and much of the content of the *Annals* affirmed Washington's belief that agricultural improvement and the exchange of knowledge might lay the foundation for new and amicable relations between Great Britain and the United States. When Young wrote of the new United States, "I am clear that we shall reap more advantages from their trade as *friends* than ever we could derive from them as *colonies,*" he implicitly rejected the calls for neo-mercantilist restrictions on the trade of the United States. Washington considered British commercial discrimination and restrictions on the trading privileges of the former colonies as grave threats to the survival of the union of states. Young's essay made clear that some influential Britons opposed commercial confrontation with the United States and saw in a particular program of agricultural improvement the potential for shared prosperity. With his stated goal of publishing an agricultural journal dedicated to repairing "the waste of war," Young presented the prospect of the two nations working together toward mutually beneficial goals of agricultural productivity and the exchange of respective advantages in trade. In Washington, he found his most avid American reader.[18]

Washington's reading of the *Annals* and his correspondence with Young taught him more about the promoters of agricultural improvement in Great Britain. He read about Thomas William Coke, the great Whig champion of the American patriots during the Revolutionary War, who introduced new husbandry at his massive Norfolk estate, motivated, according to Young, by "the most liberal and public-spirited nature." In 1786 Young published in the *Annals* two letters, signed "Ralph Robinson" but written and submitted by George III, who described his conversations with a celebrated small farmer who lived near the royal residence in Richmond. Washington probably never learned about the king's authorship, but Young in his correspondence introduced Washington to the agricultural innovations of George III. Young sent Washington a sample of wheat with the explanation that Empress Catherine of Russia had offered it to George III, who in turn shared it with the nearby farmer he wrote about in the *Annals.* In his efforts to enlist Washington into the transnational efforts to improve the breeding of sheep, Young described the collaboration of the king and Sir Joseph Banks, the renowned naturalist, in an effort to develop superior stock from Spanish Merino sheep.[19]

Young solicited from Washington a sample of wool from the Mount Vernon flocks, which he then delivered to "an ingenious person" to spin into seven samples of yarn, from coarse to fine. Washington's long-time merchant in London successfully concealed the yarn to evade what Young decried as the "abominable monopolizing laws" that prohibited its shipment from Great Britain and also forbid his sending Washington one of the South Down rams he thought would suit conditions in Virginia. Young, however, had little understanding of farming in the United States, and he was confused or incredulous about much of what Washington reported in an extensive survey of agriculture in the Middle States and the Chesapeake. In frustration, Young wrote Washington, "To analyze your husbandry has the difficulty of a problem: I cannot understand it; and the more I know of it the more surprizing it appears." Young had never purposefully gathered information about farming in North America or the Caribbean, and Washington remained his only significant correspondent in the United States.[20]

In addition to the many articles he prepared or obtained from his Suffolk neighbors, Arthur Young filled his *Annals of Agriculture* with the results of farming experiments and descriptions of improvement projects undertaken throughout Great Britain and on the European continent. The periodical depended on a steady stream of submissions, and Young was relentless in pursuing contributions from prominent and innovative estate owners, most notably George III. Early in their correspondence, Young asked Washington if he might insert in the *Annals* some extracts from his letters, attributed by name. Washington admitted it might not be thought generous or proper that any farmer "should withhold his mite of information from the general stock," but he feared that publication of his letters might be characterized as "a piece of ostentation." With the abundance of caution that increased with his fame and veneration, Washington did not want to do anything that would even risk accusations of self-promotion. To explain his reticence, he offered Young a disingenuous picture of quiet retirement at Mount Vernon and his desire "to glide silently and unnoticed through the remainder of my life." He deferred, however, to Young's prudence to do what was best.[21]

In hopes of a more explicit grant of permission, Young sought to persuade Washington that his greatest influence would come not from his many agricultural experiments but rather from public recognition that the same man who "founded an empire on the basis of human liberty" also had such a close connection "with the plough." Young esteemed those who served mankind through agricultural improvement as good citizens, and publication of Washington's letters would promote the best kind of farming. Young added that he had already shared Washington's most recent letter with several knowledgeable friends who shared his enthusiasm. When in December 1791 Washington sent Young an extensive report on farming in the United States, he emphasized, with an intended finality, that his observations on farming were written for Young's private satisfaction. "It is not my wish that they should be promulgated as coming from me."[22]

Those who knew Washington better would probably have pressed the subject no further, but Young asked permission to publish the report. He argued that the ability to promote agricultural improvement was proportional to one's fame, and "for a man on whom the eyes of the universe are fixed it is some thing for the good of agriculture to have it known that he regards, practices and studies it." This appeal arrived with a new volume of the *Annals* in which Young, with no advance notice, published the barn design he had prepared for Mount Vernon, and noted in the accompanying text that it had been prepared at Washington's request. Washington again declined permission to publish the report, insisting that his writings would only expose the defective practices of farmers in the United States. Even after he entrusted Young with his plan to reorganize his entire estate—a plan Washington considered so sensitive that he asked Young to burn the letter if he deemed it improper, Young again implored him to allow publication in the *Annals* of his survey of the nation's agriculture.[23]

In the meantime, Washington had received reports from his former secretary Tobias Lear that must have raised suspicions of Young's opportunism. Young had sought out Lear when he arrived in London, and the two spent considerable time together. Lear heard rumors that Young's reversal in political positions—"he is now as high a monarchist as any in Britain"—followed his appointment to a lucrative sinecure as secretary to the Board of Agriculture. Lear also relayed gossip claiming that Young had never made half the experiments he claimed in the *Annals,* and that his own farm was "one of the most slovenly in the part of the Country where he lives." A few days after receiving one more entreaty from Young, Washington, in November 1794, reiterated that he had prepared the survey of agriculture to answer Young's private inquiries about the possible emigration of his son, and "my present situation, adds greater reluctance than heretofore, to see, or to know that any hastily written and indigested letters of mine, should be handed, *with my name* to them, to the public." It was the last letter exchanged between Washington and Young.[24]

Washington was hardly the only person to mistrust Young; Jefferson later dismissed the *Annals* as "written merely for money," and other contemporaries questioned the evidence for many of Young's claims, just as historians since have challenged them. Washington's unwillingness to publish his observations on farming, however, arose from more than the suspected self-aggrandizement of Arthur Young. In his pursuit of agricultural improvements, Washington had circumscribed himself with the same refusal of public advocacy that marked his otherwise ardent efforts to expand the powers of the federal government and to open the Potomac to navigation. His reticence predated the concern for discretion he expressed during John Jay's negotiation of a commercial treaty, which, as Washington inferred, made Young's last appeal particularly ill-timed. Washington believed that the influence of his public image as the disinterested Cincinnatus depended on the avoidance of any appearance of self-promotion, or what he described to Young and others as "ostentation." Washington trusted instead the power of his example in the reorganization of his estate and his private influence with leading agricultural improvement advocates in the United States and Great Britain.[25]

By the time Washington closed his correspondence with Young, he had established connections with other British agriculturalists who were eager for the support of the new president. In 1790, David Erskine, the Earl of Buchan, sought Washington's patronage for a new publication proposed by James Anderson, a leading Enlightenment figure in Edinburgh. *The Bee,* its title page announced, was "a work calculated to disseminate useful Knowledge among all ranks of people at a small expence," and Anderson

Gent.Mag.May 1809. Pt.I.p.401.

J.Anderson del.   Freeman sculp.

James Anderson, L.L.D.–F.R.S.–F.A.S.–S. &c.

Fig 6.3　James Anderson, by Samuel Freeman, 1809. Anderson of Edinburgh published *The Bee,* which sought to bring knowledge of improvement to broad audiences. Washington promoted the journal in the United States and recommended Anderson for membership in the American Philosophical Society. Anderson sent Washington his publications on agriculture and plant specimens from around the world, and he hired a gardener to work at Mount Vernon. Photograph © National Portrait Gallery, London.

was intent on making advances in agriculture, manufactures, and the arts available to audiences usually neglected by literary enterprises. Washington was so impressed with the prospectus for the journal that he placed his own notice in New York's *Gazette of the United States* to promote its circulation. In September 1791, Anderson sent Washington the first four volumes "as a small testimony of respect from a lover of mankind to one of their principal benefactors." Washington became a subscriber, and Anderson became a trusted correspondent on whom Washington would continue to rely for information about agriculture and politics.[26]

Sir John Sinclair, the chairman of the British Wool Society and a tenacious proponent of agricultural improvement in his native Scotland, introduced himself to Washington in 1792 by sending several published papers along with some queries about sheep husbandry in the United States. Washington apologized that his country could offer no valuable information regarding sheep, although he reported on his own efforts to improve the stock on his farms. Washington was intrigued by Sinclair's proposal for a statistical study of Scotland, calling for a systematic collection of information about land, population, and agriculture in each county. Such a close examination must, Washington predicted, "result in greatly ameliorating the condition of the people—promoting the interests of civil society—and the happiness of Mankind at large." When Sinclair in 1793 won support from Prime Minister William Pitt for the establishment of the Board of Agriculture, he led that body as its founding president in commissioning agricultural surveys for every county in Great Britain. Sinclair was confident that the work of the Board of Agriculture would benefit the United States as much as Great Britain, an opinion with which Washington fully concurred.[27]

By the time he initiated his correspondence with Washington, Sinclair had concluded that agricultural improvement in any nation depended on more than the experiments and investments of enlightened landowners; it required the encouragement of government. Since the 1770s, more and more British proponents of improvement had called for governmental support of research in agriculture and science. Lord Kames in *The Gentleman Farmer* proposed "A Board for Improving Agriculture," in part to compensate for the anticipated loss of the American colonies, and Young's inaugural volume of the *Annals* called for governmental support of research in the natural sciences. Sinclair encouraged Washington to seek congressional approval for a board of agriculture in the United States, and sent him the outline and instructions for the county surveys initiated by the British board. The more Sinclair learned about agriculture in the United States, the more convinced he was "that the Farmers of America want *some Spur* to acquire agricultural information, as well as a Spirit to communicate to others, what they have already acquired: In short, that they should *read, speak, and write more,* upon that Subject." If Congress did not establish a board of agriculture, Sinclair suggested that a comparable private institution be established in Philadelphia to correspond with agricultural societies in each state. Washington thought that the creation of smaller societies, organized by the states, would build support for a national board, but the proposals for a Pennsylvania society, which he sent Sinclair, failed to win approval, offering further evidence that the United States fell far short of Great Britain in the organization of local agricultural societies and in governmental sponsorship of improvement.[28]

Unlike Young, who found much of what Washington reported about American farming to be incomprehensible, Sinclair quickly recognized in the agriculture of the United States a vast potential for shared knowledge and valuable trade between the new nation and Great Britain. After consulting Enoch Edwards, an accomplished Pennsylvania farmer resident in London, Sinclair in August 1793 forwarded to Washington and Jefferson a detailed account of American agricultural practices that the British should adopt and of American commodities that might be the basis of reciprocally advantageous trade. Sinclair anticipated that these agricultural and commercial ties would surely lead the two nations "to an understanding together, that a treaty of Commerce beneficial to both might be formed, & that every remnant of prejudice or jealousy would soon be completely done away." As James Anderson had similarly envisioned in his prospectus for *The Bee,* Sinclair imagined the former opponents in war joined in a new kind of empire based on culture and identity. With a proper treaty, "those who speak the language of England, might soon attain, as much power abroad and happiness at home, as any wise nation can aspire to."[29]

Although Washington recognized the same potential for reciprocal benefits of trade, he had no illusions about the obstacles to any treaty guaranteeing peaceful commerce and protection against commercial discrimination by Great Britain or France, particularly after the outbreak of war between those nations in 1793. In the spring of 1794, as John Jay traveled to Great Britain with instructions to negotiate a commercial treaty, Washington conceded to the Earl of Buchan that the conflicts in Europe, which he called "a continual state of disquietude," placed "the prospect of peace too far off & the promised millennium at an awful distance from our day."

At such time as nations abandoned their "provocations to war" and sought "to excel each other in acts of Philanthropy; industry and œconomy; in encouraging *useful* arts & manufactures," they would be able to promote a liberal exchange of "the products of one country & clime for those of another." For Washington, the shared project of improvement remained the likeliest foundation of a sustainable peace. Sinclair again emphasized to Washington the cultural bonds that remained between the nations, even in the face of commercial conflict, "for though our Governments are now distinct, the People are in fact the same, without any possible inducement to quarrel, if they knew their respective interests."[30]

Through much of Washington's presidency, Anderson, Sinclair, and Buchan offered the most influential perspectives on the British culture of improvement. Like Lord Kames in *The Gentleman Farmer,* these Scottish correspondents all felt an urgency about the project of improvement that struck a resonant note with Washington, who shared an acute sense of his own country's backwardness compared with the husbandry of England. Sinclair and Anderson offered Washington different but complementary perspectives on British agriculture in the 1790s, with Sinclair emphasizing policy and governmental support and Anderson focused on science and findings emerging from a global exchange of studies of the natural world. The Earl of Buchan, a patron rather than a practitioner of agriculture and science, emphasized political economy and the unique opportunities for the United States to escape the contests of Europe. Buchan's wish for the United States was that it be prosperous and happy enough to "be little heard of in the great world of Politics," and advised Washington that nothing was as likely to contribute to that outcome "as agricultural & mechanical improvements," and the spread of science and literature among the people. In his reply, Washington quoted those words as an expression of his own conviction that the United States should have no involvement with the contests of European nations, and should focus instead on the peaceful exchange of commodities "with all the inhabitants of the earth." Buchan further encouraged Washington to use his public office to promote a national program of education and "Union with the Red Natives," in a general policy of enlightened leadership that would make the United States a model for other nations. Anderson recognized that public affairs must be Washington's priority, but he urged Washington not to ignore agriculture, which had its own public benefit as the first among "those branches of knowledge that tend to promote the peace of society."[31]

The ongoing dialogue with the three representatives of the Scottish Enlightenment, like Washington's correspondence with Edward Newenham of Ireland, reflected a faith in a kind of universality of improvement that bound together these elite circles in Europe and the United States. Through much of the 1780s and 1790s, Newenham offered Washington his commentary on conflicts in Europe. Washington agreed that the recurring wars made clear that "Mankind are not yet ripe for the Millenial State," but soon after Virginia's ratification of the Constitution, he assured Newenham of his hope that "the United States of America will be able to keep disengaged from the labyrinth of European politics & Wars." The month before he departed for his inauguration as president, he wrote Newenham again. Through his innovations and experiments as a farmer, he explained, "I have only been made more sensible, upon every new tryal, that this *count[r]y* is susceptible of various and great improvements in its agriculture. It is on *that resource* it must depend essentially for its prosperity." Commerce and the useful arts would be important adjuncts, but farming would fix the new nation's place among nations. Washington's continued communications with these like-minded correspondents in Great Britain and Ireland reaffirmed his determination to maintain the neutrality of the United States during his presidency and deepened his conviction that his estate was uniquely prepared to demonstrate the agricultural productivity that would secure the nation's advantages in transatlantic commerce.[32]

Sinclair and Anderson, like Arthur Young before them, answered Washington's continuing demand for agricultural knowledge. Washington asked James Anderson to send any books that explained principles and combined practice with theory. Having regrettably spent so much time away from his farms, he confessed to Anderson that he felt he must rely on the experience and knowledge of others. Anderson kept Washington supplied with his own publications about farming in Great Britain, including *Essays Relating to Agriculture and Rural Affairs,* and with books that reflected his curiosity about agriculture and plant life from around the world, particularly the distant parts of the expanding British empire. Washington asked Sinclair to instruct his bookseller to continue sending the county surveys, more than eighty of which were in Washington's library at the end of his life, and Sinclair sent additional sets for Washington to distribute. Sinclair also forwarded records of the proceedings of the Board of Agriculture and his own publications, which Washington added to his library.[33]

Washington's relationships with the British agriculturalists established new ties between improvement advocates in the two countries. Young relied on Washington to deliver volumes of the *Annals of Agriculture* to the Philadelphia Society for Promoting Agriculture, and Washington offered to assist in the Philadelphia reprinting of British county surveys from the Board of Agriculture, just as he had promoted subscriptions to *The Bee*. The Board of Agriculture elected Washington and John Jay to be its first honorary members from the United States. Washington's agricultural observations reached a broader British audience when Sinclair, without Washington's knowledge, introduced their correspondence into the official minutes of the Board of Agriculture and included several letters from Washington in the published records of the board. Washington in turn introduced the board officers to Richard Peters, "one of the most judicious farmers within my reach," and he circulated Sinclair's reports among federal officeholders in Philadelphia. When an honorary board member, William Strickland, traveled to the United States to prepare an agricultural survey, Sinclair recruited Washington to advise him on his travels, which included a visit to Mount Vernon. Washington introduced Strickland to leading farmers in Maryland and Virginia, including Jefferson, who welcomed him to Monticello. Washington sponsored Anderson and Buchan as members of the American Philosophical Society, to which they were admitted in 1794, and both contributed publications and maps to the society. When Tobias Lear traveled to England and Scotland to explore private business opportunities, Sinclair welcomed him as a kind of agricultural emissary of Washington at a reception in London with leading advocates of improvement, including Arthur Young and the American expatriate Enoch Edwards. Washington stood at the center of this transatlantic community of improvement, and his stature and practical commitment to farming reinforced the ties between the two nations.[34]

The British agricultural correspondents expanded Washington's already far-reaching network of seed and plant exchange. The collection and sharing of plant material became a central object of Great Britain's expansion of its geographical reach in the decades after 1760, and this scientific curiosity about new regions was closely linked to the system of agricultural improvement based on enclosure and the management of large estates. Washington became a beneficiary of and participant in the wide net cast by the British in their pursuit of useful plants. Alexander Anderson, the director of the British botanical garden on the Caribbean island of Saint Vincent, sent Washington a parcel of seeds and a request to distribute them to Henry Laurens in South Carolina and Bishop James Madison in Virginia. Washington sent word to Jamaica that he would like a sample of the breadfruit plant recently introduced from the South Pacific, and he received thirty-nine different plants as well as catalogs of plants cultivated in Jamaica's botanical garden. James Anderson, an ardent collector and distributor of seeds, introduced himself to Washington by offering the seeds that would yield the first Swedish turnips, or rutabagas, cultivated in the United States. Anderson shared his view with Washington that the collection and exchange of plants from all over the world were essential to increasing agricultural productivity and especially food supplies, even if the great majority of experiments with them failed. The benefits of introducing broad clover, turnips, and potatoes in Great Britain, and rice to America, were so great as to demand more experiments with the sorts of exotic seeds he sent Washington—tartarian buckwheat to feed cattle and a sesame that he thought might be grown for its oil in the warmer climate of the Carolinas. Anderson sent Washington a type of turnip seed from Tibet, by way of former British governor-general of India Warren Hastings, who, "whatever may have been his conduct in his public station," was a "promoter of science and the useful arts."[35]

Improving farmers in the United States also sent Washington rare seeds, such as the Nankeen cotton seeds that John Jay forwarded after receiving them from a planter conducting experiments in South Carolina. Some seeds arrived through diplomatic channels, including the Barbary wheat and melon seeds sent by Joel Barlow when he was the American consul in Algiers. Thomas Pinckney and Rufus King, in their respective terms as United States minister to Great Britain, served as semi-official channels through which British agriculturalists transmitted to Washington their letters and gifts. Washington rarely reciprocated with gifts of his own seeds, at least beyond Virginia and Maryland, unless he received a specific request. Lafayette asked Washington to procure various seeds of trees, grasses, and curious plants from Kentucky for use in the garden of Louis XVI. Lafayette also introduced Washington to André Michaux, a prominent French botanist, who visited Mount Vernon as part of his world tour, on behalf of Louis XVI, to make a complete study of trees and plants. From France, Gouverneur Morris sent Washington seeds from the garden of the king. These varied exchanges greatly expanded Washington's knowledge of plants and connections with a world of improvement beyond the United States, and they heightened his awareness of the audience and expectations for his pursuit of the New Husbandry at Mount Vernon.[36]

The most important public demonstration of Washington's commitment to agricultural improvement was at his estate, which he designed to display his knowledge and innovation for the remarkable range of visitors who came to meet him. Like the owners of the large improved estates of Great Britain, Washington pursued an aesthetic ideal of farming that extended beyond the imposing agricultural buildings to the landscape itself, and, as on British estates, he aspired to embed agricultural improvements in the countryside as though they were part of a natural order. As early as the 1710s, Joseph Addison in *The Spectator* had proposed the erasure of distinctions between an estate's park and its farms, and the ongoing consolidation of large estates in Great Britain encouraged the placement of improved farms within a unified and carefully constructed landscape, epitomized by the expansive designs of Capability Brown. Massive drainage projects and the elimination of "wastes" were intended to beautify the countryside at the same time that they opened new land to cultivation. Trees, planted in almost unimaginable numbers, framed the working fields and further integrated the farms into their natural surroundings. Sheep pastures blurred the distinction between parks and farmyards. The success of British improvement projects would be celebrated as much for the aesthetic beauty of the agricultural landscape and the neatness of the farm buildings as for the productivity of cultivation and the utility of new breeds of livestock. The redesign of the countryside was accomplished through the application of an enormous amount of labor to create an essentially new landscape that embodied the rational order of scientific agriculture and displayed the landowner's cosmopolitan learning.[37]

Before and during the Revolutionary War, Washington made initial efforts to blend the working landscape of his estate with the more refined areas surrounding his residence by opening views from the Mansion House to outlying plantations. As he completed the redesign of Mount Vernon's plantations in the late 1780s, Washington opened other woods to create vistas to and from the Mansion House. He explained that he wanted the ground cleared outside a pasture along the road from Gum Spring "that you might see the Mansion house as soon as you should enter the little old field beyond it." Along the grandest vista, from the west gate to the Mansion House, Washington wanted the path, more than one hundred feet wide, to be plowed and sown with buckwheat, followed by timothy or orchard grass, which would place crops representative of his new farming along the route by which most visitors approached the house. Washington sketched for his farm manager a "second Visto" from the Mansion House to Muddy Hole branch, which was to be prepared provisionally, so that he could assess the view upon his next arrival home. Washington's aide and biographer, David Humphreys, described the effect of another fashioned view from the Mansion House to River Plantation; "on the opposite side of a little creek to the Northward, an extensive plain, exhibiting cornfields & cattle grazing, affords in summer a luxurious landscape to the eye."[38]

In addition to the views he devised from across the working plantations to the Mansion House, Washington ordered secondary avenues to be cut from the intersecting roads to the farmyards at the center of each plantation so that travelers could see his improvement projects. His 1793 survey of the five farms shows the bold, tree-lined avenue approaching the large barn and the surrounding buildings at Union Farm. Within the boundaries of the estate, new lanes and fences created sight lines to prominent structures, such as from the gates of Dogue Run farm to its barn and from the Union Farm barn to the gristmill along Dogue Creek. Washington redoubled the efforts, begun by Lund during the Revolutionary War, to line the principal roads and farm lanes with trees. He preferred the native cedar, which grew in abundance on the estate, and honey locust, the seeds of which he sent from Philadelphia. When seedlings from the cedar berries painstakingly gathered by enslaved workers failed to survive the summer heat, Washington instructed his farm manager to direct the work of digging mature trees out of the frozen ground and transplanting them along the new lanes. Trees were also important ornamental elements in the working parts of the estate, such as along the millrace. When Washington created new fields, he directed that scenic groves of trees remain in place, especially where they were within important lines of sight, even if they interfered with efficient plowing.[39]

Washington's attention to the appearance of the agricultural landscape went well beyond grand vistas and the architecture of barns. He was determined to maintain the neatness of fields, fences, and working areas of his estate. British visitors commented on the weed-filled fields of farms in the United States, and Washington insisted that his fields should not be hardened by "trash." In a letter to Anthony Whitting he wrote, "There is no greater eye sore to me than to see foul meadows." The concern was in part practical; the common practice of leaving a field untended for a year between grain crops only hardened the land, and the foul meadows were as destructive of plows and scythes as they were objectionable to the observer. In another letter to Whitting, Washington approvingly cited the authority of John Lambert, an English farmer who immigrated to the United States, and who attributed the poor lands and disappointing crops he saw to the weeds he found everywhere. The remedy was constant plowing to eradicate the weeds and to prepare the ground for grasses. Washington reminded a later manager, "all grasses ought to be sown on *clean* & well prepared ground, especially those near a dwelling house, w[hi]ch attract the eyes of all visitors."[40]

No component of the landscape figured more persistently in Washington's mind than living fences. In part to conserve the finite resources of timber on the estate, Washington planned to replace post-and-rail fences, which he called dead fences, with living ones created by planting hedges of an impassable mix of trees and shrubs. The decrepit condition of so many of the wooden fences was a blight on a landscape that Washington wished to make neat and clean, and their maintenance required the diversion of labor that could otherwise be applied to more productive work. During winter months, enslaved men and women at the outlying plantations regularly spent days repairing existing fences, and overseers were required to inspect wooden fences twice weekly. Rough-hewn fences, often made of fallen timber, also stood as a rude contrast to the hedging recommended by the British treatises from which Washington learned about the New Husbandry.[41]

For many British farmers, especially on the large estates consolidated in the most recent phase of enclosure, hedges were nearly synonymous with fences. Hedging fences, or hedgerows, had been used in England for centuries, but they came to define the look of the countryside only in the second half of the eighteenth century, when they were encouraged by Parliament and used to demarcate new fields and pastures on improved farms. Thomas Hale's *A Compleat Body of Husbandry,* which guided Washington's earliest improvements, declared of hedges that "no article, in the husbandman's whole concern, is of more importance, . . . they are the defence and guard of all the rest." Washington first directed a concerted effort to plant hedges as fencing during the Revolutionary War, when he instructed Lund Washington to experiment with cedar, honey locust, and hawthorn for hedging. Washington later included willows, Lombardy poplar, and sycamores in the mix, and he encouraged his manager to establish nurseries for raising the hedging plants. Once the cedar trees were transplanted and large enough, Washington wanted them plashed, a technique of interweaving branches he had seen demonstrated by William Bartram at his famous garden in Philadelphia. Washington intended to combine live fences and ditches to replace all the wooden fences that separated fields and marked the perimeters of the plantations.[42]

Hedging was one of the essential skills Washington expected of the English farmer he wanted to hire as he began his new course of farming in 1785, and he entrusted James Bloxham with the care of the honey locusts, transplanted by the thousands to establish live fences at the Ferry and French's plantations. Washington noted in his excerpts from Kames's *The Gentleman Farmer* that "the advantages of the white thorn for fence above every plant is well understood," and he subsequently ordered English seed, which he also gave to Bloxham to cultivate for fencing. From *The Farmer's Compleat Guide,* Washington copied advice on the best plants for hedging, including furse, which he ordered from Ireland for further experiments.[43]

The establishment of fencing hedges as prescribed in the British literature became a fixed determination of Washington, who accused a succession of managers of disregarding the live fences and treating them as "a Subordinate object." Washington reminded Whitting, "I mean to make hedging a *business,* and a *primary one.*" To his several white overseers, Washington wrote in 1793 with an almost inexplicable hyperbole, "There is nothing I more ardently desire; nor indeed is there anything more essential to my permanent interest, than raising of live fences . . . Yet nothing has ever been, in a general way, more shamefully neglected or mismanaged." He insisted that the planting of live fences was more important and potentially more profitable than increasing his crops of grain. If forced to choose between abandoning his lucrative fishery for a year or postponing work on his hedging projects, "I should not hesitate a moment in giving up the first; for I would make every thing yield to the latter."[44]

Washington was not alone in his expectation of the benefits of live fences. The Philadelphia Society for Promoting Agriculture in 1785 offered one of its first premiums to encourage the production of thorn and honey locust seeds for hedging, but for Washington, the transition to live fences assumed an exaggerated significance as a measure of his success as an enlightened farmer. The establishment of the hedges depended on the landowner's knowledge of plants and understanding of landscape design, as well as the close management of laborers. The hedges, enhancing the landscape with their neatness and a simulation of natural order, represented much of what Washington most prized about British husbandry and stood in stark contrast to the unkempt appearance of farms in Virginia. Washington explained to Whitting that the living fences were not just a way to conserve timber and labor, they were meant to be "ornamental to the Farm, & reputable to the Farmer."[45]

As this reference to reputation suggests, the design of the agricultural landscape at Mount Vernon framed the public display of Washington's innovative farming. In Great Britain, the most prominent estate owners who embraced agricultural improvement established "Home Farms" at which they actively participated in farming and demonstrated the results of experiments and the merits of new methods of cultivation. Washington similarly set aside the Mansion House farm for experiment and display of what he called his rural amusements, rather than commercial production of grain, but he conceived of the entire estate as a kind of Home Farm for the display of the husbandry he hoped would serve as testament to his accomplishments and as an example for the public. He fashioned the landscape of the working farms to accentuate the benefits of improvement. An Italian visitor was struck by "the spectacle of a broad expanse of cultivated terrain contrasting with the adjacent hills still clad in ancient oaks and lofty pines."[46]

Visitor after visitor noted that Mount Vernon looked different from other farms in the United States, and especially from other plantations in Virginia. Benjamin Henry Latrobe, recently arrived from England, came to Mount Vernon after a journey through Virginia and reported that "Good fences, clear grounds and extensive cultivation strike the eye as something uncommon in this part of the World." Another English visitor, Samuel Vaughan, found "the farms neat, kept perfectly clean & in prime order." A Polish statesman was surprised to learn that Washington had never left America, since the appearance of the house and estate suggested "he had seen the most beautiful examples in England of this style." A British Army officer visiting Mount Vernon several years after the death of Capability Brown recognized that Washington was "laying out his grownds with great tast in the English fashion. Brown was he alive and here would certainly say this spot had great Capabilities." The same officer paid Washington the highest compliment he might have desired by declaring, "It is the compleatest farm Yard and he appears to be the compleatest Gentleman farmer I have ever met in America and perhaps I may Add England."[47]

Many of the visitors recognized how these agricultural improvements enhanced the reputation of the great man they came to honor. When Samuel Powel, the founding president of the Philadelphia agricultural society, visited Mount Vernon with his wife, Elizabeth, they accompanied the Washingtons on a ride to four of the estate's plantations and observed the treading out of wheat. "The General," Powel found, "pays great Attention to husbandry & is, with reason I believe, said to be the best Farmer in the State." In November 1788, the new French minister to the United States, the Comte de Moustier, arrived at Mount Vernon with several prominent

Fig 6.4   Detail, frieze above the doorway in the New Room, Mount Vernon. For the completion of the largest and most refined room in the Mansion House, Washington worked with a skilled plasterer to design agricultural themes for the stuccowork. The crossed rake and scythe on the frieze complemented the images of wheat and harvest implements featured in the ceiling medallions. Courtesy of Mount Vernon Ladies' Association.

French guests and asked to see the barn being constructed according to the design of Arthur Young. From there, the party continued on foot with Washington to visit the gristmill, walking a circuit of seven miles before returning to the Mansion House. Moustier thought the model of farming at Mount Vernon, presented as an example for the citizens of the United States, heightened Washington's renown as a hero. "The Barn which you have built is a true monument of Patriotism," he concluded, "as it is intended to preserve the produce of a new mode of cultivation, which will greatly conduce to the happiness and prosperity of a people who are to form a nation." In support of Washington's improvements, Moustier went on to recommend a varnish for the wood of the barn, a preferred arrangement of the cattle stall, and, after consulting the *Encyclopédie,* a recipe for the mortar between the bricks.[48]

When visitors entered the mansion, they saw in the New Room the agricultural motifs that ornamented the most elegant space in the house. Begun in 1774 and completed only in 1787, the New Room, with its Palladian window and large collection of pictures, was a display of architectural fashion and aesthetic taste. On the walls and ceiling was stuccowork, which Washington understood to be "the present taste in England." Washington hired John Rawlins, an English-born plasterer who had executed extremely fine stuccowork in Annapolis, and on a visit to Mount Vernon in September 1785, Rawlins discussed with Washington the design for the ornamentation of the New Room. Unlike the room's English-made mantelpiece, with its classical pastoral scenes that Washington deemed too elegant for his "Republican stile of living," the agricultural imagery Rawlins developed in consultation with Washington reflected the new course of husbandry recently initiated at Mount Vernon and the georgic vision of farming. The design for the moldings in each corner of the ceiling included images of the essential implements associated with the cultivation and harvest of wheat: a rake and pitchfork; a spade and pick; a sickle with a sheaf of ripe wheat; and a scythe and flail for threshing. Surrounding the room was a frieze with a repeated pattern of a crossed rake and scythe.[49]

Atop the Mansion House, crowning the cupola that had long sat unfinished, Washington placed a weathervane of his own design. Instead of a directional arrow, Washington chose the silhouette of a bird "with an olive branch in its Mouth," and "with spread wings." The weathervane was crafted by Joseph Rakestraw in Philadelphia during the summer of the Federal Convention and delivered to Mount Vernon for installation before Washington returned home in late September 1787. The gilded dove of peace, visible on approach to the Mansion House, signaled to visitors the aspiration of Washington to offer his agricultural estate as a fulfillment of the scriptural instruction to turn swords into ploughshares and make war no more.[50]

· *7* ·

The Farmer President

Several days after signing into law the Residence Act, by which Congress designated Philadelphia as the seat of the federal government for the next ten years, Washington in July 1790 wrote a confidential note to a friend, the merchant Clement Biddle. Since the previous winter, Biddle and a business partner, Henry Drinker, had advertised in Philadelphia newspapers the availability of several small farms for purchase on the outskirts of the city. Washington, who had first read the sales notice several months earlier, proposed to exchange a much larger tract of land he owned in western Pennsylvania for one of the farms, or, if they had already been sold, to rent one of the properties. With the prospect of several years' residence in Philadelphia ahead of him, Washington hoped to find a place "for the amusement of farming, and for the benefit arising from exercise."[1]

With a candor that prompted him to request that Biddle burn the letter after reading it, Washington explained that after consulting with his physicians he had concluded that the diversion of farming would relieve the physical and intellectual pressures that had endangered his health during the first year of his presidency. Accustomed to the active pursuits "in which the mind has been agreeably amused," Washington found that his current position, with its lack of physical exercise, "and where the thoughts are continually on the stretch, has been the cause of more illness and severe attacks of my constitution, within the last twelve months, than I had undergone in 30 years preceding put together. A deviation therefore is necessary." Following a year in which he suffered three serious illnesses, Washington believed his well-being depended on a regular opportunity to farm.

Washington's complicated proposal of a land exchange and the shortage of funds for an outright purchase made acceptance of the offer unlikely, and Biddle confirmed that the sellers would consider only cash. Washington found no farm for his own management, but after moving to Philadelphia he discovered in the city and the surrounding countryside opportunities to engage with farmers and to learn about advances in cultivation. Philadelphia was the thriving center of agricultural improvement and scientific inquiry in the United States, and over the next seven years, Washington would observe the practices that made Pennsylvania farming so productive and so distinct from the agriculture of Virginia. His residence in Philadelphia, like his experience as president, would change the way Washington farmed at his own estate.[2]

◦   ◦   ◦

While the federal government was still resident in New York City, Washington in the fall of 1789 embarked on his first presidential tour, beginning with the three New England states that were part of the union. He told Secretary of the Treasury Alexander Hamilton that he wished to see the "growth and Agriculture" of the states as well as to learn about the citizens' disposition toward the new government. As he traveled from New York to New Hampshire, he noted the methods of farming that differed so significantly from those of Virginia. In New York, Washington found land so intensely cultivated that the divisions between towns and the surrounding farms were barely distinguishable. Speaking to farmers along a road outside Hartford, Connecticut, he learned the average yield per acre for wheat, corn, and oats. He found several examples of local connections between farming and manufactures. In Hartford, he visited the woolen manufactory at which he ordered a suit for himself and breeches for his enslaved servants. In Portsmouth, New Hampshire, a local clergyman showed Washington cloth dyed with Indian corn and "equal to any colours I had ever seen." In Wallingford and other Connecticut towns, he saw the cultivation of white mulberry and the production of silk in both

households and workshops. In this section of the country he had not visited since the Revolutionary War, Washington recognized a distinctive sort
of prosperity. As he passed through the farmland along the Connecticut
River, he noted "a great equality in the People of this State—Few or no op-
pulent Men and no poor."[3]

The following spring, on a short tour of Long Island, Washington focused almost exclusively on farming. Much of the land he saw was of poor
quality but made productive by the heavy application of dung carted from
New York City, and those farms closest to the city were "in a higher state
of cultivation & vegitation of Grass & grain forwarded than any place else
I had seen." According to the farmers Washington met, the regular use of
manure increased crop yields per acre by forty or even fifty percent. On
his return, Washington recorded his general observations on crop yields,
the system of plowing and rotation, and the live fences made of whatever
grew by chance.[4]

On his southern tour in the spring of 1791, Washington for the first time
viewed the very different landscape and agriculture of the Carolinas and
Georgia. Much of the land, with its sandy soil and sparse growth of pines,
appeared inhospitable to the farming he practiced and promoted. Once
he arrived in South Carolina, he found areas of rice cultivation that stood
in stark contrast to the country through which he traveled, but for much
of the journey, both along the coast and on his return to Virginia by way of
an inland route, Washington found a countryside that defied his notions
of improvement. The road from Columbia to Camden, South Carolina,
went through the most miserable pine barren he had ever seen. Only when
he traveled above Charlotte, North Carolina, did he see the first meadows
since leaving Virginia, and the beginnings of wheat cultivation. South Carolina planters had, in fact, pursued scientific farming and corresponded
with British agriculturalists before planters in the Chesapeake, but Washington fixed his interest on the grain-based agriculture that he believed
would best support commerce and the westward expansion of the United
States.[5]

Most of the southern countryside struck Washington as unfamiliar and
often crude. Outside the large towns or the low country estates in South
Carolina, he saw not a single elegant house. The accommodations along
both routes were "extremely indifferent—the houses being small and badly

provided either for man or horse." In Charleston, Washington met with the founders of the agricultural improvement society that had granted him honorary membership and with whom he agreed to share Royal Gift, but beyond that city and its environs, he noted in the three southern states little evidence of enlightened husbandry or experiment. When he found interest in improvement, he went to great lengths and personal expense to encourage it. After meeting John Chesnut in Charleston and being entertained by him at his residence in Camden, Washington sent him a drill plow of his own design, which he believed would, when applied to the sowing of indigo, "be productive of dispatch, regularity, and an abridgement of labour." If it proved useful for the planting interest of South Carolina, Washington added, "my agency therein will be most agreeably rewarded."[6]

On his tours as president, Washington was as likely to record the varieties of farming throughout the nation as to comment on the political life of the places he visited, and he returned with a greater determination to focus his improvements on the grain production that would support commerce and manufactures in the new nation and white settlement of the West. Most of what he observed in New England and the lower south had little to teach him about his own farming in Virginia, but in Pennsylvania he found advances in agriculture that he recognized as superior to what he had accomplished at Mount Vernon. In 1794, on his return from an expedition to suppress the Whiskey Rebellion that followed tax protests in the western part of that state, Washington observed the varied farming in a wide area of Pennsylvania beyond the improved estates of his friends in Philadelphia. While cultivation elsewhere in the state varied, much of it was excellent. Between Reading and Lebanon, where most of the farmers were German settlers, Washington thought "the Country is extremely fine—The lands rich—The Agriculture good—as the buildings also are, especially their Barns, which are large & fine; and for the most part of Stone." Elsewhere he saw very good land in different stages of improvement.[7]

Agriculture in Pennsylvania became a new standard that guided Washington in his weekly instructions for the management of his farms. On his rides in the countryside outside the city, Washington made inquiries of local farmers about the proper planting of potatoes and hedging. As he directed his own manager on when and how to sow crops, he cited the practice of Philadelphia area farmers. He told Anthony Whitting to use only a light cover of soil on clover, "Harrowing Clover Seed in, in the vicinity of this City is quite dis-used, and I never Saw better Clover any where than is about it." When Whitting described the drought that prevented him from preparing the ground for buckwheat, Washington admonished him that, under the same conditions for that crop near Philadelphia, "the Farmers persevered until they got in the seed & now nothing can be more promising than it is." The esteemed mills along the Brandywine and elsewhere in Pennsylvania became the model that Washington expected his own miller to follow in the production of superfine flour.[8]

Soon after his 1789 arrival in New York, Washington visited the Murray Hill farm of the Baron von Poellnitz to view his various agricultural innovations and collection of farming implements. Of particular interest was a version of the threshing machine invented by William Winlaw, which Washington had read about in the *Annals of Agriculture* in 1787. Poellnitz personally demonstrated several plows of his own design and his machine for measuring the optimal force applied to each. Washington was so impressed with the horse-hoe plow that he ordered one made to the same design to be shipped to Mount Vernon. In January 1790, Washington returned to the same farm to watch the threshing machine produce a half-bushel of clean wheat in just fifteen minutes, and he immediately thought of a way to make the work of the machine more efficient in winnowing wheat. The following year in Philadelphia, the president invited Thomas Jefferson to join him on a visit to Samuel Powel's farm for a demonstration of another threshing machine, this one invented by Arthur Anderson. Powel, in a letter to Arthur Young published in the *Annals of Agriculture,* described the machine as capable of threshing and cleaning grain from sheaves brought from the harvest field with no preliminary preparation. The model could deliver six bushels an hour, and its inventor expected a larger version to produce more than one hundred bushels a day, all fit for the miller. A threshing machine promised many efficiencies, including work for the enslaved not fully employed in other agricultural labor, and Washington thought the Winlaw thresher in particular, with its ease of operation, could be managed by women or boys aged twelve to fourteen. Washington also believed a machine was "vastly to be preferred to treading, which is hurtful to horses, filthy to the Wheat, & not more expeditious, considering the numbers that are employed in the process."[9]

The most significant technological advancement Washington adopted at Mount Vernon while president was the automated milling system invented by Oliver Evans of Delaware. In December 1790, Washington and Jefferson signed the federal government's patent number three, granting Evans the rights to his design of a system that relied on a single source of power to move grain through the entire process of milling, cooling, cleaning, and packing the flour in barrels. A diagram of the elaborate, multistory works appeared in the January 1791 edition of the *Universal Asylum and Columbian Magazine,* to which Washington subscribed. The Evans system, in addition to its speed and efficiency, operated with only one-fifth of the laborers required by traditional milling. The introduction of the Evans system coincided with increased European demand for flour, and market prices encouraged mill owners to make the significant investment in the new mills. By 1792, Mathew Carey's *American Museum* estimated the system was in use at upwards of a hundred mills.[10]

By the summer of 1791, Washington had decided to refit his existing mill with the Evans works, and he purchased a license for use of the patented design. William Ball, a millwright hired to conduct a complete repair of the Mount Vernon mill first opened in 1770, visited the Evans works operating at a mill in Occoquan, Virginia, and he determined that, with the aid of the printed plan of the system, he would be able to construct a version in Washington's mill. Washington, according to Tobias Lear, considered Ball an excellent worker, "but, as the President is desirous of having it done in the most perfect manner," he hoped Evans himself would be able to supervise the start of the work. Two of Evans's brothers spent four weeks attending to the construction and installation of the new machinery, which was completed by Ball in October 1791. During the new mill's first full season of operation, the Mount Vernon farms delivered over 4,300 bushels of wheat, which produced 288 barrels of the prized superfine flour and 362 barrels of fine flour. The Evans works made for the more efficient separation of the different grades of flour, which together sold for £1,473.[11]

While Washington learned about agricultural improvements in the Philadelphia region, he also assumed an unofficial role in coordinating the new government's communications with leading British agriculturalists.

When Arthur Young asked Washington for information about the likely costs of establishing a farm in the United States, the president seized the opportunity to compile a detailed survey of agriculture in the nation's grain-producing regions. Washington designed and conducted a survey that in many ways anticipated the statistical reports of the Board of Agriculture in Great Britain, as he solicited information from experienced farmers, several of whom were also officeholders in the federal government. Young had explained to Washington in January 1791 that he wanted information for his young son, "who urges me to let him try a plough in America," adding that he thought of moving himself but was concerned that the prosperity of the new nation had made land too expensive. Whether Young was serious about the prospects for a son who was studying theology or was instead probing for information he might publish in the *Annals of Agriculture*, Washington was eager to assist the leading agriculturalist in Great Britain and, perhaps more important, he viewed a systematic report on prices, crop yields, and local taxation as itself "an object highly interesting to our country."[12]

Almost immediately, Washington began to gather information, and he soon received from Jefferson a set of notes for Young. Jefferson described land use and crop yields in central Virginia and detailed the prices for labor, farm implements, and produce in the vicinity of Charlottesville. Following his communication with Jefferson, Washington distributed a circular to at least five individuals he considered to be "some of the most intelligent Farmers in the States of New York, New Jersey, Pennsylvania, Maryland & Virginia." Washington also spoke with Samuel Powel, who shared data on Pennsylvania prices and tax rates, which he had prepared for a separate correspondence with Young. Washington limited his canvass to the region from New York state south through Virginia. He excluded New England and the Carolinas as having neither the soil nor the climate suitable for "the pursuits of a *mere* Farmer, or congenial to the growth of the smaller Grains." His circular requested that each recipient collect information on prices for the sale and lease of farmland in their region, the average yield and market prices for grains and other crops of the New Husbandry, the costs of purchasing livestock, the sale price of meat, the costs of farming implements, and the tax rates in each state.[13]

The replies from Pennsylvania, Maryland, and Virginia offered Washington, and in turn Young, descriptions of regional economies similarly centered on wheat cultivation, but differing most notably in the legacy of tobacco and the continued reliance on enslaved labor that separated the Chesapeake states from Pennsylvania. Each of the respondents identified shortcomings of farming in their respective regions. Thomas Hartley, a member of the U.S. House of Representatives from York, Pennsylvania, drew on his own experience and that of neighbors to describe the densely-settled farms in central Pennsylvania. It was a region of natural advantages and benefited from easy access to the growing market for flour in Baltimore, but Hartley observed a general lack of interest in improvement. The farmers of York County were careful and hardworking, but disinclined "to make many innovations upon the antient practice of Agriculture." Fayette County possessed favorable soil and climate, but Hartley concluded that "the hand of Industry, with a good System is only wanting to bring it to perfection." Across the state line in Maryland, Thomas Johnson found through much of Montgomery County the destructive effects of a long dependence on tobacco cultivation and the further exhaustion of the land by corn. In his home county of Frederick, where wheat was the cash crop, the management of the land was better but still far from ideal. Johnson, whom Washington had recently appointed to the Supreme Court and who served as a commissioner for the planned federal city, expected the improved navigation of the Potomac and the commercial growth surrounding the new seat of government would stimulate interest in improved cultivation so that the land's potential could be realized, especially in the region approaching the mountains. David Stuart, also a federal city commissioner and Washington's neighbor in Fairfax County, had "never entertained any high opinion of our System of farming," but after "conversing with the most intelligent persons in my neighbourhood," was even more critical of Virginia agriculture. He attributed the lack of improvement, in part, to the reliance on "our black labourers, and the more worthless wretches we employ to overlook them." The long commitment to tobacco and corn had "no doubt had some share in rendering us slovenly farmers." The best farming in northern Virginia, Stuart reported, was to be found in Loudoun County, and he attributed this to the large number of Quakers and Germans who had moved there from Pennsylvania.[14]

Although Stuart offered a more candid discussion of slavery and its impact on farming than would have been found in any public forum in Virginia at the time, his criticisms of the state's agriculture only amplified those Washington had for several years shared with Young. Washington forwarded the three letters without revision, along with Jefferson's unsigned notes. Without waiting for replies from his New York and New Jersey correspondents, Washington advised Young that, if he himself were starting a new life of farming in the United States, he would settle in Pennsylvania, Maryland, or Virginia. His emphasis on the commercial potential of the Potomac and the expected stimulus of the federal city revealed a decided bias toward Virginia or Maryland. For all the promise of the region, however, Washington agreed with his correspondents that much remained to be done to bring farms in the United States to the standard of cultivation found in Great Britain. The average yield of wheat was just eight to ten bushels per acre, and this fact alone would give an English farmer "a contemptible opinion of our husbandry, or a horrid idea of our lands." Washington offered an explanation not mentioned in the several accompanying reports: "the aim of the farmers in this Country (if they can be called farmers) is not to make the most they can from the land, which is, or has been cheap, but the most of the labour, which is dear." As a result, land was worked without any regard for future productivity. Washington recognized that only necessity would change old habits, but the need to produce more on smaller farms would, he predicted, soon become evident.[15]

After reading the several reports and Washington's summary, Young claimed to be so confounded by the estimates of labor and land costs that he begged Washington for further explanation. He was unfamiliar with Washington's commonplace observation that American farmers paid more attention to the costs of labor rather than those of land, and wondered how it could be so when it would seem that a higher cost of labor would make crop yields all the more important. In contrast to British practice, the several reports on land prices took no account of the improvement of lands or the construction of farm buildings. Young never fully understood the regional differences within the United States, but his bewilderment also rose from an assumption that the intensity of cultivation and the interdependence of all farming activity in Great Britain were necessary in other nations. He responded with various queries that persuaded Washington to consult again with Jefferson and to solicit the advice of Richard Peters, an influential member of the Philadelphia agricultural society recently appointed by Washington to serve as a federal court judge in Pennsylvania. Peters responded with a report he had previously prepared when Alexander Hamilton requested information on the price of agricultural commodities and farmland in various parts of the nation. Washington then received several of the other reports submitted to Hamilton, which he forwarded to Young for a broader picture of farming in the Middle Atlantic states.[16]

Young's confusion inadvertently forced Washington to acknowledge the significant impact that different labor systems had in states where the same kind of farming predominated. Washington explained to Young that his earlier observation about the near-total reliance on enslaved labor applied only to Virginia, but that the reports recently delivered to him also encompassed the practices of Pennsylvania and Maryland. At Washington's request, Jefferson prepared for Young a detailed estimate of the costs of enslaved labor and conceded that he "had never before thought of calculating what were the profits of a capital invested in Virginia agriculture." He contrasted the revenue from a wheat farm reliant on hired slaves with that of one whose enslaved laborers had been purchased by the landholder, and he calculated that the latter produced the higher return on invested capital. In response to Young's assertion that the cost of enslaved labor must be higher than the cost of hired labor in England, Jefferson also calculated the long-term return on the purchase of a twenty-five-year-old enslaved male, factoring in the costs of provisions and tools for the man. Jefferson determined that the enslaved laborer who had been purchased cost half as much as the hired one, but admitted some adjustment of this estimate might be needed "to make the labour equal to that of a white man, as I believe the negro does not perform quite as much work, nor with as much intelligence."[17]

In a letter conveying Jefferson's calculations, Washington assured Young that "Blacks are capable of much labour" but he believed in general they lacked the incentive to establish a reputation for hard work. Washington offered Young his most detailed description yet of labor markets. South of Pennsylvania, wealthy farmers relied exclusively on the enslaved for agricultural labor, "whilst the poorer sort are obliged to do it themselves." Washington, who had not hired white laborers to assist in the harvest for several years, attributed the high cost of hired labor in Virginia to the opportunities for white settlers to buy land in the West, and he warned of higher expenses even beyond wages. Hired field hands in the states south of Pennsylvania expected better food than was provided to laborers of almost any other country. The enslaved "blacks, on the contrary, are cheaper: the common food of them (even when well treated) being bread, made of Indian Corn, Butter milk, Fish (pickled herrings) frequently, and meat now and then; with a blanket for bedding."[18]

Peters, in a letter that Washington also forwarded to Young, described the very different labor economy of Pennsylvania, where the population of landless laborers was small and highly mobile, and hired workers were therefore expensive. The cost of labor in the United States would, Peters thought, continue for many years to be higher than in Great Britain, in part because of the opportunities in the West and, as Washington had also recognized, because of the demands of the laborers. Hired laborers expected to eat and drink well, and to be paid enough to support a family. "Our People live better than those of the same Rank in Life in any Part of the World," Peters concluded, adding, "I am not displeased as a Citizen at this Circumstance, tho' as a Farmer it is against my Profit."[19]

Washington entrusted Thomas Pinckney, the United States minister to Great Britain, with the large package containing his own response to Arthur Young, those of Jefferson and Peters, and the reports submitted to Hamilton. Young found that the collected information "has thrown me afloat upon the High Seas." The more he learned about husbandry in the United States, the more it surprised and baffled him. Washington, determined to present his nation's farming as clearly as possible, made one more appeal to Jefferson and Peters to answer additional queries, but both appeared tired of the exchange. Jefferson promised more careful calculations once he returned to Monticello, but they were never sent. Peters sent a lengthy response filled with enough sarcasm that Washington felt obliged to explain that the author was a "man of humour" as well as "one of the best practical farmers in *this* part of the State of Pennsylvania."[20]

Peters described for Young the republican character of an agricultural economy in which land was readily available and no princes or "overgrown Nobles" were able to take "the hard Earnings of an oppressed Yeomanry." The rational calculations of land and labor costs familiar to Young would not convey the success of farming families in Pennsylvania. Their habits of farming would in Europe starve them and "leave their Children common

Labourers or Beggars. And yet here they live well & leave their Descendants the Means of obtaining the Comforts & Conveniences of Life." Peters, who often disparaged the style of husbandry employed on most Pennsylvania farms, may have been exaggerating for effect, but his answers indicated the beginnings of his more critical perspective on British husbandry and his growing skepticism about its applicability in the United States. Washington shared no such misgivings. Throughout the exchange with Young, he criticized farmers in the United States for failing to adopt the British system of farming, or any system at all. His presumption of British contempt for American agriculture, his disparaging reference to his nation's so-called farmers, and his lament that farmers in the United States had "every thing to learn that respects neat, and profitable husbandry" all reflected Washington's undiminished admiration for the culture and practices of British agricultural improvement as well as his steadily increasing disdain for most American farming.[21]

When Washington asked for comments on several reports by the Board of Agriculture and its president, Sir John Sinclair, Peters offered a more carefully considered critique of British husbandry, but one that still emphasized the republican nature of American farming. Peters praised Sinclair's model of the county agricultural surveys, but his close reading of the surveys revealed much about British farming that he condemned, largely because it perpetuated economic inequality. He believed it was regrettable "that the Country accounted the most perfect as to its general State of Agriculture; produces more of bad than of good Farming." A few farmers got rich, "but the great Body of them live not so well, nor are their Circumstances so good, as the same Proportion of ours." Peters concluded by telling Washington that "our greatest Comfort is that we can live well in a Country that will bear bad farming; for in Europe they must farm well to live at all." Peters described a society of small farmers and a broad distribution of land that bore little resemblance to Washington's Virginia or to the regions of Maryland where large, slave-owning landholders introduced diversified farming. In Washington's efforts to describe for his British correspondents a general character of farming in the wheat growing regions of the United States, he could not escape the degree to which slavery and highly concentrated landholding differentiated Virginia and Maryland from the states to the north.[22]

When Washington wrote Sinclair to acknowledge receipt of the county surveys, he copied several passages verbatim from Peters's review but omitted the more critical remarks, only acknowledging that, in the words of Peters, British forms of tenantry and heavy taxes presented impediments to improvement in that country that were not present in the United States. Washington admitted that the superior style of farming in Great Britain was far more expensive than that in the United States, but assured Sinclair that when taxes, poor rates, and other annual charges were deducted "from the produce of the land, in the two Countries, no doubt can remain in which Scale it is to be found." The British system of farming remained undiminished as Washington's model for his estate.[23]

Washington and Peters were in closer agreement in the 1790s in their advocacy of governmental support for agricultural improvement. Both had previously believed the most effective stimulus to improvement would be a combination of experiments by individual farmers and financial premiums offered by private associations, such as the Philadelphia Society for Promoting Agriculture. Washington's survey compiling information on regional farming practices for Young was a first step toward a more public and a national coordination of support for agricultural improvement. Washington called on other government officials with knowledge of farming to join him in what he described as a "common Cause." He placed himself as president at the center of the community of improvement in the United States by representing enlightened farmers in their discourse with Young and Sinclair. Peters also acknowledged the public purpose of the surveys and reports that Washington prepared for British correspondents, and he soon came to a new appreciation of how government could play a role in the promotion of agriculture. By 1794 Peters had become a leader of the effort to establish a Pennsylvania society of agriculture, to be chartered and funded by the state legislature, and Washington, in private correspondence, endorsed the proposal as a first step toward a national agricultural society or board.[24]

By the close of his presidency, Washington was prepared to give the federal government a formal role in the promotion of agricultural improvement, which was in his estimation, "a great National object." The produce of the nation's farmlands was inferior to that of other countries, even those with less fertile soils, and any systematic change in farming in the United States would require governmental encouragement. Without that public investment, Washington feared, residents of the seaboard states would migrate to the West in even greater numbers. He wanted to organize some means of persuading eastern farmers to restore their lands for sustained profit rather than abandoning depleted lands for richer soils across the mountains. The improvement of farmland would benefit the landowners themselves and infuse new wealth in neighboring communities. Mechanics would find an inexpensive source of food, and merchants would find more valuable articles of commerce. Discussing with Alexander Hamilton a draft of his last message to Congress, Washington said he would like to include a recommendation for the establishment of an agricultural board such as that advocated by Sir John Sinclair.[25]

When Sinclair informed Washington in 1793 about the formation of the Board of Agriculture in Great Britain, he expressed the hope that Congress would establish a comparable board that might initiate a similar program of statistical surveys "of your extensive & flourishing Empire." Washington in July 1794 cautioned Sinclair that it would be a long time before the Congress approved any such active governmental promotion of agricultural improvement. At the same time, however, he forwarded Sinclair's correspondence and some of the board's publications to James Madison and asked his opinion on the likelihood of congressional support for a board of agriculture. In early 1796, Washington endorsed Sinclair's separate proposal for the establishment of boards in several nations that would exchange information about agricultural improvement and provide financial support for large-scale, collaborative experiments. After sharing Sinclair's plan with Madison, Washington withheld any formal proposal, citing the advice of influential members of Congress who warned that unexpected demands on the Treasury limited the availability of funds. In his annual message to Congress in December 1796, however, Washington advocated the establishment of a national board and the appropriation of public funds for "premiums, and small pecuniary aids, to encourage and assist a spirit of discovery and improvement." The growth of a nation, he advised Congress, "renders the cultivation of the soil more and more an object of public patronage." The model of a national board, composed of prominent members, had proven a great success in other countries, and Washington thought that the great advantage of a national board in the United States would be its authority to collect information about agricultural experiments and to disseminate examples of successful practices

Fig 7.1 Sir John Sinclair, after Sir Henry Raeburn, ca. 1810. Sinclair was the founding president of the British Board of Agriculture and the originator of innovative county agricultural surveys that Washington gathered in his library. Sinclair persuaded Washington to seek congressional support for a comparable board of agriculture in the United States, and he assisted Washington in his unsuccessful efforts to recruit British tenants for the farms at Mount Vernon. Photograph © National Portrait Gallery, London.

throughout the country. He wrote Sinclair about his disappointment that Congress had taken no action before the end of its session.[26]

∘   ∘   ∘

After a controversy related to slavery first arose in the Federal Congress, Washington was satisfied the issue had "been put to sleep" for the next eighteen years, but in ways few anticipated, debates on slavery, on the condition of the enslaved, and on the ramifications of slave resistance reappeared in public affairs again and again during Washington's presidency. In the first week of February 1790, while the government was still resident in New York City, two Quaker groups and the Pennsylvania Abolition Society submitted petitions to Congress variously calling for an end to the slave trade, restrictions on ships involved in the trade, and, in the appeal of the abolition society signed by Benjamin Franklin, "the *Restoration of liberty* to those unhappy Men, who alone, in this land of Freedom, are degraded into perpetual Bondage." The Senate took no action on the petitions, but the House of Representatives referred them to a select committee, and then debated in public session the report of the committee, which endorsed many of the antislavery sentiments expressed in the petitions. While acknowledging that Congress had no authority to emancipate slaves or to interfere with state regulations of slavery, the committee expressed its confidence that state legislatures would approve measures "that may tend to the happiness of the slaves." Among the potential objects of state legislation favored by the report were the religious instruction of the enslaved, the provision of comfortable clothing and housing, the protection of slave marriages and families, proper medical care, and the shielding of free Blacks from the threat of kidnapping.[27]

On the same day that the House began its contentious debate on the report, the Quaker leader Warner Mifflin called on Washington to explain the intent of the petitioners. Mifflin had already testified before the House select committee and privately visited with Representative William Smith and Senator Ralph Izard of South Carolina to advance the cause of the petitions. Mifflin then wrote the president with assurances that he and his fellow Quakers prayed for him and for the people's attachment to the new government. Mifflin feared that frequent appeals to the president might make "such Visits too cheap" and lessen his authority, "yet I feel a strong desire to have a private interview with thee," he wrote, and Washington granted that request. By Washington's account of their meeting, Mifflin presented him with "Arguments to shew the immoral[i]ty—injustice and impolicy of keeping these people in a state of Slavery." At the same time, Mifflin assured the president that he favored gradual abolition and deferred to the Constitution. Washington, as he so often did in the face of antislavery appeals, declined to offer his own sentiments, on this occasion citing the need to remain neutral in case the issue came before him for an official decision.[28]

By late March, the House, in a compromise offered by Madison, agreed to print in the House Journal the report of the select committee, but it approved and also printed a report of the Committee of the Whole that in much more succinct language reaffirmed that the Congress had no authority to abolish the foreign slave trade before the date set in the Constitution and that only states could enact laws to abolish slavery or to regulate the treatment of slaves within their boundaries. The approved report acknowledged that Congress had the authority to prohibit citizens from supplying African slaves to foreign nations and to regulate the treatment of slaves imported on vessels owned by citizens of the United States. Washington considered the results "as favourable as the proprietors of that species of property could well have expected considering the great dereliction to Slavery in a large part of this Union," but he labeled the petitions an "ill-judged piece of business" and the House proceedings "a great waste of time." Whatever he thought of the content of the petitions, Washington was more concerned with quelling the resulting regional divisions that threatened to exacerbate those already emerging around proposals for the federal assumption of state debts incurred during the Revolutionary War.[29]

The intensity of the House debate made clear that divisions over slavery would not easily be excluded from public affairs under the new Constitution, and popular reaction to the select committee report revealed how quickly proposed restrictions on slavery or the slave trade could threaten support for the federal government in slaveholding regions of the nation. David Stuart reported to Washington that just the referral of these petitions had incensed slaveholders and depressed the price of slaves in Virginia. "The fever which the Slave business had occasioned," Stuart added, set the stage for opposition to the federal assumption of state debts. Although Washington avoided any personal identification with the congressional debates over slavery and the slave trade in 1790, he soon faced other controversies that demanded presidential decisions related to slavery.[30]

In 1791, Governor Thomas Mifflin of Pennsylvania urged Washington to recommend federal legislation that would govern interstate disputes over the rendition of fugitive slaves and the extradition of criminals. The appeal from Mifflin came after his negotiations with the governor of Virginia had reached an impasse over the requested extradition of Virginia residents accused of kidnapping and re-enslaving John Davis, who had won his freedom under the Pennsylvania abolition law of 1780. The president rejected the advice of Attorney General Edmund Randolph and forwarded Mifflin's appeal to Congress, which was empowered under the Constitution to regulate both extradition and rendition. Washington played no further role in the prolonged congressional debates that resulted in the Fugitive Slave Act that he signed in 1793, but he had already seen how attempts to recover emancipated slaves could create diplomatic conflicts as well as disputes between states within the federal union. Earlier in 1791, Washington, with the assistance of Jefferson, had acceded to the Georgia governor's request that the federal government secure the return of escaped slaves who had for many years found refuge in Spanish Florida. Washington appointed an emissary to meet with the Florida governor to negotiate the return of all persons claimed as slave property by citizens of the United States and the enforcement of a recent Spanish order to prohibit the entry of fugitive slaves. Spain did not agree to the retroactive return of fugitive slaves, and the two nations soon faced further conflict over reports that Georgia residents had kidnapped slaves in Florida. The most dramatic involvement of the federal government in slavery during Washington's administration, however, arose not out of domestic policy or diplomatic negotiations but rather in response to an international crisis.[31]

When reports of the slave rebellion in Saint Domingue reached Washington and his cabinet officers in September 1791, they offered immediate and unqualified support for the suppression of the rebellion. Washington worked closely with Hamilton, Jefferson, and Secretary of War Henry Knox to deliver the requested arms and money to French planters in Saint Domingue for their ultimately unsuccessful effort to defeat the rebels. Washington was alarmed by the uprising in the colony with the largest enslaved population in the Caribbean, and he recognized that the threat to white control would reverberate beyond the island. South Carolina governor Charles Pinckney warned Washington that the rebellion was a flame that if left unchecked would spread to neighboring islands and "may eventually prove not a very pleasing or agreeable example to the Southern

States." When a Philadelphia merchant active in the Caribbean trade sent another report of the rebellion several months later, Washington replied "Lamentable! To see such a spirit of revolt among the Blacks. Where it will stop, is difficult to say." Washington was concerned enough about the example of such a massive slave rebellion that he wrote Governor Pinckney to complain about the decision of the South Carolina legislature in 1792 to reopen the state's slave trade. He had hoped "the direful effects of Slavery which at this moment are presented" would have persuaded state lawmakers to support a complete prohibition on the importation of slaves. Exiles from the island and the enslaved people they brought with them arrived in the United States with competing and potentially subversive accounts of the rebellion, and throughout the 1790s, whites in Virginia reported slave conspiracies inspired by the uprising in Saint Domingue.[32]

The challenges for Washington and his administration continued well after the military victory of the Saint Domingue insurgents in 1793 and the subsequent emancipation of slaves by France in 1794. The rebellion, followed by British interceptions of shipping to the island, disrupted the valuable trade between the United States and Saint Domingue. The arrival in the United States of the inflammatory French envoy, "Citizen" Genet, and his advocacy of emancipation as part of a new revolutionary social order further exacerbated diplomatic tensions with France and introduced new divisions in domestic politics. Above all, the Saint Domingue rebellion following in the aftermath of the French Revolution offered Washington and other federal officials powerful evidence of how the rhetoric of liberty and revolution might inspire a slave revolt and of how disputes over slavery could inflame the already difficult relations between the United States and the competing nations of Great Britain and France. The coincidence of the rebellion with the steady rise of organized antislavery campaigns in each of those nations made clear that slavery would remain a volatile subject of domestic politics and diplomatic relations. Washington's responsibilities as president also shaped his understanding of the scope and fervor of these new challenges to slavery.[33]

Washington as a resident of Philadelphia was surrounded by antislavery activity, and as president his stature and reputation attracted varied appeals, like that of Warner Mifflin, for his public support of emancipation and even racial fairness. In what Washington called "a very unexpected address," a group of free men of color from Grenada wrote in January 1791, asking him to authenticate a pamphlet circulating throughout islands of the Caribbean and purporting to be an address by Washington, inviting free people of color to settle in the "southern parts of the States of your Excellency's Government." The committee representing the Grenadians wrote Washington that such an offer would "introduce them into a new Canaan, where they will enjoy all the Happiness of that precious Liberty, which, you gloriously and generously defended, and maintained in favor of Your illustrious Countrymen." However preposterous the letter may have seemed to Washington and to Jefferson, who also read it, the correspondence was a reminder of how powerful the image of Washington was for people of color aspiring to liberty. Such pleas for Washington's leadership on emancipation would continue for the rest of his life.[34]

Washington's personal library reflected his exposure to antislavery arguments that had emerged on both sides of the Atlantic since the close of the Revolutionary War. By the end of his life, he held in his library at least sixteen antislavery publications. At some point near the end of his second term as president, Washington added to his library a collection of matching bound volumes containing thematically organized pamphlets that he had accumulated over many years. One of the volumes, labeled "Tracts on Slavery," included works by authors from Great Britain, France, and Jamaica, as well as the United States. Among the pamphlets were Thomas Clarkson's *Essay on the Impolicy of the African Slave Trade,* the text of a speech delivered by Jacques Pierre Brissot at the founding of a French abolition society, and two antislavery appeals by American authors. The pamphlet by the Jamaican author, Bryan Edwards, was the only defense of slavery and slaveholders, which the author presented in response to a speech by British politician William Wilberforce, the text of which Washington also included in his "Tracts on Slavery" volume. Another custom-bound volume in Washington's library joined together three antislavery works by the early Quaker abolitionist Anthony Benezet, a work on another topic by Benezet, and Jeremy Bentham's *Panopticon,* which dealt with prison reform. One of the antislavery publications by Benezet had been presented to Washington by Warner Mifflin.[35]

As was his practice with almost all books, Washington made no substantive notations in the margins of the bound publications on slavery, but several of these pamphlets bore his signature and signs of use. (An earlier antislavery volume by Granville Sharp remained in the library at Mount Vernon, but with its pages left uncut after Washington received it from a visitor in 1785.) The publications bound together as "Tracts on Slavery" focused in general not on moral condemnations of slavery but rather on its deleterious impacts on a nation's economy and reputation. The 1783 pamphlet by David Cooper urged citizens of the United States to demonstrate for Europeans a commitment to the equal rights articulated in the Declaration of Independence by abolishing slavery. Wilberforce's speech similarly described slavery and the slave trade as blemishes on the honor of the British nation. Clarkson and Brissot argued for the economic advantages of free labor and the commercial benefits of replacing the slave trade with the commercial exchange of commodities with Africa. George Buchanan, a medical doctor in Maryland, wrote of slavery as an impediment to agricultural improvement. All of these authors, except Bryan Edwards, endorsed some form of gradual abolition, preferably by legislature, and even Edwards was an important proponent in Jamaica of more humane treatment of enslaved laborers. For Washington these views were all on a continuum with his own endorsement in principle of gradual abolition and his professed commitment to improving the living and working conditions of the enslaved people on his estate.[36]

The works related to slavery, like so many other publications in his library, enabled Washington to participate as a reader in a transatlantic circulation of Enlightenment thinking that had attracted his interest at least since his resignation from the Continental Army. The networks of antislavery advocates and supporters of amelioration paralleled and at times overlapped with the community of agricultural improvement with which Washington was in close correspondence. Independence for the United States and the reorganization of the British Empire led quickly to a reexamination of slavery in ostensibly enlightened, liberal nations, and a broad spectrum of proposals for the reform or abolition of slavery became a central focus of influential individuals and organizations with which Washington intersected. Among the authors of the slavery pamphlets in his library, for example, the Jamaican planter Brian Edwards and the French abolitionist Brissot were, along with Washington, members of the American Philosophical Society. Washington relied on this exchange of ideas and advocacy through print, correspondence, and association as he considered the future of slavery on his estate and in the United States.[37]

Brissot worked assiduously to establish antislavery networks, first with abolitionist organizations in Great Britain and then in the United States, where Philadelphia Quakers raised money for the joint publication of the Brissot and Clarkson pamphlets that Washington had in his library. Two months after publication of that volume and just a few months before Washington's inauguration as president, Brissot brought his appeal directly to Washington, arriving at Mount Vernon following an introduction from Lafayette. In his description of that visit, published in France in 1791, Brissot recounted conversations with Washington about slavery and the prospects for abolition in Virginia. Washington assured Brissot that he supported the establishment of an abolition society in Virginia but believed the moment was not right. "Nearly all Virginians," Brissot quoted Washington as saying, "are convinced that the general emancipation of Negroes cannot occur in the near future, and for this reason they do not wish to organize a society which might give their slaves dangerous ideas." Brissot replied that emancipation would sooner or later come to Virginia, and that the owners of slaves would best prepare for that inevitability by organizing a society that might reconcile the rights of the enslaved with the slaveholders' right to property. Were such a society established in Virginia, Brissot told Washington, "it would be fitting that the savior of America be its head and restore liberty to 300,000 unhappy inhabitants of his country."[38]

The personal appeal by Brissot followed those of Lafayette and others urging Washington to use his renown as the hero of the war for independence to promote the emancipation of slaves. Brissot, after noting Washington's efforts to make his estate an example for his fellow citizens and his relatively humane treatment of the slaves he owned, concluded that it would "be fitting that such a lofty, pure, and disinterested soul be the one to make the first step in the abolition of slavery in Virginia." The potential impact of Washington's example was only magnified by his service as the first president, and he continued to receive entreaties from antislavery advocates who recognized the influence he might have. Washington, however, was closely watched from several different perspectives, including that of Southern members of Congress alarmed by the Quaker petitions and, in all likelihood, that of the enslaved under his ownership and authority. In his private and public dealings with any matter related to slavery, Washington as president determined to avoid public controversy while attempting to maintain an almost impossible balance between reputation and self-interest.[39]

Within the presidential household were a number of enslaved domestic servants who discovered in Philadelphia a very different community from the one they knew at Mount Vernon, and they enjoyed a degree of personal autonomy unimaginable on a Virginia plantation. Hercules served as chef in the president's house in Philadelphia until late in Washington's second term, while Ona Judge and Moll served Martha Washington throughout most her time in New York and Philadelphia. Austin, the half-brother of Ona, was a valet until his death in 1794, and several other enslaved servants worked in the household in the early years of the presidency. In Philadelphia, the enslaved servants of the Washingtons mixed with free society, they shopped, and they attended the theater and circus. Hercules participated in the market himself, earning money from the sale of leftover food and purchasing clothing with the cash he earned. The enslaved servants from Mount Vernon very likely had contact with abolitionists and with the free black community. Fearing that "the idea of freedom might be too great a temptation for them to resist," Washington took extraordinary, covert measures to prevent the slaves from securing the legal rights that were theirs under Pennsylvania statute.[40]

The state's gradual abolition law, enacted in 1780, provided that any enslaved person brought into the state over the age of eighteen was eligible to apply for freedom after a six-month residence. Although the law exempted the slaves held as servants to delegates to the Continental Congress, no court or other authority had ruled on whether or not that exclusion applied to the officers of the new federal government. Washington faced the consequences of the law in 1786 when his agent sold slaves from his land in western Pennsylvania, and his intercession to recover the slave of Alexandria merchant Philip Dalby indicated his knowledge of both the law and the efforts of some Quakers to assist slaves fleeing their owners. After a discussion with Attorney General Edmund Randolph, who had also brought enslaved servants from Virginia, Washington believed he would be exempt because he was only in Philadelphia as an officer of the government, but he feared that exception would have no influence on "people who are in the practice of *enticing* slaves *even* where there is *no* colour of law for it."[41]

When Randolph informed Martha Washington that three Randolph-owned slaves intended to claim their freedom under the law, Tobias Lear asked Washington for instructions "respecting the blacks in this family." Washington, who was on his southern tour, initially thought that Lear should send all of the enslaved servants back to Mount Vernon. Even if the enslaved servants did not claim their freedom, knowledge of their rights, Washington feared, might "make them insolent in a State of Slavery." All but two of the servants in Philadelphia were dower slaves, and Washington thought it his responsibility to the Custis estate to prevent their emancipation. But Washington recognized that protection of his property rights entailed considerable risk to his reputation and his authority over the enslaved. If on further investigation Lear decided it was expedient to send the slaves to Virginia, Washington wanted "it accomplished under pretext that may deceive both them and the Public." He also requested of Lear "that these Sentiments and this advise may be known to none but *yourself & Mrs. Washington.*"[42]

After consulting again with Edmund Randolph, Lear reported that the abolition law applied to all of the enslaved servants in the president's household. The attorney general found in the law no exception for officers of the federal government, and the young enslaved servants, whom Washington thought exempt from the law, were eligible to apply for an indenture that would keep them bound to service only until they reached the age of eighteen. Randolph, however, advised Lear that if the slaves owned by Washington were temporarily transported out the state "but for a single day, a new era would commence on their return, from whence the six months must be dated." Lear then devised a plan by which each of enslaved servants would on some pretense be sent to Virginia or would accompany Martha on a short visit into New Jersey.[43]

Any expectation that the scheme would deceive the enslaved servants ended when Hercules, the president's chef, confronted Lear to say he was "mortified to the last degree to think that a suspicion could be entertained of his fidelity." Martha Washington permitted Hercules to remain in

Philadelphia past the six-month deadline, after which he traveled to Mount Vernon in June 1791. The other slaves in the household were conveyed out of the state in the spring of 1791. Randolph, in the meantime, reported that the Pennsylvania Abolition Society decided to refrain from any effort to emancipate the enslaved people owned by federal officials, and the Washingtons reduced to four the number of enslaved servants in their Philadelphia household. Washington's effort to protect his property rights in slaves, however, brought a new and very personal appeal for emancipation. Lear, Washington's trusted private secretary, explained as he organized the deception that "no consideration should induce me to take these steps to prolong the slavery of a human being, had I not the fullest confidence that they will at some future period be liberated."[44]

The confidence displayed by Hercules in his confrontation with Lear demonstrated how communications among abolitionists and among African Americans, free and unfree, might empower the enslaved and undermine Washington's authority over those he held in bondage. Hercules and the other enslaved servants who returned to Mount Vernon surely brought with them reports of life in Philadelphia and the opportunities for freedom. When he prepared to depart Mount Vernon for his inauguration in the spring of 1789, Washington was already focused on ways to maintain control over the enslaved agricultural laborers who would no longer be under his daily observation. To John Fairfax, overseer at the Mansion House farm, Washington offered an increase in wages in recognition of his additional responsibilities for coordinating the work of the enslaved at all the plantations and ensuring that the laborers "do what is reasonable & proper without suffering so much time to be spent in the house, under pretence of sickness." The management of the enslaved workers was only the most formidable of the several impediments to Washington's goal of fully implementing the new system of farming, and as president he intended to exercise some degree of the personal supervision that he always considered the prerequisite for the successful management of a Virginia estate.[45]

The work reports became the most important means by which Washington continued to direct farming and labor at Mount Vernon. Nearly every Sunday while in Philadelphia, when he could write with the fewest interruptions, Washington examined the most recent report from the overseers and prepared lengthy instructions for the farm manager. If the manager sent the weekly report on time, no more than a week separated

Fig 7.2 Junius Brutus Stearns, "Washington as a Farmer at Mount Vernon," 1851. In a painting widely reproduced in the mid-nineteenth century, Stearns set Washington in a sentimentalized scene of enslaved laborers harvesting wheat. While the nation saw intense debates about slavery in the 1850s, this and other depictions of Washington as a farmer eliminated any suggestion of harsh labor and offered no hint of the eventual freedom for the slaves he owned. Virginia Museum of Fine Arts, Richmond, Gift of Edgar William and Bernice Chrysler Garbisch. Photo Katherine Wetzel. © Virginia Museum of Fine Arts.

the dispatch of the combined overseers' reports from the receipt of Washington's response. Each white overseer received pen, ink, and paper for the preparation of their weekly reports, and Washington also expected reports from the head carpenter, the gardener, and the miller.[46]

To each new manager Washington offered advice not only on the preparation of the reports but even on the process of reading his letters so that all of his questions would be answered and his instructions carried out. Rather than trusting memory, the manager should write each query on a slate or paper and cross it off when answered. This was Washington's own method, which he thought explained why he never failed to answer a question presented by a manager. He further recommended that managers purchase pocket memorandum books to record his instructions and to write down what they needed to discuss with him in their next correspondence. Washington scrutinized the reports for any discrepancies or omissions that might indicate theft or dereliction. When one week's report from River Plantation indicated eighty bushels of wheat delivered to the mill, but the mill reported receipt of only seventy-nine, Washington urged the manager to catch these mistakes as soon as they happened and thereby "check many abuses which otherwise would be committed."[47]

George Augustine Washington was the first in a succession of managers who assumed the additional burden of running the day-to-day business of the estate during Washington's long absences. George Augustine enjoyed the trust of Washington, but he was so in awe of his uncle that he admitted to great anxiety and prolonged deliberation before making any important decision. His chronic ill health prevented active supervision of work in the fields, and when in May 1790 he hired Anthony Whitting to oversee the French's and Ferry plantations, their agreement anticipated that it might be expedient to expand the scope of Whitting's responsibilities. Within a few months, Whitting was in charge of farming across the estate, while George Augustine managed the business affairs.[48]

Washington found in Whitting a true farmer, knowledgeable in the husbandry of his native England, and it was during his service that the design of the new agricultural landscape was fully implemented. Whitting cited British practice in his recommendations, and he urged Washington to hire white laborers for jobs that he believed could not be done effectively by the enslaved laborers. The hedging that Washington so ardently wished to establish as the principal form of fencing was in England the work of specialized labor, and Whitting feared that "the Negros will never do it as it Ought." Washington resisted hiring someone to supervise hedging, but he was so frequently dissatisfied with the work of the enslaved artisans that he continued to rely on the skills of the hired carpenters, ditchers, and bricklayers who were expected to train enslaved apprentices. Washington was willing to let the enslaved bricklayers try to dig and line a new well at Union Farm, but he expected he would need to hire a well digger from Alexandria, as he recently had at another farm.[49]

The death of George Augustine Washington in February 1793, followed by that of Anthony Whitting four months later, left Mount Vernon "as a body without a head," according to Washington, who intervened to direct the work of the three white overseers. The detailed instructions sent from Philadelphia reflected Washington's attention to the improvements at every field and meadow, even at one of the most difficult times of his presidency. He closed his specific directives for each farm with the broader demand that the overseers be constantly with the laborers they supervised, "because the peace & good government of the negroes depend upon it." He warned the overseers against employing at their own house any young slaves capable of work on the fields: "So soon as they are able to work out, I expect to reap the benefit of their labour myself." While his nephew, Howell Lewis, served as an interim farm manager in the second half of 1793, Washington urged him to focus his attention on the work of the enslaved carpenters, ditchers, and the Home House gang, who were under no close supervision. Washington was convinced that Thomas Green, the head of carpenters, moved the enslaved carpenters from one nonsensical job to another, allowing the skilled carpenter Isaac to idle away his time by himself.[50]

Washington offered his new manager, William Pearce, higher wages than any previous manager, in the expectation that he would direct all of the business of the estate at a time when Washington was seldom able to visit. Pearce was the only manager with whom Washington shared his collection of agricultural treatises, and he trusted Pearce's judgment as a farmer and manager of labor. Pearce seemed intuitively to understand Washington's dictum that "to establish good rules, and a regular system, is the life, and the Soul of every kind of business." After he resigned because of illness, Pearce continued to advise Washington. The collaboration with Whitting and Pearce and their knowledge of agricultural improvement contributed to real progress toward a comprehensive system of farming during Washington's presidency, but the service of the two managers did little to alleviate Washington's fear that without his regular presence at Mount Vernon the enslaved laborers on the farms and in the workshops failed to deliver the work he demanded of them. He was certain that his absence explained the "knavery" among the enslaved and "the abuses which have crept into all parts of my business." From the distance of Philadelphia, Washington wrote his managers with a new level of suspicion and distrust of the enslaved laborers and of the overseers charged with controlling them.[51]

In exaggerated language, Washington described himself as the victim of abuse by rascally overseers whom he accused of "frolicking" at the expense of his interests. The failure of the overseers to be constantly with the enslaved under their watch was "worse even than robbing my purse, because it is also a breach of trust." Washington characterized the suspected idleness of the enslaved field laborers as a form of villainy, as was the allegedly slow pace of work among the spinners and sewers. The most alarming indication of a loss of order was the perceived increase in theft, which Washington suspected in every corner of the estate. He considered all but two or three of the slaves at Mount Vernon capable of theft, and cited his suspicions about various individuals, such as the postilion Joe, who had been caught before, and Sam, who "would not be restrained by any qualms of conscience." Washington believed Alexandria had become what he called a receptacle for stolen goods, and anything that could be sold there was subject to theft. When Sally Green, the wife of the former head carpenter, planned to open a shop there, Washington threatened to cut off his charitable support of her if she traded with any of the enslaved from Mount Vernon. He feared she would fail to distinguish between what goods were or were not stolen. Washington came to suspect even Davy Gray, the longest-serving enslaved overseer, in whom he had placed great confidence. When several missing lambs were unaccounted for in Gray's weekly report, Washington thought the loss very suspicious. It would be regrettable if Gray "betakes himself to Rogueries of that sort," but Washington worried about the influence of the field laborers at Muddy Hole. He warned Pearce to watch Gray closely: "He has some very sly, cunning & roguish negroes under him."[52]

Much of the alleged theft related directly to the work of the farms. Washington was convinced the enslaved seedsmen stole a portion of everything that passed through their hands, and he ordered his manager to mix all seeds in a bushel of sand, a practice originally devised to ensure even sowing but then enforced to prevent the seed from being sold. Washington later decided the overseers should sow the seeds themselves to eliminate any opportunity for theft. He urged the overseers to thresh or tread out wheat as quickly as possible to deter "waste and embezzlement," and the construction of the treading barn at Dogue Run was intended in part to prevent the theft of wheat left in open yards for treading. Washington was sure the decline in the potato crop during his absence was a result of theft, as was the reduced weight of fleeces from his sheep. He ordered that the sheep's fleeces be washed before rather than after shearing to reduce the chance of slaves stealing a portion of wool, and overseers were expected to deliver all fleeces directly to the manager. The insistence on a weekly count of all livestock at each of the farms would detect any animals that were stolen or surreptitiously slaughtered for food.[53]

On instructions from Washington, food for the enslaved families was distributed in regulated allotments to prevent what he labeled embezzlement. Corn was subject to "the same Spirits which attack my Wheat, Hogs, & Sheep," Washington warned Whitting, and he repeatedly ordered the close control of keys to the corn houses at the plantations and at the Mansion House, "for I know of no black person about the house that is to be trusted." Washington wanted linen distributed one piece at a time "if it is cut out by the Negro women," and the number of shirts or shifts the women made was to be checked by the manager against the total yardage given to them. Farm manager Pearce accounted precisely for the distribution of basic supplies, such as the twenty-five nails given to the carpenter Isaac to make a coffin for the infant of Annie, an enslaved spinner.[54]

Washington became equally suspicious of laborers who frequently claimed to be too sick for work. Although he continued to insist that his managers and overseers provide adequate medical care when needed, he demanded explanations for many of the prolonged illnesses recorded in the weekly reports. Washington asked what kind of lameness could keep Dick confined at Dogue Run for so many weeks, and what was the matter with Moll, who also appeared to be forever on the sick list at the same farm. When Ruth, Hannah, and Pegg, long-time field laborers at River Farm, were together reported sick over several weeks, Washington was skeptical, especially about Ruth, whom he considered "extremely deceitful." He cautioned Pearce that if the women were not made to do the work their age and strength enabled them to perform, it would "be a very bad example to others—none of whom would work if by pretexts they can avoid it." Sam at the Mansion House was sick so long that Washington wanted Pearce to examine him, but not with a doctor, "for he has had Doctors enough already, of all colours & sexes, and to no effect. Laziness Is I believe his principal ailment."[55]

James Anderson, who had managed farms and businesses in Scotland for many years before his emigration to Virginia, appeared as a different kind of manager when he succeeded Pearce near the end of Washington's presidency. With a candor and directness unprecedented in other managers, Anderson shared with Washington his reservations about enslaved labor and his emphasis on discipline and punishment. Just a few weeks before Washington again retired to Mount Vernon, Anderson bluntly acknowledged, "I am seldom pleased with the work of Negroes, being accustomed to more expedition." He also offered his assessment of the white overseers, largely based on his perception of the authority they exercised over the enslaved laborers. (Davy Gray, by then the only enslaved overseer, in Anderson's opinion did "as well as may be expected from a Negroe.") One overseer had little authority, and consequently those working under him did little; others were good overseers, who exercised the needed authority. Anderson then added, "I hope You will not be Offended by my informing that I enforce theirs and all of the Overseers Authority, by assisting in some Chastisements when needful." The enslaved, he admitted, had rights to food and clothing, "and when this is given them, the demand upon them is a Competency of work And when they fail in performing it— That they must be forced thereto."[56]

Washington, despite his earlier warnings that violent punishment created more problems than it solved and could never recover lost work, fully concurred with Anderson: "If the Negros will not do their duty by fair means, they must be compelled to do it." Far from being offended by Anderson's admission of using punishment to enforce the work regimen of the enslaved, Washington considered it part of the manager's duty. He explained to Anderson his long-standing expectation that in return for adequate provisions and medical care, slaves had a duty to labor steadily. At the close of his presidency, Washington's assent to Anderson's "chastisement" was a tacit admission that his efforts to ameliorate the conditions of enslavement had failed to secure the labor he demanded for his course of British husbandry.[57]

∘   ∘   ∘

In the midst of a correspondence focused on the exchange of publications and plant material and discussions of national boards of agriculture,

Sir John Sinclair in September 1796 sent Washington a rare private letter, asking his advice on the availability of farmland that might serve as "an asylum for my family in america." Sinclair feared the spread of revolutionary fervor from France and despaired of the lack of leadership from the "inexperienced boys," including William Pitt, the prime minister of Great Britain. Citing the "gloomy prospect" for the defense of his nation, Sinclair asked Washington to describe a farm that might be purchased in the United States for between two and three thousand pounds. He also inquired if any of the farms recently advertised for let at Mount Vernon might be available on a perpetual lease, following a Scottish model.[58]

In a response also labeled private, Washington provided a broad agricultural survey that reflected much of what he had learned on his several tours as president and in his preparation of the reports for Arthur Young. He offered Sinclair a largely positive assessment of the nation's economy, which he thought was bolstered by public confidence in the new form of government and the recent advance in market prices for the country's agricultural produce. He described patterns of farming from New England to the Carolinas and Georgia, with the advantages of each region. Farms in New England were smaller than in other states but with superior buildings and other improvements. The abundance of grass in the region supported the livestock that was one of the most valuable exports, especially to the West Indies, but the severe winters demanded that much of each summer's labor be devoted to fodder crops. A blight prevented New England farmers from cultivating wheat on a scale for export, but "They live well notwithstanding, and are a happy People." Washington was more dismissive of the coastal areas of the Carolinas and Georgia as sandy and unsuitable for the cultivation of wheat: "As I should not chuse to be an inhabitant of them myself, I ought not to say any thing that would induce others to be so."[59]

Washington focused on those areas of the nation engaged in the cultivation of wheat, which was the American crop most familiar to Sinclair and the basis of the nation's most valuable commerce. Admitting some might accuse him of partiality, Washington described the large area of Virginia between the Tidewater and the Appalachian Mountains and the part of Maryland west of the Chesapeake as together forming "the Garden of America." With soil as rich as any in Pennsylvania and with a climate "between the two extremes of heat & cold," this region was "among the most fertile lands in America, East of the Apalachian Mountains." The advantages of the region would soon be greatly multiplied with the opening of the western navigation of the Potomac, which was the most advantageous route into the Ohio country that was already attracting the settlement of farmers from New England and the Mid-Atlantic seaboard. The establishment of the seat of the federal government at the juncture of inland and tidal navigation along the Potomac, he predicted, would make "the Federal City the great emporium of the United States."

For all its natural and commercial advantages, however, the Chesapeake region did not, as Washington acknowledged to Sinclair, possess the most highly valued agricultural land in the United States. That distinction belonged to Pennsylvania farmlands, "although they are not of Superior quality." Farms in Pennsylvania were smaller than those in states to the south and more evenly distributed among the population. These farms were also more likely to have buildings and other improvements, made in large part by the many immigrants who arrived through Philadelphia and never looked beyond the opportunities available within the state. Washington identified other explanations for why land values in Pennsylvania were higher than in Virginia and Maryland. Until Congress approved the naturalization acts, Pennsylvania had attracted immigrants who preferred to settle in that state, where they found it easier to obtain the advantages of citizenship. Lastly, Washington attributed the higher value of farmland in Pennsylvania to the state laws "for the gradual abolition of Slavery, which neither of the two States abovementioned have, at present, but which nothing is more certain than that they must have, & at a period not remote."[60]

It was a remarkable concession that a continued reliance on enslaved labor threatened the improvement of agriculture and the value of land in Virginia and Maryland, while Pennsylvania's commitment to abolition had encouraged small farmers to invest in their property and to adopt a system of farming that increased the worth of the land. Washington as early as 1786 had privately expressed his support for the principle of gradual abolition by state legislature, but never before had he explicitly connected the end of slavery with the improvement of agriculture. The realization of the potential of the "Garden of America" and the dreams of commercial growth along the Potomac, both of which Pennsylvania threatened to eclipse, now made urgent some plan for the abolition of slavery in the Chesapeake. Washington remained publicly silent on the subject of abolition or any other measures to reduce the reliance of Virginia planters on enslaved agricultural labor. Privately, however, he had for several years considered plans to extricate himself from the direct management of enslaved agricultural workers on his estate and to set in place a new organization of the plantations that might allow for changes in the conditions of servitude for at least some of the enslaved at Mount Vernon. The pursuit of that new organization inspired one last attempt to transform his estate.[61]

· 8 ·

Agriculture and the
Path to Emancipation

In the fall of 1793, Washington drafted a map that documented much of what
he had accomplished since his introduction of a new system of farming
on his estate in 1785. Employing his oldest skills as a surveyor and relying
on his detailed knowledge of the landscape, Washington, probably during
his visit to Mount Vernon in September and October, confirmed the latest
improvements at each of the four working farms. The map, completed in
December, delineated the division of each farm into seven fields of roughly
equal acreage, with additional meadows and clover lots. At the center of
the map of each farm appeared suggestions of the recently clustered cabins
of the enslaved families, the overseers' houses, and the new barns. Washington included a table of the "Farms and their Contents," with the dimensions of all the fields and meadows, totaling over 3,200 acres of arable
land. In a separate table of references, he described four adjacent areas of
land that might be organized as new farms, and one that was already oc-
cupied by a family member. The map showed the location of the Mansion
House farm at the center of the estate, but the focus of the survey was the
land devoted to crop rotations and commercial agriculture. The map was
a testament to the scope of Washington's vision and his attention to every
detail in the organization of labor and farming. It was created, however,

not to record the successful implementation of the principles of British husbandry, but rather as a first step toward the breakup of the farms at Mount Vernon. The leader who so carefully staged his farewells and transitions was, by the close of 1793, thinking about how he would exit from his agricultural estate in a way that would lead to freedom for the enslaved people under his control.

The map was intended for Arthur Young, in whom Washington confided a dramatic and surprising plan to transform his estate one more time. The plans "were not even in embryo" when he had last written Young several months earlier, but in December 1793 Washington proposed to surrender his direct management of the farms and to lease all but the Mansion House farm to tenants. His stated motivation was to find a steady income that would allow him to "live free from care, and as much at my ease as possible," in what he described as the "advanced time of my life;" he also referred to other aims "not necessary to detail." He solicited Young's assistance in finding capable farmers from Great Britain to lease the farms. In Philadelphia, Washington had observed the many farmers arriving in the United States from Great Britain and Ireland, and he had received letters from individuals in Britain and Europe seeking opportunities to farm in the new nation. He hoped that Young, who had already inquired about the advantages of farming in the United States, would be able to coordinate the lease of all of the working farms and to "carry my plan into *complete* execution." Washington refused to relinquish his current system of farming "without a moral certainty of the substitute which is contemplated: for to break up these farms—remove my Negroes—and to dispose of the property on them upon terms short of this would be ruinous."[1]

Washington's preference was to lease the farms to "four substantial farmers, of wealth & strength sufficient to cultivate them." His description of the farms, which ranged in size from 476 to 1,207 acres, emphasized the advantages of renting each in its entirety, and Washington anticipated that farmers with their own capital would continue to improve the system of agriculture. Hundreds more adjoining acres might be added to those already under cultivation. The barns and other farm buildings constructed since 1785 would allow British tenants to carry on their familiar system of husbandry. Washington assumed the tenants he had in mind would not be comfortable in the existing overseers' houses and would choose to construct brick residences, and with the ready supply of mud and thatch, there would be no limitations on building. Washington would provide any tenants with a portion of his substantial holdings of livestock, including the horses, oxen, and mules trained for draft work. He added, almost as an aside, that "many of the Negroes, male & female, might be hired by the year as labourers, if this should be preferred to the importation of that class of people," but Washington did not specify any terms of hire.

In his letter to Young, Washington offered no other details about the anticipated status of the enslaved, adding only the suggestion that, if the tenants preferred to bring laborers with them, "it deserves consideration how far the mixing of whites & blacks together is advisable; especially where the former, are entirely unacquainted with the latter." Other details of the plan were still uncertain or flexible when Washington sent it to Young. If the farms were too large or the rents too high for the sort of farmers willing to emigrate, Washington would consider an association of farmers who would lease smaller units, even single fields, as long as the members of the group built the additional residences needed. If Young organized such a society of farmers, Washington stipulated that the rent would be 25 percent higher, and he insisted again that each of the four farms be included. Washington would reserve "the mansion house farm for my own residence—occupation—and amusements in agriculture."[2]

Washington made his intentions regarding the enslaved at his estate much clearer in a confidential letter to his long-time secretary, Tobias Lear. While still waiting for a response from Young, Washington in May 1794 sent Lear a duplicate copy of the letter describing the plan to lease the farms at Mount Vernon. Lear was traveling in Great Britain to explore private mercantile opportunities, and Washington correctly anticipated that Young might speak to Lear about the plan. Fearing that Young, by then secretary of the Board of Agriculture and loyal to the government of William Pitt, might be reluctant to promote the idea, Washington asked Lear to spread word of the plan during his travels through England and Scotland. He also shared with Lear, as he had not with Young, an apparently related plan to sell his settled lands in western Pennsylvania, and he explained to Lear that he hoped to establish a fixed income from the leases and sales. Then, in an extraordinary effort to preserve the confidentiality and anonymity of his message, Washington wrote on a separate, unsigned sheet of paper marked "private" the most compelling incentive for the reorganization of his estate and the sale of his western landholdings.

After describing the financial advantages of the leases and sales, Washington continued "besides these, I have another motive, which makes me earnestly wish for the accomplishment of these things—it is indeed more powerful than all the rest—namely to liberate a certain species of property which I possess, very repugnantly to my own feelings; but which imperious necessity compels; & until I can substitute some other expedient, by which expences not in my power to avoid (however well disposed I may be to do it) can be defrayed." Washington did not tell Lear or anyone else how his plans would specifically lead to the freedom of the slaves he owned, but the message to Lear was the boldest and most direct commitment to emancipation that Washington ever made before writing his will in the summer of 1799. Whatever the plan Washington had in mind, he was, by his second term as president, determined to proceed on his own without waiting for a legislative act of general abolition.[3]

In drafting what became known as the five-farms map, Washington applied to his estate a nomenclature that he and his manager had only recently adopted. Before 1793, he almost invariably referred to the agricultural units of the estate as plantations, in common with so many estates in the Chesapeake and to the south. When he joined together the adjacent Ferry and French's plantations in January 1793, Washington had told his manager the property would "henceforward be called 'Union Farm, or Plantation' instead of Ferry & French's." The subsequent weekly reports listed each division of the estate as a farm, and over the next few months the term plantation disappeared from Washington's usage when discussing agriculture at Mount Vernon. In English usage, "plantation" had before the late seventeenth century referred to colonial settlements but had since shifted in use to describe a private agricultural unit devoted to a staple crop and reliant on enslaved labor. By suddenly adopting the designation of farm, Washington made a revealing break with the language of slavery and brought his estate in accord with both the great, improving landowners in Great Britain and the employers of free labor in the United States.[4]

Most of Washington's property east of the Appalachians was leased to tenants, and he presented his plan to Young as an effort to extend a

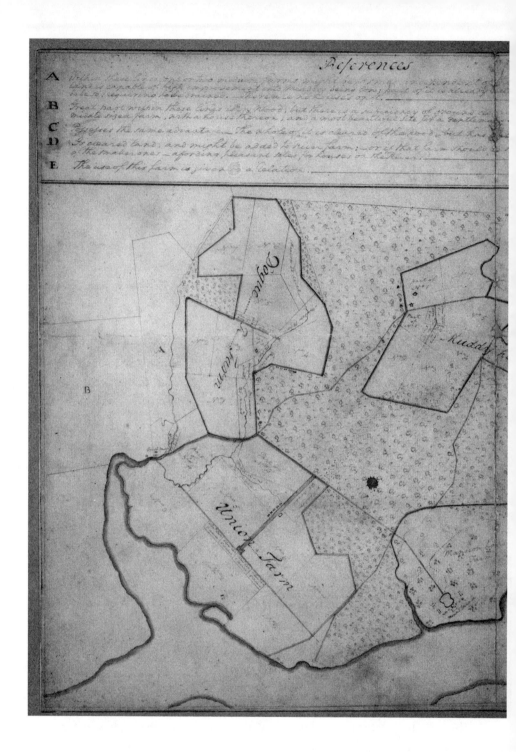

References

A Within these lines, one or two medium farms might be made, independent of the... the land is capable of high improvement into Meadow being low; part of it is already...
able to, requiring to be drained... there are no houses of...

B Great part within these lines is thy Wood, but there is a sufficiency of cleared ground to...
middle sized farm, with a house thereon; and a most beautiful site for a Gentleman...

C Possesses the same advantage... The whole of it is cleared of the Wood, but here...

D Is cleared land, and might be added to River Farm; — or if that farm should be...
of the smaller ones — affording pleasant sites for houses on the River...

E The use of this farm is given to a Relation.

Fig 8.1 "Survey and plot of Mount Vernon and neighboring farms, 1793, Dec." (Five Farms Map). The survey of 1793 documented the transformation of the agricultural landscape at Mount Vernon after the introduction of a new system of farming. Washington prepared his most detailed survey of the estate to illustrate the four farms he hoped to lease to British farmers, and he sent the map, with its description of fields under cultivation, to Arthur Young. mssHM 5995, The Huntington Library, San Marino, California.

similar organization of land to the working farms at Mount Vernon. The form of tenantry he proposed, however, bore no resemblance to the leases for his other land and had no parallel elsewhere in Virginia or in most of the United States. The tenants on Washington's lands in Virginia and Pennsylvania were small farmers who cultivated their crops with their own family labor and perhaps the assistance of a few hired or enslaved workers. When Washington divided his Bullskin Plantation in Frederick, later Berkeley, County in 1766, he created tenancies of around two hundred acres. Those in Fauquier and Loudoun Counties were even smaller. Of the twelve farms created out of the land Washington purchased in 1767, all but two comprised fewer than one hundred and sixty acres; five were just one hundred acres. Most of the leases were for three lifetimes, and although in 1794 Washington received £315 in rent from thirty-seven tenants in the Piedmont and Shenandoah counties, the collection of the rents was a chronic challenge requiring the services of an agent. Many of the tenants were frequently in arrears, and several fled to avoid payment. Improvements of the properties were modest, and even years after entering their leases, tenants would demand credit on their accounts for simple maintenance such as fence repairs.[5]

The plan for leasing entire farms at Mount Vernon more closely resembled what had become the preferred organization of large, improved estates in England and, more recently, in Scotland. British leaders of agricultural improvement, including, in England, the Duke of Bedford, the Earl of Egremont, and Thomas Coke, and in Scotland, the Duke of Buccleuch, managed Home Farms for the public display of agricultural innovations, but they relied on highly capitalized tenants to direct most of the market-oriented farming on their estates and to hire laborers as needed. On estates as expansive as thirty thousand acres, the individual farms were seldom larger than five hundred to seven hundred acres, smaller than some of the farms at Mount Vernon, and the tenants who leased these farms often introduced new methods of cultivation and shared the results of their experiments with one another. William Peacey, for whom the English farmer James Bloxham worked before arriving at Mount Vernon, typified this sort of tenant. Peacey, a highly respected farmer, rented land on Lord Sherborne's Gloucestershire estate, where he undertook experiments with crops and livestock and corresponded with the Board of Agriculture. If Washington could succeed in finding the accomplished farmers with capital, as he described them for Arthur Young, he would have moved his estate that much closer to the most advanced models in Great Britain.[6]

When he sent the plan to Young, Washington prefaced his letter with a request that if anything about the proposal was improper, such as its invitation to good farmers to emigrate from Great Britain to the United States, Young should "burn this letter and the draught which accompanies it, and the whole matter will be consigned to oblivion." Young found no such impropriety and immediately set out to inquire about farmers who might be interested. Young thought the plan worthy, with the only drawback being "the stock of negroes," but he had misinterpreted Washington's reference to the possible hire of Black laborers as a requirement of any lease. He lauded Washington's insistence on leaving the enslaved in place and pleaded ignorance of conditions in America, but observed that any such requirement "must have its difficulties." Young considered the requirement for leaseholds the most significant obstacle. Most of the farmers with whom he discussed the plan had no interest in leasing farms in the United States, since ownership of land was the primary incentive for moving there from Great Britain.[7]

Young identified a few farmers for Washington's consideration, most of whom had already decided to emigrate, but none of them appeared at Mount Vernon. Washington fully realized that the acquisition of land was among the main attractions "if not the *first* inducement to emigration to the United States," and admitted to Young, "I never was sanguine in my expectation of obtaining tenants from England." In this final letter to Young, Washington clarified the misunderstanding about his intention "respecting the Negros which reside on my farms." He had never meant to make it a condition of the lease of a farm that the laborers "should be annexed as an appendage thereto"; in fact, he added without explanation, "I had something better in view for them than that." Washington had only suggested that a farmer leasing one of his farms might "hire them, as he would do any other labourers."[8]

While at Mount Vernon in September and early October 1795, Washington discussed with David Stuart some plan regarding the future of the enslaved on the estate, and he returned in earnest to his proposal to lease the four working farms to tenants from England or Scotland. He was encouraged by the visit of an accomplished young Scottish farmer who had applied to manage a farm on the president's estate. John Bell had been recommended by Washington's correspondent in Edinburgh, James Anderson, and he had worked for Dr. Andrew Coventry, the first professor of agriculture at the University of Edinburgh. Anderson assured Washington that, in addition to understanding the business of managing a farm, Bell had considerable practical experience in agriculture. He brought the plowing skills and the knowledge of new crops that Washington was always eager to introduce from Great Britain, even though Bell presumably had no experience in supervising enslaved laborers. Washington offered Bell a position as overseer at Dogue Run farm once the agreement with the current overseer expired at the end of the year. Bell declined to wait, but before he departed, Washington shared with him the earlier plan to lease the four farms. Bell informed Washington "that a number of honest & reputable farmers were disposed to emigrate to this Country, if they could set down *at once* on *improved* farms, at a moderate rent & for a term of years." This report about the interest in emigration confirmed what Washington heard from others, including Tobias Lear, about the large number of English and Scottish farmers hoping to move to the United States. He had himself observed in Philadelphia the near daily arrival of farmers from Great Britain, but was aware that most came as families or unassociated with one another, and lacked the capital to assume management of a farm at Mount Vernon. Washington wanted assistance in attracting wealthier individuals or an association of small farmers to lease the whole of his farms.[9]

Bell's enthusiasm for that plan persuaded Washington to ask James Anderson for help in locating farmers to lease the Mount Vernon farms. In December 1795, Washington sent Anderson a copy of the original plan as outlined for Young and reiterated that he would only agree to lease the farms "provided the *whole* were taken by men of competent means," or by an association of farmers of more modest means. In the two years since he had first sent the proposal to Young, the price of American grain and the cost of land in the vicinity of the proposed federal city had risen to such heights that Washington expected a fifty percent increase in the annual rents. Even at that rate, the lease of the land made sense to Washington only because of the larger goals he was pursuing by relinquishing management of his farms.[10]

In the first weeks of 1796, as he gathered information from his manager, William Pearce, for the first public advertisement of the farms, Washington explained that he hoped to secure a fixed income and to place his "farms in the hands of a number of Tenants (if it can be accomplished agreeably to my publication) who are professed farmers, who understand and will cultivate them in the manner most approved in England, with allowance for the differences of climate." He offered Pearce no indication of the "something better" he had in mind for the enslaved laborers on the estate, but his queries revealed that he was planning some change in the status or condition of the slaves under his control. At the same time that Washington requested information about the rents paid by tenants on neighboring lands and the potential value of a lease on the gristmill, he asked Pearce to compile a list of "the Dower Negros that are grown, have husbands and wives, and who those husbands and wives are. That is—whether these connections are—one Dower Negro with another Dower Negro; whether they are with other Negros on the Estate, or whether with the Neighbouring Negros." After he received the list, Washington asked Pearce to compile similar information about all of the remaining enslaved people on the estate, distinguishing between those hired from Penelope French and the others.[11]

Once the lease of the farms was advertised, Washington offered some further hint of the changes he expected in the working conditions and lives of the enslaved. More than two years after sending his original proposal to Young, Washington told Pearce that he did not intend to lease slaves with the farms, and added, "One great object with me, is to separate the Negros from the Land; without making the condition of the former worse than it now is." Pearce apparently agreed that the lease of slaves would require his frequent attention, and Washington worried that the slaves would be subject to various kinds of abuse. Their "perpetual complaints" would "defeat in all probability the main objects which I aim at—viz.—tranquillity with a *certain* income." Although he wanted Pearce to inform him about any offers to lease the land, laborers, and livestock together, a month later he was more emphatic that he did not "want the Land and Negros to go together." Potential tenants from Virginia might well bring their own enslaved laborers or hire others, both of which possibilities Washington privately hoped to discourage. In the lease terms that Washington prepared for Pearce's instruction and sent to a few others, he commented, "although the admission of Slaves with the Tenants will not be absolutely prohibited; It would, nevertheless, be a pleasing circumstance to exclude them; If not entirely, at least in a great degree: To do which, is not among the least inducements for dividing the farms into small lots."[12]

In communication with David Stuart, Washington revealed that the fate of the enslaved at Mount Vernon was at the very center of his plan to lease the farms and sell his western lands. Washington offered Stuart his preliminary thoughts "in *confidence*" while at Mount Vernon in the early fall of 1795, and the following February, he sent Stuart a copy of the public advertisement which he described as "an essay" to ascertain the feasibility of leasing the farms and accomplishing the objectives they discussed in the fall. The lease would be only a preliminary step to a much bolder plan that he expected to carry out in two stages. The first part, which was all he expected to accomplish within the next year, was "to give up the Dower Negros . . . upon terms below what impartial men shall say their hire is worth." In his reply, Stuart made clear that the second part of the plan involved some step toward freeing the slaves Washington owned. In his written communication with Stuart, Washington avoided any direct reference to emancipation, stating only that the second part of the plan was for him the more compelling. For reasons that were political, "indeed of imperious nature," the second part of the plan would need to be delayed, presumably until the close of his term as president a year later.[13]

Washington was still considering how he might carry out this second stage when Stuart responded with extended thoughts on possible ways to manage the transition from slavery to freedom. Stuart considered Washington's proposal part of a broader movement among Virginia planters "to get released from their slaves at least," and if Washington succeeded, Stuart expected his model would inspire others who hoped to escape "from the immense trouble and small profits from lands and negroes." Stuart, like Washington, also anticipated that the growth in population and the rise in land values would soon make it possible for large landowners to live comfortably on the rent of their lands. Stuart often served as a confidante of Washington, and he had a direct interest in any decision regarding the dower slaves, since he was married to Eleanor Calvert Custis, the widow of John Parke Custis, and was thus stepfather to the four Custis children who would inherit property rights to these slaves. Washington needed to begin any discussion of the dower slaves with Stuart if he were to give them up "in any manner tolerably convenient & satisfactory" to all who had an interest in them. Stuart was also a critic of slavery as it existed in Virginia, and like Washington, believed a shift away from reliance on enslaved agricultural labor was inevitable. As indirect and veiled as much of their language was, the written exchange between Washington and Stuart opens a rare window on the type of discussions among slaveholders that were usually confined to undocumented conversations.[14]

Stuart offered Washington the outline of a plan that "would effect the abolition of slavery on terms more satisfactory to the Masters, and beneficial to the slaves too, from it's gradual operation, than any which has been tried." He acknowledged to Washington that with regard to "your intentions respecting your negroes, it is a delicate and perplexing subject," but he was convinced that both "their wellfare and the safety of the country" depended on a gradual transition. Stuart proposed to begin the plan with the selection of what he called "one of the most intelligent and responsible negroes" who would rent a farm and be provided with sufficient field laborers and implements. The laborers would each receive some compensation "as an encouragement for them to work, and do their duty without violence." If the slaves selected for the experiment "conducted themselves well they should be at perfect liberty at the expiration of two or three years either to remain on the farm, or seek employment elsewhere." Stuart reiterated his expectation "that they should enjoy perfect liberty." He thought many of the freed persons would choose to remain as tenants on the land, rendering the associations Washington sought unnecessary. "To prevent uneasiness among the rest, who have been equally deserving, and to interest them all in encouraging those with whom the first experiment was made to industry, and good behaviour," Stuart recommended that at the beginning of the plan, the slaveowner announce that all of the enslaved would in succession be offered the same opportunity until all were free.

The prospective benefits of the plan would go well beyond Mount Vernon or other estates where it was implemented; Stuart predicted that a few successful examples of the plan "would bring it into such general use, that the Legislature might ultimately recommend it, or take steps for introducing it."

Stuart anticipated not only freedom for the enslaved, but also economic self-sufficiency. Within the period of the supervised rental of a farm, "the minds of the negroes would be better prepared for directing and governing themselves at the end of the term fixed on." Payments of moderate amounts of money during the interim would teach habits of saving and frugality, and make it less likely that, as free people, they would "fall into bad habits, and become dangerous to society." Stuart went so far as to propose that, "to give this experiment a fair chance," the Virginia Assembly should grant to the slaves during the interim of the rental the right to testify against whites in a court of law, at least in cases involving trespass or robberies at their farms. He cited the example of free Blacks in Fairfax County who had been victims of theft and subsequently deprived of all redress because they were not permitted to testify against the white men they knew to be the culprits. Even with limits, this proposed grant of a legal privilege normally restricted to citizenship reflects the extent to which Stuart had considered the implications of gradual emancipation and of the presence of an increased number of free Blacks in Virginia.

In defense of the practicability of his proposal for gradual emancipation, Stuart drew an analogy between the condition of the enslaved in Virginia and that of "the lower classes of people in Europe" under feudalism. The poor of Europe were once as debased as the slaves were in Virginia, subject to their master's right to deprive them of their very lives if he saw fit, and "perhaps still more humiliating, of having the first night with the daughters of all his vassalls when married." It was not clear if Stuart was drawing an explicit parallel or was oblivious to the violence and sexual assault that the enslaved in Virginia regularly confronted, but he was one of several commentators who saw the laboring poor of Europe as a model for the future status of freed slaves. The historical lesson for Stuart was that the descendants of those poor in feudal Europe "at present form the substantial yeomanry of those Countries." "That the same will happen to our negroes," Stuart declared, "I have no doubt." He acknowledged that distinctions of color presented further obstacles to assimilation, but thought that "time which applies a remedy to all things, will no doubt soon find one for this." (Stuart appeared significantly more pessimistic and far less benevolent in a later conversation with a European visitor who recorded Stuart's account of the failed attempts to rent land to freed slaves, who, he claimed, would neither work nor pay rent. By this account, Stuart believed Blacks in Virginia would always remain a separate and inferior caste.)[15]

By the time Washington approached Stuart about his plans for the enslaved on his own estate, he was aware of several models of emancipation and employment of freed slaves as tenants or hired laborers. He was most familiar with the proposal of Lafayette, who in 1783 had invited him to join in an experiment to establish slaves as tenants on a small estate as a first step toward their freedom. Although Washington declined the offer, Lafayette kept him apprised of his similar experiment in the French colony of Cayenne. On his return to Europe, Lafayette conferred with leading antislavery advocates in France and Great Britain; he met with Wilberforce and read works by Clarkson, Sharp, and Condorcet. In December 1785, with the endorsement of Condorcet and the assistance of French colonial officials, Lafayette purchased property and slaves in Cayenne, and he prescribed a program by which the enslaved would earn an increasing share of profits from crops they produced and learn the skills that would prepare them for independence. He provided education, he encouraged marriage, and he prohibited whipping. "In a word," he summed up his objective, "the fate of the blacks will progressively become similar to that of our peasants." When he sent Washington the news of his land acquisition and decision "to free my Negroes in order to Make that Experiment which you know is My Hobby Horse," Washington replied that the announcement of "your late purchase of an Estate in the Colony of Cayenne with a view of emancipating the slaves on it, is a generous and noble proof of your humanity." Washington again shared with Lafayette his support of gradual emancipation of the enslaved: "To set them afloat at once would, I really believe, be productive of much inconvenience & mischief; but by degrees it certainly might, & assuredly ought to be effected & that too by Legislative authority."[16]

The Virginia Assembly in 1782 enacted a law that allowed slaveholders to free slaves without the legislative approval previously required for any act of manumission. The law permitted the manumission of female slaves between the ages of eighteen and forty-five and male slaves between twenty-one and forty-five. Before the law was amended in 1806 to require freed slaves to leave the state, as many as ten thousand slaves in Virginia received their freedom. Either through a deed of manumission or in a will, a wide range of slaveholders took advantage of the act. Many acted out of religious conviction, while others simply wanted to rid themselves of the responsibility of provisioning a few enslaved individuals. Most owners, especially those who owned a large numbers of slaves, provided for a gradual process of emancipation, which, like the age restrictions imposed by the law, was intended to minimize the public burden of freed persons who could not support themselves. The largest single act of emancipation, and one certainly known to Washington, was that of Robert Carter of Nomini Hall in Westmoreland County. His manumission deed submitted in a district court in 1791 provided for the eventual freedom of more than four hundred and fifty slaves. In a complicated succession of manumissions over twenty years, the enslaved at Carter's plantations in five counties were to receive not only their freedom but also wages or leases as tenants. By 1797, some of Carter's entire plantations were farmed by the freed slaves living as tenants on the land. In the face of opposition from white tenants, neighbors, and even his children, who were heirs to the estate, Carter made further efforts to protect the freedom of the former slaves and to ensure they could support themselves by their own labor.[17]

John Beale Bordley, an associate of Washington's from the Philadelphia Society for Promoting Agriculture, freed some slaves at his farms on Maryland's Eastern Shore and sold others as indentured servants, to be freed after a set term of service. Bordley, like Washington, with whom he corresponded about farming, considered enslaved labor inefficient and inadequate to the objectives of the improved husbandry they were both pursuing. He also thought that enslavement fostered a corrosive mix of indolence and dishonesty, and the families of the enslaved were a burden to the slaveholder. Bordley expected slavery would either decline or be abolished, and he was among the first to address the need to establish other organizations of labor as a replacement. In an essay published in 1801, Bordley drew on his ten years of experience in managing a transition from slavery to other forms of labor. He advocated that landowners offer freed slaves a presumably more benign kind of dependency as cottagers, based on the practice of many British estates. In return for modest housing, a small amount of land to tend gardens for their own provisions, and occasional cash or credit, the freed slaves would, as cottagers, provide a steady source of labor without imposing on the landowner the costly practice of maintaining more laborers than they needed.[18]

Carter's offer of tenancies for freed slaves and Bordley's advocacy of a system of cottagers mirrored David Stuart's expectation that most freed slaves would remain on the land as self-supporting renters. All of these ideas for private initiatives, however, stood in contrast to the several publicized proposals for general abolition in Virginia, almost all of which called for expatriation of freed slaves. Jefferson in his *Notes on the State of Virginia* and all his later writings on the subject supported abolition on the condition that freed slaves would be resettled outside the United States. Ferdinando Fairfax, a godson of Washington, in his 1790 proposal for a congressional program of gradual abolition, cited "the propriety, and even necessity of removing them to a distance from this country." St. George Tucker believed that any forced removal was impractical, but his plan for gradual abolition called for a denial of all citizenship rights, a kind of "civil slavery," which he thought would compel freed people to leave the state.[19]

Whatever precise path to freedom Washington had in mind for the enslaved, he expected that the freed slaves would remain in Virginia. Shortly after Washington's death, the Earl of Buchan recalled a more specific plan for the emancipation of the slaves at Mount Vernon and for their life in the community. Buchan, to whom Washington sent his plan to lease the Mount Vernon farms, shared some of Washington's letters with the author of an obituary published in *The Farmer's Magazine* of Edinburgh. The author described Washington's estate and reported "his black people never felt the chains of bondage; and his deeply sagacious plan was, by education and time, to render them capable of citizenship and freedom. Great difficulty he had to encounter in the cultivation of his land, where tenantry is almost unknown; but he performed much more than could have been expected: and his last aim, in corresponding with the Noble Lord [Buchan] already alluded to, was to create a free tenantry in America, upon the most liberal principles of unfettered meliorating leases, with a rent to be estimated according to the value of the fruits of the earth."[20]

Washington knew that hiring out the dower slaves from Mount Vernon would sever the family ties he had promised to protect, and he admitted that separating them from their spouses and children at his estate would be "an affecting, and trying event." Stuart agreed that this part of Washington's plan would be "more painful and perhaps difficult" than any other part, "altho' unavoidable, and what happens every day." Stuart was unwilling to commit to hiring those dower slaves, even at the low rate promised by Washington, because of his other financial commitments and reduced income from his farms, although he reaffirmed that those dower slaves would revert to the Custis heirs after the deaths of both George and Martha Washington. In the meantime, any progress toward the separation of the dower slaves or the emancipation of slaves owned by Washington depended on the lease of the farms at Mount Vernon.[21]

∘   ∘   ∘

Washington never lost sight of his parallel goal of perpetuating the system of farming he had introduced at Mount Vernon, and he insisted that any tenants continue his agricultural improvements. He defined a good tenant as one "who will do justice to the land." Tenant leases negotiated by Washington had long included requirements for such improvements as the planting of orchards and limitations on the use of timber. The terms drafted for Mount Vernon in February 1796 included those conditions and far more. The leases would protect the land from what Washington considered the most ruinous practices of Virginia farmers. Tenants would be forbidden to grow any tobacco for commercial sale, they could devote no more than one-sixth of the arable land to corn, and they were prohibited from letting hogs run wild. If the farms were leased to an association of small farmers who required new residences, the tenants would provide their own building materials, with minimal use of the surrounding timber. Washington stipulated that tenants adhere to a six-year, six-field rotation of crops that he devised, or he would consider an alternative rotation as long as it did not impose greater demands on the soil. The prescribed rotation was a distillation of much of what Washington had learned over the past decade about the soil on the farms. It specified a mix of grain crops, clover, buckwheat, and potatoes, and required one year for pasturing and manuring. Washington was now confident that such a system could be applied to a small farm of just one hundred arable acres, with fields of no more than sixteen acres. Here was a model for small, independent landowners largely dependent on their own labor. Washington even projected that tenants would be left with an annual income of £97 after paying their rent. This he hoped would be an incentive for English farmers who were accustomed to paying two-thirds of their income to taxes and rents. Washington's requirement that rents be paid in cash or wheat reaffirmed the centrality of that grain in his vision of responsible and productive agriculture.[22]

A combined advertisement for the lease of the farms at Mount Vernon and for the sale of Washington's lands to the west was printed as a broadside and appeared in numerous newspapers, from Connecticut to Virginia, and in western Pennsylvania and the Northwest Territory. Washington prefaced the advertisement with the condition that he would lease only to "real *farmers of* good *reputation and none others need apply.*" The notice described the acreage of each farm, variations in soil, existing housing for overseers and families of enslaved field laborers, and the condition of barns. Potential tenants would find level fields, free of any stones or stumps that might obstruct a plow or harrow. Those leasing the farms would be offered reasonable terms if they wished to purchase draft animals, field livestock, "ploughs, (of the best kind) harrows, and every kind of implement, necessary on a farm." The advertisement made no reference to hiring enslaved laborers currently working the land, the possibility that Washington had mentioned to Arthur Young in his first iteration of the plan. Although the advertisement indicated the number of "black labourers" usually employed on each farm, it offered no indication of their fate if the farms were leased.[23]

William Pearce would be available at Mount Vernon to show the farms and explain the terms of leases, and interested persons in Philadelphia could apply to the president's secretary to examine a copy of Washington's survey of the farms. Washington asked Jeremiah Wadsworth, an ardent proponent of agricultural improvement himself, to publish the advertisement three times in the Hartford newspaper. He called on other fellow officers from the Continental Army to distribute it in the West. Rufus Putman was asked to post it in Marietta and Cincinnati, Ohio. Washington wanted Isaac Craig to publish it three times in the Pittsburgh newspaper, and to post it at the most popular tavern.[24]

Soon after the advertisement appeared in newspapers in late winter 1796, William Pearce and Tobias Lear received multiple inquiries, but serious applicants, particularly those from Great Britain, were few. One of the first promising inquires came from Joseph Gallop and his brothers, tenants on a farm in Harford County, Maryland, one of whom visited William Pearce to inspect River Farm. The Gallop brothers offered to rent the land, the livestock, and the enslaved laborers on the farm for little more than what Washington expected for the lease of the land alone. Washington learned from mutual acquaintances in Philadelphia that the brothers were industrious and capable farmers, but he doubted he could come to any agreement with them because he did not want to lease the slaves and the offer was too low. He had already set the terms of the lease below what he estimated to be the real value of the farms because he wanted to attract good farmers who would "do justice to, and improve the premises; which will be a primary object with me." A year later, the new farm manager, James Anderson, negotiated the lease of River Farm to an English farmer, but the man failed to return. The farmer may have been Stephen Milburn, who had been referred by two Fairfax County friends and who met with Washington at Mount Vernon to discuss the plan to lease the several farms. After several days' reflection and fearing that he might never be able to rent the four advertised farms at the same time, Washington offered Milburn a lease on the River Farm alone. As further enticement and in consideration of the great expense of outfitting such a large farm, Washington was willing to advance to Milburn some or all of the stock and implements on River Farm at a reasonable valuation. Milburn worried that he would not be able to raise the capital, but he assured Washington "I would like to Farm under you as I hear you would e[n]courage the improvement of Agriculture in this Country."[25]

However wide the dissemination of the advertisement, limiting its publication to newspapers in the United States ran counter to Washington's repeatedly expressed preference for renting to farmers from Great Britain rather than to any of the "slovenly farmers of this country." Although Arthur Young and others had assured him that no laws in Great Britain restricted the emigration of farmers or artisans, Washington was hesitant to create any appearance of enticing people to move to the United States.

Anticipating that the publication of his proposal in Great Britain would attract great attention, Washington reiterated to Young, "I have *no* desire that any formal promulgation of these sentiments should be made." Washington expected, however, that its extensive publication in newspapers in the United States would increase the likelihood that some copies of the advertisement would reach Great Britain. He hoped it would encourage associations of farmers to consider the opportunity in Virginia, "for I have no idea of frittering up the farms for the accomodation of our country farmers, whose knowledge—practice at least—centres in the destruction of the land, & very little beyond it." Washington asked Tobias Lear to spread word of the plan among his English and Scottish mercantile acquaintances, and he sent the printed notice to Thomas Pinckney, the United States minister to Great Britain, so he might also share the information. Another copy went to Gouverneur Morris, then in London.[26]

More realistic efforts to recruit English or Scottish farmers would depend almost entirely on the efforts of Washington's several agricultural correspondents in Great Britain. Washington sent copies of the advertisement or broadside to his closest confidantes, with the notable omission of Arthur Young. To James Anderson, Washington described the advanced plan for leasing the farms and for selling his land in the West. For the "peaceable, industrious & skilful farmers" he hoped to find as tenants, Washington explained, "I must resort to some other country than this— where little knowledge of husbandry is possessed, and less care used in the practice of it, to keep the land from a ruinous course. For many reasons, the similarity of language not least, I would prefer those of yours." Sir John Sinclair, as president of the Board of Agriculture, was well placed to inform any farmers interested in moving to the United States, and Washington asked Sinclair to explain the terms of the offer. The Earl of Buchan had previously provided references to several persons from Scotland whom Washington had hired; now Washington sent Buchan the terms of the proposed lease that he might apprise anyone planning to move or interested in forming an association of farmers. He also sent the advertisement to William Strickland, who, alone among the British correspondents, had visited Mount Vernon when he was preparing his report on agriculture in the United States. To all of the British agriculturalists, Washington repeated some version of his "unequivocal declaration that, it is not my intention to *invite* Emigrants—even if there be no prohibitary act of your Government opposed to it."[27]

The Earl of Buchan praised Washington's intentions and promised to continue his support for emigrants to the United States. Buchan and the others promised their assistance in finding talented farmers to settle at Mount Vernon, but none of them offered much hope of success. Buchan cautioned Washington that it would be difficult to persuade farmers with capital to emigrate since their ambitions were to be owners of their own lands and cultivators of their own freeholds. Strickland had observed in his agricultural tours of Great Britain and the United States that farmers were in general unlikely to relocate. They were attached to their familiar soil, and in Great Britain they enjoyed the greatest respect of any profession. Anderson was the least optimistic. Interest in emigration had declined, and for farmers of sufficient means, the only appeal of the United States would be the opportunity to purchase land at prices far below those to be found in Great Britain. Anderson also warned that radical British supporters of the French Revolution were now the likeliest to leave for America.[28]

Whatever their misgivings, these British friends made efforts to find individual farmers for Washington and some tried to organize associations that might lease the lands on the terms set out in the advertisement. William Strickland, who lived in the East Riding of Yorkshire, visited the quayside in Hull to interview departing emigrants who might be interested in becoming tenants on the terms offered by Washington. The Earl of Buchan contacted a knowledgeable friend in the vale of Berwickshire, where he thought the land was similar to Mount Vernon's, and encouraged him to share Washington's plan with capable farmers who might be interested in moving to America. A year later, Anderson discovered renewed interest in emigration from Great Britain, and although he did not successfully recruit any tenants, he was instrumental in hiring a Scottish gardener for Washington. Sinclair presented what was surely the least expected inquiry about the plan when he suggested that he and his family might like to rent one of the farms for an extended term as a refuge from the political turmoil of Europe. In reply, Washington wrote, "to have such a tenant as Sir John Sinclair, however desirable it might be, is an honor I dare not hope for," but explained that he did not want to separate one farm from the others. He encouraged Sinclair instead to consider the neighboring Fairfax estate, Belvoir, which was one of the most beautiful properties on the Potomac and for sale.[29]

Sinclair subsequently recommended an English farmer who appeared in his letter of introduction to be an ideal prospect for the lease of one of the Mount Vernon farms. Richard Parkinson announced in the summer of 1797 that he would be greatly honored to be sponsored by such eminent men as Sinclair and Washington, and he planned to travel to Virginia to examine the farms before entering any agreement. He forwarded to Washington a prospectus for his forthcoming publication, "The Experienced Farmer," for which he claimed to have been encouraged by "the first Men in Agriculture, in this Kingdom, and by the Nobility of the first Rank." Parkinson was from Lincolnshire, a center of agricultural improvement and the advanced breeding of livestock. His brother John was the farm manager for Sir Joseph Banks, the naturalist of whom Washington had read. Parkinson's expression of interest and his request to view the farms gave Washington renewed hope of placing his farms "in the hands of skilful Agriculturalists, who are *able,* & *willing,* to manage them properly." He welcomed Parkinson to visit, and urged him to recruit other English or Scottish farmers to join in the venture. If they were farmers of sufficient capital, Washington assured Parkinson that he would be able to provide them with farming implements and stock of every kind, including draft animals, on reasonable terms. He cautioned Parkinson that, unlike Great Britain, Virginia did not have a large number of laborers available for hire and therefore the wages of workers could be expensive, "unless you were to employ slaves, and these are not to be had but by the year, and not always then." He again made no mention of the possible hire of enslaved laborers from his own estate.[30]

Whatever hope Washington had of finding a proper tenant must have been shaken by his receipt of a letter from Parkinson in November 1798. With no explanation of his delays and silence, Parkinson informed Washington that he had shipped to Mount Vernon an enormous and spectacularly expensive assortment of livestock and that he would soon be following on his own. The shipping charge alone was £850, an amount he asked Washington to forward him until he was able to sell some of the most

valuable racehorses. Parkinson was persuaded that Washington would wel-
come the best breeds of England, and the animals included "5 Stallions of
the first Blood," eight mares of "good Extraction," a hunting mare reputed
to be the fastest trotter in England, four sorts of bulls and cows, the best
kind of boars and sows, and sheep bred by Robert Bakewell, Britain's most
renowned breeder of improved livestock. With evident exasperation, Washington informed his manager that he had neither the cash to pay the freight
nor adequate facilities to house the animals and their keepers. He was, however, so eager to lease River Farm on good terms that if Parkinson agreed
to all of his lease conditions, he was inclined to accommodate the animals.
The two men, however, would never reach any terms of agreement.[31]

The only account of Parkinson's visit to Mount Vernon was his own,
published upon his return to England after a short-lived attempt to manage
a farm in Maryland. Parkinson presented *A Tour in America* as "an account
of my disappointments in America" and as a warning for any English farmer
considering a move to the United States. While its content was critical of
almost everything about farming in the United States, Parkinson reserved
his greatest scorn for the new nation's most famous farmer. Repeatedly in
his two-volume account, he criticized Washington's alleged ignorance of
English farming practices. His caustic descriptions of Mount Vernon and
of the Washingtons—he clashed with Martha as well—contradicted almost
all other visitors' accounts and holds little credibility, but the tone is surely
revealing of how thoroughly the negotiations regarding River Farm must
have broken down. Washington did not live to read the account published
in 1805, but the entire engagement with Parkinson was for him further evidence of the unlikelihood of attracting farmers of capital to lease the farms
at Mount Vernon.[32]

At every stage in the formulation of the scheme to lease the farms, Washington admitted his doubts about its practicability, yet as late as November 1798, nearly two years after resuming the full-time management of
his estate and five years after first describing his plan to Arthur Young, he
remained interested in any promising offer from an experienced British
farmer. For all of its implausibility, the plan reflected the seriousness of
Washington's determination to perpetuate his example of farming and to
end his reliance on enslaved agricultural labor. The proposed terms of the
leases were characteristically meticulous, devised in the midst of the pressures of his second term as president, but Washington left no record to explain

how he would grant freedom to the enslaved or who would subsequently provide the labor on the leased farms. He acknowledged repeatedly that white field laborers were scarce in Virginia and very expensive to hire. In some descriptions of the plan, he expected British tenants might bring laborers with them; at other times he implied the enslaved currently working the land would be available for hire like "any other labourers." The limited record of his discussion with David Stuart reflects Washington's reluctance to put in writing the specifics of any plan for emancipation, but the exchange reveals enough to indicate he had devoted considerable thought to the status and labor of the enslaved following emancipation. Whatever transition to freedom Washington envisioned, his decisions to require the continuation of his innovations in farming and to secure British rather than American farmers as tenants moved the plan from the improbable to the nearly impossible.

∘   ∘   ∘

On the evening of Washington's resignation from the presidency in March 1797, over two hundred federal officeholders, diplomats, and prominent business leaders gathered at a celebratory dinner in Philadelphia. Above the diners was displayed a large, illuminated image of Washington relinquishing the symbols of military and civil authority on the throne of liberty. With outstretched arm, the figure of Washington pointed to a recognizable depiction of Mount Vernon. In front of the mansion, an unattended plow and yoke of oxen awaited the return of Washington. On his resignation of public office and his resumption of farming at his estate, Washington was again heralded as the Cincinnatus of the age. The version of the illuminated image printed in 1799 was one of the manifold images and published references to Washington as Cincinnatus, and once again, Washington happily resumed his life as a farmer. He wrote the Earl of Buchan "At the age of 65 I am recommencing my Agricultural pursuits & rural amusements; which at all times have been the most pleasing occupation of my life, and most congenial with my temper." A dedication to farming, always the most promising art of peace, would provide the fitting close to his life. Politics yielded "to the more rational amusement of cultivating the Earth."[33]

Retirement, however, brought no end to the appeals for Washington to free his slaves, and the virtuous example of Cincinnatus could easily be

GENERAL WASHINGTON'S

RESIGNATION.

Fig 8.2 George Washington's Resignation, engraved by Alexander Lawson, after Barralet, January 1799. As Washington relinquishes the symbols of power on the throne of liberty, an unattended plow and team of oxen at Mount Vernon await his return to farming, like Cincinnatus. The Lawson engraving was based on an image originally designed as a backdrop at a dinner honoring Washington on the evening of his resignation from the presidency. Courtesy of Mount Vernon Ladies' Association.

turned against Washington the slaveholder. One of the harshest political attacks on Washington came from the Republican newspaper editor William Duane, who in December 1796 reminded his readers that "the great champion of American Freedom, the rival of Timoleon and Cincinnatus, twenty years after the establishment of the Republic, was possessed of FIVE HUNDRED of the HUMAN SPECIES IN SLAVERY, enjoying the fruits of their Labour without remuneration." In June 1797, the New York *Time Piece*, a newspaper published by the Republican editor Philip Freneau, printed a poem begging Washington to explain "How hast thou who to thousands freedom gave, Endur'd the ungrateful service of a slave?" The poet reminded Washington that the original Cincinnatus "Till'd his own ground and kept no man enslav'd." Just days earlier, the same newspaper had reprinted the Liverpool edition of Edward Rushton's scathing "Expostulatory Letter to George Washington, of Mount Vernon, in Virginia, on his Continuing to be a Proprietor of Slaves." In his preface to the letter, Rushton explained that he had sent it to Washington in the summer of 1796, only to have it returned to him "without a syllable in reply."[34]

On his return to Mount Vernon, Washington found neglect and disrepair wherever he looked across his estate, and after six months in residence he admitted that at no time in his life had he been more engaged in the recovery and the reorganization of his private affairs. He continued to bemoan the general state of agriculture in the United States—"it is indeed wretched"—but he resumed his own experiments intended to demonstrate the merits of settled agriculture and the restoration of soil fertility that too many of the nation's farmers disregarded as they abandoned exhausted grounds and moved west. His final retirement proved to be a period of enormous innovation, even as he searched for tenants who might relieve him of the daily management of the farms and make possible the first steps toward emancipation of the slaves.[35]

The famous and the curious continued their pilgrimages to Mount Vernon, and from many of them Washington learned about improved livestock and plant material collected from the farthest reaches of the British empire. Following his visit to Washington, James Athill, speaker of the Antiguan assembly, sent more than fifty plants along with a ram and four ewes from the island. In return, Washington sent five of his own sheep for an experiment about the effect of climate on the animals. A British merchant on an extended stay in the United States shipped Washington sheep, a machine for separating chaff from wheat, and several new types of farming implements. Closer to home, some Maryland estate owners known for their excellence in livestock breeding offered cattle and sheep, from which Washington expected to restore his own stock. He was disappointed that a Maryland friend had no more healthy stock of sheep imported from South Africa's Cape Colony, but the man sent Washington a young bull of his *"improved Breed."* Edward Lloyd, from Maryland's Eastern Shore, sent Washington the gift of a calf bred from the first Bakewell bull imported into the United States.[36]

At the start of his retirement, Washington considered converting much of his land to meadows for grazing, which he predicted would reduce his reliance on enslaved laborers while maintaining profit and restoring the land. He determined to improve his cattle and to obtain the good rams necessary for replenishing the flocks of sheep that he considered the most valuable of his livestock. Washington found the most satisfactory results from his decade-long effort to breed mules. After numerous disappointments, he at last had enough mules to supply each farm, and by 1797 these draft animals outnumbered working horses. He also increased his breeding stock of asses, which netted more than £50 in stud fees in 1797, and he offered jacks for sale to planters in Virginia and South Carolina.[37]

While residing in Philadelphia, Washington learned about advances in mechanized farm equipment that promised to make his laborers more efficient. Within days of Washington's return to Mount Vernon in March 1797, the enslaved carpenters were preparing hickory cogs for a threshing machine based on a model imported from Scotland by Jefferson. Washington pursued every report of improved threshing machines, searching for one "upon a simple plan & not easily put out of order in the hands of ignorant Negros, & careless Overseers." Despite his disparaging remarks, Washington relied on enslaved carpenters to construct several iterations of threshing machines and on enslaved laborers to operate the machines, which became the primary means of threshing at Union Farm and then River Farm. Washington brought William Booker, the inventor of a new threshing machine, to oversee the carpenters in its construction and in the installation of new works that proved successful. Although Washington was unsuccessful in finding the manufacturer of a wheat-raking machine he saw demonstrated at a farm outside Philadelphia, he remained alert to any innovations in harvesting. Just before the harvest of 1798, he hired a man to instruct the cradlers to cut wheat in the more efficient manner practiced on Maryland's Eastern Shore.[38]

The most notable new enterprise of Washington's retirement was the distillery that quickly became one of the largest producers of whiskey in the nation. This addition had been proposed by the new farm manager, James Anderson, originally from Scotland. Washington approved the project in January 1797 before he returned to Mount Vernon in March, and by early summer he decided to expand production. The production of whiskey added substantial value to the grains produced on the estate, and production increased so much that the operation soon required the purchase of additional grains from local farmers. The distillery was further integrated with agricultural production and livestock husbandry at the estate by feeding hogs with the mash and distributing their manure to the fields. The distillery was Anderson's most valuable contribution in what was otherwise a complicated relationship with Washington.[39]

Anderson was in many ways an unusual choice to be manager of the estate. By the time he met Washington, he was in his early fifties and had been a substantial farmer, mill owner, and grain trader in his native Scotland. Forced into bankruptcy after the widespread failure of Scottish-owned distilleries in 1788, Anderson and his family emigrated to Virginia in 1791. For two years, he rented his own farm near Mount Vernon, which he visited in Washington's absence. He then managed two larger estates in succession, where he supervised between fifteen and twenty-five enslaved laborers. At the second estate he also operated a distillery in which he had a financial interest, and he employed the services of an assistant. Anderson was accustomed to a degree of independence and discretion that no earlier managers at Mount Vernon had exercised, and he asked Washington for unprecedented benefits and wages. Washington, despite his disappointing experience with British managers, was again persuaded of the value in hiring someone who professed to have been bred since his youth to "the practical parts of Farming in Britain," and he offered Anderson a starting wage of £120, the promise of a raise within a year, horses for him and his wife, and the services of three young enslaved servants. Washington rejected Anderson's request for an assistant, but following the enormous success of the distillery he allowed the manager the services of his own writing clerk.[40]

Anderson quickly demonstrated his knowledge of farming, and he agreed to Washington's request for more regular and systematic accounting of every unit on the estate. For the first time, Washington received an annual balance of expenses and revenue for each of the four farms involved in commercial production. He also drew on his experience as president by instituting quarterly accounts. At the same time, Anderson began to chafe under Washington's demands, and in a series of lengthy letters sent the short distance from his house at Union Farm to Washington in the Mansion House, he complained about Washington's intrusive oversight and seeming distrust. Washington responded with uncharacteristic patience and offered assurances that he had no intention of replacing Anderson, but he made it clear that he remained in charge of the estate. "Strange, & singular indeed would it be, if the Proprietor of an Estate (than whom no one can be so good a judge of the resources as himself) should have nothing to say in, or controul over, his own expenditures." By May 1798, Washington proposed that Anderson assume responsibility for the operation of the distillery, the mill, and the fishery while serving as a consultant but not manager of the farms. He was confident that the full attention of Anderson might make the mill and distillery as profitable as the remainder of the estate combined. After another series of demands and concessions, Anderson remained as manager, but Washington was increasingly dissatisfied, not just with his manager's moodiness, but, more significantly, with his direction of work routines and particularly his allocation of enslaved laborers.[41]

Although he brought to Mount Vernon enormous farming experience, Anderson barely met Washington's usual requirement for familiarity with the management of enslaved laborers. Early in his service as manager, Anderson announced his aversion to working with slaves as well as his readiness to enforce with the whip his demands of their labor. He continued to exhibit a striking callousness and severity toward the enslaved. When two young children in the slave quarters died within the same week, Anderson assured Washington he had called for medical assistance, but he added the general observation that "the mothers are very inattentive to their Young." Rather than divert healthy laborers from fieldwork, Anderson proposed to Washington that he employ the elderly and infirm among the enslaved in cleaning the hedges, even if it depended on the threat of violent coercion. "If the Invalids could be made to do this work, to them it might be no hardship, And to Us a convenience, a little of the Rod would be necessary to set the business agoing." Within a few weeks, Old Sam, who had been making baskets in the spinning shop, faced a summer of weeding along the thorn tree hedges.[42]

Anderson's worst fault, from the perspective of Washington, was his lack of "system," and the inability to pursue any systematic plan of work was most evident in Anderson's supervision and control of enslaved labor, despite his harsh exercise of punishment. Washington had seen Anderson shift the ditchers from one kind of work to another, so that nothing was done well. Anderson ordered field laborers from the farms to come to the Mansion House where they waited half a day before receiving orders to work. He sent the carters to Alexandria for "trifles," with resulting injury to the teams and waste of labor. "The work of the Carpenters, & waste of their materials," Washington complained, "have suffered much by shifting them from thing to thing, & compleating nothing." The work reports submitted by Anderson revealed the near-weekly reassignment of field laborers from one farm to another, despite Washington's long-standing insistence that each farm be self-sufficient in labor except at harvest. From his long experience managing enslaved laborers who found few rewards for incentive and self-direction, Washington had concluded that "more work will be done in the *sametime* when people are kept steadily at it, than when they are taken from, & return to it again."

Washington was most concerned that Anderson failed to implement the new crop rotations, which were the foundation of any regular course of farming and without which there would be nothing but "Jumble, & confusion." Washington reminded Anderson of his guiding principle in managing an agricultural estate: "System in all things is the soul of business. To deliberate maturely, & execute promptly is the way to conduct it to advantage." He expected his manager to exercise the same foresight and determined command that he always applied to his plans for the farms. Only by adhering to a considered, long-term plan could a manager or estate owner secure the labor on which the success of farming depended. Washington suggested Anderson vary his daily ride of the estate to ensure that all was in order, livestock enclosed, farming implements protected from the weather, and fences in repair. "Examine the houses, seeing what is amiss therein—particularly the Graineries—Inspecting the Negro quarters, as well for the purpose of detecting improper conduct in them, as to see if they are kept clean (being conducive to their health)—to provide for the sick when they are really so, & to drive out those who are not so."[43]

In his own daily observation of the work of the enslaved, Washington thought he could discern the same lack of discipline and order he had suspected throughout much of his time in Philadelphia. Within six months of his return to residence at Mount Vernon, Washington rejected Anderson's proposals to save more than £120 a year by reducing the number of hired overseers and relying more on enslaved overseers or foremen. Washington advised his manager, "I have always found, however, that Negroes will either idle or slight their work if they are not closely attended to; & for that reason have doubted the propriety of one man overlooking two places." A year later, he still wanted to hire an additional overseer to avoid further empowering the enslaved foreman at Dogue Run. "When I perceive but too clearly, that Negros are growing more & more insolent & difficult to govern, I am more inclined to incur the expence of an Overseer than to hazard the management, & peace of the place to a Negro." Washington briefly considered making Will, who formerly supervised work at Dogue Run, the overseer of the Mansion House farm, but he instead hired white men for the position. Rather than accede to the hired carpenter's demand for higher wages, Anderson recommended that Isaac share management of the carpenters' work with another enslaved and skilled artisan, James, but Washington hired another white carpenter and joiner.[44]

As early as 1794, Washington had privately shared a concern with a friend about the long-term threat of unrest among the enslaved, writing, "I shall be happily mistaken, if they are not found to be a very troublesome species of property 'ere many years pass over our heads." During the winter of 1798, two of the most valuable breeding asses "died in most violent agonies," and Washington suspected they had been poisoned. When his nephew reported a runaway slave in 1797, Washington advised, "these elopements will be *much more,* before they are *less* frequent; and that the persons making them should never be retained, if they are recovered, as they are sure to contaminate and discontent others." The same report prompted another privately expressed wish by Washington for the Virginia Assembly to enact gradual abolition, but at his estate the short-term response was an enforcement of greater control and supervision. Washington advised Anderson to turn "an investigating Eye" on suspected "idleness and roguery." He also urged Anderson to establish rules for the distribution of grain and hay, "without which, wastes, if not embezzlement, is more to be expected than œconomy." Anderson redoubled efforts to prevent the theft of articles that the enslaved might sell in the local markets that increasingly provided opportunity for them to barter or obtain cash. After he discovered that the cooper Moses had sold barrels of fish in Alexandria, Anderson announced in the newspaper that to guard against those who "make improper use of their privileges," enslaved workers from Mount Vernon would henceforth carry certificates specifying the purpose of their errands in town.[45]

Anderson's shifting allocation of field laborers and tradesmen may have reflected the challenge of efficiently assigning work to the growing number of enslaved laborers on the estate. Once the new course of farming was implemented and the new division of fields was in place, the labor requirements of the farms were fixed, and the number of field laborers at each farm remained relatively stable throughout the 1790s. The number of enslaved carpenters, coopers, and bricklayers was also steady, while the number of slaves on the estate would increase by one hundred people between 1786 and 1799. Early in his service at Mount Vernon, Anderson proposed a reorganization of the farms to reduce the number of field laborers, in part by curtailing the number of acres under cultivation, but the reorganization was never put in place. The distillery provided work for relatively few laborers, and Anderson found that the transfer of field laborers to the distillery or to the larger corps of ditchers had no adverse effect on work at the farms from which they came. In 1798, Anderson proposed the establishment of a new farm and separate quarters for enslaved families on land adjacent to the mill. There the work of some ten to twelve enslaved field laborers, with equal numbers of men and women drawn from each of the existing farms, would be coordinated with the nearby distillery and produce new sources of revenue such as the breeding of thoroughbred horses. In June 1799, Anderson more explicitly addressed the dilemma of finding productive work for the larger number of enslaved on the estate. After sketching out a plan to make the Mount Vernon farms more profitable with fewer laborers, he acknowledged the proposal raised the question : "what is to be done with the Surplus hands?" Anderson's suggestion was either to hire them out "to Advantage," or perhaps to find even more profit by employing many of the slaves in settling Washington's lands in the West. There they would produce revenue within a few years, and by their improvement of the land make the property more valuable for either sale or lease.[46]

Later in the summer of 1799, Washington finally acknowledged, "it is demonstratively clear, that on this Estate (Mount Vernon) I have more working Negros by a full moiety, than can be employed to any advantage in the farming System." He refused to sell any slaves, "because I am principled against this kind of traffic in the human species," and he was reluctant to hire out the laborers because it would be impossible to do so without breaking up families. He pleaded with his nephew Robert Lewis, "What then is to be done? Something must, or I shall be ruined." Having abandoned any expectation that he might lease the four farms, Washington proposed to relocate many of the enslaved under his control. He was convinced that by placing half of them on new farms—far from Mount Vernon—he would gain more income from their labor than he currently made from the entire estate. Relying on Lewis, who had managed the collection of rents from his tenants, Washington explored the possibility of buying out leases from tenants on his lands in Virginia counties west of the Blue Ridge. He asked Lewis to visit a tract of land in Berkeley County and to assess how many laborers could be employed there. At the same time, he attempted to reduce the number of enslaved laborers under his supervision. In July he proposed to return to Penelope French the forty slaves he hired from her in accordance with a land sale agreement. In September, he offered another nephew, Lawrence Lewis, and his wife, Martha's granddaughter Nelly Custis, the lease of Dogue Run farm and adjoining property, and he proposed that they hire the enslaved laborers who worked and resided on that valuable farm. Washington valued the annual hire of six men, thirteen women, and eight working children at £192, £18 more than the annual rent for the land, and the Lewises would assume the care of fourteen younger children and three women who were infirm or "passed labor." If he could also lease the mill, the distillery, and the fishery at Union Farm, Washington thought he would be able to manage the remaining components of the estate by himself.[47]

Over the fall months, Washington offered James Anderson several opportunities to serve him in some reduced capacity while he planned for a further reduction in the number of enslaved field laborers on the remaining farms. While he continued to praise Anderson's enterprise and hard work, Washington frankly told him that the responsibility as manager of the estate was beyond his capabilities, especially given the recent decline in his health. Washington offered him a lease of the mill and distillery and the hire of the enslaved workers there, even though he preferred to put those valuable operations under Lawrence Lewis once he took up residence at Dogue Run. He also offered to let Anderson remain in his employ for another year. By late fall, Lawrence and Nelly Lewis agreed to lease Dogue Run farm, the distillery, and the mill. Anderson chose to remain as manager of the farms at Mount Vernon until Washington put them under his own direction.[48]

Washington assured Anderson, "I shall find no difficulty in superintending my Farms, myself; if not with skill, at least with œconomy." In early December he prescribed an exhaustively detailed program for managing the three remaining farms over the next four years with an anticipated reduction in the number of enslaved laborers. He asked Anderson to assist in the transition by explaining the design to the overseers and supervising their implementation of the latest revision in the system of farming. In addition to detailed instructions for every acre of cleared land on the three farms, Washington offered Anderson a summation of his lifelong approach to the combined management of improved agriculture and enslaved labor. It was the "indispensable duty" of a manager "to take a prospective, and comprehensive view of the *whole* business which is laid before him, that the several parts thereof may be so ordered and arranged, as that one sort of work may follow another sort in proper Succession, and without loss of labour, or of time." A regular course of action, "made known to *all* who are actors in it," made easier the job of the overseers and "would be less harassing to those who labour." With a system in place, "the Overseers, & even the Negros, know, what is to be done, and what they are capable of doing, in ordinary seasons: in short every thing would move like *clock work*."[49]

In the farming plan forwarded to the white overseers at River and Union Farms, Washington announced, "The hands next year may be reduced at all the Farms a little; and the year following, and thence forward, very considerably, as plowing will constitute almost the whole of the work, except at Harvest, and in getting out the Grain, and in Fencing." Once Anderson had reviewed the plans and consulted with the overseers, Washington wanted him to advise on the number of laborers who could be moved from the remaining farms to new lands as early as 1800. Washington also directed Anderson to travel in early spring to his western lands to report on their current condition and the potential for improvement. On December 12, 1799, Washington rode his customary circuit of the farms that he intended to assume the sole management of in another year, and in the worsening winter weather, he personally delivered the farming plan to the overseer at River Farm. The following morning, he awoke with symptoms of the respiratory infection of which he would die a day later. The last letter Washington ever sent was that transmitting the plan to Anderson.[50]

○   ○   ○

Following Washington's death, word quickly spread of the momentous provisions of his will. Prominently included near the beginning of the document written in his own hand and completed in July 1799 was the dramatic announcement that "it is my Will & desire that all the Slaves which I hold in my *own right,* shall receive their freedom." Washington finally granted the enslaved the liberty that he had endorsed in principle and in private for at least sixteen years. Although he "earnestly wished" to make the emancipation effective soon after his death, Washington decided to delay freedom for the enslaved until after the death of Martha so as to spare her, in his words, the "most painful sensations" that would surely accompany the disruption of the many marriages between slaves owned by Washington and those controlled by the Custis estate. Washington reminded readers of the will that it was not in "my power, under the tenure by which the Dower Negroes are held, to manumit them." Only William Lee, Washington's longtime valet, received immediate freedom and an annual stipend, "as a testimony of my sense of his attachment to me, and his faithful services during the Revolutionary War." Once Martha died, the enslaved owned by Washington would face one last condition on their freedom. In his final instruction as a farmer, Washington further delayed the freedom of the laborers until "after the Crops which may then be on the ground are harvested."[51]

In his prescribed support for the children and the elderly among the freed slaves, Washington went well beyond the requirements of Virginia law. All who were too old, too infirm, or too young to support themselves were to be clothed and fed by Washington's heirs. Washington instructed his executors to establish a permanent fund to support the former slaves as long as any required assistance. Any of the young freed people who were orphans and those whose parents were unable to support them would be bound out as indentured servants until they reached the age of twenty-five. Washington insisted that a court set the terms of servitude and determine the age of the freed children if there was no written record. Washington further required that the "Masters or Mistresses" teach the children bound to them to read and write, and that the children "be brought up to some useful occupation, agreeably to the Laws of the Commonwealth of Virginia, providing for the support of Orphan and other poor Children." Washington's choice to extend to the freed Black children the same legal protections that applied to dependent white children was the clearest indication of his expectation that the former slaves would be self-supporting and able to live independently within Virginia. The education and training of the children also made it far more likely that as adults they would be able to pay the minimal taxes and thereby avoid the risk of being detained and bound as servants under the terms of the 1782 manumission act.[52]

By the time Washington wrote his will in the summer of 1799, the first wave of emancipation in Virginia had generated popular opposition and numerous proposals to curtail manumission and restrict the rights of freed slaves. Large-scale and sweeping emancipations, like that prescribed by Robert Carter's deed of manumission, faced serious challenges from family members deprived of an inheritance of the labor that made land valuable. In various ways, the terms of Washington's will protected the freedom of the former slaves from the likeliest challenges. Washington forbid, "under any pretence whatsoever," the sale or transportation out of Virginia of any slave he owned at his death. He ordered his executors "to see that *this* clause respecting Slaves, and every part thereof be religiously fulfilled at the Epoch at which it is directed to take place; without evasion, neglect or delay." The establishment of the fund for support of the freed people was intended to eliminate the possibility of any "uncertain provision to be made by individuals." The first clause of the will required that Washington's few debts be paid "punctually and speedily," thereby shielding the estate from any claims of creditors who might be paid in slave property, as was permitted under a recent change in Virginia law. The delay of emancipation until after Martha's death protected the enslaved from any action based on a 1795 law that allowed a widow to claim a dower right to one-third of a husband's slaves, "notwithstanding they may be emancipated by his will."[53]

While preparing his will in June 1799, Washington simultaneously conducted a census of all of the enslaved people on the estate, noting those he owned, those who were dower slaves, and those hired from Penelope French. Based on that list, the will would have freed 124 persons at Mount Vernon. The census recorded more than twenty married couples that would be divided by the separation of the dower or French's slaves from those owned by Washington. In the will, Washington also provided for the eventual freedom of more than thirty slaves he had accepted ownership of in 1788 as payment on a long-standing debt owed by the estate of Martha's brother, Bartholomew Dandridge. Washington allowed Dandridge's widow to retain custody of the enslaved on her New Kent County land, without any further charge for their hire. At her death, all of the enslaved who had passed the age of forty would be freed immediately. According to the schedule determined by Washington, those between seventeen and thirty-nine would serve an indenture of seven years, and those sixteen and younger would serve until the age of twenty-five. Washington made no further provision for the kind of support or education that he had ensured for the freed slaves from Mount Vernon.[54]

By the terms of his will, Washington provided for the division of the Mount Vernon farms among several of his nephews and his adopted granddaughter. He explained each bequest in terms of family connections and obligations rather than any regard for farming abilities or commitment to agricultural improvement. Bushrod Washington, by then an associate justice on the Supreme Court, would receive the center of the estate, including the Mansion House, Union, and Muddy Hole farms, in recognition of his father John Augustine's management of the estate during the French and

Indian War and in fulfillment of Washington assurances that if he fell in battle, his favorite brother would receive Mount Vernon. The young sons born to Washington's nephew George Augustine and his wife, Martha's niece Fanny Bassett, were to receive the large River Farm and an adjacent farm of 360 acres, in consideration of their "consanguinity" with both Washingtons as well as in acknowledgment of their father's management of the estate during Washington's public service at the Federal Convention and as president. As he had informed Lawrence Lewis and his wife, Nelly, they jointly received most of Dogue Run Farm and adjoining lands, along with the gristmill and distillery. These various divisions would take effect following the death of Martha, to whom Washington bequeathed "the use, profit and benefit of my whole Estate, real and personal, for the term of her natural life."[55]

Had Washington lived long enough to remove enslaved people from the Mount Vernon farms and to settle many, perhaps half, of them on his tenancies or lands further west, it would have vastly complicated the terms of the will. He formulated the plans to reorganize the estate and reduce the number of field laborers at the remaining farms only in the months after he wrote his will and made the decision to free the slaves after his death. Throughout the fall of 1799 Washington had searched for new ways to employ the enslaved people still under his control, apparently abandoning any plan to emancipate them during his lifetime. Once he completed his will in July 1799, Washington focused on ways to reduce the number of enslaved laborers under his immediate supervision, beginning with his proposal to return those hired from the French family and continuing with his offer to let the Lewises hire the enslaved at Dogue Run, the mill, and the distillery. The anticipated removal of other field laborers to western lands would have left Washington with the minimum number of laborers and tradesmen for the experimental rotations that he outlined with such care in December 1799, but still reliant on enslaved field workers to implement his vision of improvement.[56]

◦ ◦ ◦

Freedom came to the Washington slaves at Mount Vernon on January 1, 1801, not as a result of the former president's will but rather by a deed of manumission submitted by Martha Washington in the Fairfax County court in December 1800. At least as early as the previous April, Martha indicated that she would free her husband's slaves during her lifetime, perhaps, as several contemporary accounts suggested, out of fear that as long as she stood between the slaves and their liberty, she would not be safe. By early March 1801, most of the freed people had left the estate. Many remained in Fairfax County, and some were able to purchase land. Several households of freed slaves from Mount Vernon formed the core of a sustained and cohesive free Black community not far from the estate. Some of those individuals may have been able to maintain contact with their family and friends among the dower slaves who were relocated either to the nearby estate of Lawrence and Nelly Custis Lewis or to George Washington Parke Custis's estate at Arlington. Many of the freed people who continued to live in the county or in nearby Alexandria registered as free Blacks in accordance with a Virginia statute of 1793. Washington's executors continued to provide support for the older and infirm freed people until the last of them died in the 1830s.[57]

Within six months of Washington's death, James Anderson drew a bleak picture of the farms and the burdensome costs of operating the estate. With the lease of the valuable Dogue Run farm to Lawrence and Nelly Custis Lewis, revenues from the estate fell well below expenses. Anderson wrote Martha Washington that the estate had been unproductive since he assumed management and that he now considered it "my Duty to resign," as of the end of December. Near the close of the year, Anderson placed in an Alexandria newspaper notice of his impending departure and a request to settle all debts on his or Martha Washington's accounts. As early as March 1800, the executors of Washington's estate began to sell livestock, and following the death of Martha in May 1802, much of the farm equipment was put up for sale. With the emancipation of the Washington slaves and the dispersal of the dower slaves among the Custis children, Mount Vernon lost the agricultural experience and skill of the scores of field workers and artisans. Bushrod Washington shared none of his uncle's interest in agricultural improvement, and under his ownership the farms surrounding the Mansion House went into quick decline.[58]

By the early 1830s, an agricultural reformer visiting Mount Vernon found only poignant reminders of the great ambitions of Washington. "Any, curious to mark the operation of time upon human affairs, would find much for contemplation by riding through the extensive domains of the late General Washington. A more wide spread and perfect agricultural ruin could not be imagined; yet the monuments of the great mind that once ruled, are seen throughout. The ruins of capacious barns, and long extended hedges, seem proudly to boast that their master looked to the future." The visitor recognized that Washington had directed his agricultural improvements toward the future of the nation. The legacy of Washington's commitment to improvement, however, would be found not in any enduring system of farming, but rather in the example of both his determination to make his estate a model for the nation and his belated grant of freedom to the enslaved laborers who had made possible his pursuit of enlightened farming.[59]

Epilogue

The Reputation of a Farmer

In the years following the Revolutionary War, fame and the widespread acclaim for the general-turned-farmer heightened Washington's attention to reputation and the potential legacy of his agricultural improvements. Beginning in 1785, in his most ambitious transformation of farming, Washington organized his estate not just to demonstrate the private advantages of the full course of British farming, but also to exercise a civic-minded leadership comparable to his service in the military and public office. He presented his example for the emulation of smaller farmers and exhibited for the nation the benefits of his learning and access to a global network of improving landowners and naturalists. He saw the success of his implementation of British husbandry as the measure by which this new form of leadership would be judged, and through his pursuit of agricultural improvement he sought to redefine the traditional role of the master of a large estate by reversing the shortcomings of farming in the United States. His efforts to earn the support of enlightened agricultural leaders in Great Britain and Europe and his aspiration to live up to the revolutionary era ideals invested in him as the American Cincinnatus would have their most profound and unexpected impact in his eventual decision to provide for the freedom of the slaves he owned. The response to that manumission would shape the public memory of Washington the farmer, even as it diminished the influence of a model of agricultural improvement that proved far too demanding for smaller farmers.

By dedicating himself to agricultural improvement and the practical demonstration of enlightened farming, Washington embraced an ideal that was shared by other national leaders in the North Atlantic world. The advocates of the New Husbandry equated agricultural improvement with a renewal of civic virtue, and by the last quarter of the eighteenth century, agricultural learning and farming experience had become esteemed qualities of national leaders. Arthur Young offered Washington his prediction that "the time will come when the best & fairest plume in the wing of the Great Frederick" would be his agricultural improvements rather than his military victories. Young encouraged Washington to "send new votaries to the Plough," and to serve for the "Western World" as an example similar to Frederick II, who had transformed agriculture in Prussia. Young stressed that Washington's impact would be inconsequential if he "were merely Mr George Washington planter at Mount Vernon," but his renown gave him the potential for vast influence. "For a man on whom the eyes of the universe are fixed it is some thing for the good of agriculture to have it known that he regards, practices and studies it."[1]

As Young knew well, Washington had an even closer counterpart in George III, whose agricultural experiments and mentors, including Young, closely paralleled those of Washington. Even with limited knowledge of the British monarch's dedication to farming, Washington understood agricultural improvement to be the proper pursuit of a great leader. He received support from the kings of Spain and France, and from his former French military comrades, who encouraged his return from the army to the farm. In the United States, the members of the early agricultural societies were often public officeholders or former officers in the Continental Army, and Washington shared his interest in farming with influential governmental officials, such as John Jay. Washington's most notable agricultural peer in public life was Thomas Jefferson, and their exchanges about farming formed their most amicable bond, even as the political differences between them deepened. Washington and Jefferson, like George III, used their public renown and their private estates to promote what they intended to be national models of agriculture, and for the citizens and subjects of their respective nations, the leaders became the most famous proponents of a system of enlightened farming based on scientific knowledge and practical experience.

After the close of the Revolutionary War, Washington was increasingly recognized as a leader of agricultural improvement in service to the new nation, and his image was embedded in the image of farming. At a celebration of the Treaty of Paris in Boston in March 1784, a citizen displayed on the balcony of his house a depiction of Washington not with the trappings of military command, but rather "crowned with a Laurel—at his right hand, *Commerce;* and on his left, *Agriculture* flourishing." Washington's virtuous attention to farming stood in contrast to the perceived political corruption of the mid-1780s. On the eve of the Federal Convention, "A Farmer" writing in a New Hampshire newspaper praised Washington, who, "like Cincinnatus of old, retired to his farm, and while we had been caballing, and intreaguing has busied himself in improving his lands." When Washington passed through Alexandria en route to his inauguration, citizens hailed their "improver" of agriculture, among the litany of praises for the newly elected president. The author of an early history of the United States, published in 1795, equated Washington's dedication to farming with his public leadership, noting, "President (or, as he is sometimes called, Farmer) Washington is as industrious in agricultural pursuits, as he is brave in the field, or wise in the cabinet." Washington's role as the public-spirited improver continued in retirement from the presidency, when he was toasted as "the illustrious Farmer of Mount Vernon."[2]

The centrality of farming to the public image of Washington's leadership received its most powerful representation in the sculpture commissioned from Houdon for the Virginia state capitol. After the French sculptor visited Mount Vernon in 1785, he created the standing figure of Washington in military dress, but having just removed his cloak and sword as he takes up the walking stick representative of civilian life. Behind Washington is the plow waiting for his return to life as a farmer. The plow is that of Washington, not Cincinnatus, with the visible barrel of a drill plow like that designed by Washington and manufactured by the enslaved craftsmen at Mount Vernon. Houdon's inclusion of symbols of Washington's military, civil, and agricultural leadership followed his consultations with Jefferson, Franklin, and Gouverneur Morris, and their consensus in favor of modern rather than classical dress reaffirmed that Washington's association with farming was more than an allusion to Cincinnatus and the ideals of virtue from antiquity, it was a critical component of his service to the nation.[3]

The image of Washington as Cincinnatus resonated in Great Britain as well as the United States. When the Marquess of Lansdowne in 1797 received the gift of Gilbert Stuart's standing portrait of Washington as president, he placed it near a sculpture of Cincinnatus in his London townhouse. The veneration of Washington as agricultural leader reached wider audiences in Great Britain soon after his death. William Tatham commissioned a copy of Houdon's bust of Washington for presentation to the Society for the Encouragement of Arts, Manufactures, and Commerce, in recognition of Washington's patronage of agriculture and the practical arts and his refusal of the "temptations of popular power, or selfish emoluments." When he delivered the bust in February 1802, Tatham made no reference to the general or the president, only to "George Washington Esqr. of Virginia, . . . friend of Franklin." Tatham praised Washington for his efforts "to inculcate, by practice, those lessons of industry, economy, conciliation and philanthropy, which tend to bring mankind nearer together." That same unifying effect of Washington's commitment to improvement was a central theme of the several volumes of his agricultural correspondence published in Great Britain soon after his death. Sir John Sinclair, James Anderson, and Arthur Young published many of the letters that Washington had requested be kept private during his lifetime, and each of the agricultural writers presented his respective correspondence as evidence that Washington, in his pursuit of agricultural improvement, had promoted reconciliation and the recognition of common interests among nations. Sinclair, in the introduction to his volume, paid tribute to Washington "who, though the immediate cause of the separation between Great Britain and America, yet is the person to whom, in a great measure, is to be ascribed, the good understanding which now so happily subsists between the two countries."[4]

For Sinclair, as for Anderson and Young, Washington embodied the principle that agricultural improvement should be a universal effort, removed from political disputes and national jealousies. James Anderson of Edinburgh recalled there had been no "political intrigue" in the correspondence between a "nameless individual in North Britain" and a man so exalted as Washington. Washington also served as the most compelling example of a great national leader who surrendered power for the life of a farmer. Arthur Young told readers it was "a pleasing spectacle to a reflecting mind, to see so close an attention paid to the practice of Agriculture, by men in the highest situations; who, from commanding Armies, and presiding in Senates, can descend to the humbler walk of Husbandry, and find it an employment sufficient to interest the most splendid talents." Sinclair encouraged his readers to contemplate "a person elevated by the voice of his fellow-citizens, to the summit of political authority; who, instead of wishing to aggrandize himself, and to extend his power, was anxiously bent to quit that situation." Sinclair hoped publication of Washington's agricultural letters would restrain "those, who might otherwise be induced, to dedicate themselves entirely, either to the phantoms of military fame, or the tortures of political ambition."[5]

Sinclair published his volume of letters with engraved facsimiles of Washington's distinctive handwriting, which he thought would make the edition a valuable keepsake in the United States and Great Britain "a Century or two hence." Arthur Young published most of the letters he received from Washington as an account of his farming, and he included the first published print of Washington's 1793 survey of the five farms at Mount Vernon. Young, the publisher of so many agricultural tours and national surveys, concluded that few countries had been described as well as in Washington's survey of farming in the Middle Atlantic and Chesapeake states. James Anderson first published a character study of Washington along with two letters in his monthly magazine. These and additional letters exchanged by Anderson and Washington were gathered in a volume published in Massachusetts in 1800. An Alexandria, Virginia, bookseller combined the Washington letters to Sinclair and Young in a single volume published in 1803.[6]

Sinclair wanted leaders in both nations to read the agricultural correspondence, and he distributed the volume widely. In apparent ignorance of political divisions in the United States, Sinclair in June 1800 sent the volume to John Adams and Thomas Jefferson, urging them to join one another in support of the national board of agriculture proposed by Washington. Sinclair sent the volume for inclusion in the library of George III, and he deposited the original letters from Washington in the British

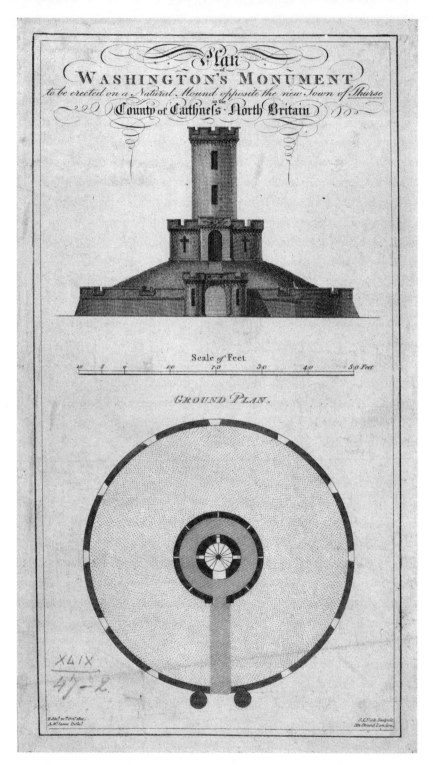

Fig E.1 "Plan of Washington's Monument to be erected . . . opposite the new Town of Thurso." Rendering by Alexander McInnes. When Sir John Sinclair in 1800 published his correspondence from Washington, he assured Martha Washington that the proceeds from the volume would fund a suitable tribute. Sinclair commissioned the design of this monument that he planned to erect in the model new town he established in the far north of Scotland, but it was never constructed. British Library, Maps K.Top.49.47.2.

Museum, "as the precious relics of a great man fit to be preserved in that valuable repository." Sinclair sent Martha Washington the published correspondence, with assurances that he would dedicate any profit from sales of the volume to some suitable tribute to Washington. Sinclair in his plan of publication had suggested to potential subscribers that he would like to fund an agricultural college or other public institution, such as Washington would have promoted. (Instead of establishing a school, Sinclair commissioned from the Scottish architect Alexander McInnes a monument to Washington, to be erected in the square of the model new town he established in a remote area of Northern Scotland, where he renamed one of his farms "Mount Vernon.")[7]

Even more than a decade after his death, Washington remained a paragon of agricultural leadership in the United States. In the preface to a Philadelphia agricultural society publication in 1811, Washington was praised for establishing "the happiness of his country" through his attention to farming. As a military leader, its writer recalled, Washington laid "the foundations of our present prosperity," and in peacetime he was, "in addition to his other virtues, distinguished for his ardent devotion to the interests of AGRICULTURE; and delighted in its practical pursuits." The figure of Fame, "long the faithful eulogist" of the departed military chief, now appeared in the garb and emblems of Ceres, and in the recital of Washington's example the goddess of agriculture called citizens and "the industrious and sober husbandman" from "subjugated portions of Europe" to the cultivation of the nation's fields. Should a monument be raised to the memory of Washington, the preface concluded, its most conspicuous tablet should read: "the encouragement of agricultural improvement, and information, was among the favourite wishes of his heart."[8]

∘   ∘   ∘

The representation of Washington as the American Cincinnatus would live on in the nineteenth century as a model of public virtue and personal integrity, but the veneration of the farmer Washington was divorced from any particular project of agricultural improvement, and the popular image of Washington in retirement at Mount Vernon almost invariably excluded any reference to the emancipation of enslaved people that had closed his life as a farmer. In the nineteenth century, as partisan politics and the pursuit of self-interest characterized so much of public life in the United States, Washington as a farmer remained an exemplary symbol of disinterested service to the nation. His practical methods of farming, however, found few followers after 1800, and his manumission of slaves became so entangled with the politics of slavery and sectionalism as to overshadow his achievements as a farmer.

In the early decades of the nineteenth century, new kinds of agricultural reform rendered the model of improvement advocated by Washington obsolete. In Virginia, collective associations promoted more rigorous scientific analysis of soil and focused on the particular challenges of the state's slave-based agriculture. In northern states, agricultural reform became more democratized and local in its organization, and it was premised on active participation by many farmers rather than demonstrations by large landholders. Washington's model of agricultural improvement had always required too great an investment of time and money for most farmers, who now gained easier access to agricultural knowledge without reliance on the examples of the wealthy few, such as Washington and his associates in the Philadelphia Society for Promoting Agriculture. Washington's emphasis on the renewal of the soil and his advocacy of the incremental settlement of farm communities held little appeal in an age of restless expansion and cheap land made possible by the steady dispossession of the territory of Indian nations west of the Appalachians.[9]

Like many of his British mentors, Washington had long believed that the widespread adoption of improved farming methods depended on the individual initiatives of wealthy landowners, like himself, who could bear the costs of experimentation and who were in a position to exchange their findings and their experience with leading agriculturalists on both sides of the Atlantic. His trust in the persuasive example of respected landowners had always been misplaced, but never more so than in the years following Independence, when farmers were disinclined to defer to the models of wealthy landowners, particularly after prices for American grain dramatically increased in the 1790s. Washington's influence was also limited by his reluctance to present his agricultural innovations to a public audience, consistently declining invitations to publish his observations in the *Annals of Agriculture* and making no contributions to the publications of the several agricultural societies with which he was in frequent contact. He was

Fig E.2   Sixteen-sided barn on Dogue Run farm, c. 1870, glass lantern slide, manufactured by A. D. Handy, Stereopticons and Supplies (Boston, MA). The innovative barn Washington designed for the treading of wheat by horses was abandoned and collapsing by the 1870s. This is the only surviving photograph of the several large barns constructed by enslaved laborers using bricks made at Mount Vernon. As early as 1833, a visitor described "the ruins of capacious barns" on Washington's estate. Courtesy of Mount Vernon Ladies' Association.

equally reticent to participate in public political debates leading up to ratification of the Constitution, but in agricultural matters his reserve may have betrayed his disdain for most common farmers. He frequently referred to the "slovenly farmers" of the United States, and he condescendingly offered his agricultural innovations as an example for "the gazing multitude, ever averse to novelty in matters of this sort, & much attached to their old customs."[10]

Washington had assumed that rural society would remain hierarchical. Among the hired white laborers and managers at Mount Vernon, he enforced categories of class that distinguished between those who might enter his house or even dine at his table and those who remained on the farms or in the workshops, in close proximity to the enslaved. On his lands across the mountains, Washington repeatedly attempted to establish a form of dependency for white settlers through the organization of tenancies that he believed would be a more profitable return on his investments than waiting for the sale of appreciated land. As they discussed the future of slavery in Virginia, David Stuart had shared with Washington his expectation that large estate owners, like Washington, would soon be able to live off the rent paid by tenants. Few were able to do so, but the persistent interest in tenancy revealed the degree to which Washington misunderstood the emergence of an increasingly democratic culture that celebrated the self-made individual. The acceptance of gradations of condition and status may, ironically, have made it easier for Washington to imagine the incorporation of freed slaves into Virginia society, in distinct contrast to Jefferson, whose commitment to equality of citizenship and opportunity for free people led him to insist that any freed slaves be expatriated.[11]

Washington's provision for the freedom of the slaves he owned was unanticipated by the public and its potential impact unclear. His widely published will initially elicited praise from abolitionists, most notably Richard Allen, the African American pastor in Philadelphia, whose eulogy in a Methodist church was one of the first public comments on the manumission. Allen linked the liberation of the enslaved at Mount Vernon to Washington's liberation of the nation, and he praised Washington for overcoming the biases of "popular opinion of the state" in which he lived. Other antislavery writers also likened Washington's act of freeing the enslaved to his defense of the nation's liberty in war. To the disappointment of abolitionists, however, Washington's manumission failed to inspire other slaveholders. Among white planters in Virginia, Washington's dramatic act was met largely with silence that only deepened after Gabriel's Rebellion in 1800 and subsequent slave conspiracies led the state assembly to restrict all manumissions in 1806. Despite his grant of freedom for the enslaved,

Washington was too closely linked to the constitutional order of government and its union with slaveholders to be embraced as a powerful symbol
by abolitionists. In his landmark address "What to the Slave Is the Fourth
of July?" Frederick Douglass in 1852 acknowledged that Washington had
freed slaves on his estate but emphasized that the physical monument then
under construction to the memory of Washington was "built up by the
price of human blood, and the traders in the bodies and souls of men."[12]

By the time Douglass spoke, Washington had become a symbol of national union, ostensibly above the conflicts of partisan or sectional politics. In the popular representation of Washington at Mount Vernon, his
lifelong reliance on enslaved labor was either ignored or presented without
any trace of the harshness of slavery. In the 1850s, two images of Washington
as a farmer set him in sentimentalized scenes of a wheat harvest, with enslaved field workers but no suggestion of forced labor. "Washington as a
Farmer at Mount Vernon," painted by Junius Brutus Stearns in 1851 and
widely reprinted as a lithograph, was part of a series Stearns called "The
Life of Washington," depicting the leader's domestic pursuits as well as
key moments of public service. The painting shows Washington "as a
Farmer" in presidential dress, speaking with a white overseer in a field, but
the painting centers clearly on a neatly dressed Black man, sickle in hand,
taking refreshment after his labor. Close at hand two white children play,
presumably the Custis grandchildren, further assuring the viewer of the
benign character of slavery and labor at Washington's Mount Vernon. In
Nathaniel Currier's "Washington at Mount Vernon 1797," published in
1852, the recently retired president sits astride his horse and respectfully
confers with an enslaved harvest worker, with no overseer as intermediary.
Printed beneath the title is an apocryphal quotation attributed to Washington, extolling agriculture as the "most healthy, the most useful, and the
most noble employment of man." Both images, created by northern art-
ists at a time of intense political controversies over slavery, eliminated any
suggestion of Washington's conflicted attitude toward the system of coerced labor and carried no hint of his grant of freedom for the enslaved.
In the midst of serious threats to the union with which Washington was
so clearly identified, the compelling image of him as a caring master of enslaved labor displaced any representation of him as an innovative farmer
or emancipator.[13]

Washington's contradictory attitude toward slavery as a system of agricultural labor had already complicated the legacy of his manumission of the slaves. At each reorganization of farming on his estate, Washington found innovative ways to adapt enslaved labor to types of work that differed significantly from the cultivation of the staple crop tobacco that had been the impetus for the introduction of slavery in colonial Virginia. Yet in his vision for agriculture in the new nation, Washington saw little future for slavery and implicitly assumed that the cultivation of grain, which he saw as the most promising prospect for farming in the United States, would neither depend upon nor benefit from enslaved labor. Whenever Washington offered his thoughts on the future of farming in the United States, he consistently excluded from consideration the Carolinas and Georgia, with their extensive reliance on enslaved labor and staple agriculture, and unlike Jefferson, he had no interest in drawing on the global exchange of plants and agricultural knowledge to support the expansion of slave-based plantations into the region west of the Carolinas and Georgia. Washington believed the model for the westward extension of commercial agriculture was to be found in the grain-producing region stretching from New York south to Virginia. The most promising practice of farming in the United States was, Washington acknowledged to Sinclair, in Pennsylvania, precisely because that state's enactment of gradual abolition of slavery had encouraged widespread agricultural improvement and increased the value of farmland.[14]

At his own estate, however, Washington, again and again, had through his management and supervision found ways to increase the value of enslaved labor in new systems of farming. In the 1760s he transferred enslaved field hands from tobacco to wheat and found profitable work for a growing number of slaves in the cultivation and processing of crops. In the 1780s he devised an original system for the allocation and supervision of enslaved labor that made possible his implementation of the complicated rotations of British husbandry, and he was largely successful in his efforts to rely more exclusively on enslaved artisans who learned the skills necessary to support the new course of farming. In his final retirement, he initiated plans to transfer slaves from Mount Vernon to work at new farms on his lands west of the Appalachians. In each successive adaptation of enslaved labor, Washington foreshadowed the decisions of other slaveholders who would perpetuate slavery as a viable labor system in Virginia and the Upper South until the Civil War. But while other plantation owners continued to profit from their use of enslaved labor in mixed agriculture, and forcefully relocated or sold many of the increasing number of slaves to new agricultural settlements in the West and Southwest, Washington instead decided to free the slaves he owned. His path to that decision revealed his very different priorities as an estate owner and his acknowledgment of the public attention to his private affairs.

Washington's renown as the hero of the American Revolution and a symbol of liberty, not only in the United States but also in Europe, exposed him to a standard of expectations that applied to no other Virginia slaveholders, and his service as a general and president introduced him to leading antislavery advocates. In Lafayette's first appeal for Washington's support of an experiment in gradual emancipation, he argued that Washington's example would motivate other slaveholders to follow his lead. Similar appeals to Washington continued through the rest of his life, many emphasizing that his stature and reputation would attract broader support for abolition. Washington refused to be a public advocate or supporter of any kind of antislavery movement, but he found instead in a system of farming the hope that he might be able to eliminate the most inhumane aspects of life for the enslaved and to demonstrate how slavery might operate as a more benevolent and productive system of agricultural labor. He aspired to implement a rational system of estate management that embodied the Enlightenment ideals of scientific farming, with an efficiency of work and the cultivation of a harmonious landscape for the betterment of all. For a few years, Washington believed he might reconfigure his estate to demonstrate the benefits of enlightened farming and to improve the lives of the enslaved. But he could never eliminate the violence or the corrosion of trust at the heart of slavery, and he recognized that Virginia was falling behind Pennsylvania, where small farmers prospered in the wake of legislation for the gradual abolition of slavery. It was only after Washington failed to achieve the ideals of improved husbandry while relying almost exclusively on enslaved labor that he finally decided to act on the antislavery principles that he professed to share as early as 1783. The ownership of slaves, he privately acknowledged more than a decade later, had become something repugnant "to my own feelings."

Washington's management of enslaved labor had since the Revolutionary War reflected his profound concern with personal reputation and public identity. In deliberating over the possible sale of slaves and his expressed wish "to get quit of Negroes," Washington wanted to disassociate himself from any public sale or any appearance of acting against the wishes of the enslaved individuals designated for sale. In his effort to ameliorate the conditions of the enslaved after 1785, he considered the inadequacy of food or medical treatment an embarrassment to him as well as an injury to his "feelings." In the recovery of an escaped slave during his presidency, he instructed his estate manager to avoid any publication of the runaway notice in newspapers published north of Virginia, in the cities where anti-slavery sentiment was growing. He ordered his secretary to deceive the enslaved and the public about his efforts to circumvent the Pennsylvania abolition law by transporting enslaved servants out of the state. The extraordinary provisions of his will went well beyond the legal requirements for support of the freed slaves and ensured that Washington would never be associated with the impoverishment of the former slaves or their return to some other form of servitude.

The costly provisions for the support of the freed slaves and the absence of any public explanation of his motivation for the manumission by his will suggest Washington did not expect other slaveholders to follow his lead. According to the account of the French abolitionist Brissot, who visited Mount Vernon in 1788, Washington had concluded that most Virginia planters were unwilling to support any form of gradual abolition, and by the time he wrote his will in the summer of 1799, he had even more reason to doubt that his example would inspire individual acts of emancipation. By 1799, the declining number of manumissions and the assembly's imposition of additional legal restrictions on slaveholders' ability to free slaves eliminated any lingering expectation that Virginia might enact the general abolition that Washington considered essential for the future prosperity of agriculture in states reliant on enslaved labor. He was left to his own choices, and in his will he at last fulfilled his pledge from 1794 "to liberate a certain species of property."

∘   ∘   ∘

By the close of Washington's life, the agricultural economy, like the political culture, had changed in ways that limited the influence of a wealthy landowner's example, even if the owner of the estate was the most revered of the founders. The model of agricultural improvement at Mount Vernon had been an essential component of the leadership Washington wanted to offer the new nation. The design of a new course of farming and its execution in collaboration with British agriculturalists reflected Washington's expectation that a particular form of agricultural improvement would help to define the nation's engagement with the wider world. The exchange of agricultural knowledge and peaceful commerce with Europe based on the produce of the United States would forge new connections to replace those of an older empire. Enlightened farming and the trade arising from it would ensure the United States' commercial strength and its respect among nations. Washington used his renown and his control of landed resources and enslaved labor to demonstrate a civic commitment in ways that would advance his private interests as well as those of the nation. The depth of his attachment to British models of farming and his further attention to reputation in the face of steady appeals from antislavery advocates finally led Washington to acknowledge that his system of improved farming could not be reconciled with slavery. In his will, Washington ensured that more than 120 enslaved persons would find freedom from their bondage at Mount Vernon, and in that action, unique among the founders in its scale, he endorsed a revolutionary legacy of liberty.

In his provision for the emancipation of enslaved people, Washington secured his reputation and affirmed his identification with enlightened advocates of improvement on both sides of the Atlantic, but he left the nation no principled statement of opposition to slavery and no practical plan that might have encouraged other planters to end their reliance on enslaved labor. The broader terms of the will, particularly the division of the farms among family members who were almost certain to continue the enslavement of agricultural laborers, represented an abandonment of both the project of agricultural improvement and the hopes for any statewide policy of gradual abolition. With the text of the will that would serve as his only public statement on the subject of slavery, Washington ensured that his name would be linked with emancipation, but the model of agricultural improvement that had transformed his own management of enslaved labor and led him to consider freeing the enslaved on his estate could not reverse the deepening commitment to slavery among landowners in Virginia and states to the south.

Washington closed his life as a farmer in much the same way that he exited from his military career and public service, with a keen awareness of his example and a sure sense of responsibility. If he could not establish a system of farming that eliminated the brutality of slavery or opened the way to free labor, he could answer the many appeals that urged him to free the enslaved people he owned as a fulfillment of his role as the most celebrated defender of American liberty. He characteristically let his actions speak for themselves, with no effort to explain himself or to persuade others of the rightness of his choice of emancipation. In ensuring the freedom of the enslaved, Washington looked beyond the interests of his family and other Virginia planters, and toward the promise of an enlightened community among nations that had originally drawn him to the transatlantic culture of agricultural improvement.

Abbreviations

Notes

Acknowledgments

Index

Abbreviations

Diaries   *The Diaries of George Washington.* Donald Jackson and
            Dorothy Twohig, eds. Charlottesville: University Press
            of Virginia, 1976–1979. 6 volumes.

Founders Online, Early Access
            https://founders.archives.gov/about/EarlyAccess

GWP, LOC   George Washington Papers, Manuscripts Division,
            Library of Congress.

Ledger A   George Washington Papers, Library of Congress,
            Manuscripts Division, Series 5, Financial Papers:
            General Ledger A, 1750–1772. Online at "The George
            Washington Financial Papers Project" of the Papers of
            George Washington Project. http://financial.gwpapers
            .org. Photostats at the Washington Library.

Ledger B   George Washington Papers, Library of Congress,
            Manuscripts Division, Series 5, Financial Papers:
            General Ledger B, 1772–1793. Online at "The George
            Washington Financial Papers Project" of the Papers of
            George Washington Project. http://financial.gwpapers
            .org. Photostats at the Washington Library.

Ledger C   General Ledger C, 1790–1799, Morristown National
                Historical Park, Morristown, NJ. Online at "The
                George Washington Financial Papers Project" of the
                Papers of George Washington Project. http://financial
                .gwpapers.org. Photostats at the Washington Library.

PGW, Col.   *The Papers of George Washington, Colonial Series.*
                W.W. Abbot, ed. Charlottesville: University Press of
                Virginia, 1983–1995. 10 volumes.

PGW, Conf.   *The Papers of George Washington, Confederation Series.*
                W.W. Abbot, ed. Charlottesville: University Press of
                Virginia, 1992–1997. 6 volumes.

PGW, Pres.   *The Papers of George Washington, Presidential Series.*
                Dorothy Twohig et al., eds. Charlottesville: University
                Press of Virginia, 1987–2020. 21 volumes.

PGW, Ret.   *The Papers of George Washington, Retirement Series.*
                W.W. Abbot, ed. Charlottesville: University Press of
                Virginia, 1998–1999. 4 volumes.

PGW, Rev.   *The Papers of George Washington, Revolutionary War
                Series.* Philander D. Chase et al., eds. Charlottesville:
                University Press of Virginia, 1985–.

Washington Library
                The Fred W. Smith National Library for the Study of
                George Washington at Mount Vernon.

Notes

INTRODUCTION

1. *Diaries,* 5: 166–168, 173, 178–179, 181–182, 243; Philadelphia Cash Accounts, 9 May—22 September 1787, *PGW, Conf.,* 5: 173–181; Andrea Wulf, *Founding Gardeners: The Revolutionary Generation, Nature, and the Shaping of the American Nation* (New York: Alfred A. Knopf, 2011), chap. 3.

2. GW to Elias Boudinot, 18 February 1784, *PGW, Conf.,* 1: 127–128; GW to Metcalf Bowler, 19 August 1786, *PGW, Conf.,* 4: 220–221; GW to Samuel Chamberline, 3 April 1788, *PGW, Conf.,* 6: 190–191; GW to Arthur Young, 20 October 1792, *PGW, Pres.,* 11: 249.

3. Philip Levy, *Where the Cherry Tree Grew: The Story of Ferry Farm, George Washington's Boyhood Home* (New York: St. Martin's Press, 2013), 31–61; Martha Saxton, *The Widow Washington: The Life of Mary Washington* (New York: Farrar, Straus and Giroux, 2019), 113–114, 158–161.

4. Lorena S. Walsh, *Motives of Honor, Pleasure, and Profit: Plantation Management in the Colonial Chesapeake, 1607–1763* (Chapel Hill: University of North Carolina Press, 2010), 472–538.

5. GW to George William Fairfax, 30 June 1785, *PGW, Conf,.* 3: 87–92; Arthur Young to Edmund Rack, 12 October 1785, enclosed in George William Fairfax to GW, 23 January 1786, *PGW, Conf.,* 3: 517–521, n. 1.

6. Washington's presentation of farming as a model for the new nation discussed in Jean B. Lee, "Mount Vernon Plantation: A Model for the Republic," in Philip J. Schwarz, ed., *Slavery at the Home of George Washington* (Mount Vernon, VA: Mount Vernon Ladies' Association, 2001), 13–45.

7. GW to Alexander Spotswood, 23 November 1794, *PGW, Pres.,* 17: 206–207; for overviews of Washington and slavery, see Philip D. Morgan, "'To Get Quit of

Negroes': George Washington and Slavery," *Journal of American Studies* 39 (December 2005): 403–429; Kenneth Morgan, "George Washington and the Problem of Slavery," *Journal of American Studies* 34, no. 2 (2000): 279–301; Mary V. Thompson, *"The Only Unavoidable Subject of Regret": George Washington, Slavery, and the Enslaved Community at Mount Vernon* (Charlottesville: University of Virginia Press, 2019); Dorothy Twohig, "'That Species of Property': Washington's Role in the Controversy over Slavery," in Don Higginbotham, ed., *George Washington Reconsidered* (Charlottesville: University Press of Virginia, 2001), 114–138; Lorena S. Walsh, "Slavery and Agriculture at Mount Vernon," in Schwarz, ed., *Slavery at the Home of George Washington,* 47–77; Henry Wiencek, *An Imperfect God: George Washington, His Slaves, and the Creation of America* (New York: Farrar, Straus and Giroux, 2003).

8. Philip D. Morgan, *Slave Counterpoint: Black Culture in the Eighteenth-Century Chesapeake and Lowcountry* (Chapel Hill: University of North Carolina Press, 1998), 659–672; Walsh, *Motives of Honor, Pleasure, and Profit,* 624–637; Ira Berlin, *Many Thousands Gone: The First Two Centuries of Slavery in North America* (Cambridge, MA: Belknap Press of Harvard University Press, 1998), 256–289; Richard S. Dunn, "Black Society in the Chesapeake, 1776–1810," in Ira Berlin and Ronald Hoffman, eds., *Slavery and Freedom in the Age of the American Revolution* (Charlottesville: University Press of Virginia, 1983), 49–82.

9. Manisha Sinha, *The Slave's Cause: A History of Abolition* (New Haven, CT: Yale University Press, 2016), 35–53, 85–86; Morgan, *Slave Counterpoint,* 665–666; Walsh, *Motives of Honor, Pleasure, and Profit,* 637; John E. Selby, *The Revolution in Virginia, 1775–1783* (Williamsburg, VA: Colonial Williamsburg Foundation, 1988), 158, 321–322.

10. Morgan, "'To Get Quit of Negroes': George Washington and Slavery," 407–408; Joseph J. Ellis, *His Excellency George Washington* (New York: Alfred A. Knopf, 2004), 256–261.

11. For overviews of recent scholarship on slavery and capitalism, see "Introduction: Slavery's Capitalism," in Sven Beckert and Seth Rockman, eds., *Slavery's Capitalism: A New History of American Economic Development* (Philadelphia: University of Pennsylvania Press, 2016), 1–27; Seth Rockman, "Review: What Makes the History of Capitalism Noteworthy?," *Journal of the Early Republic* 34, no. 3 (Fall 2014): 439–466; Caitlin Rosenthal, "Slavery's Scientific Management," in *Slavery's Capitalism,* 62–86.

12. Morgan, *Slave Counterpoint,* 662; GW to Arthur Young, 1 November 1787, *PGW, Conf.,* 5: 402–405.

13. GW to Anthony Whitting, 4 September 1791, 25 November 1792, *PGW, Pres.,* 8: 487–489, 11: 439–443; GW to William Pearce, 8 February 1795, *PGW, Pres.,* 17: 510–511; GW to James Anderson, 22 May 1798, *PGW, Ret.,* 2: 287–291; Brian Bonnyman, *The Third Duke of Buccleuch and Adam Smith: Estate Management and Improvement in Enlightenment Scotland* (Edinburgh: Edinburgh University Press, 2014), 196–197; Frederick B. Tolles, "George Logan and the Agricultural Revolution," *Proceedings of the American Philosophical Society* 95, no. 6 (1951): 589–596; Ellis, *His Excellency George Washington,* 262; on calculations of profit by Virginia planters in response to British husbandry, see Richard Lyman Bushman, *The American Farmer in the*

Eighteenth Century: A Social and Cultural History (New Haven, CT: Yale University Press, 2018), 206–207.

14. GW to Robert Morris, 1 February 1785, *PGW, Conf.*, 2: 309–315; for an examination of Washington's investments and enterprises with a greater emphasis on entrepreneurial spirit, see Edward G. Lengel, *First Entrepreneur: How George Washington Built His—and the Nation's—Prosperity* (Boston, MA: Da Capo Press, 2016).

15. GW to John Beale Bordley, 17 August 1788, *PGW, Conf.*, 6: 450–454; for networks of exchange, see Richard Drayton, *Nature's Government: Science, Imperial Britain, and the "Improvement" of the World* (New Haven, CT: Yale University Press, 2000); Anya Zilberstein, *A Temperate Empire: Making Climate Change in Early America* (New York: Oxford University Press, 2016), esp. 56–79.

16. For roots of British and settler definitions of improvement, see Zilberstein, *A Temperate Empire*, 148–160; on the importance of agricultural knowledge drawn from books, see James Daniel Fisher, "Rethinking Agricultural Books, Knowledge and Labour in Britain c. 1660–c. 1800" (Ph.D. diss., King's College London, 2018), 38, 127–165; Peter M. Jones, *Agricultural Enlightenment: Knowledge, Technology, and Nature, 1750–1840* (Oxford, UK: Oxford University Press, 2016), 6, 57–61.

17. RCIN 1047477, 1047478, 1047479, Nathaniel Kent, "Journal of the progressive improvements in Windsor Great Park," 3 vols., Royal Library, Windsor; RCIN 1047476, Nathaniel Kent, "Plan, submitted with great deference to His Majesty, upon the present State, and future Improvement of the Great Park at Windsor," Royal Library, Windsor; Nathaniel Kent, "On his Majesty's Farm upon Windsor Forest," in A. Hunter, ed., *Georgical Essays* (York: T. Wilson and R. Spence, 1803), vol. 4: 172–188; Jane Roberts, *Royal Landscape: The Gardens and Parks of Windsor* (New Haven, CT: Yale University Press, 1997), 59–75; Vincent Carretta, *George III and the Satirists from Hogarth to Byron* (Athens: University of Georgia Press, 1990), 269–294; Arthur Young, *The Autobiography of Arthur Young* (London: Smith, Elder, 1898), 132.

18. This understanding of improvement relies most importantly on Drayton, *Nature's Government*, esp. xv, 50–67, 85–89; see also Paul Warde, *The Invention of Sustainability: Nature and Destiny, c. 1500–1870* (Cambridge, UK: Cambridge University Press, 2018), 240–254; Benjamin R. Cohen, *Notes from the Ground: Science, Soil, and Society in the American Countryside* (New Haven, CT: Yale University Press, 2009), 2–12, 25–28, 37–42; Colin G. Calloway, *The Indian World of George Washington* (New York: Oxford University Press, 2018), 75–76; for contrasting experience of contemporary New England farmers, see Brian Donahue, *The Great Meadow: Farmers and the Land in Colonial Concord* (New Haven, CT: Yale University Press, 2004), 206–208.

19. Lee, "Mount Vernon Plantation: A Model for the Republic," 23–28; GW to Anthony Whiting, 2 December 1792, *PGW, Pres.*, 11: 460–464.

20. Richard Peters, "Sketches of Gen. Washington's Private Character," *Memoirs of the Philadelphia Society for Promoting Agriculture*, vol. 2 (Philadelphia: Johnson & Warner, 1811), i–ix.

21. GW to Alexander Spotswood, 13 February 1788, *PGW, Conf.*, 6: 110–113. For discussion of the georgic ethic and the ideal of enlightened landowner, see Cohen, *Notes from the Ground*, 9–12, 17–48; and Laura Browne Sayre, "Farming by the Book: British Georgic

in Prose and Practice, 1697–1820" (Ph.D. diss., Princeton University, 2002), 27–29, 375–420.

1. THE EXPERIMENTS OF A VIRGINIA PLANTER

1. *Diaries,* 1: 246, 255, 257–258, 263.
2. Invoice from Robert Cary & Company, 6 August 1759, *PGW, Col.,* 6: 332–337; GW copied notes on Tull into his diaries for May 1760, Series 1, Exercise Books, Diaries, and Surveys, ca. 1745–99, Subseries 1B, GWP, LOC; *Diaries,* 1, 250–251, 256, 261; Invoice from Richard Washington, 20 August 1757, *PGW, Col.,* 4: 376–381.
3. *Diaries,* 1: 267–268; Walsh, *Motives of Honor, Pleasure, and Profit,* 442.
4. Douglas Southall Freeman, *George Washington: A Biography,* 7 vols. (New York: Scribner, 1951), 3: 58; GW to Richard Washington, 15 April 1757, *PGW, Col.,* 4: 132–134.
5. John Carlyle to GW, 17 June 1754, 22 August 1758, *PGW, Col.,* 1: 140–145, 5: 407–408; GW to John Augustine Washington, 6 May 1755, 28 May 1755, 14 June 1755, *PGW, Col.,* 1: 266–268, 289–293, 311–314; Bruce A. Ragsdale, "George Washington, the British Tobacco Trade, and Economic Opportunity in Pre-Revolutionary Virginia," *Virginia Magazine of History and Biography* 97 (April 1989): 133–162, reprinted in Higginbotham, ed., *George Washington Reconsidered,* 67–93; GW to Richard Washington, 6 December 1755, *PGW, Col.,* 2: 207–208; Invoice from Thomas Knox, 18 August 1758, *PGW, Col.,* 5: 399–403; Invoice from Richard Washington, 20 August 1757, 10 November 1757, *PGW, Col.,* 4: 376–381, 5: 49–51; Chris Evans, "The Plantation Hoe: The Rise and Fall of an Atlantic Commodity, 1650–1850," *William and Mary Quarterly* 69, no. 1 (January 2012): 71–100.
6. Humphrey Knight to GW, 16 June, 23 August, 24 August 1758, *PGW, Col.,* 5: 217–219, 415–416, 418–419; Ledger A, 11, 14; William Poole to GW, 9 July 1758, *PGW, Col.,* 5: 274–275.
7. Slave purchases recorded in Ledger A, 10, 11, 18, 19, 21, 31, 34, 37; Humphrey Knight to GW, 2 September 1758, *PGW, Col.,* 5: 447–449; GW to John Augustine Washington, 14 June 1755, *PGW, Col.,* 1: 311–314; John Carlyle to GW, 12 January 1756, *PGW, Col.,* 2: 275–277; Christopher Hardwick to GW, 26 August 1758, *PGW, Col.,* 5: 422; Payment of threshers recorded in Ledger A, Cash Account, 1756 (no folio number), and 31; Morgan, "'To Get Quit of Negroes': George Washington and Slavery," 407–408; Donald M. Sweig, "The Importation of African Slaves to the Potomac River, 1732–1772," *William and Mary Quarterly* 42, no. 4 (October 1985): 515–518; Thompson, *"The Only Unavoidable Subject of Regret,"* 332–336.
8. Charles Smith to GW, 27 August 1758, *PGW, Col.,* 5: 423–424; Humphrey Knight to GW, 16 June 1758, 13 July 1758, 2 September 1758, *PGW, Col.,* 5: 217–219, 284–285, 447–449; Christopher Hardwick to GW, 26 August 1758, *PGW, Col.,* 5: 422; on overseers generally, see Tristan Stubbs, *Masters of Violence: The Plantation Overseers of Eighteenth-Century Virginia, South Carolina, and Georgia* (Columbia: University of South Carolina Press, 2018).
9. George William Fairfax to GW, 5 August 1758, *PGW, Col.,* 5: 371–373; John Carlyle to GW, 22 August 1758, *PGW, Col.,* 5: 407–408; Humphrey Knight to GW, 2 September 1758, *PGW, Col.,* 5: 447–449.

10. Survey Notes, 1–2 October 1759, Washington Library.

11. "The Growth of Mount Vernon, 1754–86," *Diaries,* 1: 241–242; *Diaries,* 1: 281; "Mount Vernon Estate and Gardens: Cultural Landscape Study," vol. 1, Prepared by John Milner Associates, Inc., Charlottesville, Va. (November 2004), 2.57.

12. Humphrey Knight to GW, 23 August 1758, *PGW, Col.,* 5: 415–416, n. 1; for purchases of existing leases, see for example, Cash Accounts, August 1760, Ledger A, 98; Lease to Samuel Johnston, 25 December 1761, *PGW, Col.,* 7: 100–103; George Washington, "A Plan of Mr. Clifton's Neck Land. Platted . . . by T.H. 1755 and copied by Washington in 1760," G3882.M7B5 1755 .W3, Geography and Map Division, LOC; GW to Charles Washington, 15 August 1764, *PGW, Col.,* 7: 329–331; George Washington, "A plan of my farm on Little Huntg Creek & Potomk," G3882.M7 1766 .W3, Geography and Map Division, LOC.

13. Thompson, "*The Only Unavoidable Subject of Regret,*" 13, 333; Assignment of the Widow's Dower, [ca. October 1759], *PGW, Col.,* 6: 217–220.

14. Slave purchases for 1759 recorded in GW's Cash Accounts, *PGW, Col.,* 6: 197–200, 313, 321; in his account with the estate of Daniel Parke Custis and in correspondence with the Hanburys, Washington recorded his draft on Capel and Osgood Hanbury for £99, payable to Champe & Hunter, Ledger A, 57, and GW to Capel and Osgood Hanbury, 26 August 1759, *PGW, Col.,* 6: 338–339; John Champe & Company advertised a sale of 350 African slaves to begin on 20 August 1759 (*Maryland Gazette,* 16 August 1759). Washington entered the costs of ferriage to and within Maryland on 20 August, Cash Accounts, *PGW, Col.,* 6: 331–332. In a runaway advertisement of 11 August 1761, Washington described Neptune and Cupid as slaves bought from an African ship in August 1759, *PGW, Col.,* 7: 65–68). Washington often failed to record the names of individual slaves at the time of purchase, making it impossible to determine where they lived and what work they did. For marriage of Hannah and Morris, Thompson, "*The Only Unavoidable Subject of Regret,*" 131.

15. Most of the slave purchases between 1760 and 1764 recorded in Cash Accounts, *PGW, Col.,* 7: 1–11, 104–111, 335–337; Ledger A, 173; *Maryland Gazette,* 16 August 1759, 30 July 1761; Thompson, "*The Only Unavoidable Subject of Regret,*" 332–336; Sweig, "Importation of African Slaves to the Potomac River," 507–524; Gregory E. O'Malley, *Final Passages: The Intercolonial Slave Trade of British America, 1619–1807* (Chapel Hill: University of North Carolina Press, 2014), 322.

16. Memorandum, Division of Slaves, 1762, *PGW, Col.,* 7: 172–174; Account of Carpenters Work, 1760–1764, Washington Library; new slaves and their work at Mount Vernon recorded in GW's Memorandum Lists of Tithables, beginning in 1760, *PGW, Col.,* 6: 428, 7: 45, 139, 227–228, 313, 376–377.

17. GW to Robert Cary & Company, 1 May 1759, *PGW, Col.,* 6: 315–317; for correspondence between Martha Custis and the English tobacco merchants, see Joseph E. Fields, *Worthy Partner: The Papers of Martha Washington* (Westport, Conn: Greenwood Press, 1994), 3–61. The variety of goods imported through Robert Cary & Company described in the numerous invoices, *PGW, Col.,* vols. 6–9; GW to Robert Cary & Company, 20 September 1759, *PGW, Col.,* 6: 348–352.

18. GW to Robert Cary & Company, 20 September 1759, *PGW, Col.,* 6: 348–352; GW to James Gildart, 20 September 1759, *PGW, Col.,* 6: 348.

19. Editorial Note, *PGW, Col.*, 6: 201–209; Fields, *Worthy Partner,* 8–9; Joseph Horrell and Richard W. Oram, "George Washington's 'Marble Colour'd Folio Book': A Newly Identified Ledger," *William and Mary Quarterly* 43, no. 2 (1986): 252–266; Washington's Appointment as Guardian, 21 October 1761, *PGW, Col.,* 7: 84.

20. GW to Burwell Bassett, 9 August 1759, Washington Library; General Account of the Estate, 1758–1759, *PGW, Col.*, 6: 266–270.

21. Combined County Inventory of Slaves and Personal Property in the Estate, 1757–58, *PGW, Col.*, 6: 220–232; List of Books at Mount Vernon, 1764, *PGW, Col.*, 7: 343–350; Walsh, *Motives of Honor, Pleasure, and Profit,* 440–446.

22. Assignment of the Widow's Dower, [ca. October 1759], *PGW, Col.*, 6: 217–220; Appendix C, List of Artisans and Household Slaves in the Estate [ca. 1759], *PGW, Col.*, 6: 282; Schedule B: General Account of the Estate, c. October 1759, *PGW, Col.*, 6: 252–261; Walsh, *Motives of Honor, Pleasure, and Profit,* 447.

23. "Mount Vernon Estate and Gardens: Cultural Landscape Study," 1: 2.48–71; Organization of plantations at Mount Vernon in Memorandum List of Tithables, May 1760, 4 June 1761, *PGW, Col.*, 6: 428, 7: 45; Ledger A, 120, 148, 149; for marriage and family patterns among the enslaved, see Thompson, *"The Only Unavoidable Subject of Regret,"* 127–131.

24. *Diaries,* 1: 215, 251–252, 265, 270–273, 280; Ledger A, 163, 185; sometime between 1760 and June 1761, two slaves, Ned Holt and Perros, were moved from the Custis estates to Mount Vernon, see List of Dower Slaves, *PGW, Col.*, 6: 311–13; Memorandum List of Tithables, 4 June 1761, *PGW, Col.*, 7: 45.

25. T. Williamson, *The Transformation of Rural England: Farming and the Landscape, 1700–1870* (Exeter, UK: University of Exeter Press, 2002), 3–19, 170; Joel Mokyr, *The Enlightened Economy: An Economic History of Britain, 1750–1850* (New Haven, CT: Yale University Press, 2009), 171–197; Jones, *Agricultural Enlightenment,* 1–29, 57–97; Mark Overton, *Agricultural Revolution in England: The Transformation of the Agrarian Economy, 1500–1850* (Cambridge, UK: Cambridge University Press, 1996), 70–132.

26. The literature on agricultural improvement and the emergence of a new rural order in eighteenth-century Britain is extensive; see Jones, *Agricultural Enlightenment,* chaps. 3 and 4; Mokyr, *The Enlightened Economy,* introduction and chap. 9; Williamson, *The Transformation of Rural England,* chap. 1; and especially, Fisher, "Rethinking Agricultural Books, Knowledge and Labour in Britain c. 1660–c. 1800."

27. Fisher, "Rethinking Agricultural Books"; Jones, *Agricultural Enlightenment,* 11; Mokyr, *The Enlightened Economy,* 192.

28. Jones, *Agricultural Enlightenment,* 60; Fisher, "Rethinking Agricultural Books," 123–134.

29. Sayre, "Farming by the Book: British Georgic in Prose and Practice," 4–5, 67; Edward Lisle, *Observations in Husbandry,* 2 vols., 2nd ed. (London: L. J. Hughs, etc., 1757), 1: xi, xix.

30. Jones, *Agricultural Enlightenment,* 14–15, 112–119; Mokyr, *The Enlightened Economy,* 185.

31. GW to Robert Cary & Company, 1 May 1759, 24 October 1760, *PGW, Col.*, 6: 315–317, 471–473; Invoice to Robert Cary & Company, 1 May 1759, 31 March 1761, *PGW, Col.*, 6:

317–318, 7: 22–31; Invoice from Robert Cary & Company, 6 August 1759, 31 March 1761, *PGW, Col.,* 6: 332–337, 7: 22–31; Cash Accounts, April 1764, *PGW, Col.,* 7: 298–300; Kevin J. Hayes, *George Washington: A Life in Books* (New York: Oxford University Press, 2017), 91–109; Amanda C. Isaac, *Take Note!: George Washington the Reader* (George Washington's Mount Vernon, 2013), 61–74.

32. The American Correspondence of the Royal Society of Arts, London, 1755–1840, Guard Books (1755–70) and Loose Archives (1755–1840), Virginia Historical Society microfilm, ViH Mss 10: no. 92; Robert Leroy Hilldrup, "A Campaign to Promote the Prosperity of Colonial Virginia," *Virginia Magazine of History and Biography* 67 (October 1959): 410–428; Walsh, *Motives of Honor, Pleasure, and Profit,* 526, 532–537; Subscription for Maurice Pound, October 1759, *PGW, Col.,* 6: 368–370.

33. Walsh, *Motives of Honor, Pleasure, and Profit,* 527–537; Rhys Isaac, *Landon Carter's Uneasy Kingdom: Revolution and Rebellion on a Virginia Plantation* (New York: Oxford University Press, 2004), 76–84, 101–103; Hayes, *George Washington: A Life in Books,* 91–109.

34. *Museum Rusticum et Commerciale,* vol. 1 (London: Printed for R. Davis, 1764), 1, 4; Francis Home, *Principles of Agriculture and Vegetation,* 2nd ed. (London: A. Millar, 1757), iii–iv; Robert Maxwell, *The Practical Husbandman: Being a Collection of Miscellaneous Papers on Husbandry, &c.* (Edinburgh: C. Wright and Company, 1757), v–vi.

35. Maxwell, *The Practical Husbandman,* iii–iv; *Museum Rusticum,* preface; Thomas Hale, *A Compleat Body of Husbandry,* 4 vols. (London: T. Osborne, 1758–1759), 1: v; Jethro Tull, *Horse-Hoeing Husbandry: Or, An Essay On the Principles of Vegetation And Tillage,* 3rd ed. (London: Printed for A. Millar, 1751), ix.

36. *The Farmer's Compleat Guide* (London: G. Kearsly, 1760), 2.

37. Notes on Tull in Diaries for May 1760, GWP, LOC; Home, *Principles of Agriculture and Vegetation,* 81–103; Hayes, *George Washington: A Life in Books,* 98–100; *Diaries,* 1: 266–268; Hale, *A Compleat Body of Husbandry,* 1: 105–106; *Diaries,* 1: 296; Invoice to Robert Cary & Company, 12 October 1761, *PGW, Col.,* 7: 77–80; *A Practical Treatise of Husbandry,* 2nd ed. (London: C. Hitch and L. Hawes, 1762), 49; Alan Fusonie and Donna Jean Fusonie, comps., "A Selected Bibliography on George Washington's Interest in Agriculture," Agricultural History Center, University of California at Davis, January 1976, typescript at Washington Library, 8–9. Maxwell's *The Practical Husbandman,* which Washington acquired at about the same time as he bought Duhamel, included a diagram and detailed description of the "Rotheran" plow but associated it with Scotland.

38. Tull, *Horse-Hoeing Husbandry,* 14; *Diaries,* 1: 266–268, 275, 282–283.

39. *Diaries,* 1: 256, 260–261, 269, 282, 296, 300.

40. GW to Richard Washington, 7 May 1759, *PGW, Col.,* 6: 319–320; Indenture with John Askew, 1 September 1759, *PGW, Col.,* 6: 340–341; Account of Carpenters' Work, Washington Library; Ledger A, 102.

41. *Diaries,* 1: 232–234.

42. *Diaries,* 1: 227, 230, 253, 296; Ledger A, 120.

43. Indenture with John Askew, 1 September 1759, *PGW, Col.,* 6: 340–341; Account of Carpenters' Work, Washington Library; Agreement with Burgis Mitchell, 1 May 1762,

PGW, Col., 7: 131–132; *Diaries,* 1: 304; Washington paid Mitchell 10 shillings when he was hired, and he paid the tithable for Mitchell in June 1762, but he never paid Mitchell any portion of the £6 offered in the letter of agreement; for overseer contracts in Virginia generally, see Stubbs, *Masters of Violence,* 55–63.

44. Agreement with Edward Violet, 5 August 1762, *PGW, Col.,* 7: 143–146; Agreement with Nelson Kelly, 1 September 1762, *PGW, Col.,* 7: 148–151; *Diaries,* 1: 313–314.

45. Agreement with Edward Violet, 5 August 1762, *PGW, Col.,* 7: 143–146; Agreement with Nelson Kelly, 1 September 1762, *PGW, Col.,* 7: 148–151.

46. GW to Robert Cary & Company, 3 April 1761, 12 October 1761, 28 May 1762, 18 September 1762, 26 April 1763, *PGW, Col.,* 7: 33–35, 76–77, 135–137, 153–155, 202–205; Ledger A, 148.

47. Ledger A, 104, 120, 148–149, 161–164, 206–207; GW to Robert Cary & Company, 27 September 1763, *PGW, Col.,* 7: 251–253.

48. GW to Robert Cary & Company, 20 June 1762, 18 September 1762, 26 April 1763, 22 January 1764, *PGW, Col.,* 7: 140–141, 153–155, 202–205, 284–285; Ragsdale, "George Washington, the British Tobacco Trade, . . . ," 73–74, 77.

49. Bruce A. Ragsdale, *A Planters' Republic: The Search For Economic Independence in Revolutionary Virginia* (Madison, WI: Madison House, 1996), 10–18, 29–36; GW to Robert Cary & Company, 20 September 1759, 10 August 1764, *PGW, Col.,* 6: 348–352, 7: 323–326.

50. GW to Robert Cary & Company, 1 May 1764, 10 August 1764, *PGW, Col.,* 7: 305–306, 323–326; Ledger A, 67, 154, 198.

51. Tobacco Accounts, Ledger A, 233; Ragsdale, "George Washington, the British Tobacco Trade, . . . ," 79–80.

52. George Washington, John Carlyle, and Robert Adam, Contract for Wheat, 18 January 1763, Series 4, GWP, LOC.

53. Harold B. Gill, "Wheat Culture in Colonial Virginia," *Agricultural History* 52, no. 3 (1978): 380–393; David Klingaman, "The Significance of Grain in the Development of the Tobacco Colonies," *Journal of Economic History* 29, no. 2 (1969): 268–278; Ledger A, 180; for overseers' shares, see e.g., Nelson Kelly, Ledger A, 139; John Alton, Ledger A, 179; John Chowning, Ledger A, 185.

54. G. Melvin Herndon, "Hemp in Colonial Virginia," *Agricultural History* 37, no. 2 (1963): 86–93; *Diaries,* 1: 337, 340; Ledger A, 73, 131, 195, 203, 205, 269.

55. Edward Burn & Sons to GW, 26 June 1765, *PGW, Col.,* 7: 375; Agreement with Christopher Hardwick, 22 January 1763, *PGW, Col.,* 7: 182–185; Ledger A, 91, 138; Memorandum List of Tithables, 9 June 1762, *PGW, Col.,* 7: 139.

56. Book of Accounts, 1762–1784, of Lund Washington, Overseer of Mount Vernon for General Washington, U.S. Naval Academy Museum; Ledger A, 153, 190; Joseph Davenport to Lund Washington, September 1765, 16 October 1765, 22 November 1765, *PGW, Col.,* 7: 405–408, 414–415; GW to Charles Washington, 15 August 1764, *PGW, Col.,* 7: 329–331.

57. *Diaries,* 1: 235, 256, 311; Ledger A, 132, 179, 185.

58. Agreement with Nelson Kelly, 1 September 1762, *PGW, Col.,* 7: 148–151; Advertisement for Runaway Slaves, 11 August 1761, *PGW, Col.,* 7: 65–68; Memorandum List of Tithables,

9 June 1762, *PGW, Col.,* 7: 139; Ledger A, 210; Philip D. Morgan and Michael L. Nicholls, "Slave Flight: Mount Vernon, Virginia, and the Wider Atlantic World," in Tamara Harvey and Greg O'Brien, eds., *George Washington's South* (Gainesville: University of Florida Press, 2004), 197–222.

59. GW to Joseph Thompson, 2 July 1766, *PGW, Col.,* 7: 453–454; Ledger A, 245. On 13 June 1766, Washington paid £2 currency for "taking up Negroe Tom," Cash Account, *PGW, Col.,* 7: 441–442 (this is the only record of him running away); Cash Accounts, April 1766, *PGW, Col.,* 7: 434–435; Cloe had been at Mount Vernon at least since 1760; Abram was first listed on the tithables at River Plantation on 16 June 1766; both remained at River Plantation for many years. Morgan and Nicholls, "Slave Flight" discusses the case of Sam, a carpenter offered for sale by Washington in 1767 after numerous incidents of running away over eight or nine years. Washington also authorized the sale to San Domingue of Will Shag, an enslaved worker on the York River plantation of John Parke Custis. Will Shag had run away and assaulted a white overseer. Morgan and Nicholls, "Slave Flight," 198–200.

60. Joseph Valentine to GW, 21–23 November 1770, *PGW, Col.,* 8: 400–402; GW to Charles Washington, 15 August 1764, *PGW, Col.,* 7: 329–331.

61. Indenture with John Askew, 1 September 1759, *PGW, Col.,* 6: 340–341; Memorandum List of Tithables, May 1760, *PGW, Col.,* 6: 428; GW to George William Fairfax, 25 July 1763, *PGW, Col.,* 7: 233–235, n. 2; Memorandum List of Tithables, 9 June 1762, 2 July 1765, 16 June 1766, *PGW, Col.,* 7: 139, 376–377, 442–443; *Diaries,* 1: 215, 252, 264–265, 280.

62. GW to Crosbies & Trafford, 6 March 1765, *PGW, Col.,* 7: 358–359; Ledger A, 206, 212.

63. GW to Robert Cary & Company, 22 August 1766, *PGW, Col.,* 7: 460; Thomas Symes described in *Newcastle Courant,* 14 July 1764; for farm implements from Theodosia Crowley and Symes & Company, see esp. Invoices from Robert Cary & Company, 10 April 1762, 13 February 1764, and 13 February 1765, *PGW, Col.,* 7: 124–131, 287–295, 353–357; Evans, "The Plantation Hoe."

2. THE AGRICULTURAL FOUNDATIONS OF INDEPENDENCE

1. GW to Robert Cary & Company, 20 September 1765, *PGW, Col.,* 7: 398–402.

2. GW to Robert Cary & Company, 20 September 1765, *PGW, Col.,* 7: 398–402; Invoice to Robert Cary & Company, 20 September 1765, *PGW, Col.,* 7: 402–404; Ragsdale, *Planters' Republic,* 58–59, 67–68; Weaving Accounts, 1767–1771, Series 5, Financial Papers, GWP, LOC; Spinning and Weaving Records, 1768, *PGW, Col.,* 8: 154–155.

3. GW to Robert Cary & Company, 20 September 1765, *PGW, Col.,* 7: 398–402; GW to Capel and Osgood Hanbury, 20 September 1765, *PGW, Col.,* 7: 393–394; GW to James Gildart, 20 September 1765, *PGW, Col.,* 7: 397.

4. GW to Robert Cary & Company, 21 July 1766, *PGW, Col.,* 7: 456–457; GW to Capel & Osgood Hanbury, 25 July 1767, *PGW, Col.,* 8: 14–16.

5. The *Diaries* include numerous references to clearing new ground, see e.g., 2: 36, 125; GW to Carlyle & Adam, 9 March 1765, *PGW, Col.,* 7: 359–361; GW to Robert Cary &

Company, 1 June 1774, *PGW, Col.,* 10: 82–85; Lund Washington to GW, 17 August, 22 August, 5 September 1767, *PGW, Col.,* 8: 17–20, 25–26; *Diaries,* 2: 36, 73–74.

6. Lund Washington, Book of Accounts, 1762–1784, USNA Museum, 46; *Diaries,* 2: 260, 3: 37.

7. *Diaries,* 1: 343–344, 3: 135; Walsh, "Slavery and Agriculture at Mount Vernon," 57–58; *Diaries,* 2: 17–18.

8. GW to Robert Cary & Company, 20 July 1771, *PGW, Col.,* 8: 503–507; GW to Robert Cary & Company, 10 July 1773, *PGW, Col.,* 9: 271–273, enclosure printed in n. 1.

9. *A Practical Treatise of Husbandry . . . by Duhamel,* 65–72; *The Farmer's Compleat Guide,* 14–55, see esp. 30; *Diaries,* 2: 82, 185–186, 3: 50; GW's signed and annotated copy of *A Practical Treatise of Husbandry* is in the collection of the Virginia Historical Society.

10. Harvest details recorded throughout the *Diaries,* see esp. 2: 5, 74–77, 157–160, 162–165, 171–172, 3: 39.

11. *Diaries,* 2: 171–172.

12. Ledger A, 292; *Diaries,* 2: 82–83, 171–172, 3: 44, 122–123.

13. *Diaries,* 2: 17, 57, 164; Indenture with Peter Gollatt, 19 March 1770, *PGW, Col.,* 8: 320; Benjamin Buckler and George Washington, Contract for Carpenter, 25 February 1771, Series 4, GWP, LOC.

14. Contract with Benjamin Buckler; Caleb Stone and George Washington, Contract for Carpenter, 8 February 1773, Series 4, GWP, LOC.

15. *Diaries,* 2: 49–50, 57, 67, 23; Ledger A, 195; for hiring out of carpenters, see e.g., account with George William Fairfax, Ledger A, 1, 105; account with John Posey, Ledger A, 92; and account with William Triplett, Ledger A, 72.

16. Washington first recorded "Morrice" as a carpenter, age 29, in "List of Artisans and Household Slaves in the [Custis] Estate, c. 1759," *PGW, Col.,* 6: 282; for Morris at Mount Vernon, see *Diaries,* 1: 214; Account of Carpenters Work, 1760–1764, Washington Library; Memorandum List of Tithables, 12 June 1766, *PGW, Col.,* 7: 442–443, lists Morris's name first at Dogue Run, and for the first time no white overseer was designated. The number of field laborers was recorded in subsequent lists of tithables. Hannah was also listed for the first time. For references to Morris as overseer, see e.g., *Diaries,* 2: 6, 17, 164; payments to Morris in Ledger A, 262, 286, 302, 335, 350; Susan P. Schoelwer, ed., *Lives Bound Together: Slavery at George Washington's Mount Vernon* (Mount Vernon, VA: Mount Vernon Ladies' Association, 2016), 80–81.

17. Memorandum List of Tithables, 1770–1774, *PGW, Col.,* 8: 356–357, 479–480, 9: 54–55, 238–239, 10: 137–138; Ledger A, 350; Ledger B, 82, 98; Lund Washington Account Book, 1772–1786 (typed transcription by Gwendolyn White and Maureen Connors, 2009), Washington Library, 4, 19. Washington recorded payments to Morris, Davy, and "Mike" as a grouping under heading "Negro" in 1771, and "Overseer" in 1773.

18. GW to John Posey, 24 June 1767, *PGW, Col.,* 8: 1–4; GW to Carlyle & Adam, 15 February 1767, *PGW, Col.,* 7: 482–491; Memorandum List of Tithables and Taxable Land and Property, 2 July 1765, *PGW, Col.,* 7: 376–377; Memorandum List of Tithables, July 1774, *PGW, Col.,* 10: 137–138.

19. Ledger A, 204, 255, 261, 310; Ledger B, 86; Memorandum List of Tithables, 20 June 1768, 16 July 1770, 9 June 1773, *PGW, Col.,* 8: 104, 356–357; 9: 238–239.

20. GW to Daniel Jenifer Adams, 20 July 1772, *PGW, Col.,* 9: 69–71.

21. Joseph Valentine to GW, 21–23 November 1770, *PGW, Col.,* 8: 400–402.

22. Memorandum List of Tithables, 14 June 1771, *PGW, Col.,* 8: 479–480; GW to John Posey, 11 June 1769, *PGW, Col.,* 8: 211–216; for purchase of lands from Posey and West, see notes in *Diaries,* 2: 143, 189, 271.

23. Memorandum List of Tithables, 14 June 1771, *PGW, Col.,* 8: 479–480; *Diaries,* 3: 45; Ledger A, 340.

24. Memorandum List of Tithables and Taxable Land and Property, 16 June 1766, *PGW, Col.,* 7: 442–443, for new adult slaves at Mount Vernon, eight of whom were at River Plantation. No list of slaves at Bullskin Plantation survives, but the overseer's account named two slaves, Neptune and Walley, who ran away and were recaptured. Both appear on the list for River Plantation in 1766, Ledger A, 210, 221. Among the earliest tenants at Bullskin were David Kennedy and Joseph Thomson, Ledger A, 248; Joseph Davenport served as overseer at Bullskin until late 1765, Ledger A, 221; Joseph Davenport to Lund Washington, September 1765, 16 October 1765, 22 November 1765, *PGW, Col.,* 7: 405–408, 414–415.

25. *Virginia Gazette* (Purdie & Dixon), 19 November 1767, 4; Ledger A, 283; *Diaries,* 2: 133–135; Lease to Francis Ballinger, 17 March 1769, *PGW, Col.,* 8: 171–177; Willard F. Bliss, "The Rise of Tenancy in Virginia," *Virginia Magazine of History and Biography* 58, no. 4 (1950): 427–441. Washington periodically visited his tenants in Fauquier, Loudoun, and Frederick Counties, see e.g., *Diaries,* 3: 239.

26. GW to George Mason, 5 April 1769, *PGW, Col.,* 8: 177–181; Ragsdale, *Planters' Republic,* ix-xi, 73–78.

27. Ragsdale, *Planters' Republic,* 78, 103–104, 191–194; GW to George Mason, 5 April 1769, *PGW, Col.,* 8: 177–181.

28. GW to Charles West, 6 June 1769, *PGW, Col.,* 8: 208–211; *Diaries,* 2: 204, 214, 217, 234–235; 3: 24; Ledger A, 324, 333.

29. William Roberts and George Washington, Contract for Miller, 13 October 1770, Series 4, GWP, LOC; *Diaries,* 3: 51, 59. The next highest wage was £40 per annum, paid to Jonathan Palmer and Caleb Stone, Ledger A, 294; Caleb Stone and George Washington, 8 February 1773, Contract for Carpenter, Series 4, GWP, LOC.

30. GW to Robert Cary & Company, 12 August 1771, *PGW, Col.,* 8: 516–517; "John Cooper," in A.W. Skempton, ed., *A Biographical Dictionary of Civil Engineers in Great Britain and Ireland,* vol. 1 (London: Thomas Telford, 2002), 149; John G. Gazley, "Arthur Young and the Society of Arts," *Journal of Economic History* 1, no. 2 (November 1941): 129–152.

31. GW to Carlyle & Adam, 15 February 1767, *PGW, Col.,* 7: 482–491. This letter is the only surviving document from a series in which Washington apparently threatened to sue Carlyle & Adam and in which the merchants responded with comments that Washington quoted in the surviving letter.

32. GW to Carlyle & Adam, 15 February 1767, *PGW, Col.,* 7: 482–491; GW to Capel & Osgood Hanbury, 25 July 1769, *PGW, Col.,* 8: 228–229.

33. GW to Carlyle & Adam, 15 February 1767, *PGW, Col.*, 7: 482–491; GW to Daniel Jenifer Adams, 20 July 1772, *PGW, Col.*, 9: 69–71; GW to Robert McMickan, 12 January 1773, 20 July 1773, 10 May 1774, *PGW, Col.*,, 158–159, 283, 10: 55–58; Ledger B, 127.

34. GW to Robert McMickan, 10 May 1774, *PGW, Col.*, 10: 55–58; Thomas Newton, Jr., to GW, 21 December 1774, *PGW, Col., 10:* 209–210; *Diaries*, 3: 319; Lund Washington Account Book, 1772–1786, 36, 39; Thomas Contee to GW, 11 April 1775, *PGW, Col.*, 10: 336.

35. *Diaries*, 3: 99–100; William Waller Hening, ed., *The Statutes at Large, Being a Collection of all the Laws of Virginia . . .* , vol. 8 [1-8] (Richmond: Printed by J. & G. Cochrane, 1821), 511–514; Washington recorded his brand with the Fairfax County clerk, 21 December 1772, in n. 1, Thomas Newton, Jr., to GW, 11 January 1773, *PGW, Col.*, 9: 156–157; Henry Hill to GW, 22 June 1773, *PGW, Col.*, 9: 244–245; GW to Lamar, Hill, Bisset & Company, 15 July 1773, *PGW, Col.*, 9: 280–282; GW to Thomas Newton, Jr., 10 July 1773, *PGW, Col.*, 9: 270–271; GW to Robert Cary & Company, 15 July 1773, in n. 4, GW to Lamar, Hill, Bisset & Company, *PGW, Col.*, 9: 282. Lamar, Hill, Bisset & Company were leading Madeira traders to the Chesapeake and Mid-Atlantic colonies, David Hancock, *Oceans of Wine: Madeira and the Emergence of American Trade and Taste* (New Haven, CT: Yale University Press, 2009), 151–155.

36. GW to Thomas Newton, Jr., 23 January 1773, 27 January 1773, 12 February 1773, *PGW, Col.*, 9: 165–167, 175–176; Thomas Newton to GW, 27 June 1774, *PGW, Col.*, 10: 101–102; Ledger B, 85; GW to Robert Cary & Company, 1 June 1774, *PGW, Col.*, 10: 82–85.

37. Capel & Osgood Hanbury to GW, 20 November 1765, *PGW, Col.*, 7: 413–414; James Gildart to GW, 22 April 1766, 12 April 1768, 31 October 1768, *PGW, Col.*, 7: 435, 8: 80–81, 138–140.

38. "The Growth of Mount Vernon, 1754–86," in *Diaries*, 1: 240–242; "The Growth of Mount Vernon," in *The Mount Vernon Ladies' Association of the Union, Annual Report, 1982*, 21–23; *Diaries*, 2: 222, 3: 12.

39. George Washington, "A Plan of My Farm on Little Huntg Creek & Potomk R.," 1766, Geography and Map Division, LOC; letter to scythe maker, in GW to Robert Cary & Company, 10 July 1773, n. 1, *PGW, Col.*, 9: 271–273; *Diaries*, 2: 165–168, 3: 70, 102–104, 109.

40. The *Diaries* are filled with numerous, sometimes daily, references to foxhunting, from January 1768 to late winter 1775, and again in the 1780s. See esp. *Diaries*, 2: 30–32, 93–96; Jane Bevan, "Agricultural Change and the Development of Foxhunting in the Eighteenth Century," *The Agricultural History Review* 58, no. 1 (2010): 49–75; Raymond Carr, *English Fox Hunting*, rev. ed. (London: Weidenfeld and Nicolson, 1986), 45–50; Invoice from Robert Cary & Company, 29 October 1767, *PGW, Col.*, 8: 44–50; Invoice to Robert Cary & Company, 10 July 1773, *PGW, Col.*, 9: 273–276. GW's last recorded fox hunt was 15 February 1788, *Diaries*, 5: 277. A new generation of British agricultural writers decried blood sports as antithetical to enlightened farming. GW would have read Lord Kames on the subject: "His [landed gentlemen] train of ideas was confined to dogs, horses, hares, foxes; not a rational idea entered the train, not a spark of patriotism, nothing done for the public, his dependents enslaved and not fed, no husbandry," *The Gentleman Farmer* (Dublin: James Williams, 1779), xviii.

41. Ragsdale, *Planters' Republic,* 144–146; *Diaries,* 2: 199–204; GW to Thomas Johnson, 20 July 1770, *PGW, Col.,* 8: 357–360; Advertisement of Western Lands, 15 July 1773, *PGW, Col.,* 9: 278–280. Washington's interest in Potomac navigation dated back to 1754 when, at the request of Charles Carter, he examined the natural obstacles along a stretch of the river. See GW to Charles Carter, August 1754, *PGW, Col.,* 1: 196–198; GW to a Participant in the Potomac River Enterprise, 1762, *PGW, Col.,* 7: 175–178.

42. GW to James Tilghman, Jr., 17 February 1774, *PGW, Col.,* 9: 484–485; GW to William Crawford, 17 September 1767, *PGW, Col.,* 8: 26–32; Calloway, *The Indian World of George Washington,* 184–190.

43. GW to William Crawford, 17 September 1767, *PGW, Col.,* 8: 26–32; GW to John Armstrong, 21 September 1767, *PGW, Col.,* 8: 32–33; John Armstrong to GW, 3 November—20 December 1767, *PGW, Col.,* 8: 55–58. Armstrong advised GW that the limit on land granted to individuals in Pennsylvania "has not been generally adher'd to."; *Diaries,* 2: 290.

44. *Diaries,* 2: 294–318; Calloway, *The Indian World of George Washington,* 196–199.

45. GW to Charles Washington, 31 January 1770, *PGW, Col.,* 8: 300–304; GW to Botetourt, 8 December 1769, *PGW, Col.,* 8: 272–277; Petition to Botetourt, 15 December 1769, *PGW, Col.,* 8: 277–279; GW to Henry Riddell, 22 February 1774, *PGW, Col.,* 9: 493–496; Calloway, *The Indian World of George Washington,* 195–203.

46. Ledger A, 81; Ledger B, 87; Gilbert Simpson to GW, 5 October 1772, 26 December 1772, *PGW, Col.,* 9: 113–115, 148–149; GW to Gilbert Simpson, 23 February 1773, *PGW, Col.,* 9: 185–187.

47. Gilbert Simpson to GW, 11 April 1773, 20 May 1773, 14 June 1773, July 1773, 6 February 1775, *PGW, Col.,* 9: 216–217, 234, 241–242, 290–293, 10: 256–257; Ledger B, 87; GW to Lund Washington, 20 August 1775, *PGW, Rev.,* 1: 334–340; GW to Gilbert Simpson, 10 July 1784, *PGW, Conf.,* 1: 496–498; Ledger B, 138.

48. W.W. Abbot, "George Washington, the West, and the Union," in Higginbotham, ed., *George Washington Reconsidered,* 202–203; Calloway, *The Indian World of George Washington,* 191–192.

49. Advertisement of Western Lands, 15 July 1773, *PGW, Col.,* 9: 278–280; GW to Henry Riddell, 22 February, 1 March, 5 March 1774, *PGW, Col.,* 9: 493–496, 506–508, 509–510; *Diaries,* 3: 199–200; Richard Thompson to GW, 30 September 1773, *PGW, Col.,* 9: 337–340; William McGachen to GW, 13 March 1774, *PGW, Col.,* 9: 519; Promissory Note to John Harper, 18 February 1775, *PGW, Col.,* 10: 269; Ledger B, 133.

50. Contract and Instructions, GW and James Cleveland, 10 January 1775, Series 4, GWP, LOC; Agreement with William Skilling, 25 February 1775, *PGW, Col.,* 10: 272–273; GW to William Stevens, 6 March 1775, *PGW, Col.,* 10: 288–292; GW to James Cleveland, March 1775, *PGW, Col.,* 10: 314–315; James Cleveland to GW, 21 May, 7 June 1775, *PGW, Col.,* 10: 365–367, 371–373.

51. GW to James Cleveland, March 1775, *PGW, Col.,* 10: 314–315; James Cleveland to Lund Washington, 1 October 1775, Series 4, GWP, LOC; Lund Washington to GW, 5 November 1775, *PGW, Rev.,* 2: 304–308; James Cleveland to GW, 16 November 1775, *PGW, Rev.,* 2: 381–384; Ledger B, 137; an unspecified number of slaves were returned to Mount Vernon from William Crawford's property in April 1778, Ledger B, 153.

52. GW to Edward Montagu, 5 April 1775, *PGW, Col.,* 10: 328–330.

53. GW to Edward Montagu, 5 April 1775, *PGW, Col.,* 10: 328–330; GW to James Mercer, 12 December 1774, *PGW, Col.,* 10: 201–205; James Mercer to GW, 6 September 1771, *PGW, Col.,* 8: 525–526; Ledger A, 151, Ledger B, 46; and with Thomas Moore, Ledger A, 204; GW to John Posey, 24 June 1767, *PGW, Col.,* 8: 1–4.

54. GW to John Posey, 24 June 1767, *PGW, Col.,* 8: 1–4; Bernard Moore to GW, 21 October 1766, *PGW, Col.,* 7: 467; James Mercer to GW, 6 September 1771, *PGW, Col.,,* 8: 525–526.

55. Thomas Moore to GW, 24 October 1766, *PGW, Col.,* 7: 468–469; James Mercer to GW, 23 August 1773, *PGW, Col.,* 9: 311–313; GW to James Mercer, 19 July 1773, *PGW, Col.,* 9: 282–283; Bernard Moore to GW, 12 January 1771, *PGW, Col.,* 8: 427–428; Ledger B, 46.

56. *Diaries,* 2: 246, 200–202; Ledger A, 204; Washington listed as a manager for Bernard Moore's lottery in *Virginia Gazette* (Rind), 14 April 1768, and 23 November 1769; advertisement for Posey's sale in GW to Hector Ross, 9 October 1769, n. 1, *PGW, Col.,* 8: 254–257.

57. GW to John Posey, 11 June 1769, *PGW, Col.,* 8: 211–216; GW to Hector Ross, 9 October 1769, *PGW, Col.,* 8: 254–257; GW to Robert Hanson Harrison, 7 October 1769, *PGW, Col.,* 8: 252–254; Ledger A, 256. Washington remained involved with Posey, to whom he hired out the enslaved field laborer, Jack, for six months in 1770. Posey returned Jack to Mount Vernon, for fear that one of his Maryland creditors would take possession of the slave owned by Washington. In his last engagements with Posey, Washington in 1773 and 1774 gave him cash for "charity." John Posey to GW, 25 May 1771, 9 August 1773, *PGW, Col.,* 8: 470–473, 9: 301; Ledger B, 93, 106.

58. Ledger A, 242; *Diaries,* 2: 11; Ledger B, 21; Memorandum List of Tithables, 9 June 1773, *PGW, Col.,* 9: 238–239.

59. Washington oversaw the auctions of Mercer's estate from 21–30 November 1774, *Diaries,* 3: 292–293; GW to John Tayloe, 30 November 1774, *PGW, Col.,* 10: 191–192; notice of the sale printed in *Virginia Gazette* (Purdie & Dixon) from 30 June 1774 until 24 October 1774; William Dawson to GW, 5 October 1789, *PGW, Pres.,* 4: 134–137.

60. *Diaries,* 3: 297; meeting of trustees of Potomac River company, *Virginia Gazette* (Dixon & Hunter), 7 January 1775, 3.

61. GW to Bryan Fairfax, 24 August 1774, *PGW, Col.,* 10: 154–156.

3. MOUNT VERNON IN WARTIME

1. GW to Lund Washington, 26 November 1775, 28 February 1778, *PGW, Rev.,* 2: 431–433, 13: 699–700; GW to Lund Washington, 30 April 1781, 12 February 1783, Founders Online, Early Access.

2. Lund Washington to GW, 24 November 1775, *PGW, Rev.,* 2: 421–424.

3. Lund Washington to GW, 29 October 1775, 14 November 1775, 17 January 1776, *PGW, Rev.,* 2: 256–260, 373–377, 3: 126–132; Flora Fraser, *The Washingtons: George and Martha, "Join'd by Friendship, Crown'd by Love"* (New York: Alfred A. Knopf, 2015), 118–120; Patricia Brady, *Martha Washington: An American Life* (New York: Penguin Books, 2005), 100–101.

4. Lund Washington to GW, 29 October 1775, *PGW, Rev.*, 2: 256–260; Lund Washington to GW, 31 January 1776, *PGW, Rev.*, 3: 230–233.

5. Woody Holton, *Forced Founders: Indians, Debtors, Slaves, and the Making of the American Revolution in Virginia* (Chapel Hill: University of North Carolina Press, 1999), 144–158; Lund Washington to GW, 29 September 1775, 5 November 1775, 3 December 1775, *PGW, Rev.*, 2: 64–66, 304–308, 477–482; Fielding Lewis to GW, 14 November 1775, *PGW, Rev.*, 2: 371–373.

6. Lund Washington to GW, 3 December 1775, 17 January 1776, *PGW, Rev.*, 2: 477–482, 3: 126–132; GW to Richard Henry Lee, 26 December 1775, *PGW, Rev.*, 2: 610–613; GW to Lieutenant Colonel Joseph Reed, 15 December 1775, *PGW, Rev.*, 2: 551–554; GW to John Hancock, 18 December 1775, *PGW, Rev.*, 2: 573–575.

7. Impact of Dunmore's Proclamation described in: Alan Taylor, *The Internal Enemy: Slavery and War in Virginia, 1772–1832* (New York: W.W. Norton, 2013), 23–27; Cassandra Pybus, *Epic Journeys of Freedom: Runaway Slaves of the American Revolution and their Global Quest for Liberty* (Boston: Beacon Press, 2006), 8–11; Gary B. Nash, *The Forgotten Fifth: African Americans in the Age of Revolution* (Cambridge, MA: Harvard University Press, 2006), 25–29; and Michael A. McDonnell, *The Politics of War: Race, Class, and Conflict in Revolutionary Virginia* (Chapel Hill: University of North Carolina Press, 2007), 155–161; Philip D. Morgan and Andrew Jackson O'Shaughnessy, "Arming Slaves in the American Revolution," in Christopher Leslie Brown and Philip D. Morgan, eds., *Arming Slaves: From Classical Times to the Modern Age* (New Haven, CT: Yale University Press, 2006), 189–190; Master's Log of *H.M.S Roebuck*, in William James Morgan, ed., *Naval Documents of the American Revolution*, vol. 5 (Washington, DC: Naval History Division, 1970), 1250. At least one of those who boarded the *Roebuck*, a convict servant named Henry Young, escaped from the ship and presented himself to Washington in New York in October 1776. Young returned to work for wages at Mount Vernon from 1778 to 1781, see GW to Lund Washington, 6 October 1776, *PGW, Rev.*, 6: 493–495; Sylvia R. Frey, *Water From the Rock: Black Resistance in a Revolutionary Age* (Princeton, NJ: Princeton University Press, 1991), 145–149.

8. GW to Lund Washington, 20 August 1775, *PGW, Rev.*, 1: 334–340; Lund Washington to GW, 17 January 1776, 31 January 1776, 15 February 1776, 1 April 1778, *PGW, Rev.*, 3: 126–132, 230–233, 317–320, 14: 381–384; Lund Washington Account Book, 1772–1786, Washington Library, 45, 68, 69, 78, 84.

9. GW to Lund Washington, 20 August 1775, *PGW, Rev.*, 1: 334–340; GW to Samuel Washington, 1 October 1775, *PGW, Rev.*, 2: 78–79; Ragsdale, *Planters' Republic*, 194–195, 199–203, 216–218; Lund Washington to GW, 29 February 1776, *PGW, Rev.*, 3: 393–398; GW to Lund Washington, 26 August 1776, *PGW, Rev.*, 6: 135–137; Brooke Hunter, "Wheat, War, and the American Economy during the Age of Revolution," *William and Mary Quarterly* 62, no. 3 (July 2005): 505–526.

10. Lund Washington, Book of Accounts, 1762–1784, USNA Museum, 46; Mill Account Book, 1776–1785 (Photostat of original in the Tennessee Historical Society), Washington Library; Lund Washington to GW, 31 January 1776, 24 December 1777, 2 September 1778, *PGW, Rev.*, 3: 230–233, 12: 698–700, 16: 496–502.

11. Lund Washington to GW, 3 December 1775, 2 September 1778, *PGW, Rev.*, 2: 477–482, 16: 496–502.

12. Wheat purchases recorded in Ledger B, 148–149, 152–154; wheat sales in Lund Washington's accounts with GW, Ledger B, 144–173; Lund Washington to GW, 17 January 1776, *PGW, Rev.*, 3: 126–132.

13. Lund Washington to GW, 14 November 1775, 24 December 1777, 19 August 1778, 2 September 1778, *PGW, Rev.*, 2: 373–377, 12: 698–700, 16: 333–335, 496–502; GW to Lund Washington, 15 August 1778, *PGW, Rev.*, 16: 315–317; Lund Washington Account Book, 1772–1786, Washington Library, 118; Ledger B, 145.

14. Ledger B, 151, 163; Lund Washington Account Book, 1772–1786, Washington Library, 75, 76; Lund Washington to GW, 1 April 1778, *PGW, Rev.*, 14: 381–384.

15. John Parke Custis to GW, October 1777, *PGW, Rev.*, 12: 73–74; Lund Washington to GW, 18 March 1778, 1 April 1778, 22 April 1788, *PGW, Rev.*, 14: 220–222, 381–384, 588–590; Lund Washington Account Book, 1772–1786, Washington Library, 61, 81, 109; Rental Account, Lund Washington to GW, 25 December 1775, in the hand of Lund Washington, records 24 tenants in four counties, Washington Library; Lund Washington to GW, 30 December 1775, *PGW, Rev.*, 2: 620–621; Lund Washington to GW, 15 February 1776, *PGW, Rev.*, 3: 317–320; Lund Washington to GW, 29 February 1776, *PGW, Rev.*, 3: 393–398; Holton, *Forced Founders*, 175–184; McDonnell, *Politics of War*, 189–196; Lund Washington to GW, 1 April 1778, *PGW, Rev.*, 14: 381–384; Lund Washington to GW, 1 October 1783, Founders Online, Early Access.

16. Ledger B, 147, 156, 161, 170; Lund Washington Account Book, 1772–1786, 45; Lund Washington to GW, 24 November 1775, 31 January 1776, 24 December 1777, *PGW, Rev.*, 2: 421–424, 3: 230–233, 12: 698–700; GW to Lund Washington, 10–17 December 1776, *PGW, Rev.*, 7: 289–292.

17. GW to Lund Washington, 28 February 1778, 18 December 1778, *PGW, Rev.*, 13: 699–700, 18: 459–463; Lund Washington to GW, 5 November 1775, 18 March 1778, *PGW, Rev.*, 2: 304–308, 14: 220–222.

18. GW to Lund Washington, 29 May 1779, 17 August 1779, 14 September 1779, *PGW, Rev.*, 20: 688–690, 22: 165–166, 427–428.

19. GW to Lund Washington, 15 August 1778, 24–26 February 1779, *PGW, Rev.*, 16: 315–317; 19: 257–259.

20. GW to Lund Washington, 15 August 1778, 24–26 February 1779, *PGW, Rev.*, 16: 315–317, 19: 257–259; Lund Washington to GW, 11 March 1778, 8 April 1778, *PGW, Rev.*, 14: 150–152, 429–431.

21. Lund Washington to GW, 2 September 1778, *PGW, Rev.*, 16: 496–502; GW to Lund Washington, 24–26 February 1779, *PGW, Rev.*, 19: 257–259; Ledger B, 156. On 20 April 1778, Lund Washington paid Alexander Cleveland for "going over the Alegana Mountains, & Bringing your Negroes doun from Colo. Crawfords," Ledger B, 153.

22. GW to Lund Washington, 15 August 1778, *PGW, Rev.*, 16: 315–317; Lund Washington to GW, 2 September 1778, *PGW, Rev.*, 16: 496–502.

23. Council of War, 18 October 1775, *PGW, Rev.*, 2: 185–190; General Orders, 30 December 1775, *PGW, Rev.*, 2: 620; GW to John Hancock, 31 December 1775, *PGW, Rev.*, 2: 622–626; Twohig, "'That Species of Property': Washington's Role in the Controversy

over Slavery," 118–120; Morgan and O'Shaughnessy, "Arming Slaves in the American Revolution," 192–194; Frey, *Water From the Rock,* 78–80; Edward G. Lengel, *General George Washington: A Military Life* (New York: Random House, 2005), 313–318; John Laurens quoted in Gregory D. Massey, "The Limits of Antislavery Thought in the Revolutionary Lower South: John Laurens and Henry Laurens," *Journal of Southern History* 63, no. 3 (1997): 495–530.

24. GW to Lund Washington, 24–26 February 1779, *PGW, Rev.,* 19: 257–259; GW to Gilbert Simpson, 23 February 1773, *PGW, Col.,* 9: 185–187; Sale of "Negro Man Will" to Dr. James Craik, 1 February 1777, Ledger B, 148.

25. GW to Henry Laurens, 20 March 1779, *PGW, Rev.,* 19: 542–543; GW to Continental Congress Camp Committee, 29 January 1778, *PGW, Rev.,* 13: 376–409; Morgan, "'To Get Quit of Negroes': George Washington and Slavery," 416.

26. Pybus, *Epic Journeys,* 45–47; Morgan and Nicholls, "Slave Flight," 200–201; Fritz Hirschfeld, ed., "'Burnt All Their Houses': The Log of HMS *Savage* during a Raid up the Potomac River, Spring 1781," *Virginia Magazine of History and Biography* 99, no. 4 (1991): 513–530; Lafayette to GW, 23 April 1781, Founders Online, Early Access; GW to Lafayette, 4 May 1781, Founders Online, Early Access; François Jean, Marquis de Chastellux, *Travels In North-America, In the Years 1780, 1781, And 1782,* 2nd ed. (London: G. G. J. and J. Robinson, 1787), vol. 2, 170–171.

27. GW to Lund Washington, 30 April 1781, Founders Online, Early Access.

28. Sylvia R. Frey, "Between Slavery and Freedom: Virginia Blacks in the American Revolution," *Journal of Southern History* 49, no. 3 (1983): 375–398; Morgan and Nicholls, "Slave Flight," 200–201, 207; Lund Washington, List of slaves returned from British, 1781, Washington Library. Lund enclosed a copy of this list in a letter, now lost, to GW of 18 April 1781.

29. Lund Washington, List of slaves returned from British, 1781, Washington Library; Morgan and Nicholls, "Slave Flight," 201; list of slaves, 18 February 1786, in *Diaries,* 4: 277–283.

30. Account of a Conference between Washington and Sir Guy Carleton, 6 May 1783, Founders Online, Early Access; GW to Benjamin Harrison, 7 May 1783, Founders Online, Early Access. For Washington's efforts to recover slaves claimed by Harrison, Lund Washington, and himself, see GW to Daniel Parker, 28 April 1783, Founders Online, Early Access, and GW to Benjamin Harrison, 30 April 1783, Founders Online, Early Access; Lund Washington recorded payment of "your prop[ortio]n of Mr. Wm Tripletts Exps. Going to New Yk after Negroes," 6 June 1783, Ledger B, 172; Benjamin Quarles, *The Negro in the American Revolution* (Chapel Hill: University of North Carolina Press, 1961), 167–172; Christopher Leslie Brown, *Moral Capital: Foundations of British Abolitionism* (Chapel Hill: University of North Carolina Press, 2006), 298–303.

31. GW to Lund Washington, 19 August 1776, 3 April 1779, *PGW, Rev.,* 6: 82–87, 19: 734–736; "Mount Vernon Estate and Gardens: Cultural Landscape Study," 1, 2.18–21.

32. GW to Lund Washington, 10–17 December 1776, 17 December 1778, 3 April 1779, *PGW, Rev.,* 7: 289–292, 18: 438–442, 19: 734–736; Lund Washington to GW, 23 December 1775, *PGW, Rev.,* 2: 593–596; on Washington's memory of the landscape, see Bushman, *The American Farmer in the Eighteenth Century,* 204–205.

33. GW to Lund Washington, 10–17 December 1776, *PGW, Rev.,* 7: 289–292; Lund Washington to GW, 28 January 1778, 1 April 1778, 8 April 1778, *PGW, Rev.,* 13: 374–376; 14: 381–384, 429–431; Ledger B, 153–155, 158–159; Lund Washington Account Book, 1772–1786, Washington Library, 75; GW to Lund Washington, 28 March 1781, Founders Online, Early Access.

34. GW to Lund Washington, 15 August 1778, 17 December 1778, 18 December 1778, *PGW, Rev.,* 16: 315–317, 18: 438–442, 459–463; GW to Lund Washington, 21 November 1782, Founders Online, Early Access; *Diaries,* 1: 240–242; Indenture deed of William and Sarah Barry to George Washington for Mount Vernon land, 16 June 1783, Washington Library.

35. "Mount Vernon Estate and Gardens: Cultural Landscape Study," vol. 1, 2.51.

36. GW to Lund Washington, 17 July 1780, 21 November 1782, Founders Online, Early Access; GW to Robert Townsend Hooe, 18 July 1784, *PGW, Conf.,* 2: 1–2.

37. GW to The States, 8 June 1783, Founders Online, Early Access; *Diaries,* 4: 66–67; GW to Lafayette, 15 August 1786, *PGW, Conf.,* 4: 214–216.

38. GW to James Duane, 7 September 1783, in Founders Online, Early Access; Paul K. Longmore, *The Invention of George Washington* (Charlottesville: University Press of Virginia, 1999), 302n40; GW to Chastellux, 5 September 1785, *PGW, Conf.,* 3: 228–229; GW to Lafayette, 15 August 1786, *PGW, Conf.,* 4: 214–216.

39. Lafayette to GW, 5 February 1783, Founders Online, Early Access.

40. GW to Lafayette, 5 April 1783, Founders Online, Early Access; William Gordon to GW, 30 August 1784, *PGW, Conf.,* 2: 63–65.

41. Between 1776 and 1798, Washington referred to some variation of life under vine and fig tree at least 37 times, with two additional references to turning swords into ploughshares. These references drew on both the prophet Micah and the prophet Isaiah. Many of these references to vine and fig tree appear at the time of Washington's resignation from the Continental Army and again at his retirement from the presidency. See e.g., GW to Edmund Randolph, 7 November 1780, GW to Bartholomew Dandridge, 18 December 1782, GW to Chastellux, 12 October 1783, Founders Online, Early Access; Daniel L. Dreisbach, "The 'Vine and Fig Tree' in George Washington's Letters: Reflections on a Biblical Motif in the Literature of the American Founding Era," *Anglican and Episcopal History* 76 (September 2007): 299–326.

42. Washington's Sentiments on a Peace Establishment, 1 May 1783, Founders Online, Early Access; Washington's Farewell Address to the Army, 2 November 1783, Founders Online, Early Access.

43. GW to Chastellux, 25 April–1 May 1788, *PGW, Conf.,* 6: 227–230.

4. NEW FARMING IN A NEW NATION

1. GW to George William Fairfax, 10 November 1785, *PGW, Conf.,* 3: 348–351; GW to Charles Carter, 20 January 1788, *PGW, Conf.,* 6: 48–49.

2. GW to George William Fairfax, 30 June 1785, *PGW, Conf.,* 3: 87–92; *An Address from the Philadelphia Society for Promoting Agriculture, with a Summary of Its Laws and Premiums Offered,* 1785; Samuel Powel to GW, 5 July 1785, *PGW, Conf.,* 3: 106.

3. GW to Arthur Young, 6 August 1786, 1 November 1787, *PGW, Conf.,* 4: 196–200, 5: 402–405.

4. GW to George William Fairfax, 30 June 1785, *PGW, Conf.,* 3: 87–92.

5. Bath and West Society minutes of annual and ordinary meetings, 1777–1791, Acc. 38/1/1, Bath Record Office; Edmund Rack to George William Fairfax, 3 October 1785, and Arthur Young to Edmund Rack, 12 October 1785, enclosed in George William Fairfax to GW, 23 January 1786, *PGW, Conf.,* 3: 517–521, n. 1; "Excerpts from two original Letters of General Washington, and Mrs. Macaulay," printed in, among others: *The Gentleman's Magazine,* February 1786, 59: 109; *The Edinburgh Magazine,* March 1786, 3: 202–203; *The Scots Magazine,* 1 March 1786, 48: 112; and *Bath Chronicle and Weekly Gazette,* 23 March 1786, 4. The letters then appeared in *Columbian Herald* (Charleston, SC), 8 June 1786, and *Pennsylvania Packet* (Philadelphia), 23 June 1786.

6. John Wilton to GW, 31 March 1786, *PGW, Conf.,* 3: 617; George William Fairfax to GW, 23 January 1786, with enclosure of William Peacey to Edmund Rack, 27 December 1785, *PGW, Conf.,* 3: 517–521; agricultural experiments by Peacey described in Thomas Rudge, *General View of the Agriculture of the County of Gloucester* (London: R. Phillips, 1807), 253–255, 271–272.

7. *Diaries,* 4: 315; Articles of Agreement with James Bloxham, 31 May 1786, *PGW, Conf.,* 4: 86–88; GW to William Peacey, 5 August 1786, with enclosure, James Bloxham to William Peacey, 23 July 1786, *PGW, Conf.,* 4: 192–195.

8. GW to William Peacey, 5 August 1786, *PGW, Conf.,* 4: 192–195; GW to George William Fairfax, 25 June 1786, *PGW, Conf.,* 4: 126–129; Articles of Agreement with James Bloxham, 31 May 1786, *PGW, Conf.,* 4: 86–88; GW to Arthur Young, 6 August 1786, *PGW, Conf.,* 4: 196–200.

9. Arthur Young to GW, 7 January 1786, *PGW, Conf.,* 3: 498–500.

10. GW to Arthur Young, 6 August 1786, 15 November 1786, *PGW, Conf.,* 4: 196–200, 371–372; Washington had ordered Young's *Tour in Ireland* in 1783, see GW to William Stephens Smith, 15 May 1783, Founders Online, Early Access, and, more recently, Young's *A Six Month's Tour through the North of England,* see GW to Clement Biddle, 10 February 1786, *PGW, Conf.,* 3: 553–554; Arthur Young to GW, 1 February 1787, *PGW, Conf.,* 5: 3–6.

11. GW to Clement Biddle, 10 February 1786, *PGW, Conf.,* 3: 553–554; Ledger B, 244. Washington owned the Dublin edition of Kames: Henry Home, Lord Kames, *The Gentleman Farmer. Being an Attempt to Improve Agriculture, By Subjecting it to the Test of Rational Principles* (Dublin: James Williams, 1779), see esp. preface, ix–xix, Plate 2; Abstract of "The Gentleman Farmer by Henry Home," in Series 8d., Extracts, Abstracts, and Notes, 1760–1799, GWP, LOC; Ian Simpson Ross, *Lord Kames and the Scotland of His Day* (Oxford, UK: Clarendon Press, 1972), chap. 16; T. C. Smout, "A New Look at the Scottish Improvers," *The Scottish Historical Review* 91, no. 231 (2012): 125–149. Washington's Scottish agricultural correspondents included David Erskine, Earl of Buchan; James Anderson; and Sir John Sinclair.

12. Abstract of "The Gentleman Farmer by Henry Home," GWP, LOC; "Extracts and Notes on Agriculture," GWP, LOC; Kames, *The Gentleman Farmer,* 114; GW to Charles Carter, 20 January 1788, *PGW, Conf.,* 6: 48–49; RA Geo/Main/6359, George III,

Sequence of crop rotations for 1787–1789, Royal Archives, Windsor; RA Geo / Main / 6933, George III, Rotation of Crops at Richmond and Windsor, January 1792, Royal Archives, Windsor. For economic and cultural impact of crop rotations in the eighteenth century, see: Mokyr, *The Enlightened Economy,* 172–174; Williamson, *The Transformation of Rural England,* 6–17, 170; John Brewer, *The Pleasures of the Imagination: English Culture in the Eighteenth Century* (New York: Farrar, Straus and Giroux, 1997), 341–343.

13. GW to Charles Carter, 20 January 1788, *PGW, Conf.,* 6: 48–49; Lund Washington to GW, 23 December 1775, *PGW, Rev.,* 2: 593–596; GW to Lund Washington, 13 August 1783, Founders Online, Early Access; in 1782, Lund offered overseer Hezekiah Fairfax compensation for fallowing land an extra year for wheat, rather than planting corn, Lund Washington Account Book, 1772–1786, Washington Library, 123; GW to Robert Anderson, 3 November 1784, *PGW, Conf.,* 2: 113–114.

14. Abstract of "The Gentleman Farmer by Henry Home," GWP, LOC; GW to Charles Carter, 20 January 1788, *PGW, Conf.,* 6: 48–49; Partial survey of Ferry Plantation, with two crop rotation tables, 1787, Washington Library; Rotation of crops for Dogue-run and Rotation for the other Farms, n.d., Washington Library; Table of Crop Rotations, 11 July 1790, Series 4, GWP, LOC.

15. GW to Tench Tilghman, 10 March 1786, *PGW, Conf.,* 3: 595–596; GW to Clement Biddle, 10 February 1786, *PGW, Conf.,* 3: 553–554; William Peacey to GW, 2 February 1787, *PGW, Conf.,* 5: 6–7.

16. *Diaries,* 4: 257; GW to William Triplett, 25 September 1786, *PGW, Conf.,* 4: 268–274; Partial survey of Ferry Plantation, with two crop rotation tables, 1787, Washington Library; Agreement with James Lawson, 18 November 1786, Series 4, GWP, LOC; GW to Philip Marstellar, 27 November 1786, *PGW, Conf.,* 4: 402–403; *Diaries,* 5: 70, 113, 141–142, 227, 286–287; Ledger B, 237, 245.

17. James Martin Robinson, *Georgian Model Farms: A Study of Decorative and Model Farm Buildings in the Age of Improvement, 1700–1846* (New York: Oxford University Press, 1983), especially chaps. 1, 2, 4, and 5; *An Address from the Philadelphia Society for Promoting Agriculture, with a Summary of Its Laws and Premiums Offered,* 1785; GW to Samuel Powel, 25 May 1786, *PGW, Conf.,* 4: 75–76.

18. GW to Arthur Young, 15 November 1786, *PGW, Conf.,* 4: 371–372; Arthur Young to GW, 1 February 1787, *PGW, Conf,* 5: 3–6; plan for a barn, 28 October 1792, Series 4, GWP, LOC. (The plan in the Library of Congress mistakenly joins the farmyard with the later drawing of the treading barn at Dogue Run Farm. See Orlando Ridout IV and John Riley, "George Washington's Treading Barn at Dogue Run Farm: A Documentary and Architectural Analysis," February 1993, Staff report, Appendix II, 88, Washington Library); *Annals of Agriculture,* 2: 381–383. Washington's notes on the *Annals* indicate he had read Young's article on Thomas William Coke, "Extracts from Young's Annals of Agriculture," Series 8d., Extracts, Abstracts, and Notes, GWP, LOC. Arthur Young published his plan for the barn in the *Annals of Agriculture* (Bury St. Edmunds, 1791), 16: 149–155.

19. GW to Arthur Young, 1 November 1787, *PGW, Conf.,* 5: 402–405; GW to Arthur Young, 4 December 1788, *PGW, Pres.,* 1: 159–163; Samuel Powel to GW, 10 May 1786, *PGW, Conf.,* 4: 45–46; Enclosure, "Essay and Plans for Buildings," 10 May 1786, Series 4, GWP, LOC; George Morgan's plan for a barnyard was published in *The*

Columbian Magazine (Philadelphia, 1787), 1: 77–82, to which Washington subscribed; J.P. Brissot de Warville, *New Travels in the United States of America, 1788,* Mara Soceanu Vamos and Durand Echeverria, trans., Durand Echeverria, ed. (Cambridge, MA: Belknap Press of Harvard University Press, 1964), 237–239; Ridout and Riley, "George Washington's Treading Barn at Dogue Run Farm," 9–18, Washington Library; Plan for a Barn, 28 October 1792, GWP, LOC; Orlando Ridout V, "Agricultural Buildings," in Cary Carson and Carl Lounsbury, eds., *The Chesapeake House: Architectural Investigation by Colonial Williamsburg* (Chapel Hill: University of North Carolina Press, 2013), 179–203.

20. *Diaries,* 5: 271–272, 304, 331, 349; GW to Peterson & Taylor, 5 January 1788, *PGW, Conf.,* 6: 10–13; Memorandum of an Agreement between GW and Charles Hagan, January 5, 1788, Series 4, GWP, LOC; Ledger B, 271.

21. GW to George Augustine Washington, 31 March 1789, *PGW, Pres.,* 1: 472–476; Memorandum from GW, June 1791, printed in n. 1 to GW to Tobias Lear, 26 June 1791, *PGW, Pres.,* 8: 300–302; *Diaries,* 5: 64; GW to George Augustine Washington, 24 July 1787, *PGW, Conf.,* 5: 269–271.

22. Cross section and specifications of Dogue Run treading barn, in Plan for a Barn, 28 October 1792, GWP, LOC; Enclosure: Washington's Plan for a barn, 28 October 1792, *PGW, Pres.,* 11: 278–282; GW to Carlyle & Adam, 15 February 1767, *PGW, Col.,* 7: 482–491; *Diaries,* 2: 90; GW to Samuel Chamberline, 3 April 1788, *PGW, Conf.,* 6: 190–191; Ridout and Riley, "George Washington's Treading Barn at Dogue Run Farm," 19–28; George Morgan, "An Essay, exhibiting a plan for a Farm-Yard."

23. Enclosure: Washington's Plan for a barn, 28 October 1792, *PGW, Pres.,* 11: 278–282; GW to Anthony Whitting, 28 October 1792, 6 January 1793, 3 March 1793, 28 April 1793, *PGW, Pres.,* 11: 273–278, 594–599, 12: 257–260, 488–493; GW to William Pearce, 16 February 1794, *PGW, Pres.,* 15: 238–241.

24. GW to William Pearce, 23 December 1793, 16–17 March 1794, 30 March 1794, 13 April 1794, 10 May 1795, 24 May 1795, 29 November 1795, *PGW, Pres.,* 14: 606–616, 15: 395–398, 469–471, 575–577, 18: 136–139, 167–169, 19: 191–193; "Calculation of the number of Bricks wanting for the Barn at River Farm," 1795 May, enclosed in GW to William Pearce, 10 May 1795, *PGW, Pres.,* 18: 136–139; Weekly Report, 16 April 1796, Photostat, Washington Library.

25. Memorandum from GW, June 1791, printed in n. 1 to GW to Tobias Lear, 26 June 1791, *PGW, Pres.,* 8: 300–302.

26. Farm Reports, 26 November 1785–15 April 1786, *PGW, Conf.,* 3: 389–410; David Humphreys described the process of compiling the weekly reports: "Every week, On Saturday in the afternoon, reports are made by all his Overseers & registered in books kept for the purpose; so that at the end of the year, the quantity of labour & produce may be accurately known," in *David Humphreys' "Life of General Washington" with George Washington's "Remarks,"* Rosemarie Zagarri, ed. (Athens: University of Georgia Press, 1991), 37–39.

27. GW to Lund Washington, 20 November 1785, 20 December 1785, *PGW, Conf.,* 3: 373–375, 478–479; Lund Washington was conducting business at Mount Vernon for GW until 8 April 1786, Ledger B, 228; by 1784, Lund was constructing a house at Hayfields on the land he had acquired from GW, Lund Washington, Book of Accounts, 1762–1784, USNA Museum, 68.

28. Mount Vernon Weekly Reports of Managers, November 18, 1786—April 28, 1787 (typed transcriptions), Washington Library; GW to George Augustine Washington, 17 May 1787, 27 May 1787, 10 June 1787, 1 July 1787, *PGW, Conf.,* 5: 189, 196–199, 224–227, 241–244.

29. Weekly Report, September 18, 1790, Washington Library.

30. Justin Roberts, *Slavery and the Enlightenment in the British Atlantic, 1750–1807* (New York: Cambridge University Press, 2013), 56–68; Caitlin Rosenthal, *Accounting for Slavery: Masters and Management* (Cambridge, MA: Harvard University Press, 2018), 9–12, 28–31; Rosenthal, "Slavery's Scientific Management," 63–69, 328, n. 75.

31. Articles of Agreement with Anthony Whitting, in n.1, GW to Anthony Whitting, 14 April 1790, *PGW, Pres.,* 5: 330–333; Agreement with William Pearce, 23 September 1793, *PGW, Pres.,* 14: 120–123; Articles of Agreement with James Anderson, 5 October 1796, *PGW, Pres.,* 21: 52–53; GW to Howell Lewis, 18 August 1793, *PGW, Pres.,* 13: 485–490; Samuel Vaughan Journal, 1787, 55–56, Washington Library. When one of the enslaved overseers was sick, such as Will at Muddy Hole in February 1786, Washington noted that he received no account from that farm, Farm Reports, 1785–1786. A receipt signed with Davy Gray's mark indicates he could not write; receipt, Mrs. Washington in account with Davie Gray, 12 January 1801, Peter Family Papers, Box 34, Washington Library. No surviving document indicates that other enslaved overseers submitted written reports. For importance of enslaved overseers in gathering work reports on Caribbean plantations, see Rosenthal, *Accounting for Slavery,* 35–36.

32. Roberts, *Slavery and the Enlightenment in the British Atlantic,* 26–79, esp. 56–68; Rosenthal, *Accounting for Slavery,* 27–31; Mount Vernon Weekly Reports, April 19, 1789—September 17, 1791, Photostats, Washington Library; *Diaries,* 4: 223–233, 237–240; Articles of Agreement with William Garner, 10 December 1788, *PGW, Pres.,* 1: 171–173; Overseer's Account Book, 1785–1798, Washington Library; Mount Vernon Store Book, 1787, Washington Library; later store accounts found in Mount Vernon Ledger, January 1794–December 1796, Series 5, Financial Papers, GWP, LOC.

33. "Notes & Observations [1785–1786]," Photostat, Washington Library (original in GWP, LOC); see also "Summary for 1788," Photostat, Washington Library; for organization of agricultural knowledge, see Bushman, *The American Farmer in the Eighteenth Century,* 203–209.

34. Slave census in *Diaries,* 4: 277–283; Brenda E. Stevenson, *Life in Black and White: Family and Community in the Slave South* (New York: Oxford University Press, 1996), 210–212; Thompson, *"The Only Unavoidable Subject of Regret,"* 128.

35. *Diaries,* 5: 3–4, 42, 66; GW to William Peacey, 16 November 1786, 7 January 1788, *PGW, Conf.,* 4: 375–376, 6: 13–14; William Peacey to GW, 2 February 1787, *PGW, Pres.,* 5: 6–7; Wakelin Welch to William Peacey, 17 January 1787, Washington Library.

36. *Diaries,* 5: 42, 54, 111, 120, 131–132, 317; GW to George Augustine Washington, 3 June 1787, 29 July 1787, *PGW, Conf.,* 5: 217–219, 276–279; George Augustine Washington to GW, 27 April 1789, *PGW, Pres.,* 2: 140–142; GW to James Bloxham, 1 January 1789, *PGW, Pres.,* 1: 208–215.

37. George Augustine Washington to GW, 5 March 1790, 26 March 1790, *PGW, Pres.,* 5: 202–206, 279–284; Ledger B, 237, 303; Wilbur Cortez Abbott, "James Bloxham, Farmer," *Massachusetts Historical Society Proceedings* 59 (1925–1926): 177–203.

38. GW to William Pearce, 25 January 1795, *PGW, Pres.,* 17: 435–439.

39. *Diaries,* 4: 119, 244, 252; Overseer's Account Book, 1785–1798, Washington Library, 1, 2, 3, 4, 17, 38–42; Isaac first appears as lead carpenter in Weekly Report for 6 May 1786, Photostats, Washington Library.

40. Ledger B, 260; Articles of Agreement with William Garner, 10 December 1788, *PGW, Pres.,* 1: 171–173; Articles of Agreement with Anthony Whitting, in n.1, GW to Anthony Whitting, 14 April 1790, *PGW, Pres.,* 5: 330–333; GW to William Pearce, 18 December 1793, *PGW, Pres.,* 14: 558–564; GW to Howell Lewis, 11 August 1793, *PGW, Pres.,* 13: 417–423.

41. GW to Lund Washington, 21 November 1782, Founders Online, Early Access; GW to William Triplett, 25 September 1786, *PGW, Conf.,* 4: 268–274; Ledger B, 27, 355; For Washington's later description of the transaction and the value of the slaves rented from French, see GW to David Stuart, 12 December 1790, *PGW, Pres.,* 7: 59–61.

42. GW to William Triplett, 25 September 1786, *PGW, Conf.,* 4: 268–74; *Diaries,* 5: 73–74; Williamson, *The Transformation of Rural England,* 6–19, 170.

43. *Diaries,* 5: 101–102, 115, 121–122, 226; Weekly Reports, 13 January, 17 February, 10 March 1787, Washington Library; John Robertson and George Washington, Memorandum of Agreement, 24 October 1786, Series 4, GWP, LOC.

44. *Diaries,* 4: 268–269, 307–308; 5: 94–96, 320.

45. Crop notes in Series 8d., Extracts, Abstracts, and Notes, GWP, LOC; Arthur Young to GW, 1 February 1787, *PGW, Conf.,* 5: 3–6; GW to Arthur Young, 1 November 1787, *PGW, Conf.,* 5: 402–405. GW consulted: *The Farmer's Complete Guide,* 1760; *Museum Rusticum,* 1764; John Wynn Baker, *Experiments in Agriculture,* 1764–1773; *A Practical Treatise of Husbandry, from Duhamel,* 1762; Kames, *The Gentleman Farmer,* 1779; Philip Miller, *The Abridgement of the Gardeners Dictionary,* 1763; Tull, *Horse-Hoeing Husbandry,* 1751; Charles Varlo, *A New System of Husbandry,* 1785.

46. Brissot de Warville, *Travels in North America,* 237–239; GW to John Beale Bordley, 17 August 1788, *PGW, Conf.,* 6: 450–454; GW to Samuel Powel, 21 February 1790, *PGW, Pres.,* 5: 165–166.

47. GW to John Beale Bordley, 17 August 1788, *PGW, Conf.,* 6: 450–454; GW to Samuel Powel, 19 July 1785, 2 November 1785, *PGW, Conf.,* 3: 139–140, 338–339; Olive Moore Gambrill, "John Beale Bordley and the Early Years of the Philadelphia Agricultural Society," *Pennsylvania Magazine of History and Biography* 66 (1942): 410–439; John Beale Bordley, *A Summary View of the Courses of Crops in the Husbandry of England & Maryland* (Philadelphia: C. Cist, 1784).

48. Crop Rotations, 1790, and Crop Rotations, 1794 (this document is misdated and is part of the 1790 notes), Series 4, General Correspondence, GWP, LOC.

49. GW to Anthony Whitting, 4 September 1791, *PGW, Pres.,* 8: 487–489; GW to William Pearce, 18 December 1793, 2 November 1794, 8 February 1795, *PGW, Pres.,* 14: 558–564, 17: 129–132, 17: 510–511; GW to James Anderson, 22 May 1798, *PGW, Ret.,* 2: 287–291.

50. Rotation of Crops for Dogue Run, 1793, *PGW, Pres.,* 14: 660–667; GW to William Pearce, 18 December 1793, *PGW, Pres.,* 14: 558–564; Enclosure: Crop Rotations for Mount Vernon Farms, 1793, *PGW, Pres.,* 14: 566–580.

51. GW to George William Fairfax, 30 June 1785, *PGW, Conf.,* 3: 87–92; GW to Arthur Young, 1 November 1787, *PGW, Conf.,* 5: 402–405; GW to George Augustine Washington, 1 July 1787, 29 July 1787, *PGW, Conf.,* 5: 241–244, 276–279; GW to Alexander Spotswood, 13 February 1788, *PGW, Conf.,* 6: 110–113; Roberts, *Slavery and the Enlightenment in the British Atlantic,* 92–93; Corn purchases between 1786 and 1789 recorded in Ledger B, 221, 224, 246, 269; Corn sold to Alexander Smith in 1795, Mount Vernon Farm Ledger, January 1794—December 1796, Washington Library, 66, 90; GW to William Augustine Washington, 26 June 1798, 3 October 1798, *PGW, Ret.,* 2: 360–362, 3: 76–77.

52. "Notes & Observations," Photostat, Washington Library; GW to Arthur Young, 6 August 1786, *PGW, Conf.,* 4: 196–200; GW to Arthur Young, 4 December 1788, *PGW, Pres.,* 1: 159–163; *Diaries,* 4: 304–306, 5: 126; Weekly Reports, 24 March, 31 March, 13 May 1786, Washington Library.

53. GW to Arthur Young, 1 November 1787, *PGW, Conf.,* 5: 402–405; Arthur Young to GW, 1 July 1788, *PGW, Conf.,* 6: 368–370; GW to John Beale Bordley, 17 August 1788, *PGW, Conf.,* 6: 450–454; GW to Levi Hollingsworth, 20 September 1785, *PGW, Conf.,* 3: 267–268; Arthur Donaldson to GW, 1 October 1785, *PGW, Conf.,* 3: 286–288; GW to Arthur Donaldson, 16 October 1785, *PGW, Conf.,* 3: 307. Washington continued to experiment with river mud as a manure, but he had no further correspondence with the inventor. The plan of the machine enclosed in: Arthur Donaldson to George Washington, 1 October 1785, Series 4, GWP, LOC.

54. GW to Robert Lewis, 6 September 1783, in Founders Online, Early Access; GW to Robert Lewis & Sons, 1 February 1785, *PGW, Conf.,* 2: 317–318; in an appeal to extend his contract, Roberts offered his contrition for his abuse of his wife, to GW, 25 November 1784, *PGW, Conf.,* 2: 151–153. This incident was the last recorded problem before Washington decided to dismiss Roberts.

55. GW to Robert Lewis & Sons, 1 February 1785, 12 April 1785, *PGW, Conf.,* 2: 317–318, 493–494; Robert Lewis & Sons to GW, 5 April 1785, *PGW, Conf.,* 2: 480–482; Memorandum of Agreement with Joseph Davenport, 23 May 1785, *PGW, Conf.,* 3: 11–12; Census of Slaves, *Diaries,* 4: 279; GW to Robert Lewis & Co., 18 May 1786, *PGW, Conf.,* 4: 56–57; GW to Anthony Whitting, 13–14 January 1793, *PGW, Pres.,* 11: 625–631.

56. GW to Arthur Young, 4 December 1788, *PGW, Pres.,* 1: 159–163; GW to Bushrod Washington, 25 November 1788, *PGW, Pres.,* 1: 126–127.

57. GW to George Augustine Washington, 31 March 1789, *PGW, Pres.,* 1: 472–476; GW to John Fairfax, 1 January 1789, *PGW, Pres.,* 1: 216–225; GW to James Bloxham, 1 January 1789, *PGW, Pres.,* 1: 208–215.

58. GW to John Fairfax, 1 January 1789, *PGW, Pres.,* 1: 216–225; GW to James Bloxham, 1 January 1789, *PGW, Pres.,* 1: 208–215; GW to David Stuart, 25 November, 2 December 1788, *PGW, Pres.,* 1: 125–126, 147–149.

59. GW to John Fairfax, 1 January 1789, *PGW, Pres.,* 1: 216–225.

5. ENSLAVED AGRICULTURAL LABOR AT MOUNT VERNON

1. *Diaries,* 5: 3–10.

2. *Diaries,* 5: 8–10; Note for 15 July 1786, in "Notes & Observations, 1785–1786," Photostat at Washington Library (original in GWP, LOC).

3. Summary of annual cycles of work drawn from Weekly Reports, Summary for 1788, "Notes & Observations, 1785–1786," Photostats at Washington Library, and *Diaries,* 5. See esp. Mount Vernon Weekly Reports, November 26, 1785—December 30, 1786, Photostats at Washington Library, original in GWP, LOC; Overseer's Account Book, 1785–1798, Washington Library.

4. Washington began to use the term "hoe people" in 1787 as other enslaved workers took on more specialized work, see e.g., *Diaries,* 5: 98, 207, 399, 407, 410; GW to John Fairfax, 1 January 1789, *PGW, Pres.,* 1: 216–225; GW to Anthony Whitting, 23 December 1792, 19 May 1793, *PGW, Pres.,* 11: 543–546, 12: 610–616; Lois Green Carr and Lorena S. Walsh, "Economic Diversification and Labor Organization in the Chesapeake, 1650–1820," in Stephen Innes, ed., *Work and Labor in Early America* (Chapel Hill: University of North Carolina Press, 1988), 144–188. Carr and Walsh describe Washington as "a true agricultural innovator," and describe Mount Vernon as an important example of the gendered division of labor that followed diversification in the Chesapeake.

5. Roberts, *Slavery and the Enlightenment in the British Atlantic,* 180–189; Thompson, *"The Only Unavoidable Subject of Regret,"* 135–138.

6. The slave census of February 1786 named four carpenters at the Home House: Isaac, James, Sambo, and Tom Nokes, *Diaries,* 4: 278; Carpenter's account for June 1786 in Mount Vernon Weekly Reports, November 26, 1785—December 30, 1786, Photostats at the Washington Library (original in GWP, LOC).

7. Agreement between James Lawson and George Washington, 18 November 1786, Series 4, GWP, LOC; See e.g., Weekly Reports for 30 December 1786, 22 August 1789, 17 September 1791, 14 April 1792, Washington Library; GW to Anthony Whitting, 2 December 1792, *PGW, Pres.,* 11: 460–465.

8. Thompson, *"The Only Unavoidable Subject of Regret,"* 177–182; Overseer's Account Book, Washington Library.

9. GW to Anthony Whitting, 26 May 1793, *PGW, Pres.,* 12: 631–637; Overview of harvests drawn from *Diaries* and Weekly Reports. The most detailed account of Washington's direct management of the harvests is for the summer of 1788 in *Diaries,* 5: 337–371; Thompson, *"The Only Unavoidable Subject of Regret,"* 116–117.

10. Robert Hunter, quoted in Lee, ed., *Experiencing Mount Vernon,* 31.

11. *Diaries,* 4: 78, 145; Elkanah Watson and Winslow C. Watson, *Men and Times of the Revolution: Or, Memoirs of Elkanah Watson, Including Journals of Travels in Europe and America* (New York: Dana and Company, 1856), 232–233; Samuel Drew, *The Life of Rev. Thomas Coke, LL.D.: Including In Detail His Various Travels and Extraordinary Missionary Exertions, In England, Ireland, America, And the West-Indies* (New York: J. Soule and T. Mason, for the Methodist Episcopal Church in the United States, 1818), 138; James Madison to GW, 11 November 1785, *PGW, Conf.,* 3: 355–358; Robert

McColley, *Slavery and Jeffersonian Virginia* (Urbana: University of Illinois Press, 1964), 141–162.

12. Robert Pleasants to GW, 11 December 1785, *PGW, Conf.,* 3: 449–451.

13. GW to Robert Morris, 12 April 1786, *PGW, Conf.,* 4: 15–17; GW to Lafayette, 10 May 1786, *PGW, Conf.,* 4: 41–45.

14. Amelioration, and particularly its appearance in North America, is discussed in Roberts, *Slavery and Enlightenment in the British Atlantic,* 44–56; and Christa Dierksheide, *Amelioration and Empire: Progress and Slavery in the Plantation Americas* (Charlottesville: University of Virginia Press, 2014), esp. 10–19; for Joshua Steele, see David Lambert, *White Creole Culture, Politics and Identity during the Age of Abolition* (Cambridge, UK: Cambridge University Press, 2005), c. 2; for the impact of early antislavery efforts in the Anglophone world, see Brown, *Moral Capital;* Thomas Jefferson to Thomas Mann Randolph, 18 February 1793, *Papers of Thomas Jefferson,* 25: 230.

15. GW to John Francis Mercer, 6 November 1786, *PGW, Conf.,* 4: 336–338; see notes to GW to Burwell Bassett, Jr., 3 February 1788, *PGW, Conf.,* 6: 78–79; GW to John Dandridge, 2 October 1791, *PGW, Pres.,* 9: 41–43; Ledger B, 280; Ledger C, 9.

16. GW to Thomas Freeman, 16 October 1785, *PGW, Conf.,* 3: 308–310; Thomas Freeman to GW, 18 December 1786, *PGW, Conf.,* 4: 463–465; Thomas Freeman, Bill of Sale of Slaves, 5 October 1786, Series 4, GWP, LOC.

17. GW to John Francis Mercer, 6 November 1786, 24 November 1786, 19 December 1786, 1 February 1787, *PGW, Conf.,* 4: 336–338, 393–395, 465–467, 5: 2–3; List and description of slaves, with values assigned, in Mercer Family Papers, Virginia Historical Society, Mss1 M5345, a446 (previously unidentified document with docket: "Letters to Genl Washington").

18. GW to Henry Lee, Jr., 4 February 1787, *PGW, Conf.,* 5: 10–11; John Lawson to GW, 17 March 1787, 18 April 1787, 25 April 1787, *PGW, Conf.,* 5: 91–92, 150, 154–155; GW to John Lawson, 10 April 1787, *PGW, Conf.,* 5: 138; *Diaries,* 5: 131.

19. GW to John Fowler, 2 February 1788, *PGW, Conf.,* 6: 77–78; GW to David Stuart, 22 January 1788, *PGW, Conf.,* 6: 54; GW to Betty Lewis, 13 September 1789, *PGW, Pres.,* 4: 32–36. In 1786, Washington discharged the execution of a debt owed him by the widow of William Crawford to avoid her sale of slaves to pay the debt; GW to Thomas Freeman, 8 May 1786, *PGW, Conf.,* 4: 36; see also note to Francis Willis, Jr., to GW, 24 September 1788, *PGW, Pres.,* 1: 10–13.

20. GW to Anthony Whitting, 19 May 1793, *PGW, Pres.,* 12: 610–616; Stevenson, *Life in Black and White,* 210–212; Thompson, *"The Only Unavoidable Subject of Regret,"* 127–131.

21. GW to Anthony Whitting, 28 April 1793, 12 May 1793, 26 May 1793, *PGW, Pres.,* 12: 488–493, 566–570, 631–637; GW to William Pearce, 23 December 1793, 20 April 1794, *PGW, Pres.,* 14: 606–616; 15: 624–628; on diet of the enslaved generally, see Thompson, *"The Only Unavoidable Subject of Regret,"* 221–246.

22. GW to Anthony Whitting, 26 May 1793, *PGW, Pres.,* 12: 631–637; Overseer's Account Book, 1785–1798, Washington Library; [William Pearce], Mount Vernon Ledger, 1794–1796, Store Account, 22–36, Series 5, Financial Papers, GWP, LOC [Photostat at Washington Library]; Thompson, *"The Only Unavoidable Subject of Regret,"* 232–234.

23. Articles of Agreement with William Garner, 10 December 1788, *PGW, Pres.*, 1: 171–173; Agreement with Henry Jones, in n. 3 to GW to Anthony Whitting, 14 August 1791, *PGW, Pres.*, 8: 425–428; GW to Anthony Whitting, 14 October 1792, *PGW, Pres.*, 11: 222–231; GW to William Pearce, 18 May 1794, *PGW, Pres.*, 16: 87–92.

24. GW to Anthony Whitting, 5 May 1793, *PGW, Pres.*, 12: 523–529; GW to James Anderson, 20 February 1797, *PGW, Pres.*, 21: 721–723; GW to William Pearce, 12 January 1794, *PGW, Pres.*, 15: 60–67; GW to William Augustine Washington, 23 November 1794, *PGW, Pres.*, 17: 207–209; GW to John Fairfax, 1 January 1789, *PGW, Pres.*, 1: 216–225.

25. "Estimate of the cost of Mrs French's Land and Negroes on Dogue Creek," in n. 3 to GW to William Triplett, 25 September 1786, *PGW, Conf.*, 4: 268–274; GW to David Stuart, 12 December 1790, *PGW, Pres.*, 7: 59–61.

26. Overseer's Account Book, Washington Library; the daily work of the carpenters in the harvest of 1786 was valued at 2/6, although the hired white mowers that year received 4/per day, Ledger B, 231.

27. Circular to William Stuart, Hiland Crow, and Henry McCoy, 14 July 1793, *PGW, Pres.*, 13: 220–226; GW to Anthony Whitting, 6 January 1793, 5 May 1793, *PGW, Pres.*, 11: 594–599, 12: 523–529.

28. GW to William Pearce, 18 December 1793, 30 March 1794, *PGW, Pres.*, 14: 558–564, 15: 469–471; George Augustine Washington to GW, 7 December 1790, *PGW, Pres.*, 7: 40–45; GW to Anthony Whitting, 24 February 1793, *PGW, Pres.*, 12: 212–215; overview of punishment in Thompson, *"The Only Unavoidable Subject of Regret,"* 247–259.

29. GW to William Pearce, 30 March 1794, *PGW, Pres.*, 15: 469–471; GW to Burgess Ball, 27 July 1794, *PGW, Pres.*, 16: 440–442; Thompson, *"The Only Unavoidable Subject of Regret,"* 251.

30. GW to Anthony Whitting, 16 December 1792, 20 January 1793, 19 May 1793, 2 June 1793, *PGW, Pres.*, 11: 519–524, 12: 31–36, 12: 610–616, 13: 6–13; Anthony Whitting to GW, 16 January 1793, *PGW, Pres.*, 12: 5–14.

31. GW to Anthony Whitting, 16 December 1792, 3 March 1793, *PGW, Pres.*, 11: 519–523, 12: 257–260; GW to William Pearce, 30 March 1794, 1 March 1795, 7 June 1795, 14 November 1796, *PGW, Pres.*, 15: 469–471, 17: 600–602, 18: 198–199, 21: 217–220; Thompson, *"The Only Unavoidable Subject of Regret,"* 132.

32. GW to Robert Morris, 12 April 1786, *PGW, Conf.*, 4: 15–17; GW to James McHenry, 11 November 1786, *PGW, Conf.*, 4: 358–359; GW to William Drayton, 20 November 1786, *PGW, Conf.*, 4: 389–390. Jack escaped again in Baltimore and was recaptured in Philadelphia, see Edward Moyston to GW, 4 April 1787, *PGW, Conf.*, 5: 123–124.

33. GW to William Pearce, 22 March 1795, 5 April 1795, *PGW, Pres.*, 17: 678–680, 18: 10–12; Erica Armstrong Dunbar, *Never Caught: The Washingtons' Relentless Pursuit of their Runaway Slave, Ona Judge* (New York: 37 Ink / Atria, 2017), 110–113; GW to Frederick Kitt, 10 January 1798, 29 January 1798, *PGW, Ret.*, 2: 16, 60.

34. Ledger B, 336; GW to Anthony Whitting, 24 February 1793, 3 March 1793, *PGW, Pres.*, 12: 212–215, 257–260; GW to John Dandridge, 28 May 1795, *PGW, Pres.*, 18: 180; Ledger C, 22; for slaves Washington acquired from the Dandridge estate, see Morgan, *"'To Get Quit of Negroes': George Washington and Slavery,"* 404–405.

35. Enslaved overseers identified in Overseer's Account Book, Washington Library; GW to Thomas Green, 31 March 1789, *PGW, Pres.,* 1: 467–469; Weekly Report, 25 April 1789, Washington Library.

36. GW to Anthony Whitting, 30 December 1792, 13–14 January 1793, *PGW, Pres.,* 11: 568–573, 625–631; GW to Burgess Ball, 27 July 1794, *PGW, Pres.,* 16: 440–442.

37. GW to William Pearce, 18 December 1793, *PGW, Pres.,* 14: 558–564.

38. GW to William Pearce, 23 December 1793, 20 April 1794, *PGW, Pres.,* 14: 606–616, 15: 624–628; GW to Burgess Ball, 27 July 1794, *PGW, Pres.,* 16: 440–442; George Augustine Washington to GW, 26 March 1790, *PGW, Pres.,* 5: 279–284; GW to Anthony Whitting, 26 May 1793, *PGW, Pres.,* 12: 631–637.

39. George Augustine Washington to GW, 5 March 1790, *PGW, Pres.,* 5: 202–206; GW to James Anderson, 18 June 1797, *PGW, Ret.,* 1: 191–195; GW to Anthony Whitting, 3 February 1793, *PGW, Pres.,* 12: 95–100.

40. Articles of Agreement with William Garner, 10 December 1788, *PGW, Pres.,* 1: 171–173; Articles of Agreement between Anthony Whitting and George Augustine Washington, on behalf of George Washington, 20 May 1790, in note to GW to Whitting, 14 April 1790, *PGW, Pres.,* 5: 330–333; Hiland Crow, Articles of Agreement with George A. Washington, 15 September 1790, Series 4, GWP, LOC; Articles of Agreement between Henry McCoy and Anthony Whitting, on behalf of the President of the United States, 17 December 1792, in Series 4, GWP, LOC; GW to William Pearce, 3 August 1794, *PGW, Pres.,* 16: 463–467.

41. Book of Memorandums Inventories and Miscellaneous Transactions of the Exter [Executor] to the Estate of John Cadwalader Esqr. begun March 1786, in Collection 3831, Historical Society of Pennsylvania; Lambert Cadwalader and Philemon Dickinson in account with Anthony Whitting, February 1786 to February 1790, in Cadwalader Family Papers, collection 1454, Box 18, Folder 7, Historical Society of Pennsylvania; An Inventory or Schedule of Negroes, Stock, Farming Utensils of every kind, . . . left at Shrewsbury Farm, 1 January 1790, John Cadwalader Estate Volume, Collection 3831, Historical Society of Pennsylvania; George Augustine Washington to GW, 26 March 1790, *PGW, Pres.,* 5: 279–284; Articles of Agreement between Anthony Whitting and George Augustine Washington, on behalf of George Washington, 20 May 1790, in note to GW to Whitting, 14 April 1790, *PGW, Pres.,* 330–333; GW to Anthony Whitting, 14 October 1792, 16 December 1792, *PGW, Pres.,* 11: 222–231, 519–524.

42. GW to Anthony Whitting, 14 April 1790, *PGW, Pres.,* 5: 330–333; GW to William Pearce, 18 December 1793, 25 January 1795, *PGW, Pres.,* 14: 558–564, 17: 435–439.

43. GW to William Tilghman, 21 July 1793, *PGW, Pres.,* 13: 262–265.

44. Thomas Jefferson to Jacob Hollingsworth, 22 November 1792, *Papers of Thomas Jefferson,* 24: 656; Thomas Jefferson to Thomas Mann Randolph, 18 February 1793, *Papers of Thomas Jefferson,* 25: 230; Jacob Hollingsworth to Thomas Jefferson, 9 December 1792, *Papers of Thomas Jefferson,* 24: 713–714; Thomas Jefferson to GW, 28 June 1793, *PGW, Pres.,* 13: 152–154.

45. Agreement with William Pearce, 23 September 1793, *PGW, Pres.,* 14: 120–123; GW to William Pearce, 18 December 1793, *PGW, Pres.,* 14: 558–564; Walsh, "Slavery and Agriculture at Mount Vernon," 65, 77n32. Pearce had since 1778 worked at Hopewell Plantation in Kent County, Galloway Account Books, Ringgold Estate, 1777–90, Box 87, Galloway-Maxcy-Markoe Families Papers, Library of Congress.

46. GW to George Augustine Washington, 29 July 1787, *PGW, Conf.,* 5: 276–279; GW to Anthony Whitting, 6 January 1793, 12 May 1793, *PGW, Pres.,* 11: 594–599, 12: 566–570; GW to William Pearce, 18 December 1793, 19 January 1794, *PGW, Pres.,* 14: 558–564, 15: 84–86; certificate, in n. 3 to GW to William Pearce, 7 September 1794, *PGW, Pres.,* 16: 650–652.

47. GW to Anthony Whitting, 6 January 1793, *PGW, Pres.,* 11: 594–599; GW to George Augustine Washington, 29 July 1787, *PGW, Conf.,* 5: 276–279; GW to William Pearce, 20–21 July 1794, 28 September 1794, *PGW, Pres.,* 16: 391–392, 731–733.

48. GW to William Pearce, 28 September 1794, 25 January 1795, *PGW, Pres.,* 16: 731–733, 17: 435–439; GW to William Augustine Washington, 28 September 1794, 23 November 1794, *PGW, Pres.,* 16: 733–734, 17: 207–209.

49. Agreement with James Donaldson, 29 September 1794, *PGW, Pres.,* 16: 734–735; Agreement between James Lawson and George Washington, 18 November 1786, Series 4, GWP, LOC; John Knowles and George Washington, Articles of Agreement, 7 July 1789, Series 4, GWP, LOC; Indenture with Thomas Green, 9 November 1790, *PGW, Pres.,* 6: 641–644.

50. GW to William Pearce, 18 December 1793, 2 November 1794, 16 November 1794, 7 December 1794, 22 March 1795, *PGW, Pres.,* 14: 558–564, 17: 129–132, 165–168, 248–251, 678–680; Indenture with Thomas Green, 9 November 1790, *PGW, Pres.,* 6: 641–644; Robert F. Dalzell, Jr., and Lee Baldwin Dalzell, *George Washington's Mount Vernon: At Home in Revolutionary America* (New York: Oxford University Press, 1998), 145–147.

51. GW to William Pearce, 18 December 1793, *PGW, Pres.,* 14: 558–564; for social division of whites, see GW to George William Fairfax, 30 June 1785, *PGW, Conf.,* 3: 87–92.

52. Note for 16 May 1786, in "Notes & Observations, 1785–1786," Photostat at Washington Library; GW to James Bloxham, 1 January 1789, *PGW, Pres.,* 1: 208–215; GW to George Augustine Washington, 24 April 1786, *PGW, Conf.,* 4: 28–29; GW to Arthur Young, 4 December 1788, *PGW, Pres.,* 1: 159–163.

53. GW to Benjamin Dulany, 15 July 1799, *PGW, Ret.,* 4: 189–190; "A list of Negros the property of Mrs. French, in possession of George Washington," 15 July 1799, Washington Library. Benjamin Dulany acknowledged Washington's proposal but after waiting to consult with his mother-in-law, Penelope French, he apparently did not respond before Washington's death five months later.

54. "A list of Negros the property of Mrs. French, in possession of George Washington," Washington Library; George Augustine Washington to GW, 20 August 1790, *PGW, Pres.,* 6: 311–315; Washington's Slave List, June 1799, *PGW, Ret.,* 4: 527–542; Stevenson, *Life in Black and White,* 211–212; GW to William Pearce, 8 March 1795, *PGW, Pres.,* 17: 632–634.

55. *Diaries,* 4: 124; GW to George Augustine Washington, 26 August 1787, *PGW, Conf.,* 5: 303–305; GW to Anthony Whitting, 28 October 1792, 21 April 1793, 5 May 1793, *PGW, Pres.,* 11: 273–278, 12: 463–468, 523–529.

56. GW to George Gilpin, 29 October 1785, *PGW, Conf.,* 3: 324–325; GW to Henry Lee, 16 October 1793, *PGW, Pres.,* 14: 224–225; Tobias Lear to Charles Vancouver, 5 November 1791, in n. 2 to Vancouver to GW, 5 November 1791, *PGW, Pres.,* 9: 142–144.

57. GW to William Pearce, 22 February 1795, *PGW, Pres.,* 17: 555–558; GW to Anthony Whitting, 6 January 1793, 3 March 1793, *PGW, Pres.,* 11: 594–599, 12: 257–260.

58. GW to William Pearce, 1 June 1794, *PGW, Pres.*, 16: 176–178; GW to John Fairfax,
      1 January 1789, *PGW, Pres.*, 1: 216–225; Articles of agreement between George
      Washington and House carpenter and joiner, 1793, Washington Library.

59. GW to Thomas Green, 31 March 1789, *PGW, Pres.*, 1: 467–469; GW to Arthur Young,
      18–21 June 1792, *PGW, Pres.*, 10: 460–467; Thompson, "*The Only Unavoidable Subject
      of Regret*," 260.

6. CINCINNATUS AND THE WORLD OF IMPROVEMENT

1. Chevalier de la Luzerne to Rayneval, 12 April 1784, in "Early Descriptions of Mount
     Vernon," Washington Library; R.W.G. Vail, ed., "A Dinner at Mount Vernon: From the
     Unpublished Journal of Joshua Brookes (1773–1859)," *The New-York Historical Society
     Quarterly* 31 (April 1947): 72–85; Robert Hunter, Latrobe, and Niemcewicz quoted in
     Lee, ed., *Experiencing Mount Vernon*, 31, 63–64, 81.

2. Robert Hunter quoted in Lee, ed., *Experiencing Mount Vernon*, 31; Garry Wills,
     Cincinnatus: George Washington and the Enlightenment (Garden City, NY: Doubleday,
     1984), see esp. 13–16, 23; Carl J. Richard, *The Founders and the Classics: Greece, Rome,
     and the American Enlightenment* (Cambridge, MA: Harvard University Press, 1994),
     50–56, 69–72.

3. GW to Chastellux, 1 February 1784, *PGW, Conf.*, 1: 85–86; GW to Lafayette, 1 February
     1784, *PGW, Conf.*, 1: 87–90; GW to Rochambeau, 1 February 1784, *PGW, Conf.*, 1:
     101–102; GW to Adrienne, Marquise de Lafayette, 4 April 1784, *PGW, Conf.*,
     1: 257–259.

4. GW to Robert Townsend Hooe, 18 July 1784, *PGW, Conf.*, 2: 1–2; GW to Diego Joseph
     Navarro, 30 April 1780, in n. to GW to La Luzerne, 28 April 1780, *PGW, Rev.*, 25:
     507–511.

5. William Carmichael to GW, 3 December 1784, 25 March 1785, *PGW, Conf.*, 2: 163–164,
     460–461; Enclosure, Floridablanca to William Carmichael, 24 November 1784, *PGW,
     Conf.*, 2: 165; William Carmichael to Thomas Jefferson, 25 November 1784, *Papers of
     Thomas Jefferson*, 7: 548–550; Thomas Jefferson to GW, 10 December 1784, *Papers
     of Thomas Jefferson*, 7: 566–567.

6. GW to Lafayette, 15 February 1785, *PGW, Conf.*, 2: 363–367; GW to William Carmichael,
     19 December 1785, *PGW, Conf.*, 3: 471–472; GW to Floridablanca, 19 December 1785,
     in n. 1 to GW to William Carmichael, 19 December 1785, *PGW, Conf.*, 3: 471–472;
     James McHenry to GW, 5 November 1786, 18 November 1786, *PGW, Conf.*, 4: 330–331,
     380–381; GW to James McHenry, 11 November 1786, 29 November 1786, *PGW, Conf.*,
     4: 358–359, 408–410; GW to Lafayette, 19 November 1786, *PGW, Conf.*, 4: 385; Lafayette
     to GW, 7 February 1787, *PGW, Conf.*, 5: 13–15.

7. GW to Lafayette, 25 July 1785, *PGW, Conf.*, 3: 151–155; Boston *Continental Journal*,
     6 October 1785; Thomas Cushing to GW, 7 October 1785, *PGW, Conf.*, 3: 296–298;
     GW to Thomas Cushing, 26 October 1785, *PGW, Conf.*, 3: 319–320; GW to John
     Fairfax, 26 October 1785, *PGW, Conf.*, 3: 320–323.

8. *Weatherwise's Town and Country Almanack, for the year of our Lord, 1786* (Boston,
     1785); Tench Tilghman to GW, 18 November 1785, *PGW, Conf.*, 3: 371–372; Farm

Reports, 11 February 1786, *PGW, Conf.,* 3: 397; Advertisement, 23 February 1786, *PGW, Conf.,* 3: 571–572.

9. *Diaries,* 4: 303; GW to Bushrod Washington, 13 April 1786, *PGW, Conf.,* 4: 18; GW to William Fitzhugh, Jr., 15 May 1786, *PGW, Conf.,* 4: 52–53; GW to William Fitzhugh, Sr., 2 July 1786, *PGW, Conf.,* 4: 146–147; GW to Lafayette, 10 May 1786, *PGW, Conf.,* 4: 41–45; GW to Richard Sprigg, 28 September 1787, *PGW, Conf.,* 5: 344–345.

10. *Diaries,* 5: 68; Correspondence with William Lyles & Company and Samuel Brandon regarding the jenny from Surinam in n. 1, John Fitzgerald to GW, 7 February 1786, *PGW, Conf.,* 3: 549–551; Account of Stock, 24 November 1785, *Diaries,* 4: 236–240; GW to Henry Lee, 30 November 1788, *PGW, Pres.,* 1: 139–140; GW to Abraham Hunt, 20 July 1789, *PGW, Pres.,* 3: 245–246; GW to Thomas Hartley, 29 September 1789, *PGW, Pres.,* 4: 109–112; George Augustine Washington to GW, 16 July 1790, *PGW, Pres.,* 6: 88–95; GW to William Pearce, 23 December 1793, *PGW, Pres.,* 14: 606–616; Ledger B contains many entries for cash received for pasturage and stud fees, see e.g., 269, 270, 275.

11. GW to Lafayette, 1 September 1785, *PGW, Conf.,* 3: 215–218; GW to Arthur Young, 4 December 1788, *PGW, Pres.,* 1: 159–163; Arthur Young to GW, 19 May 1789, *PGW, Pres.,* 2: 341–344.

12. GW to Arthur Young, 4 December 1788, *PGW, Pres.,* 1: 159–163; GW to Anthony Whitting, 2 June 1793, 9 June 1793, *PGW, Pres.,* 13: 6–13, 48–52; Richard Sprigg to GW, 1 June 1786, *PGW, Conf.,* 4: 90–91; John Jay to GW, 3 February 1788, 20 April 1788, *PGW, Conf.,* 6: 79–81, 217; GW to John Jay, 3 March 1788, *PGW, Conf.,* 6: 138–139; Tobias Lear to GW, 15 May 1791, *PGW, Pres.,* 8: 188–193; Tobias Lear to Jeremiah Wadsworth, 13 July 1791, in n. 3 to Tobias Lear to GW, 15 May 1791, *PGW, Pres.,* 8: 188–193; GW to William Pearce, 22 February 1795, *PGW, Pres.,* 17: 555–558; Chester McArthur Destler, "The Gentleman Farmer and the New Agriculture: Jeremiah Wadsworth," *Agricultural History* 46, no. 1 (1972): 135–153.

13. Accounts & papers relating to Royal Gift, 1792–1795, Photostat in the Washington Library (originals in the Chicago Historical Society); William Washington to George Augustine Washington, 15 October 1792, in n. 1 to GW to William Washington, 30 January 1793, *PGW, Pres.,* 12: 65–68; GW to William Washington, 14 July 1795, *PGW, Pres.,* 18: 346–347; William Washington to GW, 23 July 1796, *PGW, Pres.,* 20: 479–480; Agricultural Society of South Carolina records, South Carolina Historical Society, 251.01 (P) 01–74.

14. Samuel Powel to GW, 5 July 1785, *PGW, Conf.,* 3: 106; William Drayton to GW, 23 November 1785, *PGW, Conf.,* 3: 380–381; GW to William Drayton, 25 March 1786, *PGW, Conf.,* 3: 605–606; Philadelphia County Society for Promotion of Agriculture and Domestic Manufactures to GW, 4 May 1789, *PGW, Pres.,* 2: 207; GW to Robert R. Livingston, 16 February 1795, *PGW, Pres.,* 17: 533–534.

15. GW to Samuel Powel, 25 May 1786, *PGW, Conf.,* 4: 75–76; GW to John Beale Bordley, 17 August 1788, *PGW, Conf.,* 6: 450–454; Brian Bonnyman, "Agrarian Patriotism and the Landed Interest: The Scottish 'Society of Improvers in the Knowledge of Agriculture', 1723–1746," in Koen Stapelbroek and Jani Marjanen, eds., *The Rise of*

Economic Societies in the Eighteenth Century: Patriotic Reform in Europe and North America (New York: Palgrave Macmillan, 2012), 26–51; Zilberstein, *A Temperate Empire,* 61–67; Manuela Albertone, "The American Agricultural Societies and the Making of the New Republic, 1785–1830," in Stapelbroek and Marjanen, eds., *The Rise of Economic Societies in the Eighteenth Century,* 339–369; Gambrill, "John Beale Bordley and the Early Years of the Philadelphia Agricultural Society," 410–439; GW to Landon Carter, 17 October 1796, *PGW, Pres.,* 21: 104–106.

16. GW to James Warren, 7 October 1785, *PGW, Conf.,* 3: 298–301; GW to Alexander Spotswood, 13 February 1788, *PGW, Conf.,* 6: 110–113.

17. GW to Samuel Powel, 19 July 1785, 2 November 1785, 25 May 1786, *PGW, Conf.,* 3: 139–140, 338–339; 4: 75–76; Samuel Powel to GW, 10 May 1786, *PGW, Conf.,* 4: 45–46; *Diaries,* 5: 173, 175; Deborah Norris Logan, *Memoir of Dr. George Logan of Stenton* (Philadelphia: Historical Society of Pennsylvania, 1899), 44–45; *Memoirs of the Philadelphia Society for Promoting Agriculture,* vol. 1 (Philadelphia: Johnson & Warner, 1815), v; Tolles, "George Logan and the Agricultural Revolution," 589–596; GW to Robert R. Livingston, 16 February 1795, *PGW, Pres.,* 17: 533–534; GW to Landon Carter, 17 October 1796, *PGW, Pres.,* 21: 104–106.

18. Arthur Young to GW, 7 January 1786, *PGW, Conf.,* 3: 498–500; [Arthur Young], "An enquiry into the Situation of the Kingdom on the Conclusion to the Late Treaty," in *Annals of Agriculture, and Other Useful Arts* (Bury St. Edmunds: J. Rackham, 1786), vol. 1: 9–89; RA Geo / Add / 32 / 2010–2011, [George III], "America is lost!," Essay on America and Future Colonial Policy, Royal Archives, Windsor.

19. *Annals of Agriculture* (London, 1784), 2: 353–383; GW notes on wheat cultivation at Coke's estate, from the *Annals,* in Series 8, Subseries 8D, Extracts, Abstracts, and Notes, GWP, LOC; *Annals of Agriculture* (Bury St. Edmunds, 1786), 7: 65–71, 332–336; RA Geo / Add / 32 / 2016, draft letter, George III to Mr. Ducket, Essays of George III, Royal Archives, Windsor; Arthur Young to GW, 1 February 1787, 1 July 1788, *PGW, Conf.,* 5: 3–6, 6: 368–370.

20. Arthur Young to GW, 19 May 1789, 18 January 1792, 17 January 1793, *PGW, Pres.,* 2: 341–344, 9: 471–481, 12: 18–26; Wakelin Welch & Son to GW, 6 May 1791, *PGW, Pres.,* 8: 157–158.

21. Young's biographer estimates he wrote about one-third of the articles in the *Annals,* John G. Gazley, *The Life of Arthur Young, 1741–1820* (Philadelphia: American Philosophical Society, 1973), vii; Arthur Young to GW, 1 July 1788, *PGW, Conf.,* 6: 368–370; GW to Arthur Young, 4 December 1788, *PGW, Pres.,* 1: 159–163.

22. Arthur Young to GW, 19 May 1789, *PGW, Pres.,* 2: 341–344; GW to Arthur Young, 5 December 1791, *PGW, Pres.,* 9: 253–258.

23. Arthur Young to GW, 18 January 1792, 2 June 1794, *PGW, Pres.,* 9: 471–481, 16: 179–181; GW to Arthur Young, 18–21 June 1792, 12 December 1793, *PGW, Pres.,* 10: 460–467, 14: 504–514; *Annals of Agriculture* (Bury St. Edmunds, 1791), 16: 149–155.

24. Tobias Lear to GW, 26–30 January 1794, *PGW, Pres.,* 15: 115–125; GW to Arthur Young, 9 November 1794, *PGW, Pres.,* 17: 154–156.

25. Thomas Jefferson, Catalogue of Books on Agriculture, ca. 3 March 1817, *Papers of Thomas Jefferson, Retirement Series,* 11: 164–165; P.M. Jones, "Arthur Young (1741–1820): For and Against," *English Historical Review* 127, no. 528 (October 2012): 1100–1120;

critical review of the *Annals* by Washington's correspondent, James Anderson, quoted in Gazley, *Life of Arthur Young*, 197–198.

26. Earl of Buchan to GW, 27 March 1790, *PGW, Pres.*, 5: 284–285; GW to Earl of Buchan, 30 June 1790, *PGW, Pres.*, 5: 569–570; "Prospectus for *The Bee*," *The Bee: Or Literary Weekly Intelligencer*, vol. 1 (Edinburgh: Printed by Mundell and son, [1790]), vi–ix; James Anderson to GW, 28 September 1791, in n. 1 to GW to James Anderson, 20 June 1792, *PGW, Pres.*, 10: 468–471; political and agricultural activities of Anderson discussed in Frederik Albritton Jonsson, *Enlightenment's Frontier: The Scottish Highlands and the Origins of Environmentalism* (New Haven, CT: Yale University Press, 2013), 88–89, 93–94, 102–109.

27. Sir John Sinclair to GW, 18 May 1792, *PGW, Pres.*, 10: 397; GW to Sir John Sinclair, 20 October 1792, 15 March 1793, *PGW, Pres.*, 11: 247–248, 12: 322–324; Rosalind Mitchison, "The Old Board of Agriculture (1793–1822)," *English Historical Review* 74 (1959): 41–69; Rosalind Mitchison, *Agricultural Sir John; The Life of Sir John Sinclair* (London: Geoffrey Bles, 1962); Jonsson, *Enlightenment's Frontier*, 54–56, 223–226.

28. Kames, *The Gentleman Farmer*, Appendix, Article II, 337–342; *Annals of Agriculture*, 1: 83; Drayton, *Nature's Government*, 65–67; Sir John Sinclair to GW, 10 September 1796, *PGW, Pres.*, 20: 670–673; Jones, *Agricultural Enlightenment*, chap. 2.

29. Sir John Sinclair to GW, 15 August 1793, *PGW, Pres.*, 13: 463–466; Enclosure, Sir John Sinclair to Enoch Edwards, 13 August 1793, Series 4, GWP, LOC, also published with minor variations in *Papers of Thomas Jefferson*, 26: 680–684; James Anderson in his prospectus for *The Bee* expected the journal would find its way "Into all nations, therefore, where the English language is in any way known," Prospectus for *The Bee*, ix.

30. GW to Earl of Buchan, 26 May 1794, *PGW, Pres.*, 16: 127–129; Sir John Sinclair to GW, 10 September 1796, *PGW, Pres.*, 20: 670–673.

31. Earl of Buchan to GW, 22 October 1792, *PGW, Pres.*, 11: 253–255; GW to Earl of Buchan, 22 April 1793, *PGW, Pres.*, 12: 468–471; Earl of Buchan summary of letter to GW, 18 June 1793 (letter not found), in note to GW to Earl of Buchan, 22 April 1793, *PGW, Pres.*, 12: 468–471; James Anderson to GW, 6 December 1794, *PGW, Pres.*, 17: 242–248.

32. GW to Edward Newenham, 29 August 1788, *PGW, Conf.*, 6: 486–489; GW to Edward Newenham, 2 March 1789, *PGW, Pres.*, 1: 354–356.

33. GW to James Anderson, 24 December 1795, *PGW, Pres.*, 19: 290–294; James Anderson to GW, 15 August 1793, 6 December 1794, *PGW, Pres.*, 13: 455–460, 17: 242–248; GW to Sir John Sinclair, 20 July 1794, *PGW, Pres.*, 16: 394–397; Sir John Sinclair to GW, 6 February 1794, *PGW, Pres.*, 15: 187; Appleton P. Griffin, comp., *A Catalogue of the Washington Collection In the Boston Athenæum* (Cambridge, MA: University Press: J. Wilson and Son, 1897), 91–95. Washington's library included among other publications of Sinclair: *Account of the Origin of the Board of Agriculture, and Its Progress For Three Years After Its Establishment* (London: W. Bulmer, 1796); *Specimens of Statistical Reports; Exhibiting the Progress of Political Society, from the Pastoral State, to that of Luxury and Refinement* (London: T. Cadell, 1793).

34. GW to Earl of Buchan, 22 April 1793, *PGW, Pres.*, 12: 468–471; James Anderson to GW, 6 December 1794, *PGW, Pres.*, 17: 242–248; GW to David Rittenhouse, 20 April 1794, in n. 4 to James Anderson to GW, 6 December 1794, *PGW, Pres.*, 17: 242–248; British

Board of Agriculture to GW, 6 April 1795, *PGW, Pres.*, 18: 14–16; Register of Official, Ordinary, Honorary and Corresponding Members of the Board of Agriculture commencing the 4th of September 1793, SR RASE/B/XI, Archive of the Royal Agricultural Society of England, 1793–1960, Museum of English Rural Life; *Communications to the Board of agriculture, on subjects relative to the husbandry and internal improvement of the country*, vol. 1 (London: Printed by W. Bulmer, 1797), 367–375; GW to Sir John Sinclair, 20 July 1794, 20 February 1796, *PGW, Pres.*, 16: 394–397, 19: 480–482; Sir John Sinclair to GW, 5 July 1794, *PGW, Pres.*, 16: 311–312; GW to James Madison, 10 January 1794, *PGW, Pres.*, 15: 54–55; Richard Peters to GW, 14 April 1794, *PGW, Pres.*, 595–596; GW to Thomas Jefferson, 30 March 1795, *PGW, Pres.*, 17: 703; William Strickland, *Journal of a Tour in the United States of America, 1794–1795*, ed., Rev. J.E. Strickland (New York: New-York Historical Society, 1971), 240; notes on "Chit Chat," February 1794, in Sinclair of Ulbster Letterbooks (microfilm), f. 211, National Library of Scotland.

35. Drayton, *Nature's Government*, xiv–xv, chap. 3, 111–112; GW to Henry Laurens, 12 October 1789, *PGW, Pres.*, 4: 161; GW to Alexander Anderson, 18 November 1789, *PGW, Pres.*, 14: 303–304; Fairlie Christie to GW, 25 March 1795, *PGW, Pres.*, 17: 682–684; James Anderson to GW, 28 September 1791, in n. 1 to GW to James Anderson, 20 June 1792, *PGW, Pres.*, 10: 468–471; James Anderson to GW, 15 August 1793, *PGW, Pres.*, 13: 455–460.

36. John Jay to GW, 1 March 1794, *PGW, Pres.*, 15: 302–303; Timothy Pickering to GW, 27 April 1797, *PGW, Ret.*, 1: 126; Lafayette to GW, 17 December 1784, 3 September 1785, *PGW, Conf.*, 2: 194, 3: 224–225; GW to Lafayette, 25 July 1785, *PGW, Conf.*, 3: 151–155; Gouverneur Morris to GW, with enclosure: list of seeds, January 1790, *PGW, Pres.*, 5: 82–83; GW to Fairlie Christie, 25 May 1795, *PGW, Pres.*, 18: 171.

37. Drayton, *Nature's Government*, see esp. chap. 3; Robinson, *Georgian Model Farms*, 1–16; Brewer, *Pleasures of the Imagination*, 615–630; Pat Gardner, "Landscape, follies and villages," in Christopher Christie, *The British Country House in the Eighteenth Century* (Manchester, UK: Manchester University Press, 2000), 139–151; Roy Porter, "'England's Green and Pleasant Land': The English Enlightenment and the Environment," in Kate Flint and Howard Murphy, eds., *Culture, Landscape, and the Environment: The Linacre Lectures, 1997* (Oxford, UK: Oxford University Press, 2000), 15–43; Williamson, *The Transformation of Rural England*, chap. 7.

38. GW to Anthony Whitting, 4 July 1792, 16 December 1792, 13–14 January 1793, 24 March 1793, *PGW, Pres.*, 10: 517–518, 11: 519–524, 625–631, 12: 373–375; Joseph Manca, *George Washington's Eye: Landscape, Architecture, and Design at Mount Vernon* (Baltimore, MD: Johns Hopkins University Press, 2012), 85–95, 150–155; *David Humphreys' "Life of General Washington" with George Washington's "Remarks,"* Zagarri, ed., 40–41. Manca observes that "Washington spent much of his life measuring views as a surveyor and relying on them in military planning," 148.

39. GW to William Pearce, 23 December 1793, 16 November 1794, *PGW, Pres.*, 14: 606–616, 17: 165–168; GW to Anthony Whitting, 14 October 1792, 4, 11, 18, and 25 November 1792, 20 January 1793, *PGW, Pres.*, 11: 222–231, 330–334, 370–376, 400–406, 439–443, 12: 31–36.

40. GW to Anthony Whitting, 11 November 1792, 27 January 1793, *PGW, Pres.,* 11: 370–376, 12: 54–57; GW to William Pearce, 22 March 1795, *PGW, Pres.,* 17: 678–680.

41. Hiland Crow, articles of agreement with George A. Washington, 15 September 1790, Series 4, GWP, LOC; Articles of Agreement between Henry McCoy and Anthony Whitting, on behalf of the President of the United States, 17 December 1792, Series 4, GWP, LOC.

42. W.G. Hoskins, *The Making of the English Landscape* (1955; reprint, Little Toller Books, 2013), 166–171, 179–184; Jones, *Agricultural Enlightenment,* 157, 159, 189–190; Hale, *A Compleat Body of Husbandry,* 1: 230; GW to Lund Washington, 19 August 1776, *PGW, Rev.,* 6: 82–87; GW to Anthony Whitting, 14 October 1792, 9 December 1792, 10 February 1793, *PGW, Pres.,* 11: 222–231, 485–491, 12: 126–129.

43. GW to George William Fairfax, 30 June 1785, *PGW, Conf.,* 3: 87–92; Abstract of "The Gentleman Farmer by Henry Home," 99–103, Series 8d., Extracts, Abstracts, and Notes, 1760–1799, GWP, LOC; extracts from *The Farmer's Compleat Guide,* Series 8d., Extracts, Abstracts, and Notes, 1760–1799, GWP, LOC; GW to Anthony Whitting, 20 January 1793, *PGW, Pres.,* 12: 31–36.

44. GW to Anthony Whitting, 2 December 1792, 6 January 1793, 13–14 January 1793, *PGW, Pres.,* 11: 460–465, 594–599, 625–631; GW to William Pearce, 22 November 1795, *PGW, Pres.,* 19: 178–181; GW Circular to William Stuart, Hiland Crow, and Henry McCoy, 14 July 1793, *PGW, Pres.,* 13: 220–226..

45. *An Address from the Philadelphia Society for Promoting Agriculture, with a Summary of Its Laws and Premiums Offered* (1785), 15; GW to Anthony Whitting, 14 October 1792, *PGW, Pres.,* 11: 222–231.

46. An extensive literature discusses the importance of the Home Farm in late-eighteenth century Great Britain, see e.g., Brewer, *Pleasures of the Imagination,* 627–628; David Brown, "Reassessing the Influence of the Aristocratic Improver: The Example of the Fifth Duke of Bedford (1765–1802)," *Agricultural History Review* 47, no. 2 (1999): 182–195; Susanna Wade Martins, *Coke of Norfolk, 1754–1842* (Woodbridge: Boydell Press, 2009), 102; Jane Roberts, *Royal Landscape: The Gardens and Parks of Windsor* (New Haven, CT: Yale University Press, 1997), chap. 15; Robinson, *Georgian Model Farms,* chap. 2; *Luigi Castiglioni's Viaggio: Travels in the United States of North America, 1785–1787,* Antonio Pace, ed. (Syracuse, NY: Syracuse University Press, 1983), 112.

47. Lee, ed., *Experiencing Mount Vernon,* 56–57, 75–76; Samuel Vaughan Journal, 1787, 55–56, Washington Library; *The American Journals of Lt. John Enys,* Elizabeth Connetti, ed. (Syracuse, NY: Syracuse University Press, 1976), 245–249.

48. Lee, ed., *Experiencing Mount Vernon,* 47–53; *Diaries,* 5: 418–419; Moustier to GW, 26 November 1788, *PGW, Pres.,* 1: 127–130.

49. Thomas A. Reinhart and Susan P. Schoelwer, "'Distinguished by the Name of the New Room': Reinvestigation and Reinterpretation of George Washington's Grandest Space," in Carol Borchert Cadou, ed., with Luke J. Pecoraro and Thomas A. Reinhart, *Stewards of Memory: The Past, Present, and Future of Historic Preservation at George Washington's Mount Vernon* (Charlottesville: University of Virginia Press, 2018), 45–46; Susan P. Schoelwer, "George Washington's 'New Room': Evidence and Interpretation at Mount Vernon," unpublished report, Washington Library; GW to Benjamin

Vaughan, 5 February 1785, *PGW, Conf.,* 2: 325; Account with John Rawlins, Ledger B, 222; Dalzell and Dalzell, *George Washington's Mount Vernon,* 114–115, 121; GW to Samuel Vaughan, 14 January 1784, *PGW, Conf.,* 1: 45–46.

50.   GW to Joseph Rakestraw, 20 July 1787, *PGW, Conf.,* 5: 267; GW to George Augustine Washington, 12 August 1787, 9 September 1787, *PGW, Conf.,* 5: 286–289, 321–323.

7. THE FARMER PRESIDENT

1.   The Residence Act (1 Stat. 130), was signed by Washington on 16 July 1790. GW to Clement Biddle, 20 July 1790, *PGW, Pres.,* 6: 104–106; "For Sale," *Pennsylvania Packet,* 12 January 1790, 3; 9 February 1790, 4.

2.   Clement Biddle to GW, 23 July 1790, *PGW, Pres.,* 6: 117–118.

3.   *Diaries,* 5: 452–453, 460–497, see esp. 461–462, 467–468, 490, 496; T.H. Breen, *George Washington's Journey* (New York: Simon & Schuster, 2016).

4.   *Diaries,* 6: 63–67.

5.   *Diaries,* 6: 113–159, see esp. 147, 151, 156–158; Chaplin, *An Anxious Pursuit,* 134–158.

6.   *Diaries,* 6: 113–159, see esp. 123, 156–158; GW to John Chesnut, [26 June 1791], in n. 1 to GW to Charles Cotesworth Pinckney, 26 June 1791, *PGW, Pres.,* 8: 302–303.

7.   *Diaries,* 6: 190–191.

8.   GW to Anthony Whitting, 4 September 1791, 4 November 1792, 6 January 1793, 27 January 1793, *PGW, Pres.,* 8: 487–489, 11: 330–334, 594–599, 12: 54–57.

9.   "Improvements in Agriculture," *Pennsylvania Mercury,* 2 June 1789; *Diaries,* 6: 12; GW to Thomas Jefferson, 21 August 1791, *PGW, Pres.,* 8: 448–449; *Annals of Agriculture* (1792), 17: 206–208.

10.   *Universal Asylum and Columbian Magazine* (January 1791), 3–6; *The American Museum* (Philadelphia: Mathew Carey, 1792), 225–226; Hunter, "Wheat, War, and the American Economy during the Age of Revolution," 505–526.

11.   William Ball and George Washington, Agreement, 16 April 1791, Series 4, GWP, LOC; Tobias Lear to Oliver Evans, 29 August 1791, *PGW, Pres.,* 8: 463–464; GW to Anthony Whitting, 4 September 1791, *PGW, Pres.,* 8: 487–489; Tobias Lear to Oliver Evans, 4 September 1791 and 9 September 1791, in n. 3 to Lear to Evans, 29 August 1791, *PGW, Pres.,* 8: 463–464; Ledger B, 333, 334; Anthony Whit[t]ing to George Washington, Accounts, May 1793, Series 4, GWP, LOC.

12.   Arthur Young to GW, 25 January 1791, *PGW, Pres.,* 7: 283–287; GW to Arthur Young, 15 August 1791, 5 December 1791, *PGW, Pres.,* 8: 431–432, 9: 253–258.

13.   Thomas Jefferson to GW, 3 August 1791, *Papers of Thomas Jefferson,* 20: 716; Enclosure: Notes on Virginia Lands, 3 August 1791, *Papers of Thomas Jefferson,* 20: 716–717; Circular on the State of American Agriculture, 25 August 1791, *PGW, Pres.,* 8: 453–454 (GW sent the circular to David Stuart of Virginia, Philip Schuyler of New York, Thomas Johnson of Maryland, Thomas Hartley of Pennsylvania, and Thomas Lowrey of New Jersey); Samuel Powel to GW, 24 October 1791, *PGW, Pres.,* 9: 107–108; GW to Arthur Young, 5 December 1791, *PGW, Pres.,* 9: 253–258.

14.   Thomas Hartley to GW, 24 September 1791, *PGW, Pres.,* 9: 5–12; Thomas Johnson to GW, 10 November 1791, *PGW, Pres.,* 9: 169–175; David Stuart to GW, 18 November 1791, *PGW, Pres.,* 9: 197–205.

15. GW to Arthur Young, 5 December 1791, *PGW, Pres.,* 9: 253–258.
16. Arthur Young to GW, 18 January 1792, *PGW, Pres.,* 9: 471–481; Richard Peters to GW, 22 June 1792, *PGW, Pres.,* 10: 495–496. Hamilton on 13 August 1791 sent a Treasury Department Circular to Peters, Henry Wynkoop, Timothy Pickering, John Neville, and John Beale Bordley, asking each to complete an enclosed form with information on the value and product of "cultivated farms of *middling* quality," *Papers of Alexander Hamilton,* Harold C. Syrett, ed. (New York: Columbia University Press, 1965), 9: 35–37. Washington received copies of the replies from Wynkoop, Neville, and Bordley as well as that of Peters. Henry Wynkoop to Hamilton, with enclosure, 29 August 1791, *Papers of Alexander Hamilton,* 9: 123–124; John Neville to Alexander Hamilton, with enclosure, 27 October 1791, *Papers of Alexander Hamilton,* 9: 419–420; John Beale Bordley to Alexander Hamilton, with enclosure, 11 November 1791, *Papers of Alexander Hamilton,* 9: 490–492.
17. GW to Arthur Young, 18–21 June 1792, *PGW, Pres.,* 10: 460–467; [Thomas Jefferson] Notes on Arthur Young's Letter to GW, 18 June 1792, *Papers of Thomas Jefferson,* 24: 95–99
18. GW to Arthur Young, 18–21 June 1792, *PGW, Pres.,* 10: 460–467.
19. Richard Peters to GW, 20 June 1792, *PGW, Pres.,* 10: 484–488.
20. GW to Arthur Young, 18–21 June 1792, *PGW, Pres.,* 10: 460–467; Arthur Young to GW, 17 January 1793, *PGW, Pres.,* 12: 18–26; GW to Thomas Jefferson, 13 May 1793, *PGW, Pres.,* 12: 570; "Observations on an Extract of a Letter dated 17. January 1793 from Arthur Young Esqr to The President," in n. 1 to Richard Peters to GW, 20 June 1793, *PGW, Pres.,* 13: 113–119; GW to Arthur Young, 1 September 1793, *PGW, Pres.,* 14: 3–4.
21. "Observations on an Extract," in n. 1 to Richard Peters to GW, 20 June 1793, *PGW, Pres.,* 13: 113–119; GW to Arthur Young, 18–21 June 1792, 1 September 1793, *PGW, Pres.,* 10: 460–467, 14: 3–4
22. Richard Peters to GW, 16 July 1794, *PGW, Pres.,* 16: 362–366.
23. GW to Sir John Sinclair, 20 July 1794, *PGW, Pres.,* 16: 394–397.
24. GW to Richard Peters, 16 May 1793, *PGW, Pres.,* 12: 598–599; Richard Peters to GW, 20 June 1793, 14 February 1794, *PGW, Pres.,* 13: 113–119, 15: 232–233; GW to Sir John Sinclair, 20 July 1794, *PGW, Pres.,* 16: 394–397.
25. GW to Alexander Hamilton, 2 November 1796, *PGW, Pres.,* 21: 152–158; GW to Landon Carter, 17 October 1796, *PGW, Pres.,* 21: 104–106; Draft of George Washington's Eighth Annual Address to Congress, 10 November 1796, *Papers of Alexander Hamilton,* 20: 382–388.
26. Sir John Sinclair to GW, 15 June 1793, *PGW, Pres.,* 13: 88; GW to Sir John Sinclair, 20 July 1794, 20 February 1796, *PGW, Pres.,* 16: 394–397, 19: 480–482; GW to James Madison, 10 January 1794, 6 December 1795, *PGW, Pres.,* 15: 54–55, 19: 213; Eighth Annual Message, December 6, 1796, *Journal of the House of Representatives of the United States, Being the Second Session of the Fourth Congress* (Washington: Gales and Seaton, 1826), 609; GW to Sir John Sinclair, 6 March 1797, *PGW, Ret.,* 1: 13–15.
27. GW to David Stuart, 28 March 1790, *PGW, Pres.,* 5: 286–288; William C. DiGiacomantonio, "'For the Gratification of a Volunteering Society': Antislavery and Pressure Group Politics in the First Federal Congress," *Journal of the Early Republic* 15, no. 2 (1995): 169–197; Richard S. Newman, *The Transformation of American Abolitionism:*

Fighting Slavery in the Early Republic (Chapel Hill: University of North Carolina Press, 2002), 39–45; George William Van Cleve, *A Slaveholders' Union: Slavery, Politics, and the Constitution in the Early American Republic* (Chicago: University of Chicago Press, 2010), 191–199; *Journal of the House of Representatives of the United States*, 1: 179–181.

28. *Diaries*, 6: 47–48; Warner Mifflin to GW, 12 March 1790, *PGW, Pres.*, 5: 222–224; Gary B. Nash, *Warner Mifflin: Unflinching Quaker Abolitionist* (Philadelphia: University of Pennsylvania Press, 2017), 170; DiGiacomantonio, "'For the Gratification of a Volunteering Society,'" 188.

29. DiGiacomantonio, "'For the Gratification of a Volunteering Society,'" 192; *Journal of the House of Representatives of the United States*, 1: 179–181; GW to David Stuart, 28 March 1790, 15 June 1790, *PGW, Pres.*, 5: 286–288, 523–528.

30. David Stuart to GW, 2 June 1790, *PGW, Pres.*, 5: 458–464; Van Cleve, *Slaveholders' Union*, 187–188.

31. Paul Finkelman, "The Kidnapping of John Davis and the Adoption of the Fugitive Slave Law of 1793," *Journal of Southern History* 56, no. 3 (1990): 397–422; Van Cleve, *Slaveholders' Union*, 203–205; Don E. Fehrenbacher, *The Slaveholding Republic: An Account of the United States Government's Relations to Slavery*, ed. Ward M. McAfee (New York: Oxford University Press, 2001), 98–99, 209–213; GW to James Seagrove, 20 May 1791, *PGW, Pres.*, 8: 198–200.

32. Timothy M. Matthewson, "George Washington's Policy Toward the Haitian Revolution," *Diplomatic History* 3, no. 3 (1979): 321–336; Charles Pinckney to GW, 20 September 1791, *PGW, Pres.*, 8: 542–546; GW to John Vaughan, 27 December 1791, *PGW, Pres.*, 9: 339; GW to Charles Pinckney, 17 March 1792, *PGW, Pres.*, 10: 128–130; Alexander Dun, *Dangerous Neighbors: Making the Haitian Revolution in Early America* (Philadelphia: University of Pennsylvania Press, 2016), 69–70; James Sidbury, "Saint Domingue in Virginia: Ideology, Local Meanings, and Resistance to Slavery, 1790–1800," *Journal of Southern History* 63, no. 3 (1997): 531–552.

33. Matthewson, "George Washington's Policy Toward the Haitian Revolution"; Ashli White, *Encountering Revolution: Haiti and the Making of the Early Republic* (Baltimore, MD: Johns Hopkins University Press, 2010); Dun, *Dangerous Neighbors*, 90–99, 125–133.

34. Paul J. Polgar, *Standard-Bearers of Equality: America's First Abolition Movement* (Chapel Hill: University of North Carolina Press, 2019), 52–67; Gary B. Nash and Jean R. Soderlund, *Freedom by Degrees: Emancipation in Pennsylvania and its Aftermath* (New York: Oxford University Press, 1991), 101–128; Louis Lagrenade et al. to GW, 24 January 1791, *PGW, Pres.*, 7: 274–277; Thomas Jefferson to GW, 20 June 1791, *Papers of Thomas Jefferson*, 20: 558–559; Edward L. Cox, "The British Caribbean in the Age of Revolution," in Eliga H. Gould and Peter S. Onuf, eds., *Empire and Nation: The American Revolution in the Atlantic World* (Baltimore, MD: Johns Hopkins University Press, 2005), 275–294.

35. François Furstenberg, "Atlantic Slavery, Atlantic Freedom: George Washington, Slavery, and Transatlantic Abolitionist Networks," *William and Mary Quarterly* 68, no. 2 (2011): 247–286. Furstenberg is the first scholar to examine Washington's organization of the "Tracts on Slavery." See also Hayes, *George Washington: A Life in*

Books, 228–241, and Griffin, comp., *A Catalogue of the Washington Collection In the Boston Athenæum.* The pamphlets authored by Americans were David A. Cooper, *A Serious Address to the Rulers of America* (1783), and George Buchanan, *An Oration Upon the Moral and Political Evil of Slavery* (1793). Although no surviving evidence identifies who selected the pamphlets for binding, Furstenberg finds physical evidence in the volumes and their subject matter that strongly supports the conclusion that Washington organized the pamphlets for the bound volumes. Washington received Bentham's *Panopticon* from Benjamin Vaugham, who sent copies to Jefferson and John Jay at the same time; see note to Thomas Pinckney to Thomas Jefferson, 29 August 1792, *Papers of Thomas Jefferson,* 24: 329–331. Lucia Stanton, "Perfecting Slavery: Rational Plantation Management at Monticello," in *"Those who Labor for My Happiness": Slavery at Thomas Jefferson's Monticello* (Charlottesville: University of Virginia Press, 2012), 71–89, suggests the Bentham publication may have influenced Jefferson's supervision of enslaved laborers.

36. Summaries of the pamphlets drawn largely from Furstenberg, "Atlantic Slavery, Atlantic Freedom"; for Bryan Edwards and amelioration, see Roberts, *Slavery and the Enlightenment in the British Atlantic,* 77–78, 142, 171.

37. Furstenberg, "Atlantic Slavery, Atlantic Freedom"; J.R. Oldfield, *Transatlantic Abolitionism in the Age of Revolution: An International History of Anti-slavery, c. 1787–1820* (Cambridge, UK: Cambridge University Press, 2013), 13–41.

38. Furstenberg, "Atlantic Slavery, Atlantic Freedom"; Oldfield, *Transatlantic Abolitionism,* 49–50; Brissot to GW, 10 August 1788, *PGW, Conf.,* 6: 437; Brissot de Warville, *New Travels in the United States of America, 1788,* 237–239.

39. Lafayette to GW, 5 February 1783, Founders Online, Early Access; Brissot, *New Travels in the United States of America,* 238.

40. Polgar, *Standard-Bearers of Equality,* 63–76; Dunbar, *Never Caught,* 49–59, 75–86; George Washington Parke Custis, *Recollections and Private Memoirs of Washington* (Philadelphia: J. W. Bradley, 1861), 422–424; GW to Tobias Lear, 12 April 1791, *PGW, Pres.,* 8: 84–86; Nash and Soderlund, *Freedom by Degrees,* 170–180.

41. Thomas Freeman to GW, 18 December 1786, *PGW, Conf.,* 4: 463–465; GW to Robert Morris, 12 April 1786, *PGW, Pres.,* 4: 15–17; Tobias Lear to GW, 5 April 1791, *PGW, Pres.,* 8: 67–68; GW to Tobias Lear, 12 April 1791, *PGW, Pres.,* 8: 84–86; Newman, *Transformation of American Abolitionism,* 45–46.

42. Tobias Lear to GW, 5 April 1791, *PGW, Pres.,* 8: 67–68; GW to Tobias Lear, 12 April 1791, *PGW, Pres.,* 8: 84–86.

43. GW to Tobias Lear, 12 April 1791, *PGW, Pres.,* 8: 84–86; Tobias Lear to GW, 24 April 1791, *PGW, Pres.,* 8: 129–134.

44. Tobias Lear to GW, 5 June 1791, *PGW, Pres.,* 8: 231–235.

45. GW to John Fairfax, 31 March 1789, *PGW, Pres.,* 1: 465–467.

46. GW to Anthony Whitting, 14 October 1792, 11 November 1792, 2 December 1792, *PGW, Pres.,* 11: 222–231, 370–376, 460–465; GW to William Pearce, 23 December 1793, *PGW, Pres.,* 14: 606–616.

47. GW to Anthony Whitting, 4 November 1792, 19 May 1793, *PGW, Pres.,* 11: 330–334, 12: 610–616; GW to Howell Lewis, 11 August 1793, *PGW, Pres.,* 13: 417–423; Weekly Report, 27 October 1792, Washington Library.

48. George Augustine Washington to GW, 20 August 1790, 7 December 1790, *PGW, Pres.,* 6: 311–315, 7: 40–45; Articles of Agreement between Anthony Whit[t]ing and George Augustine Washington, on behalf of George Washington, 20 May 1790, in n. to GW to Whitting, April 14, 1790, *PGW, Pres.,* 5: 330–333.

49. Anthony Whitting to GW, 22 January 1792, 16 January 1793, *PGW, Pres.,* 9: 496–499, 12: 5–14; GW to Howell Lewis, 3 November 1793, *PGW, Pres.,* 14: 332–337; Ledger B, 347.

50. GW to Henry Lee, 21 July 1793, *PGW, Pres.,* 13: 260–262; Circular to William Stuart, Hiland Crow, and Henry McCoy, 14 July 1793, *PGW, Pres.,* 13: 220–226; GW to Howell Lewis, 11 August 1793, 18 August 1793, *PGW, Pres.,* 13: 417–423, 485–490.

51. Agreement with William Pearce, 23 September 1793, *PGW, Pres.,* 14: 120–123; GW to William Pearce, 18 December 1793, 8 June 1794, 25 October 1795, 3 April 1796, *PGW, Pres.,* 14: 558–564, 16: 201–204, 19: 72–74, 20: 9–12; GW to James Anderson, 18 August 1796, *PGW, Pres.,* 20: 590–592.

52. GW to Anthony Whitting, 18 November 1792, 2 December 1792, *PGW, Pres.,* 11: 400–406, 460–465; Circular to William Stuart, Hiland Crow, and Henry McCoy, 14 July 1793, *PGW, Pres.,* 13: 220–226; GW to William Pearce, 1 June 1794, 3 August 1794, 16 November 1794, 30 November 1974, 7 June 1795, *PGW, Pres.,* 16: 176–178, 463–467, 17: 165–168, 221–222, 18: 198–199. Between the weekly report of 30 May 1795 and those of 18 June and 11 July, the number of sheep and lambs at Muddy Hole dropped from 38 and 17 to 36 and 13, respectively, Weekly Reports, Washington Library.

53. GW to Anthony Whitting, 25 November 1792, 24 February 1793, 21 April 1793, 2 June 1793, *PGW, Pres.,* 11: 439–443, 12: 212–215, 463–468, 13: 6–13; Circular to William Stuart, Hiland Crow, and Henry McCoy, 14 July 1793, *PGW, Pres.,* 13: 220–226; GW to Howell Lewis, 11 August 1793, *PGW, Pres.,* 13: 417–423.

54. GW to Anthony Whitting, 9 December 1792, 28 April 1793, *PGW, Pres.,* 11: 485–491, 12: 488–493; GW to William Pearce, 25 October 1795, 29 November 1795, *PGW, Pres.,* 19: 72–74, 191–193; Mount Vernon Ledger, January 1794–December 1796, 28, Photostat at Washington Library (original at GWP, LOC).

55. GW to William Pearce, 12 January 1794, 27 July 1794, 8 March, 1795, *PGW, Pres.,* 15: 60–67, 16: 442–444, 17: 632–634; GW to Howell Lewis, 11 August 1793, *PGW, Pres.,* 13: 417–423.

56. James Anderson to GW, 14 February 1797, *PGW, Pres.,* 21: 688–692.

57. GW to James Anderson, 20 February 1797, *PGW, Pres.,* 21: 721–723.

58. Sir John Sinclair to George Washington, 11 September 1796, in note to Sinclair to GW, 30 May 1796, *PGW, Pres.,* 20: 215.

59. GW to Sir John Sinclair, 11 December 1796, *PGW, Pres.,* 21: 346–354.

60. GW to Sir John Sinclair, 11 December 1796, *PGW, Pres.,* 21: 346–354

61. For earlier support of abolition, see GW to Robert Morris, 12 April 1786, *PGW, Conf.,* 4: 15–17.

8. AGRICULTURE AND THE PATH TO EMANCIPATION

1. GW to Arthur Young, 12 December 1793, *PGW, Pres.,* 14: 504–514.

2. GW to Arthur Young, 12 December 1793, *PGW, Pres.,* 14: 504–514.

3. GW to Tobias Lear, 6 May 1794, *PGW, Pres.*, 16: 22–28; Tobias Lear to GW, 5 September 1794, *PGW, Pres.*, 16: 641–645. Washington did not include the private excerpt to Lear in his letterpress of letter-book copies. The 6 May letter to Lear did not arrive in Great Britain until after Lear had left in June. John Jay, concerned about the confidentiality of any correspondence from the president, returned the letter to Washington, who then forwarded it to Lear on 28 August.

4. GW to Anthony Whitting, 27 January 1793, *PGW, Pres.*, 12: 54–57; S. Max Edelson, *Plantation Enterprise in Colonial South Carolina* (Cambridge, MA: Harvard University Press, 2006), 2–3.

5. Note to Lease to Francis Ballinger, 17 March 1769, *PGW, Col.*, 8: 171–177; Status of George Washington's Rental Accounts, December 1791, Washington Library; Rental Account, Robt Lewis to George Washington for 1794, Washington Library; for comparable size of tenant holdings in Virginia, see Thomas J. Humphrey, "Conflicting Independence: Land Tenancy and the American Revolution," *Journal of the Early Republic* 28, no. 2 (2008): 159–182.

6. Mokyr, *The Enlightened Economy*, 175, 183, 191–193; Susanna Wade Martins, "Farmers of the Holkham Estate," in Richard Hoyle, ed., *The Farmer in England, 1650–1980* (Farnham: Ashgate, 2013), 193–220; Robinson, *Georgian Model Farms*, 19; Pamela Horn, "The Contribution of the Propagandist to Eighteenth-Century Agricultural Improvement," *The Historical Journal* 25, no. 2 (1982): 313–329; Bonnyman, *The Third Duke of Buccleuch and Adam Smith*, 87–92, 150–151; Rudge, *General View of the Agriculture of the County of Gloucester*, 253, 271; To Mr. Peacey, 28 November 1798, Letterbook, September 1793–14 October 1800, Archive of the Old Board of Agriculture, 1793 - 1822, Museum of English Rural Life.

7. Arthur Young to GW, 2 June 1794, *PGW, Pres.*, 16: 179–181.

8. GW to Arthur Young, 9 November 1794, *PGW, Pres.*, 17: 154–156.

9. James Anderson to GW, 10 May 1795, 24 December 1795, 15 February 1796, *PGW, Pres.*, 18: 129–131, 19: 290–294, 464–465; Tobias Lear to GW, 5 September 1794, *PGW, Pres.*, 16: 641–645; GW to William Strickland, 20 February 1796, *PGW, Pres.*, 19: 482–483.

10. GW to James Anderson, 24 December 1795, *PGW, Pres.*, 19: 290–294.

11. GW to William Pearce, 27 January 1796, 7 February 1796, *PGW, Pres.*, 19: 392–393, 437–440.

12. GW to William Pearce, 13 March 1796, 20 March 1796, 17 April 1796, *PGW, Pres.*, 19: 555–559, 572–574, 20: 52–53; Lease Terms, 1 February 1796, *PGW, Pres*, 19: 422–426.

13. GW to David Stuart, 7 February 1796, *PGW, Pres.*, 19: 441–442.

14. GW to David Stuart, 7 February 1796, *PGW, Pres.*, 19: 441–442; David Stuart to GW, 25 February 1796, *PGW, Pres.*, 19: 496–500.

15. David Stuart to GW, 25 February 1796, *PGW, Pres.*, 19: 496–500; Thompson, *"The Only Unavoidable Subject of Regret,"* 307–309, 445n54; for comparison of the enslaved with the laboring poor of Europe, see Thomas Jefferson to Edward Bancroft, 26 January 1789, *Papers of Thomas Jefferson*, 14: 492–494.

16. Lafayette quoted in Patrick Villiers, "'The Freedom of All the Blacks on the Plantation': Lafayette and His Fight for Emancipation in French Guiana, 1785–1802," in Olga Anna Duhl and Diane Windham Shaw, eds., *"A True Friend of the Cause": Lafayette and the*

Antislavery Movement (Grolier Club and Lafayette College, 2016), 33–41; John Stauffer, "'I Have Been So Long the Friend of Emancipation': Lafayette as Abolitionist," in Duhl and Shaw, *"A True Friend of the Cause,"* 1–15; Lafayette to GW, 6 February 1786, *PGW, Conf.,* 3: 538–547; GW to Lafayette, 10 May 1786, *PGW, Conf.,* 4: 41–45.

17. Eva Sheppard Wolf, *Race and Liberty in the New Nation: Emancipation in Virginia from the Revolution to Nat Turner's Rebellion* (Baton Rouge: Louisiana State University Press, 2006), 28–35, 53–62, 121–127; Louis Morton, *Robert Carter of Nomini Hall* (Williamsburg, VA: Colonial Williamsburg, 1941), 263–269; Andrew Levy, *The First Emancipator: The Forgotten Story of Robert Carter, the Founding Father who Freed his Slaves* (New York: Random House, 2005), 140–159; for broader patterns of emancipation in post-Revolutionary Virginia, see also McColley, *Slavery and Jeffersonian Virginia,* 141–162.

18. John Beale Bordley, *Husbandry and Rural Affairs,* 2nd ed. (Philadelphia: Printed by Budd and Bartram, for Thomas Dobson, 1801), 387–396; *Biographical Sketches of the Bordley Family of Maryland, for their Descendants. By Elizabeth Bordley Gibson, Edited by her niece, Elizabeth Mifflin* (Philadelphia: Henry B. Ashmead, 1865), 133–134; Jennifer Hull Dorsey, *Hirelings: African American Workers and Free Labor in Early Maryland* (Ithaca, NY: Cornell University Press, 2011), 22–32; David Hackett Fischer, "John Beale Bordley, Daniel Boorstin, and the American Enlightenment," *Journal of Southern History* 28, no. 3(August 1962): 327–342.

19. Dierksheide, *Amelioration and Empire,* 27, 37–44; Ferdinando Fairfax, "Plan for liberating the negroes within the United States," 6 March 1790, *American Museum, or, Universal Magazine,* vol. 8 (Philadelphia: Carey, Stewart, 1790), 285–287; Wolf, *Race and Liberty in the New Nation,* 101–107; Van Cleve, *A Slaveholders' Union,* 206–211.

20. *The Farmer's Magazine,* vol. 1, no. 2, 14 April 1800, published in 5th ed. (Edinburgh: Archibald Constable, 1802), 234–236.

21. GW to David Stuart, 7 February 1796, *PGW, Pres.,* 19: 441–442; David Stuart to GW, 25 February 1796, *PGW, Pres.,* 19: 496–500.

22. Lease Terms, 1 February 1796, *PGW, Pres.,* 19: 422–426; GW to William Pearce, 13 March 1796, *PGW, Pres.,* 19: 555–559.

23. Advertisement, 1 February 1796, *PGW, Pres.,* 19: 414–422.

24. Advertisement, 1 February 1796, *PGW, Pres.,* 19: 414–422; GW to Jeremiah Wadsworth, 11 February 1796, *PGW, Pres.,* 19: 451–452; GW to Rufus Putnam, 13 February 1796, *PGW, Pres.,* 19: 462–463; GW to Isaac Craig, 13 February 1796, *PGW, Pres.,* 19: 457.

25. GW to William Pearce, 17 April 1796, 24 April 1796, *PGW, Pres.,* 20: 52–53, 72–74; GW to Tobias Lear, 11 September 1797, *PGW, Ret.,* 1: 345–347; GW to Stephen Milburn, 15 May 1797, *PGW, Ret.,* 1: 141–142; Stephen Milburn to GW, 24 May 1797, in n. 2 to GW to Stephen Milburn, 15 May 1797, *PGW, Ret.,* 1: 141–142.

26. GW to Arthur Young, 12 December 1793, *PGW, Pres.,* 14: 504–514; Arthur Young to GW, 2 June 1794, *PGW, Pres.,* 16: 179–181; GW to James Anderson, 24 December 1795, *PGW, Pres.,* 19: 290–294; GW to David Stuart, 7 February 1796, *PGW, Pres.,* 19: 441–442; GW to William Pearce, 7 February 1796, *PGW, Pres.,* 19: 437–440; GW to Tobias Lear, 13 March 1796, *PGW, Pres.,* 19: 554–555; GW to Thomas Pinckney, 20

February 1796, *PGW, Pres.,* 19: 477–478; GW to Gouverneur Morris, 4 March 1796, *PGW, Pres.,* 19: 527–529.

27. GW to James Anderson, 15 February 1796, *PGW, Pres.,* 19: 464–465; GW to Sir John Sinclair, 20 February 1796, *PGW, Pres.,* 19: 480–482; GW to Earl of Buchan, 20 February 1796, *PGW, Pres.,* 19: 476–477; GW to William Strickland, 20 February 1796, *PGW, Pres.,* 19: 482–483.

28. Earl of Buchan to GW, 1 July 1796, *PGW, Pres.,* 20: 341–343; William Strickland to GW, 30 May 1796, *PGW, Pres.,* 20: 216–219; James Anderson to GW, 30 May 1796, *PGW, Pres.,* 20: 206–210.

29. GW to William Strickland, 15 July 1797, *PGW, Ret.,* 1: 253–259; Earl of Buchan to GW, 1 July 1796, *PGW, Pres.,* 20: 341–343; James Anderson to GW, 3 August 1797, *PGW, Ret.,* 1: 284–287; GW to James Anderson, 25 July 1798, *PGW, Pres.,* 2: 452–454; Sir John Sinclair to GW, 11 September 1796, in note to Sinclair to GW, 30 May 1796, *PGW, Pres.,* 20: 215; GW to Sir John Sinclair, 11 December 1796, *PGW, Pres.,* 21: 346–354.

30. Richard Parkinson to GW, 28 August 1797, *PGW, Ret.,* 1: 323–325; Richard Parkinson to GW, 27 September 1797, in n. 3 to Richard Parkinson to GW, 28 August 1797, *PGW, Ret.,* 1: 323–325; GW to Richard Parkinson, 28 November 1797, 15 December 1797, *PGW, Ret.,* 1: 488–489, 517–518. Richard Parkinson is frequently and incorrectly identified as the steward of Banks' estate, see H.B. Carter, *His Majesty's Spanish Flock: Sir Joseph Banks and the Merinos of George III of England* (Sydney: Angus & Robertson, 1964), 287.

31. Richard Parkinson to GW, 28 August 1798, *PGW, Ret.,* 2: 567–568; GW to James Anderson, 3 November 1798, *PGW, Pres.,* 3: 173–175.

32. Richard Parkinson, *A Tour in America, in 1798, 1799, and 1800: Exhibiting Sketches of Society and Manners, and a Particular Account of the American System of Agriculture, with its Recent Improvements,* 2 vols. (London: J. Harding, 1805), 1: 5–9, 50–64, 2: 419–442.

33. Laura Auricchio, "Two Versions of *General Washington's Resignation:* Politics, Commerce, and Visual Culture in 1790s Philadelphia," *Eighteenth-Century Studies* 44, no. 3 (2011): 383–400; GW to Earl of Buchan, 4 July 1797, *PGW, Ret.,* 1: 235–237; GW to James Anderson, 7 April 1797, *PGW, Ret.,* 1: 79–82.

34. Jasper Dwight [William Duane], "A Letter to George Washington, . . . ," (Philadelphia, 1796), 47–48; Padraig Riley, "Slavery and the Problem of Democracy in Jeffersonian America," in John Craig Hammond and Matthew Mason, eds., *Contesting Slavery: The Politics of Bondage and Freedom in the New American Nation* (Charlottesville: University of Virginia Press, 2011), 229–230; Jeffrey L. Pasley, *"The Tyranny of Printers": Newspaper Politics in the Early American Republic* (Charlottesville: University of Virginia Press, 2001), 181–183; New York *Time Piece,* 26 May 1797; "To Matilda," New York *Time Piece,* 23 June 1797, cited in White, *Encountering Revolution,* 138; Ralph Eddowes to GW, 21 October 1796, n. 1, *PGW, Pres.,* 21: 122–124.

35. GW to William Gordon, 15 October 1797, *PGW, Ret.,* 1: 406–409; GW to William Strickland, 15 July 1797, *PGW, Ret.,* 1: 253–259.

36. James Athill to GW, 21 July 1798, *PGW, Ret.,* 2: 435–437; GW to James Athill, 4 September 1798, *PGW, Ret.,* 2: 584; William Russell to GW, 8 September 1798, *PGW,*

Ret., 2: 593–594; Gustavus Scott to GW, 16 June 1797, *PGW, Ret.,* 1: 189–190; Harry Dorsey Gough to GW, 17 August 1797, *PGW, Ret.,* 1: 302.

37. GW to James Anderson, 18 August 1796, *PGW, Pres.,* 20: 590–592; GW to William Strickland, 15 July 1797, *PGW, Ret.,* 1: 253–259; GW to Harry Dorsey Gough, 23 August 1797, *PGW, Ret.,* 1: 316; GW to Robert Lewis, 23 January 1799, *PGW, Ret.,* 3: 333–334; GW to William Washington, 31 March 1799, *PGW, Ret.,* 3: 462–463; Farm Reports, 2–8 April 1797, *PGW, Ret.,* 1: 60–66; Mount Vernon Farm Ledger, 1797–1798, 87–88, Washington Library.

38. GW to William Booker, 26 June 1797, *PGW, Ret.,* 1: 216–217; GW to Thomas Coleman Martin, 3 October 1797, PGW, Ret., 1: 381–382; GW to Clement Biddle, 28 April 1799, *PGW, Ret.,* 4: 28–29; GW to William Pearce, 6 May 1798, *PGW, Ret.,* 2: 254–255; Weekly Reports, 11 March, 15 April, 15 July 1797, 6 January, 20 October, 27 October 1798, Washington Library.

39. Dennis J. Pogue, *Founding Spirits: George Washington and the Beginnings of the American Whiskey Industry* (Buena Vista, Va.: Harbour Books, 2011), 111–126; Distillery Ledger, Washington Library.

40. James Anderson to GW, 28 August, 11 September 1796, *PGW, Pres.,* 20: 623, 673–675; bankruptcy proceedings and record of business in Sequestration Records of James Anderson, CS 231 / Seq. / A / 1 / 7, National Records of Scotland; Agreement with James Anderson, 5 October 1796, *PGW, Pres.,* 21: 52–55; GW to James Anderson, 11 June 1798, *PGW, Ret.,* 2: 319–323; Mount Vernon Farm Ledger, 1797–1798, 13–14.

41. GW to James Anderson, 21 December 1797, 6–7 February, 22 May, 11 June, 16 September 1798, *PGW, Ret.,* 1: 523–527, 2: 74–75, 287–291, 319–323, 3: 1–4; Mount Vernon Farm Ledger, 1797–1798, 87–88, Washington Library; James Anderson to GW, 19 June 1798, *PGW, Ret.,* 2: 343–348.

42. James Anderson to GW, 14 February 1797, *PGW, Pres.,* 21: 688–692; Weekly Reports, 18 February 1797, July and August 1798, Washington Library; James Anderson to GW, 19 June 1798, *PGW, Ret.,* 2: 343–348.

43. GW to James Anderson, 21 December 1797, 22 May, 11 June 1798, *PGW, Ret.,* 1: 523–527, 2: 287–291, 319–323; for GW complaints about the irregular order and tardiness of Anderson's reports, see Weekly Report, 15 September 1798, with note by Washington, dated 22 September, Washington Library,.

44. James Anderson to GW, 21 June 1797, *PGW, Ret.,* 1: 199–201; GW to James Anderson, 18 June 1797, *PGW, Ret.,* 1: 191–195; GW to Alexander Spotswood, 14 September 1798, *PGW, Ret.,* 2: 612–615; Overseers at Mansion House after 1797 included Samuel Brewer and R. Farrell, Weekly Reports, 3 November 1798 and 5 January 1799, Washington Library; Ledger C, 50; entry for 5 October 1798, Cash Memoranda, 1797–1799, Photostats, Washington Library (originals in the John Carter Brown Library, Providence, RI).

45. GW to Alexander Spotswood, 23 November 1794, *PGW, Pres.,* 17: 206–207; GW to John Tayloe, 23 January 1799, *PGW, Ret.,* 3: 334–336; GW to Lawrence Lewis, 4 August 1797, *PGW, Ret.,* 1: 288–289; James Anderson to GW, 22 May 1798, *PGW, Ret.,* 2: 291–292, advertisement of 21 June 1798 printed in n. 7.

46. GW to James Anderson, 18 June 1797, *PGW, Ret.,* 1: 191–195; James Anderson to GW, 23 June 1799, *PGW, Ret.,* 4: 145–149; James Anderson, Crop Rotation Plans, 1798, in Series 4, GWP, LOC; 1786 slave census in *Diaries,* 4: 276–83; Washington's Slave List, June 1799, *PGW, Ret.,* 4: 527–542.

47. GW to Robert Lewis, 17 August 1799, *PGW, Ret.,* 4: 256–258; GW to Benjamin Dulany, 15 July, 12 September 1799, *PGW, Ret.,* 4: 189–190, 295–296; GW to Lawrence Lewis, 20 and 28 September 1799, *PGW, Ret.,* 4: 311–315, 324–326; Memorandum of land and Dogue Run Hands, 1799, Washington Library.

48. GW to James Anderson, 10 September, 16 September, 1 October 1799, *PGW, Ret.,* 4: 291–294, 305–306, 331–333; GW to William Augustine Washington, 29 October 1799, *PGW, Ret.,* 4: 379.

49. GW to James Anderson, 10 December 1799, in n. 1, GW to James Anderson, 13 December 1799, *PGW, Ret.,* 4: 455–457; Enclosure: Washington's Plans for his River, Union, and Muddy Hole Farms, 10 December 1799, *PGW, Ret.,* 4: 458–477.

50. Plans for Farms, second version, 10 December 1799, Series 4, GWP, LOC; GW to James Anderson, 10 December 1799, in n. 1, GW to James Anderson, 13 December 1799, *PGW, Ret.,* 4: 455–457.

51. George Washington's Last Will and Testament, *PGW, Ret.,* 4: 479–511. Martha Washington received rights to all of her husband's property with the exception of a few immediate bequests, such as the house in Alexandria, and the immediate emancipation of William Lee.

52. George Washington's Last Will and Testament, *PGW, Ret.,* 4: 479–511; the most recent Virginia statute regulating orphans and servants was enacted in 1792: William Waller Hening and Samuel Shepherd, *The Statutes At Large of Virginia* (Richmond: Printed by S. Shepherd, 1835), 1: 103–106; Wolf, *Race and Liberty in the New Nation,* 34.

53. Wolf, *Race and Liberty in the New Nation,* 115–117; Levy, *The First Emancipator,* 157–159; Hening and Shepherd, *Statutes,* 1: 363–365.

54. Washington's Slave List, June 1799, *PGW, Ret.,* 4: 527–542; Thompson, *"The Only Unavoidable Subject of Regret,"* 309–310. Washington in 1788 acquired 33 slaves from the Dandridge estate. One of the enslaved men, Anderson, had been sold as punishment for running away, but presumably the number of slaves owned by Washington and held by Dandridge's widow had increased by 1799. List of the slaves by name and assessed value in 1788 in Ledger B, 280. No subsequent list of the Dandridge-held slaves has been identified; Morgan, "'To Get Quit of Negroes': George Washington and Slavery," 404–405.

55. George Washington's Last Will and Testament, 9 July 1799, *PGW, Ret.,* 4: 479–511.

56. Morgan, "'To Get Quit of Negroes': George Washington and Slavery," 424, emphasizes Washington's shifting attitudes toward slave ownership, even after he wrote his will.

57. Thompson, *"The Only Unavoidable Subject of Regret,"* 310–319; Bushrod Washington wrote on 27 December 1799 that he had advised Martha to get "clear of her negroes & her plantation cares & troubles," in Fields, *Worthy Partner,* 328–330; Edna Greene Medford, "Beyond Mount Vernon: George Washington's Emancipated Laborers and their Descendants," in Schwarz, ed., *Slavery at the Home of George Washington,* 137–157; Susan Hellman and Maddy McCoy, "Soil Tilled by Free Men: The Formation of a Free Black Community in Fairfax County, Virginia," *Virginia Magazine of History*

and Biography 125, no. 1 (2017): 38–67; François Furstenberg, *In the Name of the Father: Washington's Legacy, Slavery, and the Making of a Nation* (New York: Penguin Press, 2006), 72–74.

58. James Anderson to Martha Washington, 21 July 1800, Peter Family Papers, Box 34, Washington Library; *Alexandria Advertiser and Commercial Intelligencer,* 23 December 1800–10 January 1801; Public Sales made by the Executors of Genl. George Washington, Appendix III, in Eugene E. Prussing, *The Estate of George Washington, Deceased* (Boston: Little, Brown, and Company, 1927), 449–459.

59. "To the Editor, signed by "F," Fairfax County, Dec. 28th, 1833, Edmund Ruffin, ed., *Farmers' Register* (Shellbanks, VA, 1834), 552–553.

EPILOGUE

1. Cohen, *Notes from the Ground,* 9; Arthur Young to GW, 18 January 1792, *PGW, Pres.,* 9: 471–481.

2. *Salem Gazette,* 11 March 1784, 4; "Agriculture," *New Hampshire Spy,* 15 May 1787; "Address to George Washington," *Pennsylvania Packet,* 28 April 1789, 3; John M'Culloch, *A Concise History of the United States, from the discovery of America till 1795* (Philadelphia, 1795), 198; Boston *Federal Gazette,* 23 January 1798, 3.

3. Garry Wills, "Washington's Civic Virtue: Greenough and Houdon," *Critical Inquiry* 10, no. 3 (March 1984): 420–441. Washington offered Jefferson his own preference for modern dress in GW to Thomas Jefferson, 1 August 1786, *PGW, Conf.,* 4: 183–185; Thomas Jefferson to GW, 14 August 1787, *PGW, Conf.,* 5: 290–293.

4. Elizabeth Angelicoussis, *Reconstructing the Lansdowne Collection of Classical Marbles* (Munich: Hirmer, 2017), vol. 2: 453; William Tatham to Charles Taylor, 11 February 1802, RSA / AD / MA / 305 / 10 / 55, RSA Archives, London; Sir John Sinclair, *Letters from His Excellency George Washington, President of the United States of America, to Sir John Sinclair, Bart. M.P. on Agricultural, and other interesting topics* (London: W. Bulmer and Co., 1800), 17.

5. Arthur Young, comp., *Letters from His Excellency General Washington, to Arthur Young, Esq. F.R.S., containing An Account of His Husbandry, with a Map of His Farm* (London: B. McMillan, 1801), vi; [James Anderson], *Selections from the Correspondence of George Washington, and James Anderson* (Charlestown, MA: Samuel Etheridge, 1800), 8; Sinclair, *Letters from His Excellency George Washington,* 9–10, 53.

6. Plan of publication, Letters of Sir John Sinclair of Ulbster, Bart., 1789–1811, National Library of Scotland, MS 9812; Sir John Sinclair to Thomas Jefferson, 22 June 1801, *Papers of Thomas Jefferson,* 34: 414; Young, *Letters from His Excellency General Washington,* vi; *Recreations in Agriculture, Natural-History, Arts, and Miscellaneous Literature* (London: T. Bensley, 1800), 2: 460–473; *Selections from the Correspondence of George Washington, and James Anderson; Letters from His Excellency George Washington, to Arthur Young, esq., F. R. S., and Sir John Sinclair, bart., M. P. : containing an account of his husbandry, with his opinions on various questions in agriculture; and many particulars of the rural economy of the United States* (Alexandria, VA: Cottom and Stewart, 1803).

7. John Sinclair to John Adams, 5 June 1800, Founders Online, Early Access; Sir John Sinclair to Thomas Jefferson, 6 June 1800, *Papers of Thomas Jefferson*, 32: 13–14; Sinclair, *Letters from his Excellency George Washington, to Sir John Sinclair,* King's Library, 91.K.11, British Library; Sir John Sinclair, *The Correspondence of the Right Honourable Sir John Sinclair . . .* 2 vols. (London: H. Colburn & R. Bentley, 1831), 2: 15–16; Sir John Sinclair to Martha Washington, 2 June 1800, Box 2, Peter Family Papers, Washington Library; Plan of Publication, Letters of Sinclair, National Library of Scotland; Sir John Sinclair to Thomas Jefferson, 3 June 1802, *Papers of Thomas Jefferson*, 37: 536–537; "An Account of the Improvements Carried on by Sir John Sinclair, Bart., Founder, and First President, of the Board of Agriculture, on his Estates in Scotland," Extracted from the *Agricultural Report of the County of Caithness* (London: B. McMillan, 1812), 6–7; Plan of Washington Monument, 20 October 1801, Cartographic Items, Maps K.Top. 49.47.2., British Library.

8. *Memoirs of the Philadelphia Society for Promoting Agriculture,* vol. 2 (Philadelphia: Johnson & Warner, 1811), vi–viii.

9. Cohen, *Notes from the Ground,* 127–165; Emily Pawley, *The Nature of the Future: Agriculture, Science, and Capitalism in the Antebellum North* (Chicago: University of Chicago Press, 2020), introduction; Timothy K. Minella, "A Pattern for Improvement: Pattern Farms and Scientific Authority in Early Nineteenth-Century America," *Agricultural History* 90, no. 4 (Fall 2016): 434–458.

10. Hunter, "Wheat, War, and the American Economy," 505–526; GW to Arthur Young, 6 August 1786, *PGW, Conf.,* 4: 196–200.

11. For settlement of tenants on western lands, see e.g., Enclosure: Advertisement: Ohio Lands, 10 March 1784, *PGW, Conf.,* 1: 201–204; Peter S. Onuf, "Domesticating the Captive Nation: Thomas Jefferson and the Problem of Slavery," in John Milton Cooper, Jr., and Thomas J. Knock, eds., *Jefferson, Lincoln, and Wilson: The American Dilemma of Race and Slavery* (Charlottesville: University of Virginia Press, 2010), 34–60; Dierksheide, *Amelioration and Empire,* 33–47.

12. Thompson, *"The Only Unavoidable Subject of Regret,"* 293–295; Furstenberg, *In the Name of the Father,* 86–87; Douglass quoted in David W. Blight, *Frederick Douglass: Prophet of Freedom* (New York: Simon & Schuster, 2018), 232.

13. Furstenberg, *In the Name of the Father,* 92–101; Junius Brutus Stearns, "Washington as a Farmer at Mount Vernon," 1851, Virginia Museum of Fine Arts; N. Currier, "Washington at Mount Vernon 1797," lithograph (New York: N. Currier, 1852), LOC, Prints and Photographs; the quotation on the Currier print appeared as the masthead of *The American Agriculturalist,* A.B. Allen, ed. (New York, 1848).

14. For Jefferson's interest in food for the provisioning of enslaved laborers, see e.g., Thomas Jefferson to William Drayton, 30 July 1787, *Papers of Thomas Jefferson,* 11: 644–650; "Summary of Public Service," [after 2 September 1800], *Papers of Thomas Jefferson,* 32: 122–125.

Acknowledgments

The idea for this books dates back to 1996, when I was invited to present a paper at Mount Vernon's inaugural George Washington Symposium. The topic was the business affairs of Washington, and in a review of the literature, I recognized that the full story of Washington's innovations in agriculture remained unwritten. I subsequently benefited from conversations with Jean B. Lee, who had done so much innovative research on Washington the farmer and the enslaved laborers at Mount Vernon. Service on the Advisory Council of George Washington Scholars at Mount Vernon and participation in a planning symposium for the George Washington financial papers project gave me further opportunities to consider the outlines of a book. Any book project, however, was on hold while I served as director of the history office at the Federal Judicial Center. Not surprisingly, this book is very different from the one I envisioned long ago, but I remain convinced that a full understanding of Washington depends on a narrative of his life as a farmer and a manager of enslaved labor.

A research fellowship from the Washington Library at Mount Vernon provided the opportunity to begin the project in earnest. I was fortunate to be at the library when the founding director, Doug Bradburn, initiated the programs that quickly made the library an important center for scholarly research and public outreach. As president and chief executive officer of Mount Vernon, Doug has continued to ensure that the interpretation of the past reflects the best scholarship and encourages civic engagement. I am grateful for Doug's important support of my work on this book, and especially for his friendship.

I received enormous help from the staff at the Washington Library and Mount Vernon. For many years, anyone who has researched the enslaved community at Mount Vernon has been indebted to Mary Thompson for her remarkable knowledge of Washington and the enslaved individuals who labored under his control. Mary generously shared her research and previews of her landmark book on slavery at Mount Vernon. Curt Viebranz, the former president and chief executive officer of Mount Vernon, invited me to speak at a meeting of the Mount Vernon Ladies' Association and to participate in other programs. Stephen McLeod flawlessly manages the fellowship program at the Washington Library and coordinated several conferences in which I participated. Susan Schoelwer, the executive director for historic preservation and collections at Mount Vernon, readily answered my many questions and has become a valued colleague. Dawn Bonner, manager of visual resources, provided the images for many presentations and for inclusion in this publication. Sara Myers, former access librarian, and Samantha Snyder, reference librarian, opened up the full range of resources at the Washington Library. Michele Lee, as special collections librarian, introduced me to important collections of Washington-related manuscripts and books. Allison Wickens and the education staff at Mount Vernon gave me the opportunity to talk about my research with teachers. Jessie MacLeod offered me a preview of her work on the landmark exhibit "Lives Bound Together," and directed me to resources for the history of slavery at Mount Vernon. Steve Bashore, director of historic trades, shared his knowledge of farming and milling in the eighteenth century. Mary Jongema made everything at the library work smoothly. Kevin Butterfield, the executive director of the Washington Library, has offered continuing support of my research and writing. I am especially grateful for the support and encouragement of the Mount Vernon Ladies' Association.

My fellowship at the Washington Library was greatly enriched by the support of the other long-term fellows, Kate Brown and Dana Stefanelli, and by enlightening conversations with Cassandra Good, with whom I shared an office for a month.

As Mount Vernon's inaugural fellow with the Georgian Papers Programme, I had the opportunity to research the agricultural improvements of George III and to expand my understanding of the culture of British husbandry that so interested Washington. At the Royal Archives in the Round Tower at Windsor Castle, I benefited from the assistance of Oliver Walton, Lynnette Beech, Rachel Krier, and Bill Stockting, among others. I appreciated the support of Oliver Urquhart Irvine, who was Librarian and Deputy Keeper of the Queen's Archives while I was at Windsor. Oliver Walton arranged a memorable tour of the Royal Farms and Windsor Great Park with Oliver Hampton of the Crown Estate Commissioners and Emma Clarke, a farm manager. During many lunches with the staff at the Royal Archives, the other fellows and I were able to discuss our research in what was then a largely uncharted collection of documents.

I am grateful for the permission of Her Majesty Queen Elizabeth II to access and publish materials from the Royal Library and Royal Archives.

At King's College London, Arthur Burns, the academic director of the Georgian Papers Programme, provided me with the opportunity to present my research to faculty and other researchers, and continues to support the community of fellows. I especially appreciate the comments and suggestions from the audience at the public talk I gave at King's College London. Angel-Luke O'Donnell, as academic liaison for the Georgian Papers Programme, encouraged my participation in a number of events, and he invited me to meet with his students to discuss Washington. James Fisher, then the administrator for the Georgian Papers Programme, generously shared his research and knowledge of the British agricultural literature that influenced Washington. James has since given me access to his completed dissertation, which helped me to rethink various parts of this book, and I learned a great deal from our conversations when he was a fellow at the Washington Library.

A fellowship at the International Center for Jefferson Studies at Monticello allowed me to research the other founding farmer from Virginia, and to explore the agricultural collaborations of Washington and Jefferson. Andrew O'Shaughnessy, the Saunders Director of the center, offered important encouragement for my work. Anna Berkes, Endrina Tay, and Jack Robertson made for a more efficient use of resources at the Jefferson Library, and Whitney Pippin ensured I was able to make the most of my fellowship. I particularly enjoyed the informal lunches with the staff of the Center and other fellows, and I received very helpful responses to my presentation at the Fellow's Forum. I thank Frank Cogliano for our conversations about Washington and Jefferson.

Jennifer Stertzer at the Papers of George Washington gave me an early preview of the George Washington Financial Papers Project, and Erica Cavanaugh guided me through the navigation of the site. I would never have been able to write this book without the ability to search Washington's financial ledgers. Near the close of work on this book, Jennifer provided important assistance when so many libraries remained inaccessible.

At the Virginia Museum of History and Culture, Frances Pollard and John McClure of the Research Library provided me with access to collections, and I thank Jamie Bosket, president and chief executive officer of the museum, for his support. Julie Miller of the Manuscripts Division at the Library of Congress answered my queries about unpublished agricultural records in the George Washington Papers and provided images while the Library was closed to researchers. Stanley Cushing, curator of Rare Books and Manuscripts at the Boston Athenaeum, facilitated my research in the volumes from Washington's collection of agricultural treatises. James Cheevers, senior curator at the US Naval Academy Museum, gave me access to Lund Washington's Book of Accounts. Evelyn Watson, head of archive at the Royal Society of Arts in London, assisted me in research on the Society for the Encouragement of Arts, Manufactures, and Commerce.

Flora Fraser directed me to the farm-related correspondence of the daughters of George III, and she shared her valuable perspective shaped by her research on the Washingtons as well as the king. Lady Jane Roberts graciously shared materials from her research on George III and his agricultural enterprises at Windsor. I thank Karin Wulf for inviting me to present my research at a conference of the British Group for Early American History and to participate in a Georgian Papers Programme symposium.

Denver Brunsman and Edward Lengel read an early proposal for this book and offered helpful comments based on their expert knowledge of Washington. Cynthia Kierner provided important assistance and good advice. Steven Lawson provided timely help at a critical stage of the project. François Furstenberg offered an extremely helpful review of the manuscript.

My book agent, Christopher Rogers, provided invaluable advice on sharpening my proposal and demonstrated his formidable editorial skills, always with encouraging good cheer. At Harvard University Press, Kathleen McDermott understood the value of this book project and has been unerring in her editorial advice.

My greatest debt in writing this book, as in every part of my life, is to my husband, Richard Scobey. For nearly thirty years, he has always encouraged me to pursue the kind of historical research and writing that I find most rewarding.

Index

Page numbers in italics refer to illustrations.

abolition and abolitionists, 10, 90, 100, 217–218, 220–224, 289–291; appeals to GW, 11, 98–100, 140–142, 223, 259–261, 289; gradual abolition proposals, 143, 217, 239, 247–251; GW support for, 98–99, 142, 234–235, 267; Pennsylvania Abolition Act, 144–145, 219, 224–226, 234, 288–290; response to GW's will, 286–287

Adam, Robert, 42, 66. *See also* Carlyle & Adam

Adams, Daniel Jenifer, 58, 65

Addison, Joseph, 172, 194

agricultural books, 14–17, 21, 29, 31–36, 103, 110, 140; GW acquisition of, 48, 191–192; GW reliance on, 52–54, 107–108, 125–126, 181, 197, 229

agricultural exchanges, 6, 14, 31, 97, 215, 232, 284; improvement societies and, 179–180; and national cooperation, 2, 183, 190, 291; of plants and livestock, 192–194, 261–262, 288

agriculture societies, 178–181, 189, 205, 214, 278, 284; British, 34–35, 105, 181, 188. *See also* Philadelphia Society for Promoting Agriculture

Alexandria, VA, 61, 80, 91, 148–149, 228, 265, 274, 279; indentured servants purchased in, 71; market for stolen goods, 169, 230, 267; merchants in, 22, 66, 85, 156, 173, 224; shipbuilder in, 65; GW's house in, 161; wheat and flour sold in, 42, 63, 84, 177

Allen, Richard, 286

American Philosophical Society, 192, 223

Anderson, James (manager), 127, 232, 254, 263–270, 274

Anderson, James (of Scotland), 186–193, 244, 255–256, 280–281

Annals of Agriculture, 107, 188, 192, 208; and anti-mercantilism, 181, 183; GW reliance on, 110–111, *112*, 129, 183–184, 206; GW refusal to publish in, 184–186, 284

Asbury, Francis, 141

Bakewell, Robert, 258, 262

Banks, Sir Joseph, 184, 257

barley, 30, 36, 109, 120, 125, 136, 168

barns, 51, 60, 136, 146, 196, 205, 236–237, 253; British models of, 110–111; at River Plantation, 94, 115; ruins of, 275; treading

351